D0874049

THE VICTORIANS AND THEIR READING

THE VICTORIANS AND THEIR READING

by

AMY CRUSE

HOUGHTON MIFFLIN COMPANY BOSTON
THE RIVERSIDE PRESS CAMBRIDGE

*Published in Great Britain as "The Victorians
and their Books"*

Fourth Printing R

PRINTED IN THE U.S.A.

PREFACE

THIS book is concerned with that side of the history of literature which tells of the readers rather than of the writers of books. It attempts to show what books, good and bad, were actually read by the Victorians during the first fifty years of the Queen's reign, what they thought of them, and how their reactions influenced the future output. The material has been drawn from the biographies, autobiographies, correspondence, novels, essays, and periodical literature of the time. It would be impossible to mention here all the books to which the author is indebted.

The author and publishers wish to thank the following for permission to quote passages from copyright works:—

> Messrs. Wm. Heinemann, from John Galsworthy's *Maid-in-Waiting*; Messrs. John Murray, from *The Diary of Lady Frederick Cavendish*; Mr. Humphrey Milford, from Austin Dobson's poem *Incognita*; Messrs. A. R. Mowbray, from Mrs. Ethel Romanes' *Charlotte Yonge*; Messrs. Grayson and Grayson, from George Gissing's *Thyrza*; Messrs. Macmillan, from *Memorials of Burne-Jones*.

In spite of careful search one or two owners of copyright remain unidentified, and apologies are offered to any whose rights have therefore not been acknowledged.

CONTENTS

THE VICTORIANS AND THEIR READING

THE VICTORIAN READER

"The Victorian Reader" is not a term used merely to denote a reader who lived during a certain epoch. It stands for one who bears quite definite marks of a unique and powerful influence. From that June morning in 1837 when England knew that an eighteen-year-old girl claimed her allegiance, to the great day, fifty years later, when the nation gathered to do homage to a widowed, indomitable old lady of sixty-eight, that curious emanation known as Victorianism was acting with ever-increasing power on the national life, and setting, for good or ill, a characteristic mark on its every department. After 1887 it began to weaken before the new influences brought to bear upon the country, and the 'nineties saw it on the way to being overpowered.

The reading habits of Her Majesty's subjects during those fifty years bore quite unmistakably the Victorian impress. Not that the Queen was a great reader, or aspired to lead the literary fashions of her reign; in this, as in many other things, she influenced her subjects not so much by specific acts as by the general fashion of her life and conversation. She set a high standard of morality; and her people responded by demanding books whose morality was perhaps over-emphasized. Her family life was well-ordered and affectionate; and domestic stories became the means of conveying those ideals of nobility and heroism which had been found previously only in wild and romantic melodrama. She had strong prejudices, which she did not hesitate to make known; and this helps to account for the fact that the Victorian reader was more apt than any of his predecessors or successors to make a tremendous outcry when a book was published which offended his susceptibilities. Also—and this is sometimes overlooked—the Queen had a keen brain and a deep and sincere interest in questions that affected the nation's highest good; and a large section of her subjects followed her, and responded eagerly to the stimulation of books that required a real mental effort to read, and that opened up new lines of thought. Quite early in her reign, in 1851, Tennyson, speaking for the nation, said—

> Her court was pure; her life serene;
>> God gave her peace; her land reposed;
>> A thousand claims to reverence closed
> In her as Mother, Wife and Queen.

It was thus that most of her people saw her to the end; and it was this conception which gave to Victorianism its strength and its effectiveness.

Of the other important influences brought to bear upon the Victorian reader something is said in the chapters that follow. It was a time of great movements both in life and in thought, and, in many of these books played an important part. No attempt is here made to describe those movements or to estimate their value. They are regarded simply in relation to the reader of the day, and only so much is said about them as will indicate their influence upon him.

The Victorian reader—and in this he resembles the reader of all other ages—did not confine himself to "great" books. It is the great books, we know, that make up the literature of a country, but there is a sense in which the lesser books are equally important. For a book does not become effective, does not really come to life, except in its contacts with the reader, and it happens sometimes in the case of even very great books that these contacts are comparatively few and slight. The books that figure largely in histories of literature are, in many households, those which are placed respectfully behind the glass doors of the best bookcase, to protect their beautiful and expensive bindings, and are looked at with satisfaction as repositories of the higher culture, available when required, though required but seldom; while the family reads and re-reads old favourites in tattered covers, and devours by dozens new volumes from the circulating library. Many of these, too, are probably great books, but certainly not all. There are some that have no tincture of the quality that confers immortality or even of that which promises long life. Yet their contacts are many and close. Their lives, though short, are active and potent. From the point of view of their readers they are as important as those which take the higher rank.

It is the reader's point of view that is to be considered here.

This book aims at telling, not what great books were written between 1837 and 1887, but what works, great or small, were read by the subjects of Queen Victoria during the first fifty years of Her Most Gracious Majesty's reign. With the writers of these books we are concerned only so far as to try to see them through the eyes of their public. We shall disregard the opinions of the critics except when these can be shown to have had a real influence on the reading of a section of the public. The opinion of a particular book expressed by some ordinary man or woman will receive more consideration than a review of the work in the *Athenaeum* or the *Quarterly*. We shall be interested in sales, because the number of copies sold gives some indication of the number of a book's readers, but we shall be more interested in finding out who bought the copies and what they thought of the work when they had read it.

It is unfortunate for our purposes that so few Victorian readers have put their reactions to the books they read on record; though for that most of us cannot fairly blame them, for few of us probably are setting down how we were affected by *The Forsyte Saga* and which of Mr. Edgar Wallace's thrillers caused our hair to rise most perceptibly upon our heads; how we wrestled and overcame in an encounter with Mr. Stephen Spender, and retired discomfited before a poem of Miss Gertrude Stein; how Sir James Jeans set us as dizzy specks in the midst of an illimitable universe, while a host of Freudian writers revealed to us vast unexplored tracts in our own minds and hearts. The diary habit is not a common one, and even industrious diarists often make little mention of books. Only a few, like Lady Frederick Cavendish and Miss Mary Gladstone, give full and interesting details concerning their reading. Biographies, for our purpose, are equally disappointing. Even if they give, as they often do, the weighty works which their subject studied as part of his education, they make only casual mention of a few of the books he read for his pleasure and entertainment. Often from a lengthy *Life and Letters* it is only possible to gather a few meagre scraps of information on this point; sometimes even these are lacking. Autobiographies are a little more fruitful, but in many of these the writer, after raising our hopes by telling us some really interesting things concerning the reading of his boyhood and youth, drops the subject altogether when he comes to the period of his manhood.

Even the diaries, biographies, and autobiographies that do yield some kind of harvest do not give us just what we require. The people who write, or are written about in these works are the exceptional people, and cannot be taken as representative of readers in general. We are in search of that elusive person the ordinary man, and it is exceedingly difficult to find him. We come nearest to him, perhaps, in the novel, that is, in the particular class of novel in which the writer attempts to depict the society of his day. Society is, for the most part, made up of ordinary people, so that when, as sometimes, though all too seldom, happens, the characters of a novel are to be found reading or talking about books, we may reasonably suppose that we have discovered something concerning the tastes and opinions of the objects of our search.

Let us, with the help of data carefully gathered from all these sources of information, try to see some of those ordinary readers as they existed in the year of the Queen's accession—readers for whom Victorianism was to be, during the coming years, a guiding and inspiring influence. We will imagine a household of the upper middle class—the class which at that period was quickly rising into special prominence. In the solidly furnished drawing-room of such a household, under the blaze of an ornate chandelier, sat one autumn evening four persons. Papa was in his arm-chair by the fire, mamma opposite to him, with her worsted work. Caroline, the eldest daughter of the house, lately returned from a genteel boarding-school, sat on the sofa industriously tatting, and beside her sat Edward, her newly affianced lover. Caroline was very pretty, fair and small, with a waist that looked even less than its actual twenty inches in comparison with the circumference of her extended skirts, worn over the fashionable corded petticoat, soon to be superseded by the even more widely spreading crinoline. Edward was tall, with magnificent dark whiskers and an intelligent countenance. He was reading aloud an instructive article on The New Steam Plough, from *Chambers's Journal*. Mamma listened approvingly, not that she understood a great deal of what was being read, but it sounded entirely moral and sensible, with no sort of frivolity about it. Mamma hated frivolity. She was strongly Evangelical in her opinions, and would have much preferred that Edward should read something from the *Christian Observer* or from Pollok's *Course of Time*, both of which lay on the polished centre table, among a number of other carefully arranged and handsomely bound volumes. But she knew that neither papa nor Edward would welcome such an exchange. Papa had no sympathy with what he called Methodist ranting. He was of a jovial temperament and favoured a more robust type of literature. He loved to talk of the time when he and his young companions went wild over *Lara* and *Don Juan*, and wore their hair long and their shirt collars open in imitation of the noble author. All Byron's poems—the volumes tattered with much use—were even then in his own room. Mamma protested against their being admitted to the drawing-room, lest Caroline should be corrupted. He had all Walter Scott's works, too, almost equally worn and shabby; but there was another set, in resplendent bindings on the same shelf with Shakespeare and Milton and *Pilgrim's Progress* and *Robinson Crusoe* in the bookcase that stood in the dining-room. Mamma did not object to Sir Walter, and in this believed that she showed great liberality, for some of the members of the congregation of the very Low Church that she attended would admit no novels at all to the house, believing them, Sir Walter's included, to be works of the Evil One.

Edward was also unwilling to read "Methodist rant," but for reasons somewhat different from those of papa. He had lately finished his career at Oxford where he had been strongly influenced by Newman and the *Tracts*, and he had become an ardent High Churchman. If he had not been such an excellent match for Caroline, belonging to such a well-to-do and highly respected mercantile family, mamma would have been louder in her protests against the engagement than she had, under the circumstances, ventured to be. But she knew that papa would hear nothing against the young man, and her wifely obedience obliged her to content herself with occasional sighs and mournful ejaculations and hopes that Caroline, after they were married, would lead him back to the right way.

It was, however, most unlikely that Caroline would ever lead Edward anywhere. She was of the type that follows, not leads, and, like most young ladies of her day, had been brought up to believe unquestioningly in the superiority of the male and the obligation of the wife to obey her husband. As she sat on the sofa and listened to Edward reading, she thought admiringly how very clever he was to understand all those long words and difficult explanations. It sounded to her very much like something out of the lesson books which she had been obliged to read at school, and which she had so joyfully closed for ever on leaving; but Edward's voice made it quite delightful. It was almost as good as the novels which she read by stealth, smuggling them up into her bedroom, and finding ingenious hiding-places for them where mamma would never think of looking. At that moment Mrs. Gore's *Cecil: a Peer* was lying under masses of tissue paper at the bottom of the bandbox that held her best bonnet. Her friend, Miss Emily Robinson, whose very fashionable mamma loved novels and had quantities of them from Hookham's Library, in Bond Street, had brought it to her the day before, ingeniously hidden in her muff, and Caroline had had several delicious snatches at it and was longing for more.

Edward finished the article on the Steam Plough, and then turned to a poem of Mrs. Hemans, printed on the last page of the *Journal*. It was called *The Adopted Child*, and began—

> Why wouldst thou leave me, oh gentle child,
> Thy home on the mountain is bleak and wild.

Caroline listened eagerly now, for, like all young ladies of that day, she adored Mrs. Hemans, and had several song-books filled with that lady's mournful ditties, which she could scarcely ever sing without breaking down in tears. There were tears in her eyes now, before Edward had finished, and tears in mamma's eyes too. But papa was growing impatient. All this time there had been lying on his knee a thin, green paper-covered volume, of which he had been unable to resist reading snatches, though he knew himself to be transgressing the drawing-room code of politeness. "Here, let's have some *Pickwick* now," he said; and Edward, with brightening eyes, took the slim green number from his hand. Caroline's eyes brightened too, for she, with thousands of other people in England, was following the career of the stout little spectacled gentleman and his lanky cockney serving-man with keenest interest. There followed a delightful half-hour, with peals of laughter from papa and Edward, and soft, ladylike titters from Caroline. Mamma set her lips, and tried to think of the Rev. Josiah Banks' last Sunday's sermon, but nevertheless she managed to hear a good deal about Mrs. Bardell's arrival at the Fleet Prison, and her reception by Mr. Samuel Weller, and enjoyed the story— though she would never have owned to having done so—almost as much as did the others.

Ten o'clock came, and Edward closed the book and rose to say good-night. Mamma went down to the kitchen to dismiss the servants to bed. She had given them a fresh supply of tracts that afternoon, including that soul-stirring one by Mr. Banks entitled, *To-morrow you may wake up in Hell*. She hoped they had spent an improving evening over these; but when she reached the basement she heard shouts of laughter, and opening the kitchen door, saw Jane, the housemaid, with the obnoxious number of *Pickwick* in her hand, reading aloud to the cook and Henry the boot-boy. Mamma sighed, but since papa welcomed *Pickwick* in the drawing-room, she could not, as a dutiful wife, forbid its entrance to the kitchen.

Meantime Edward was making his way home, his head full of his beloved Caroline. How delightful when they were married to teach her to appreciate some of the books he loved himself—not all of them, of course, for a woman could not be expected to rise to the higher realms of literature, nor was it fitting she should do so. But she had, he thought, a taste for poetry. He had given her *The Christian Year* for a birthday present, and she had declared that some of its poems were "sweetly pretty." At Christmas he would give her Newman's *Lyra Apostolica*, or perhaps a volume of Wordsworth's. She would surely love *Lucy Gray* and *Ruth*. Edward himself had been an admirer of Wordsworth since his boyhood, and had been delighted to see how, of late, appreciation of the poet's works had been spreading. Edward had a fine though not a very cultivated literary taste, and an eager intellectual curiosity that drew him towards a new book as towards a promising adventure. He thought now of several of these that he wanted to read: of *The French Revolution* by Carlyle, whose *Sartor Resartus* had excited and puzzled him; of the new poet, young Mr. Tennyson, in whose poems, contained in the little volume of 1833, he had recognized a new music; of Boz and the *Pickwick Papers*; of Disraeli and *Henrietta Temple*. "There is a good time coming for people who like reading," Edward reflected joyfully. "All these men are young and just at the beginning of their work. Who knows what they will give us before they have done?"

Edward was right. There was a good time coming. The forces that were to shape the Victorian reader were gathering, and the writers who were to supply his needs were ready. As we go on to the consideration of these we will think of Edward and Caroline, and of the large family which, according to Victorian custom, will inevitably grow up around them. They shall stand for those ordinary Victorian readers who, in such vast numbers, seclude themselves behind the more prominent figures, and whose acquaintance, with all our pains, we can only make in a partial and superficial fashion.

CHAPTER II

THE TRACTARIANS

TRACTS had, since the days when Miss Hannah More sent out her *Shepherd of Salisbury Plain*, been regarded as a form of religious literature pertaining especially to the Evangelical party in the English Church, and addressed to the uninstructed and the careless. Everyone knew the little leaflets with their heavily weighted moral stories and their fervid appeals to the consciences of their readers. They had been distributed in enormous numbers throughout the country, and everyone, the scoffers as well as the believers, had learnt to attach to the term "tract" a definite and specialized meaning.

This meaning persisted until the closing months of 1833, and then, suddenly, the word gained a new and arousing significance. The first number of a series of *Tracts for the Times* was sent out in the September of that year from the University of Oxford. The copies of this tract were not left at cottage doors, or scattered broadcast in the hope that they might meet the eye of the unconverted. They were delivered at rectories and vicarages and clerical lodgings, and other places where clergy of the Established Church might be found. Most of the distributors were members of Oxford University, and many of them were young clergymen. Thomas Mozley, a graduate of Oriel, who had been ordained deacon in 1831, and was in 1833 working in a Northamptonshire parish, tells how, "putting on a great-coat and mounting a shaggy pony at the dawn of a winter's day," he rode about the country, calling at one parsonage after another, surprising the inmates of the first one he visited while they were at breakfast; and there were many other young Oxford men doing the same thing in other districts. Some tracts, also, were sent by post; some were taken by the booksellers and sold for a penny each. Great efforts were made to reach every clergyman, however humble his position or remote his parish.

The title of the tract—*Thoughts on the Ministerial Commission, respectfully addressed to the Clergy*—surprised and possibly startled a good many of those who received it, and made them turn curiously to the opening page, where they read—

I am but one of yourselves—a Presbyter—and therefore I conceal my name lest I should take too much on myself by speaking in my own person. Yet speak I must; for the times are very evil, yet no one speaks against them. Is not this so? Do not we "look upon one another" yet perform nothing?. . . Now then, let me come at once to the subject which leads me to address you. Should the Government and the Country so far forget their God as to cast off the Church, to deprive it of its temporal honours and substance, *on what* will you rest the claim of respect and attention which you make upon your flocks?

The Church, the writer said, was not a creation of man, but a divinely appointed society through which God showed Himself to His people. Governments had no authority over her. Her clergy were the ministers of God, not the servants of the State.

I fear we have neglected the real ground on which our authority is built—OUR APOSTOLIC DESCENT. We have been born, not of blood, nor of the will of the flesh, nor of the will of man, but of God. The Lord Jesus gave His Spirit to His Apostles; they in turn laid their hands on those who should succeed them; and these again on others; and so the sacred gift has been handed down to our present bishops, who have appointed us as their assistants, and in some sense representatives.

This was the main purpose of the tract—to uphold the doctrine of the Apostolic Succession. Would the clergy of the Church forgo their high inheritance—resign the heaven-given authority which had been handed on to them down the centuries, and become, like the Dissenting ministers, "the creatures of the people"? "Choose your side, since side you shortly must with one or other party even though you do nothing."

It was not a long tract, only four pages, and it looked much the same as those which had been coming for years from the Religious Tract Society. But it did well what it set out to do. It was plain and direct and carefully reasoned, the work of a scholar and a thinker; the work, too, of a man simple and sincere, who was under the strongest conviction of the necessity to speak out the truth that he believed.

There could be no doubt of the quarter from which the tract had come. The mind of each reader went back to the sermon that had been preached at St. Mary's, Oxford, on the fourteenth of the previous July, by John Keble, before the judges of assize. Its subject was "National Apostasy," and the preacher had, with quiet but intense fervour, denounced the recent action of the Government in abolishing certain Irish sees, and had lamented that such a thing should be possible in a land that professed to honour the Church of Christ. His words had come with force, first, because there were many in the country who felt as he did, that a determined attack was being made upon the rights of the Church; and next, because John Keble was a man widely known and reverenced. He was a Fellow of Oriel, and Professor of Poetry in the University; and he worked as a curate to his father, who was vicar of Fairford, a little village on the edge of the Cotswolds. Six years before he preached his famous sermon Keble had published a little volume of religious poetry, called *The Christian Year*, which had become a manual of devotion to hundreds of Church people, and had caused him to be reverenced as a poet and a saint in hundreds of homes all over the country.

It was not Keble, however, who had written the *Tract*; it was another member of the group to which he belonged—John Henry Newman. The members of this group all held the views which Keble had put forward in his assize sermon, and they were united in a firm resolve to win back for the Church the authority and the reverence that had been hers in times past, and to which they fervently believed she was divinely entitled. Newman was, like Keble, a Fellow of Oriel, and was, besides, vicar of the University church of St. Mary's.

Other *Tracts* followed. Month by month they came, all of them dealing with some aspect of the same subject—the restoration of the ancient privileges and practices of the Church. Most of them were written by Newman, eight were by Keble, the rest by various other members of the Tractarian group. They were addressed not to the clergy only, but to the public generally; and, as time went on, they contained less of warning and more of instruction. At first the Tractarians had written "as a man might give notice of a fire, or an inundation, to startle all who heard him," but, the alarm having been given, there came the calmer setting forward of principles and arguments.

At the beginning of 1834 the group was joined by Edward Bouverie Pusey, and his reputation as a scholar and a theologian gave added weight to the movement. He wrote eight of the *Tracts*, and to one of them he put his initials; and, since the other writers remained anonymous, his name became associated in the public mind with the *Tracts*. The term "Puseyism" was coined, and was taken as standing for the system of religious belief and practice advocated by the *Tracts* as a whole.

In many of the parsonages throughout England the *Tracts* were read with enthusiasm, and regarded as a call to a holy conflict. High Church doctrines, it must be remembered, did not come in with the Tractarians; a considerable number of the clergy had long held them. In other clerical homes, like that of Archdeacon Froude, of the parish of Darlington, in Devon, the *Tracts* were read with approval, but without any great stirring of emotion. The Archdeacon, so his son James Anthony tells us, was a High Churchman of the old school, but he was "too solid a man to be carried off his feet by the Oxford enthusiasm"; and this although his elder son, Hurrell, was one of the most prominent figures in the movement. Many of the clergy felt little interest in the Tractarians and their doings, and were not moved to take either side. Florence Nightingale says that most of the parsons she met in the late 'thirties were neither Evangelical nor Puseyite, but just country gentlemen or men of the world performing their clerical duties with decent diligence, but without any kind of fervour.

But there were some clergymen who regarded the *Tracts* with downright horror. Dr. Thomas Arnold, in his schoolhouse at Rugby, read them, and denounced them as being entirely mischievous. He himself had been writing and preaching for some years on Church reform, but it was not the reform advocated by the *Tracts*. "I cannot say," he wrote to his friend, Mr. Serjeant Coleridge—

how I am annoyed, both on public and private grounds, by these extravagances at Oxford; on private grounds, from the gross breaches of charity to which they lead good men; and on public, because if these things do produce any effect on the clergy, the evil consequences to the nation are not to be calculated; for what is to become of the Church if the clergy begin to exhibit an aggravation of the worst superstitions of the Roman Catholics, only stripped of that consistency which stamps even the errors of the Romish system with something of a character of greatness.

Arnold, Coleridge, and Keble had, twenty years before, been undergraduates together at Corpus Christi College, and they had remained close friends ever since. Both Arnold and Coleridge looked upon Keble as one of the saintliest of men; both loved the *Christian Year* and used it as a manual of devotion. Coleridge, although he was not an ardent Tractarian, belonged to the High Church party. He stood, he said, half-way between Arnold and Keble, and was able to sympathize with both. But since Arnold and Keble differed on points that both considered vital, it was impossible that they should continue on the old happy terms "I learn," wrote Dr. Arnold to Coleridge, in 1841—

what I never knew before, the special ground of Keble's alienation from me; it appears that he says that I "do not believe in the Holy Catholic Church." Now that I do not believe in it in Keble's sense is most true; I would just as soon worship Jupiter; and Jupiter's idolatry is scarcely farther from Christianity, in my judgment, than the idolatry of the priesthood.

Charles Kingsley read the *Tracts* while he was an undergraduate at Cambridge, and denounced them vigorously. Some years later he wrote in the Introduction to a book to be given to his wife on their marriage day—

You know what first turned my attention to the Oxford *Tracts*; but you do *not* know that my own heart strangely yearned towards them from the first; that if they had not struck at the root of wedded happiness, I too had been ensnared! . . . But when I read I soon saw that the Oxford writings contained only half truths: that if what they said was true, much more what they did *not* say was true also! . . . that Popery was their climax—the full development of their theory—the abyss to which they were hurrying, dallying on the brink, afraid to plunge in and be honest.

Arnold and Kingsley, with most of the clergy belonging to that party in the Church which was beginning to be known as "Broad," were, throughout, the determined opponents of the Oxford Movement. They wrote against the *Tracts*, and preached against them, striving with all their might to combat what they fervently believed to be an evil influence. Most of them agreed with Frederick Denison Maurice when he said, "To me they are, for the most part, more unpleasant than I quite like to acknowledge, to myself or others."

At Oxford, the birthplace of the *Tracts*, the excitement rose highest and the battle raged most fiercely. Nearly all the older members of the University were opposed to the movement; the heads of Colleges, except old President Routh of Magdalen, showed their hostility to it in every way they could. James Anthony Froude, who went up to Oxford in 1836, said that then "the controversial fires were beginning to blaze, but not as yet hotly." The flames rose to their fiercest during the five years that followed. Keble no longer lived in Oxford, and was seen there only occasionally, but Newman was still Vicar of St. Mary's, and still preached week by week to the undergraduates. Many of them knew him personally, and felt for him a passionate devotion. To all he was an object of interest, and to most of veneration. As he passed with swift, noiseless step along Oriel Lane, "head thrust forward and gaze fixed as though on some vision seen only by himself," light-hearted undergraduates would, we are told, drop their voices and whisper, "There's Newman." Many of them received the doctrines that he preached largely because it was he who preached them. "*Credo in Newmannum* was," says Froude, "for hundreds of young men the genuine symbol of faith."

Newman's sermons were as important a part of the Oxford Movement as the *Tracts* themselves. Sunday after Sunday he preached to a congregation that never more than half filled the big church; for the authorities discouraged the undergraduates from attending, and the dinner hour of the Colleges was so arranged—some said purposely—that those who had been to the four o'clock service could not get back in time for the meal. Anxious Evangelical fathers and mothers and schoolmasters were on the side of the dons. When the lads came home for the vacation, talking of nothing but Newman and his sermons, they took alarm, and warned their sons and pupils solemnly against the snares set for them at St. Mary's.

We sent our sons to Oxford nice honest lads, educated in the principles of the Church of England, and at the end of the first term they came home puppies, talking Popish nonsense, which they had learnt from the pedants to whose care we had entrusted them,

fumed George Borrow. Dr. Arnold wrote warningly to his favourite pupil, Arthur Penrhyn Stanley, who went up to Oxford in 1834—

Now with regard to the Newmanites. I do not call them bad men, nor would I deny their many good qualities. . . . But it is clear to me that Newman and his party are idolaters; they put Christ's Church and Christ's Sacraments and Christ's Ministers in the place of Christ Himself. . . . I have been looking through the *Tracts* which to me are a memorable proof of their idolatry.

Yet in spite of warnings and discouragements, many undergraduates—Arthur Stanley and Dr. Arnold's son Matthew among them—were eager to listen to the words of the man who was calling Oxford and England to a higher loyalty to the Church of their fathers. None of them ever forgot those quiet, solemn Sunday afternoons; many have told of them in words which show how deep was the impression received. The service was a very simple one, short and with no ritualistic observances. The sermon, too, was simple. Newman left alone controversial subjects. He did not talk about the Apostolic Succession, or the rights of the Church; he made no attacks on Dissent. "His power showed itself," said John Campbell Shairp, a young undergraduate from Glasgow, "in the new and unlooked-for ways in which he touched into life old truths." "Eloquent" was not the word to describe his sermons; they were the "high poems of an inspired singer or prophet."

And the tone of voice in which they were spoken, once you grew accustomed to it, sounded like a fine strain of unearthly music. Through the stillness of the high Gothic building the words fell on the ear like the measured drippings of water in some vast, dim cave. After hearing these sermons you might come away still not believing the tenets peculiar to the High Church system; but you would be harder than most men if you did not feel more than ever ashamed of coarseness, selfishness, worldliness; if you did not feel the things of faith brought closer to the soul.

James Anthony Froude tells of a sermon that he heard in which Newman dwelt on some of the incidents of our Lord's Passion.

He then paused. For a few moments there was a breathless silence. Then, in a low, clear voice, of which the faintest vibration was audible in the farthest corner of St. Mary's, he said, "Now I bid you recollect that He to whom these things were done was Almighty God." It was as if an electric stroke had gone through the church, as if every person present understood for the first time the meaning of what he had all his life been saying. I suppose it was an epoch in the mental history of more than one of my Oxford contemporaries.

Among these contemporaries was Arthur Stanley. He came up to Oxford from Rugby a devoted worshipper of the great headmaster he had just left. "Loving him and admiring him as I do," wrote the young undergraduate in his diary, "to the very verge of all love and admiration that can be paid to man, I fear that I have passed the limit and have made him my idol, and that in all I may be but serving God for man's sake." Yet this devotion to Arnold could not prevent Stanley from falling under the spell of the man whom Arnold denounced. He heard Newman preach at St. Mary's and was impelled to offer him the highest tribute it was in his power to pay. The Tractarian preacher, said Stanley, was like Arnold. The two men, though they seemed directly antagonistic, were really of the same essence. They were alike in their preaching —in the general tone, the manner, the simple language, the overpowering conviction conveyed that the speaker was a true and earnest Christian. Stanley never joined the High Church party and he remained a devoted disciple of Dr. Arnold; but Newman's sermons left their mark upon him.

Both Dr. Arnold's sons, Matthew and Thomas, were undergraduates at Oxford during the most agitated years of the Tractarian movement. Thomas almost entirely disregarded it. His daughter, Mrs. Humphry Ward, says that although he had rooms opposite St. Mary's, he only once crossed the road to hear Newman preach. But more than ten years later, when he was living in New Zealand, the claims of the Christian faith, which he had put aside at Oxford, made a strong appeal to him. He remembered Newman, and he sent to England for the *Tracts for the Times*. In 1854 he was received into the Church of Rome.

His brother Matthew was attracted by Newman's gift of language rather than by the doctrines he preached. He went to hear the sermon on Sunday afternoons as he would have gone to hear a fine poem, or to see a stirring drama, and, years afterwards, described what he had heard with convincing eloquence.

Who could resist the charm of that spiritual apparition, gliding in the dim afternoon light through the aisles of St. Mary's, rising into the pulpit, and then, in the most entrancing of voices breaking the silence with words and thoughts that were a religious music— subtle, sweet, mournful? I seem to hear him still, saying, "After the fever of life, after wearinesses and sicknesses, fightings and despondings, languor and fretfulness, struggling and succeeding;

after all the changes and chances of this troubled and unhealthy state—at length comes death, at length the white throne of God, at length the beatific vision."

Thus Newman's sermons became famous throughout Oxford. Year by year the influence of the Tractarian movement on the general life of the University was more clearly seen. Richard Church (afterwards Dean of St. Paul's) says that when he came up in 1833, going to service at St. Mary's on Sunday afternoons was looked upon as "rather a fashion of a set who talked a kind of religious philosophy—Evangelico-Coleridgean, and claimed at once to admire Newman, whom the common set decried, and to admire with reserve." By 1841, when Thomas Hughes went up to Oriel, the set had grown into a party. In *Tom Brown at Oxford*, Hughes tells of his hero's experiences, which were probably, at least in this connection, his own. The best men of his College were "diligent readers of *Tracts for the Times*" and followers of the able leaders of the High Church party, which was then a growing one. Hughes, as a Broad Churchman, was not likely to be biased in favour of this party; yet he says that even the worst of its members was making "some sort of protest for self-denial and against self-indulgence."

A large number had, indeed, definitely declared themselves members of Newman's party. Mark Pattison, who came up in 1832, says that he became "a declared Puseyite, then an ultra-Puseyite." Anthony Trollope, in *Barchester Towers*, tells of young Francis Arabin, who from a boy had been on the side of the Tractarians, and who

at Oxford sat for a while at the feet of the great Newman. To this cause he lent all his faculties. For it he concocted verses, for it he made speeches, for it he scintillated the brightest sparks of his quiet wit. For it he ate and drank and dressed and had his being.

Richard Church came more slowly, but no less surely, to the state of a whole-hearted Tractarian. At first he went only occasionally to hear Newman preach. After he had taken his degree he went more often, and in 1836 a sermon, "Make Ventures for Christ's Sake," impressed him very deeply. He joined the group of young men who by this time had gathered round Newman, and henceforward was among the most ardent of the band.

One of these young men was Frederick Faber, who had come up to Oxford at about the same time as Church. He was a singularly handsome youth, full of life and spirit, a scholar and a poet. In the Long Vacation of 1837, when he was not quite twenty-four years old, he took a reading party of Oxford undergraduates to Ambleside. There they met a reading party of Cambridge men, nearly all of them youths of great talent, destined to make a mark in the world. Among them were John Manners, George Smythe, and Beresford Hope. They were full of all sorts of romantic notions, and devotedly attached to the Church. They dreamt of a revival of the days of chivalry, and of an ideal order of knighthood that should go out into the world to fight against evil and misery. To them the brilliant, ardent Faber, coming from Oxford, with the halo of the great Movement about him, seemed the inspired leader they had looked for. When he preached on Sunday morning in Ambleside church, where thirty-five University men sat among the country congregation, his passionate eloquence thrilled and uplifted his hearers. The sermon, said John Manners, was "eloquent, earnest, and gorgeous beyond what I had anticipated, expressions and similes drawn from nature, glowing and glorious."

Manners and Smythe spent the next Epiphany season at Oxford, and there they fell under the spell of Newman; and when they went back to Cambridge they took with them much Tractarian literature, and became missionaries of the cause among their fellows. On the Feast of St. John the Evangelist Faber sent Manners seven volumes of Newman's works, saying, "A refuge from all party and controversial thoughts you will find in these volumes. . . . Whenever you want thoughts akin to God and greatness you will find them here."

Meantime, outside the Universities, the *Tracts* were finding an increasing number of readers. Isaac Williams, who had come, a clever, eager boy from Wales, to be Keble's pupil, and had become Newman's curate at St. Mary's, says that when the *Tracts* were first published little or no notice of them was taken by the general public. He asked one of the undergraduates to inquire for them at any large towns he visited during the vacation, and he himself did the same; and their inquiries showed that very few were on sale. But as time went on more cheering news came in. When Williams paid his daily visit to Newman's rooms there was often something to be told which showed the *Tracts* were making their way. The laity as well as the clergy were beginning to read them. One morning there was a mention of them in *The Times*, and this gave Newman great delight. Soon Pusey was able to say—

The *Tracts* found an echo everywhere. Friends started up like armed men from the ground. I only dread our being too popular. It was like the men from the heath in *The Lady of the Lake*.

Public opinion was fully aroused. Each *Tract* as it appeared became the subject of eager, even fierce discussion. The Tractarians saw the increasing success of their efforts to arouse the country with astonishment as well as satisfaction.

We did but light a beacon fire on the summit of a lonely hill, and now we are amazed to find the firmament on every side red with the light of some responsive flame.

The Duke of Newcastle, one of the Tory leaders, was ardent in support of the movement. The Liberal Lord John Russell was strongly opposed to it. He looked on "Newmania" as nothing more than a new kind of Toryism, and declared that the "economy of truth" recommended by the Tractarians made him physically sick. Gladstone, though he sympathized, was never fully in accord with Newman. A good many years later he declared that the Oxford Movement had had no direct effect on him. "I did not see the *Tracts*, and to this hour I have read but few of them." He was a High Churchman, but it seemed to him that the means used by Newman and his friends were not the best that could have been chosen to touch the national conscience. Lord Melbourne, who became Prime Minister in 1834, considered that a great deal too much stir was being made about the *Tracts*. He had not read them, he wrote to Dr. Pusey, but he had heard that they set forward doctrines which were not in accordance with those generally held.

I do not myself dread bold inquiry and speculation. I have seen too many new theories spring up and die away to feel much alarm on such a subject. If they are founded on truth they establish themselves, and become part of the established belief. If they are erroneous they decay and perish.

The Tractarians were quite willing to accept this test. They had faith that the truth would prevail, and they believed that the truth they upheld was prevailing. By the young especially it was being received with ardour; all over the country eager young converts were looking to Oxford and the *Tracts* for guidance in their spiritual life. At Killerton, in Devon, the two sons of Sir Thomas Acland declared themselves Tractarians, to the intense distress of their Evangelical mother. Edward Freeman, the future historian, read the *Tracts* while he was at school at Cheam, and went on to read all the ancient and modern literature connected with the principles of the movement that he could find; and he upheld the cause of the Tractarians against mocking schoolfellows and disapproving masters. Sixteen-year-old Walter Bagehot was won over by hearing Newman preach, while on a visit to Oxford. Elizabeth Sewell, the author of *Amy Herbert*, tells how, in 1836, when she was twenty-one years old and living with her parents in the Isle of Wight, she saw one day, lying on the counter of a bookseller's shop at Newport, some numbers of *Tracts for the Times*. She had heard of the *Tracts* from her brother William, who was an undergraduate at Oxford and one of Newman's disciples. She bought the numbers, took them home, and read them. The rest of the family—there were twelve brothers and sisters in all—read them too, and they agreed that here was teaching which showed the way to a high and holy life more clearly than any they had received before. It needed only some discussion with the enthusiastic Newmanite brother to bring them entirely to his way of thinking. Elizabeth had never felt quite happy in the Evangelical faith in which she had been brought up. She had read Mrs. Sherwood's tales—the far-famed *Fairchild Family* and *Little Henry and his Bearer*—and similar stories by other writers, but she had disliked the way in which the children were represented as "quoting texts and talking of their feelings in an unnatural way, or what seemed to me unnatural."

I had really suffered so much at school from things said to me that jarred upon my taste, that it was perfect rest to be able to talk upon religious subjects without hearing or using cant phrases.

There was, as Miss Elizabeth Rigby (afterwards Lady Eastlake) wrote in 1843, plenty of young fervour and devotion gathering round "Puseyism, so called."

Mary Ann Evans (George Eliot) read the *Tracts* in 1839, but felt none of the comfort and relief that came to Elizabeth Sewell. She was then a girl of nineteen, keeping house for her father at Griff, cumbered by all sorts of domestic cares, and troubled exceedingly by religious doubts. She read many theological works, trying to find some "comfortable repose" on a firm religious conviction as to "the nature of the visible Church." In May 1839 she wrote to Miss Lewis, her old schoolmistress—

The authors of the Oxford *Tracts* . . . evince . . . a disposition rather to fraternize with the members of a Church carrying on her brow the prophetical epithets applied by St. John to the scarlet beast, the mystery of Iniquity, than with pious Nonconformists. It is true that they disclaim all this, and that their opinions are seconded by the extensive learning, the laborious zeal and the deep devotion of those who propagate them; but a reference to facts will convince us that such has generally been the character of heretical teachers. Satan is too crafty to commit his cause into the hands of those who have nothing to recommend them to approbation.

Nevertheless, she still felt the *Tracts* worth reading. A year later she wrote to Miss Lewis saying she was beginning a new volume of the Oxford *Tracts*, though she shrank from the labour of conning. This was not long before her removal to Coventry, which brought her under entirely new religious influences, and we hear no more of the *Tracts*.

In some districts colonies of Tractarians were growing up. One such colony was being formed round about Keble's parish of Hursley. In 1836, on the death of his father, he had become vicar of Hursley, had married, and devoted himself to parochial work. His influence was felt beyond the village which he served so faithfully. The Bishop of Winchester held decidedly Evangelical views, and most of the clergy in his diocese followed him, so that for those who accepted the Tractarian teaching the services at Hursley had a strong attraction. Among those who came to them were the Yonge family—father, mother, son, and daughter— living at Otterbourne, four miles from Winchester. They had read the *Tracts* with enthusiasm, and were eager to take John Keble for their spiritual guide. When he came as vicar to Hursley, Charlotte Yonge, the daughter, was twelve years old, a bright, happy, clever girl, sharing already her parents' deep interest in matters of religion. With Keble, she said, came in the chief spiritual influence of her life. He prepared her for confirmation. His *Christian Year* she knew by heart. She read the books he advised her to read, and held the truths that he taught. He was in all things her mentor and guide.

John Taylor Coleridge, who was a cousin of Mr. Yonge's, came often from his Devonshire home to stay at Otterbourne. He was, as has been said, only partially in sympathy with the Tractarians, but his two daughters were almost as enthusiastic as Charlotte Yonge. Another of Keble's College friends, Charles Dyson, was vicar of the little village of Dogmersfield, not far from Hursley, and he and his invalid sister were both ardent readers of the *Tracts*. George Moberly, Fellow of Balliol, who was appointed Headmaster of Winchester School in 1836, was another member of the High Church society.

Keble's presence at Hursley kept this society closely in touch with Oxford and with Newman. Elizabeth Sewell tells of a dinner at Mr. Yonge's house in 1840, on the occasion of the consecration of the new church which he had given to the parish. Keble and Newman and Isaac Williams and other notabilities from Oxford were there also, and she listened with delighted awe to the gay talk of the dinner table. When this turned on the Waverley novels, Newman praised the great Sir Walter and *Guy Mannering*. All through his long life Newman read and loved the works of Scott. He acknowledged—and other writers have enlarged upon the theme—how much the Tractarians owed to Sir Walter, whose books had prepared men's minds to receive their teaching. There was, in many things, a strong and close sympathy between them. Both had an ardent love of the historic past; an imagination ready to be kindled by brave tales of deeds done by their forefathers; a delight in the romantic side of life, and in things beautiful, stately, and impressive; a loyalty to the powers that they believed appointed by God to rule over them. Scott was a Jacobite at heart, though his patriotism and his common sense made him a faithful subject of the reigning king. To the Tractarians, Charles I was a saint and a martyr. Every year, as the twenty-ninth of January came round, they joined in mournful commemoration of his death, and read with sad and loyal devotion Keble's poem for that day in the *Christian Year*—

Our own, our royal saint; thy memory rests
On many a prayer, the more for thee endear'd,
True son of our dear Mother, early taught
With her to worship and for her to die,
Nursed in her aisles to more than kingly thought,
Oft in her solemn hours we deem thee nigh.

The opponents of the Tractarians recognized this alliance with Scott, and included Sir Walter in their denunciations.

Whence did the pedants get the Popish nonsense with which they have corrupted youth? Why, from the same quarter from which they got the Jacobite nonsense with which they have inoculated those lads who were not inoculated with it before—Scott's novels. Jacobitism and Laudism, a kind of half Popery, had at one time been very prevalent at Oxford, but both had been long consigned to oblivion there, and people at Oxford cared as little about Laud as they did about the Pretender. Both were dead and buried there as everywhere else, till Scott called them out of their graves, when the pedants of Oxford hailed both—ay, and the Pope, too, as soon as Scott had made the old fellow fascinating through particular novels, more especially the *Monastery* and *Abbot*.

Thus, in dire indignation, George Borrow; and he drew out his argument at length, attempting to show that all the misfortunes of poor, brave Sir Walter's life were a punishment for this resuscitation of Popery and Jacobitism. But the High Church party remained faithful to the Waverley novels, and read them with almost as great a sense of edification as they felt in reading the definitely religious publications that came from Oxford. When the first volume of Newman's *Parochial Sermons* was published in 1834, Thomas Mozley declared—

It was as if a trumpet had sounded through the land. All read and admired even if they dissented or criticized. The publishers said that the volume put all other sermons out of the market, just as *Waverley* and *Guy Mannering* had put all other novels.

Nobody felt that there was anything incongruous in the comparison. The two men might well stand side by side.

Several volumes of Newman's sermons were published between 1834 and 1843, and all of them were eagerly read. Thackeray and Edward FitzGerald both declared them to be the best that ever were written. Frederick Robertson, who later became himself a famous preacher, read them when he came up to Brasenose College, Oxford, in 1837. They made a great impression upon him, and he continued to read them with pleasure and profit to the day of his death. Mrs. Gaskell, the wife of a Unitarian minister, wrote in 1842 that she was "taking a course of Newman's sermons." Sara Coleridge, daughter of the poet, read them, and in spite of her High Church sympathies, found much in them for criticism.

I trust they are likely to do great good by placing in so strong a light as they do the indispensableness of an orthodox belief, the importance of sacraments as the main channels of Christian privileges, and the powers, gifts, and offices of Christian ministers derived by Apostolic Succession. But then these views are often supported, as I think, by unfair reasonings, and are connected with other notions that appear to me superstitious, unwarranted by any fair interpretation of Scripture, and containing the germ of popular errors.

These published sermons, with those of Keble, Pusey, and other Tractarians, had a larger circulation than the *Tracts*. But still there remained some classes of readers whom neither sermons nor tracts had reached, and the Oxford leaders were unceasing in their efforts to provide literature suitable for these. "We hope," said Pusey, "to publish tracts for hawkers' baskets in time." They proposed to found these tracts on interesting legends and stories of the saints, such, for instance, as the story of St. John and the robber he had baptized in youth. "These are popular in their nature, and to the people we must come."

The *Lyra Apostolica*, a collection of poems that had appeared originally in the *British Magazine*, was published in 1836. Most of the poems were written by Newman, the rest by Keble, Williams, and others. The book had not the immediate and enthusiastic recognition that had been given to the *Christian Year*, but it became one of the treasured possessions of those who loved Newman and revered his words. Some of the poems it contained —pre-eminently *The Pillar of the Cloud*, commonly known by its opening words, "Lead, kindly Light"—made a strong appeal to all readers of a devotional temperament, High Church and Low Church, educated and uneducated alike. The *Lyra Apostolica* was one of the books that Walter Bagehot and his wife read together on their honeymoon. Mary Ann Evans was attracted to it "by some highly poetical extracts I have picked up in various quarters." James Anthony Froude read it before he went up to Oxford, and was greatly struck by it. The poems, he said—

> were unlike any other religious poetry that was then extant. It was hard to say why they were so fascinating. They had none of the musical grace of the *Christian Year*. They were not harmonious; the metre halted, the rhymes were irregular, yet there was something in them that seized the attention and would not let it go.

Meantime the *Tracts* had been regularly appearing. For seven years and a half they were sent out from Oxford month by month, until, on February 27, 1841, came the ninetieth of the series. It was written by Newman, and dealt with the assertion made by some of his opponents that the doctrines taught by the Tractarians were not in agreement with the Thirty-nine Articles; and it endeavoured to show, by reference to the history of the Church, that certain Articles, rightly considered, might bear an interpretation different from that usually given to them. Although this was an undoubted historic fact, since the Articles were framed by Cranmer and his assistants in a spirit of compromise, in order that men of varying shades of religious belief might conscientiously subscribe to them, it was one that had been lost sight of in the fervour of Protestantism that marked the seventeenth century. Newman's re-statement of it came as a shock to the larger part of the nation.

The effect of *Tract 90* was startling. The disapproval, the opposition, the hatred that the Oxford Movement had provoked caught fire at it and blazed up in a fierce outbreak of antagonism; while on the other side love and devotion glowed with fresh intensity. All England seemed aflame. Newman and his friends were amazed. They had expected nothing more than the ordinary chorus of dissent with which each *Tract* as it appeared had been received. Isaac Williams says that the first intimation they had of what was happening came when William Ward, a Fellow of Balliol, and an eager, outspoken Tractarian, came into Newman's room, and said, "There is an immense demand for that *Tract*, and it is creating a tremendous stir, I find, in Parker's shop." The startled group of friends saw the stir spread from Oxford all over the country; they heard of large orders for it being given by booksellers, and they learnt that by the end of a fortnight two thousand five hundred copies had been sold. But before that time they knew that the sensation the *Tract* was causing did not mean approval but bitter condemnation.

Within the University the condemnation was fiercest. All the heads of Colleges, except the President of Magdalen and the Rector of Exeter, denounced the *Tract*. The morning following its publication four College tutors—including Tait of Balliol, who, later, became Archbishop of Canterbury—met and drew up a letter calling on the author to disclose his name. Tait was especially active. He became, Richard Church says, "a purchaser of *No. 90* to such an extent that Parker could hardly supply him," and he sent copies to all the bishops and to other influential Churchmen. On March 12th the Heads of Houses decided that the *Tract* should be censured. They gave the author no opportunity to explain or defend his work. On March 16th the official condemnation of the *Tract*, with the author's name appended, was posted up in the Schools and in the College Butteries.

Thirteen years later, in his *Apologia*, Newman told the story of those sad and stormy days—

> In the universal storm of indignation with which the *Tract* was received throughout the country on its appearance I recognize much of real religious feeling, much of honest and true principle, much of straightforward, ignorant common sense. . . . I was quite unprepared for the outbreak and was startled by its violence. I do not think I had any fear. Nay, I will add I am not sure that it was not in one point of view a relief to me.
>
> I saw indeed clearly that my place in the movement was lost. Public confidence was at an end; my recognition was gone! It was simply an impossibility that I could say anything henceforth to good effect, when I had been posted up by the Marshal on the buttery hatch of every College of my University after the manner of discommoned pastrycooks, and when in every part of the country and every class of society, through every organ and occasion of opinion, in newspapers, in periodicals, at meetings, in pulpits, at dinner-tables, in coffee-rooms, in railway carriages I was denounced as a traitor who had laid his train, and was in the very act of firing it against the time-honoured Establishment.

Charles Kingsley, writing from Cambridge to his mother in June 1841, put into words what hundreds of men and women in the country were thinking about *Tract 90* when he said—

Whether wilful or self-deceived, these men are Jesuits, taking the oath to the Articles with moral reservations which allow them to explain them away in senses utterly different from those of their authors. All the worst doctrinal features of Popery Mr. Newman professes to believe in.

It was this idea—that Newman was acting unfairly and meanly, was twisting the words of the Articles to his own ends that he might still remain in the English Church though he was not her loyal son—which roused the wrath of the country against him. It was this which moved Dr. Arnold to denounce the *Tract* with violence, both in his sermons and his writings, and which made him say in a letter to an old pupil—

My feelings towards a Roman Catholic are quite different from my feelings towards a Newmanite, because I think the one a fair enemy, the other a treacherous one. The one is the Frenchman in his own uniform, and within his own praesidia; the other is the Frenchman disguised in a red coat, and holding a post within our praesidia for the purpose of betraying it. I should honour the first and hang the second.

Some of those who condemned the *Tract* did so unwillingly, and only after careful study of the text. F. W. Robertson annotated his copy with answers to its arguments drawn from works of theology dealing with the subject. In the end he decided against the Tractarians, though he kept a deep respect for their manliness and devotion and for the practical work they had done in arousing the Church. Benjamin Jowett, Fellow of Balliol, also studied the *Tract* carefully, and wrote out reasons for and against its arguments. On the whole he saw no reason to depart from the position he had taken up three years before, when he had said—

I do not agree with or understand many of Newman's principles, but cannot help thinking they will have, on the whole, a salutary effect on the Protestant Church in bringing back men's minds to a class of duties which have been too much neglected.

James Anthony Froude said that fifty years after the *Tract* was published he found a copy of it, scored over with pencil marks and interjections, among the papers of a friend. Mr. Gladstone read *No. 90* carefully, and absolved its author of duplicity, though he deplored the tendency of his writing—

The most serious feature of the *Tract* to my mind is that, doubtless with very honest intentions, and with his mind turned for the moment so entirely towards those inclined to defection, and therefore occupying their point of view exclusively, he has in writing it placed himself quite outside the Church of England in point of spirit and sympathy.

Martin Tupper was less charitable. As the most popular poet of the day, whose books of rhymed moral platitudes were selling by thousands, he obviously thought himself entitled to sit in judgment upon anyone who showed a presumptuous desire to share with him the office of spiritual guide and leader.

In matters theological I was strongly opposed to the Tractarians, especially denouncing Newman and Pusey for their dishonest non-naturalness and *No. 90*.

The months went on and the storm showed no signs of dying down. It did not drive Newman's disciples from him; rather it braced them to set their feet more firmly upon the path along which he was leading. There was a large body of opinion on Newman's side, although his opponents made the most noise. The papers, as Richard Church put it, were "full of the row," but *The Times*, under the editorship of John Walter, was, as Charles Greville, the diarist, recorded, "decidedly Puseyite"; and the High Church organs were staunch. "People in the country," said Church—

have in general backed us up manfully. Newman has had most kind letters of approval and concurrence from W. Palmer of Worcester, A. Perceval, Hook, Todd, and Moberly.

But in spite of all this support, Newman, as he said, saw clearly that his place in the movement was lost. When the Bishop of Oxford desired him to issue no more tracts, he agreed at once. At the beginning of 1842 he left Oxford and went to live at Littlemore, three miles away, though he still sometimes preached at St. Mary's Church. Doubts began to trouble him, and he could find no rest in the Anglo-Catholic doctrines he had upheld so strenuously. In September 1843 he resigned his living, and in October 1845 he was received into the Church of Rome.

Eight months before this Oxford had witnessed the last scene in the history of *Tract 90*. When Convocation met on February 13th a motion of censure on the *Tract* was brought forward. It was hotly discussed, and excitement rose very high. There was obviously a majority in favour of the motion, but the proctors (of whom Richard Church was one) exercised their right of veto, and the formal censure was thus avoided.

There followed for the Anglo-Catholics a period of deep depression. Faber and Ward and Hope-Scott and several others followed Newman to Rome, and there were fears of a much larger secession. But Keble and Pusey remained, and with them as guides the party rallied and took heart. It never ceased to mourn for Newman, for no one who had known him could forget his devotion, his selflessness, his strange endearing charm. The seed he had helped to sow grew up and flourished. Year by year the High Church party increased in numbers and in influence, until it was strong enough to have a real effect on the national life.

CHAPTER III

THE WORLD OF MISS CHARLOTTE YONGE

FROM Newman to Miss Charlotte Yonge may seem a somewhat depressing descent. Yet, as Newman represents and explains the forces engaged in the great battle of the *Tracts*, so through Miss Yonge is revealed the state of the High Church kingdom when the worst of the strife was over, and, in the dangerous days of peace, the effort to maintain the ideals and use the privileges that had been fought for so gallantly must form part of the daily life of each loyal subject. The girl who had been brought up under Keble's guidance, and in the midst of the Anglican colony of Hursley, became the historian and interpreter of this stage of the Movement to a later generation; while to her own she appeared as a great story-teller and an inspired teacher.

Miss Yonge's stories—her historical novels being omitted—dealt mainly with well-ordered households of the upper middle class. The members of these households were not always well-to-do, they were sometimes actually poor, but they were refined, highly principled, well-educated, and devotedly attached to the Anglican Church. Their lives were filled with such small daily acts of self-discipline and obedience to the higher law as made them ready for great deeds when occasion called. The villains of the stories came from outside the Church's pale, and, apart from the machinations of these aliens, the chief causes of sorrow and disaster were shown to be spiritual pride in various forms, and neglect or misuse of Church privileges. Occasionally Miss Yonge extended the boundaries of her world to take in the mansions of the nobility—as in *Heartsease*—or the cottages of country labourers —as in *Tales of Langley Village*—but in these, too, life was ordered in accordance with the same ideals and principles.

In *Samuel Butler and his Family Relations*, the author, speaking of Miss May Butler, says—

I think her prototype is to be met in the novels of Charlotte M. Yonge; the perfect Churchwoman, spiritual, intellectual, devoted; strong in her faithful following of duty; sweet-tempered, serene, and cheerful from an active and disciplined life.

The description might well stand for Charlotte Yonge herself and for many of her readers, as well as for the characters in her books. It would be difficult to find another writer whose characters and whose readers bore so close a resemblance to each other as did those of Charlotte Yonge in the early days of her fame. It is, indeed, quite possible to imagine them changing places. Ethel May of *The Daisy Chain* would have delighted in reading *The Heir of Redclyffe*, and Dr. Moberly's large family—who adored Miss Yonge's novels—might quite fittingly have figured in a new story on the lines of *The Pillars of the House*.

There were other authors who wrote for and about the High Church party, though none of them with the insight and success of Charlotte Yonge. Elizabeth Sewell's *Amy Herbert* appeared in 1844. It was, its author said, "the outcome of the influence that the Oxford Movement had not only upon myself but upon all about me." It contrasted the lives led by worldly and by religious people, and in a time when the claims of the Church were being so strongly and so eloquently urged it attracted a good deal of attention. There was much discussion as to how these claims should be met.

Everyone seemed waking up to a sense of unfulfilled duties, and the question constantly discussed was which had the primary claim—home, or church services and works of charity. I heard it said that young ladies rushed about to visit the poor, and were constant at daily services, while they were neglectful of their parents.

This suggested to Miss Sewell the subject for her next book, *Gertrude*, in which she gave her views on these contending claims, and she followed this with other books on similar lines. For some years she had the field almost to herself, for Charlotte Yonge, who was still in her early twenties, was writing only a few children's stories for the *Monthly Packet*, a High Church magazine which she edited, and the circulation of which never rose above fifteen or sixteen hundred.

All through the 'forties and the early 'fifties the impulse given by the Oxford Movement was being more and more widely felt. Everywhere neglected churches were being put in order, services were becoming more frequent, as well as more seemly and beautiful, parishes were being stirred out of the apathy in which for years they had been sunk. In the large towns new churches were rising to serve the needs of crowded industrial districts. At Leeds, Walter Farquhar Hook and his devoted band of curates were making a great fight against the ignorance and irreligion of the factory population. Even into remote country districts like the tiny Cornish village of Aberalva, of which Kingsley tells in *Two Years Ago*, there came ardent young Anglican priests eager—perhaps over-eager—to do battle against Dissent as well as against wickedness. In 1845 Edward FitzGerald, who although he admired Newman and had some sympathy with the Oxford Movement, was always irritated by what he considered the excesses of the High Church party, wrote from Dorsetshire—

I found the churches much occupied by Puseyite parsons; new chancels built, with altars and painted windows that officiously displayed the Virgin Mary, etc. The people in those parts call that party "Puyicides" and receive their doctrines and doings peacefully. I am vexed at these silly men who are dishing themselves and their Church as fast as they can.

But instead of "dishing" the Church, the "silly men" by their labours and their enthusiasm were steadily raising it in the estimation of many even among their opponents. That great national organ, *The Times*, continued under the editorship of Mr. John Walter to give them strong support. Newman's influence was still powerful, although he no longer spoke from the pulpit of St. Mary's. In 1848 he established the Oratory at Birmingham, and there, in the vacation of that year, Edward White Benson, a schoolboy of nearly nineteen, heard him preach. Benson's schoolfellow, Joseph Lightfoot, had entreated him not to go, but the boy had read the *Tracts for the Times*, and was too much interested in the Oxford Movement to miss a chance of seeing and hearing the man who had led and then forsaken it. Afterwards he wrote to Lightfoot—

Do not say anything to me about conscientiously formed opinions as to the propriety of going to hear Newman preach, for I have none. I went one Sunday in Lent, because I wished to hear him, and I am very glad that I did. He is a wonderful man, truly, and spoke with a sort of Angel eloquence, if you comprehend me. Sweet, flowing, unlaboured language, in short, very short and pithy and touching sentences. Such a style of preaching I never heard before, never hope again to hear. Yet it reminded me very forcibly of Arnold. . . . To think that this timid-looking, little, weak-voiced man had so moved England.

In this same year of 1848 a fifteen-year-old schoolboy, Edward Burne-Jones, went from his home in Birmingham to visit a friend who lived at Hereford. There he met John Goss, a young High Church clergyman who had been at Oxford at the time of Newman's secession. At Birmingham he had been used to attend with his father a church where the services were of a pronounced Evangelical character. The beauty and dignity of Mr. Goss's Anglican services touched the boy's imagination, and he was eager to learn all the clergyman could teach him of High Church faith and practice. Mr. Goss lent him Newman's works, and he left Hereford an ardent Anglican. Thirty years afterwards he wrote to a friend—

When I was fifteen or sixteen he (Newman) taught me so much that I do mind—things that will never be out of me. In an age of sofas and cushions he taught me to be indifferent to comfort, and in an age of materialism he taught me to venture all on the unseen. . . . So if this world cannot tempt me—and it can't—or anything that it has in its trumpery treasure house, it is most of all because he said it in a way that touched me—walking with me a step in front. So he stands to me as a great image or symbol of a man who never stooped, and who put all this world's life in a splendid venture, which he knew, as well as you or I, might fail, but with a generous scorn of everything that was not his dream.

Almost at the same time another boy, William Morris, a year younger than Burne-Jones, was leaving his home at Walthamstow to enter Marlborough College. The school, which had only lately been founded, had no formal attachment to any religious party, but its tone was definitely High Church, and William Morris was quick to respond to its teaching. When he left the school he spent a year with a devout Anglican tutor, and his influence completed the work. The boy was an eager reader, with a special attraction towards what was ideal and romantic, and he found much to please his taste in the literature with which his Anglican guides supplied him.

There was growing up also a small company of younger boys

who were to meet later at Eton, and form there a fervent High Church group—Vincent Coles, son of the rector of Shepton Beauchamp, Archibald Primrose, afterwards Lord Rosebery, Digby Mackworth Dolben, the poet, and Robert Bridges, the future poet-laureate. Coles, said Dr. Bridges—

pre-eminent for his precocious theological bent and devotion to the cause was indeed the recognized authority, and our leader, in so far as universal esteem and confidence could give anyone such a position among us.

Lucy Lyttelton, afterwards Lady Frederick Cavendish, has told us something about the books upon which she and her eight brothers and three sisters were being brought up in the late 'forties and the 'fifties, and her account may be taken as applying to many other families whose heads were, like Lord Lyttelton, staunchly Anglican.

Not much of High Church doctrine was ever definitely taught to us as children, but the utmost care was taken as to the choice of our books and hymns. The quaint doggerel to which Watts thought it necessary to stoop when writing for children, the dismal Calvinism of *The Fairchild Family*, the irreverent familiarity of the *Peep of Day* and *Line upon Line*, were unknown in our nursery and schoolroom. Our earliest "Bible Book" was one containing the history of the Fall and the Gospel story in the words of Scripture, compiled by Bishop Samuel Wilberforce, and we were brought up upon his allegories and those of Adams and Monro, upon Mrs. Alexander's hymns—as devout, spiritual, and tender as they are dogmatic; upon the *Christian Year*, Neale's *Stories of Saints and Martyrs*, Paget's *Tales of the Village Children*, and among other beloved books *Ivo and Verena* and *The Birthday*. I am glad to say, however, that *Pilgrim's Progress*, unabridged and delightfully illustrated, was among our great favourites. But while conscious that all these had their marked effect, I should certainly place in the first rank of books that influenced my girlhood Miss Sewell's and Miss Yonge's.

In working-class homes there was to be found the same spiritual atmosphere. Miss Octavia Hill tells how, in 1859, she visited one of the pupils who came to the Working Men's College. The family of eight lived at the top of a house in rather a wretched neighbourhood. They had seen better days, and they tried hard to make the best of their poor home. "They are earnest High Church people," said Miss Hill; "the baby is called Amy Herbert after Miss Sewell's heroine, and also because Mrs. —— is so fond of George Herbert's poems. Brave, faithful little home!"

Thus there was being formed in the country a company of readers whose members were drawn from all parts and from all classes, and had certain common tastes and common interests, and a common attraction to particular books.

First among these books came the *Christian Year*. It was the Anglican's treasure, highly valued and reverently loved. The Oxford Movement had, said John Campbell Shairp, bequeathed to England "two permanent monuments of genius, Newman's sermons and the *Christian Year*. The little book became the daily companion of thousands of High Church people. Children were brought up upon it, and there must have been many who, like Thackeray's Arthur Pendennis, remembered reading it with their mothers, "whispering it to each other in awe."

Faint, very faint and seldom in after life Pendennis heard that solemn church music; but he always loved the remembrance of it, and of the times that it struck on his heart, and he walked over the fields, full of hope and void of doubt as the church bells rang on Sunday morning.

Mr. Robert Bridges in his boyhood was given the *Christian Year* on Sunday and set to learn its poems by heart. In the Lyttelton family the book was a loved and familiar possession. The verses for the week were read aloud each Sunday morning; Lucy Lyttelton and Lord Frederick Cavendish read them together after they became engaged. When they were married, in 1864, her father gave Lord Frederick Cavendish a Communion book in which he wrote the last verse of the *Christian Year* poem on marriage, and eighteen years later, in the first terrible days of mourning for her murdered husband, Lady Frederick was able to find some comfort in the beautiful familiar words read to her by her cousin, Mary Gladstone.

High Church people turned naturally to the *Christian Year* when they were in trouble. In the more solemn moments of life its help and counsel were often sought. "Arthur received his first Communion to-day. He has been reading to me the *Christian Year* for the day," said Kitty Moberly, the eldest of the sixteen children of the Headmaster of Winchester School. "Scraps of the *Christian Year* have been of great comfort to me," wrote Pusey; and Bishop Westcott declared that a verse of Keble was worth volumes of Tennyson.

James Smethan, architect and poet, called Keble a "sweet poet," and quoted with delight "New every morning is the love." Florence Nightingale loved the *Christian Year*. Mr. Holt White has told us how his father used to learn verses from it while he combed and burnished his beautiful Victorian beard. Even Ouida's flippant reference in her story, *Fitz's Election*, where she represents Mr. Le Hoop Smith, the Liberal-Conservative candidate, as winning the favour of the clergy by quoting freely from the *Christian Year*, is a testimony to the esteem in which the book was held. It was for several generations a favourite gift book; and in High Church bookshops, such as that of which Mrs. Oliphant tells us in *Salem Chapel*, there were editions suitable for all recipients—tiny miniature copies, "just made to slip within the pocket of an Anglican waistcoat," big, red-leaved and morocco-bound volumes for family use, and "something pretty with a little ornament and gilding" to delight young ladies. Ninety-five editions were sold during Keble's lifetime, and the new church at Hursley was built with the profits that they brought. We can understand, therefore, Lady Frederick Cavendish's surprise and almost horror as she wrote in her diary on August 31, 1864—

Mr. Lionel Ashley came and made my hair stand on end by announcing that he had just heard for the first time of Keble and the *Christian Year*.

A similar hair-raising effect would have been produced in a company of Anglican readers if one of their number had confessed that he knew nothing of the works of Scott. Sir Walter was not, like Keble, the particular property of the Anglicans; he belonged to the nation. Yet they could claim that in one sense he was peculiarly their own, since he was to them more fully than to any other body of readers a teacher and a spiritual guide. Charlotte Yonge in one of her later works, *The Trial*, shows clearly this side of the relation between Scott and his High Church readers. *The Trial* is to some extent a sequel to *The Daisy Chain*, and continues the history of the May family, though its hero is Leonard Ward, one of their friends. This youth at the age of sixteen was but slightly acquainted with Sir Walter. "You who taught us to love our Walter Scott next to our *Christian Year*," wrote Ethel May to her father, "and who gave us half-crowns for rehearsing him when other children were learning the *Robin's Petition*, what think you of this poor boy Leonard knowing few of the novels and none of the poems?" With headlong enthusiasm Ethel set to work to remedy this defect in the boy's education. She and her brother Aubrey spent a wet afternoon in reading *Marmion* to Leonard—

Aubrey snatching it from me at all the critical passages for fear I should not do them justice, and thundering out the battle, which stirred the other boy like a trumpet sound. Indeed, Leonard got Mab (the dog) into a corner, and had a very bad cold in the head when De Wilton was re-knighted; and when "the hand of Douglas was his own" he jumped up and shouted out, "Well done, old fellow!" Then he took it to himself and read it all over again, introductions and all, and has raved about it ever since.

Afterwards the three had a serious discussion as to why Heaven had not shown the right in the encounter between Marmion and De Wilton. Was it, as the poem suggested, because

> Perchance some form was unobserved,
> Perchance in prayer or faith he swerved?

Ethel had, as she said, to "plunge deep" in her efforts to prove that divine justice was certain, though it might be delayed, and that human injustice might be allowed for some high and hidden purpose.

Then came Leonard's troubles. Before he was eighteen he was accused of a murder of which he knew nothing, tried, and condemned to death. In the terrible time that followed the boy was comforted by thinking of "the happy days when we read *Marmion*," as well as by Keble's hymn, "Sun of my soul." Almost at the last moment his sentence was commuted to penal servitude for life, and he was imprisoned for three years before his innocence was established and he was released. On the morning after his return home he went with Ethel to the early Communion service, and as they entered the church she could not help repeating the long-treasured lines—

Grieve not for thy woes
Disgrace and trouble;
For He who honour best bestows,
Shall give thee double.

And Leonard replied, "I've never ceased to be glad that you read *Marmion* with me."

Not all the High Church party read Scott in this devout spirit, but in most cases a touch of reverence mingled with the affectionate admiration that was given to him. Yet this did not prevent them from enjoying to the full the thrills that both the Waverley novels and the poems can give. "We delighted in the Waverley novels," said Kitty Moberly—

from the time when Alice and George, as small children, rushed out into the street to greet their father who was just alighting from the omnibus with the excited announcement, "Such good news! the Black Knight has got into the castle!" to the time when Annie entreated Emily and me to say nothing against the Vehme Gericht while undressing at night, lest our beds should be drawn by pulleys into the larder below.

If the Anglicans could claim but a partial interest in Sir Walter Scott, they could boast that Charlotte Yonge was peculiarly and entirely their own. To compare the two would seem, to any later generation, an impertinence, but Miss Yonge's contemporaries saw in it nothing incongruous. Canon Dixon declared that *The Heir of Redclyffe* was "unquestionably one of the finest books in the world." When it appeared in 1853 it had a reception such as has been given to no other book in our language. Miss Elizabeth Wordsworth, who at that time was thirteen years old, says—

It is difficult for people of this generation to understand the enthusiasm with which it was received. It was, as regards fiction, what to the Tractarian Movement the *Christian Year* and some of Newman's poems had been to poetry. . . . It is hardly too much to say that Charlotte Yonge's work, open to criticism as it undoubtedly is, yet seems likely to remain as the high-water mark of English society at its very best. *The Heir of Redclyffe* won instant popularity, not only with girls in the schoolroom, but with grown men, scholars, artists, and men of the world.

To the High Church party it was not only a beautiful story, but also a confession of faith, a noble picture of an ideal life. Sir

Guy Morville, its young hero, became the model for hundreds of youths growing up to manhood. His unfortunate ancestry, the doom that hung over him, his high spirits, his violent passions, his courage, his charm, his misfortunes, and his early death appealed to the same love of romance that caused readers to delight in the novels of Scott; while his high principles, his struggles against temptation, his self-sacrifice, his devout attachment to the Church, made him the ideal Tractarian hero.

The book was read and discussed everywhere. Alice Moberly declared herself in love with Sir Guy, and she was the first of a large number of young ladies who lost their hearts to the all-conquering heir of Redclyffe. Justice Coleridge waxed indignant at Philip, the hero's immaculate cousin, and declared that when Philip came to Oxford to inquire into Guy's debts, Guy should have kicked him downstairs. Julian Yonge added that he should have horsewhipped him round the quad. Julian was Charlotte's brother, and an officer in the Rifle Brigade. All the young men in his regiment, he said, had a copy of *The Heir of Redclyffe*, and all were captivated by the story. When the Crimean War sent many officers to hospital, the book that was in the greatest demand among them was *The Heir of Redclyffe*.

Keble admired the book greatly, and Mrs. Keble read it many times over. She liked best, she said, the part that told of Guy's retirement at Redclyffe. Mrs. Wilson, the wife of Keble's curate, declared that when she had finished the book she felt as if she had lost a dear friend. Many tears were shed over Guy's sorrows, and more over his early death—not only by sentimental young ladies, but also, we are told, by elderly and scholarly gentlemen and high-spirited youths. In 1857 George Lawrence published his notorious *Guy Livingstone*, which described a way of life the exact opposite of that shown by Miss Yonge—the life of a rich, dissipated, reckless young man, who defied all conventions and cared nothing for morality. Yet even in this book *The Heir of Redclyffe* received a tribute of respectful admiration—

Very old and very young women, in the plenitude of their benevolence, are good enough to sympathize with any tale of woe, however absurdly exaggerated; but men, I think, are most moved by the simple and quiet sorrows. . . . We yawn over the wailings of Werter and Raphael; but we ponder gravely over the last chapters of *The Heir of Redclyffe*.

There was, in particular, one set of young men upon whom the book had a great and lasting influence. William Morris went up to Oxford in 1853, in the same year as Edward Burne-Jones. The two met, and quickly formed a friendship which lasted to the end of their lives. Burne-Jones had other friends at Oxford who had been his schoolfellows at King Edward's School, Birmingham—Cornell Price, Richard Watson Dixon, William Fulford, and Harry Macdonald. A little group was formed whose members read and talked and studied together, and among the books that they read was *The Heir of Redclyffe*. It exercised upon them an extraordinary fascination. They took it, with devout seriousness, as their inspiration and their guide, and Morris, in particular, resolved to model himself upon its hero. Later, they found that their idol, Dante Gabriel Rossetti, and the Pre-Raphaelite group of which he was the leading spirit, also loved and reverenced Miss Yonge's masterpiece, and this confirmed them in their own allegiance.

The group to which John Manners and George Smythe belonged was almost equally affected. To them Sir Guy Morville seemed the embodiment of their vision of a latter-day knight, and they recognized him as their leader in deeds of chivalry and high adventure. His sympathy with the Stuart cause made the hearts of those whom Borrow had scornfully stigmatized as Jacobites turn eagerly towards him. Here was one who, like themselves, revered the memory of "our own, our royal saint," King Charles I. "How one would have loved him," said Sir Guy, "loved him for the gentleness so little accordant with the rude times and the part he had to act—served him half like a knight's devotion to his lady-love, half like devotion to a saint."

Some readers did not care for the book, but these were outside the High Church pale. Hester Cholmondley, sister of Mary Cholmondley, and youngest of the eight children of the Evangelical rector of Hodnet, Shropshire, complained that it was sentimental and feeble, and went on too long after Guy's death; but Hester was an impatient, precocious young genius, apter to blame than to praise. Few Dissenters, probably, read the book, but they heard it talked about and learnt something of its story. Mrs. Austin, daughter of the Unitarian Mrs. John Taylor, who in the early years of the nineteenth century had held her brilliant literary salon at Norwich, probably expressed the views of her circle when she wrote—

The Heir of Redclyffe I have not read. It sounded too good for me. I am not worthy of superhuman flights of virtue—in a novel. I want to see how people act and suffer who are as good-for-nothing as I am myself. Then I have the sinful pretension to be amused, whereas all our novelists want to reform us, and to show us what a hideous place the world is.

But no criticism from outsiders, to whom Sir Guy was only an over-good and rather tiresome young man, could affect the hero-worshippers. He remained their model and high exemplar, whom they were eager to copy in every particular. They read the books that he had read and approved; and chief among these was Sintram and his Companions, by La Motte Fouqué, a French writer of the late eighteenth century. The story was one of a series of four, each of which dealt allegorically with one of the four seasons. It had been well known in England long before the publication of The Heir of Redclyffe. Newman had read it in his boyhood, and had been so overcome by it that he had rushed away to finish it in the garden by himself. Bishop Thirlwall, Mrs. Carlyle, and Edward Freeman had all read and admired it. Macaulay considered it odd and extravagant, and rebuked his fifteen-year-old niece for praising it, but Macaulay's sympathies and tastes were, definitely, not those of the Anglicans. After the appearance of The Heir of Redclyffe, Sintram became one of the treasures of the High Church party. William Morris and Edward Burne-Jones read it eagerly and remembered it to the end of their lives. In 1874 Burne-Jones wrote to his son, who was at school at Marlborough—

I send you a little book I used to love very much, called Fouqué's Seasons. I have not read them for twenty years, but I still think they must be very good. I believe Undine is the best, but I used to like Sintram most.

A little before the publication of The Heir of Redclyffe, the first instalment of another novel by Miss Yonge, called The Daisy Chain, appeared in the Monthly Packet. This little magazine had become very popular in its own special circle. "In our large family it was fairly read to pieces," said Lucy Lyttelton. The Daisy Chain made it more popular still. The story ran for two years, and then, as there seemed a likelihood of its running for two more, it was discontinued, and in 1856 was published in a complete form.

This time it was the heroine—Ethel May—who became the idol of the book's many readers. Hundreds of schoolgirls adored the "thin, lank, angular, sallow" girl of fifteen to whom they were introduced in the opening passage of the new book. She was so clever, so unselfish, so loyal a daughter of the Church, so full of great and noble schemes for the good of others. Her untidiness, her clumsiness, her short sight, her brusque manners were all so many endearing qualities that established her still more firmly in her admirers' affections. One girl who had fallen in love with Ethel wrote to Miss Yonge saying, "You are the mother of all my good thoughts." Another, who was an orphan and lonely, said that she had found her first real friends in *The Daisy Chain*. The wife of Bishop Summer told how she had introduced to Miss Yonge yet another young girl who had conceived a passion for her through *The Heir of Redclyffe* and *The Daisy Chain*; and a certain Mr. Butterfield was said to be going about searching for an Ethel May that he might make her his wife.

The Moberlys were greatly excited over the new book, which they had begun in the *Monthly Packet*. The fact that it was about a large family, though one not quite as large as their own, quickened their interest. Miss Yonge delighted in large families, and in that, as in other things, she reflected the tendencies of her age. There were eleven Mays, and in *The Pillars of the House*, that came later, there were thirteen Underwoods.

Dr. May shared the honours with Ethel. As the head of his motherless household he was considered by sober, grown-up opinion to have done all that a devout High Church father could do; while his lovable recklessness and quick temper gained him the favour of younger readers. Even Hester Cholmondley was subjugated. "Dr. May is charming," she said, though she thought the tale as a whole "too long and too dull," with "some characters good and lifelike, but others solemnly exaggerated and unnatural." When Miss Yonge began writing sequels to her stories Dr. Moberly made her promise that she would never allow Ethel May to be married or Dr. May to die. That promise she kept. When, eight years later, she wrote *The Trial*, Dr. May was as active and hot-tempered as ever, and Ethel having reached the mature age of twenty-five, was ready, in Victorian fashion, to describe herself as "an elderly, despised spinster."

Soon after *The Trial* appeared, Henry Sidgwick, then a Fellow of Trinity College, Cambridge, wrote to his friend, Roden Noel—

There is a new story by the authoress of *The Heir of Redclyffe* which I have read with all my old enthusiasm. I thought it was quite gone off as the last two of her books rather bored me, but I can't get *The Trial* out of my head. Did you ever read *Madame Bovary*? It is a very powerful book, and Miss Yonge reminds me of it by force of contrast. It shows how the ennui of mean French domestic life drags down women, whereas Miss Yonge makes one feel how full of interest the narrowest sphere of life is. I think her religion is charming, and it mellows with age, the *âpre* Puseyism wears off.

It says much for the qualities of the new book that it found, as it did, many readers as appreciative as Henry Sidgwick; for it came at a time when there was great excitement in the Anglican party, and when the attention of most of its members was given to a book of a very different character. The cause of the excitement was a controversy between Kingsley and Newman. Kingsley's strong sense of what he believed to be the soul-destroying effects of the Romish doctrines would not let him rest. To fight those doctrines with all his strength was, as he saw it, his plain duty. In a review of Froude's *History* he stated that the Roman Catholic clergy did not regard truth as one of the highest virtues, and that this had been acknowledged by Father Newman. Newman demanded when he had made such an admission, and Kingsley, instead of owning that he had spoken hastily and made too strong a statement, attempted to defend what he had said. In reply Newman wrote his *Apologia pro vita sua*.

He wrote it, he said, straight on, for many hours at a time, weeping sometimes, feeling always that he had that to say which must be said. The result was a marvellous history of his spiritual life, vivid, sincere, convincing, told in the same fine, simple language that had helped to give his sermons their charm. It gave him the victory in the controversy with Kingsley, and it did far more than that. It came to those who had loved him and sorrowed for his loss almost as a voice from the dead, arousing in them the same fervour of devotion that they had felt when his words had come to them week by week from St. Mary's. They read of their leader's doubts and sufferings and learnt with what anguish of soul he had taken those last steps in which they had not been able to follow. Keble, who had grieved bitterly over Newman's secession, found great reason for rejoicing in the *Apologia*; Church was profoundly moved by it.

Lady Frederick Cavendish wrote in her diary on August 28, 1864, ten weeks after her marriage—

I have just read a book which Newman has written in answer to a very feeble and spiteful attack on him by Kingsley. The title is *Apologia pro vita sua*, and it is an account of his religious opinions, and what led him to Rome. I was often beyond my depth, but I think I see something of the principle that influenced him, viz., that unity is more to be valued than pure doctrine; and he got into a dilemma between Rome on the one hand and scepticism on the other. He is as little controversial as possible, and defends none of the great errors, except indirectly. It is written very fairly and modestly, and in his beautiful clear style.

There were some who had once been Newman's ardent disciples, but who had later renounced their allegiance to the Anglican Church; yet even these kept a tender and reverent memory of their old leader's personality, and read his book with sincerest admiration. One such was Mark Pattison, another was James Anthony Froude. Of Pattison Mrs. Humphry Ward says that though in the sceptical and agnostic talk of his later years he never spared either the Anglican priesthood or the Roman converts, she never heard him mention "the great name of John Henry Newman" with the slightest touch of disrespect, but that, on the other hand, she had seen him receive a message brought by a friend from Newman "with an eager look and a start of pleasure." Froude, though his sympathies in the controversy were mainly with Kingsley, yet acknowledged that that Protestant champion had entirely misunderstood Newman's character. "Newman's whole life had been a struggle for truth. . . . To represent such a person as careless of truth was neither generous nor even reasonable." The *Apologia*, Froude said, was "the most beautiful of autobiographies."

It touched every heart. It made High Churchmen treasure more lovingly and reverently Newman's earlier teaching; and to those who were not so deeply concerned with the religious issue it showed a man single-hearted and saintly who compelled their respect and admiration. George Eliot said that the *Apologia* "breathed much life into me when I read it." Edward FitzGerald was enthusiastic about it, praising especially its sincerity. Tennyson read and pondered over it. Horace Moule, a friend of Thomas Hardy's, was so impressed by it that he induced Hardy, then a young man of twenty-four, to read it. In July 1865 Hardy wrote in his diary—

Worked at J. H. Newman's *Apologia* which we have all been talking about lately. A great desire to be convinced by him, because Moule likes him so much. Style charming and his logic really human, being based not on syllogisms but on converging probabilities. Only—and here comes the fatal catastrophe—there is no first link to his excellent chain of reasoning, and down you come headlong.

One of the characters in George Gissing's *Born in Exile*, an agnostic, read the book, and made a criticism similar to that of Hardy—

When I first got hold of Newman's *Apologia* I began to read it with the utmost eagerness, flattering myself that now at length I should understand how a man of brains could travel such a road. I was horribly disappointed, and not a little enraged when I found he began by assuming the very beliefs I thought he was going to justify.

To no reader in Miss Yonge's world would such an objection have occurred. To them as to Newman the "first link" was a matter of faith, not capable of, or needing, logical proof. The last links were those which they rejected, and in this, too, faith rather than pure reason was their guide.

None of Miss Yonge's later books had quite the popularity or influence of the first two, though *Heartsease*, published in 1854, approached them very nearly. Lord Raglan read *Heartsease* amid the terrible distractions of the Crimean War. It was the last book he ever read. That stout opponent of Tractarianism, Charles Kingsley, said it was the most delightful and wholesome novel he had met with, and wrote to Miss Yonge to tell her so.

Never mind what *The Times* or anyone else says; the book is wise and human as well as Christian, and will surely become a standard book for aye and a day.

Keble, in a letter to Dr. Moberly, said—

> I do think Mrs. Moberly will enjoy little John Martindale even more this time than before. Mrs. Keble is very fond of him.

John Martindale, the heroine's little son, was perhaps too much like the preternaturally good children of the Evangelical tracts to please all tastes. Hester Cholmondley may have been thinking of him when she said that *Heartsease* was "good, but excessively annoying." Unlike those other prodigies, however, he did not make an edifying end at an early age, but lived to grow strong, and almost boylike.

Miss Rhoda Broughton, who was a girl of fifteen when *Heartsease* appeared, obviously read it, then or later, for in her novel, *Red as a Rose is She*, published in 1870, she makes her heroine, Esther, when told she is too young for love or marriage, reply—

> "I was seventeen last May, if you call that young," . . . her thoughts recurring to *Heartsease*, the heroine of which is wooed and married and a' before her sixteenth birthday.

It does not seem certain, however, that Miss Broughton admired Miss Yonge's works with the whole-heartedness of a true devotee. A slight note of disparagement may perhaps be detected in a remark she made towards the end of her literary career, "I began life as Zola, I finish it as Miss Charlotte Yonge" —a reference to the fact that her works, at first esteemed unfit for young ladies' reading, came later to be regarded as innocuous.

By the time the 'sixties came Miss Yonge's books were being read not only by her own High Church circle, but by the general reading public also; which, if it did not find itself in entire harmony with their religious tone, was yet attracted by the picture that they gave of a disciplined and devout family life. Miss Yonge had become a celebrity. When she came to London and attended evening parties people crowded to see her, and many of her admirers made pilgrimages to Hursley in the hope of catching a glimpse of the creator of Guy Morville and Ethel May.

In 1865 Miss Yonge paid a visit to Oxford, "where the enthusiasm for her among the undergraduates was wonderful." On another visit she met the learned mathematician and theologian, Charles Lutwidge Dodgson, who had lately acquired fame in a new direction by his *Alice in Wonderland*, and who, we are told, had long delighted in Miss Yonge's novels. In 1868 Henry Kingsley, another of her admirers, wrote, "Miss Yonge is as lovely as ever," referring presumably to the latest published of her works, *The Clever Woman of the Family*. In 1870 Miss Wordsworth recorded that at the opening of Keble College she "saw Miss Yonge, *the* Miss Yonge." Tennyson read Miss Yonge's books and admired them, though he sometimes allowed himself a kindly gibe at their strong Church bias. Mr. Palgrave said that once when he was on a visit to the poet, Tennyson was absorbed in *The Young Stepmother* and one night was reading it in bed. The story tells of the deferred confirmation of one of the grown-up characters, Mr. Kendal, the rite only being administered after many agitations and delays. For a long time Tennyson read on with absorbed attention. Then Mr. Palgrave heard him call out, "I see land! Mr. Kendal is just going to be confirmed"; after which the light was extinguished and the poet slept.

Tennyson's friend, Edward FitzGerald, had no sympathy with this taste for Miss Yonge. "I cannot get on with Books about the Daily Life which I find rather insufferable in practice about me," he complained; "I can't read the *Adam Bedes* and *Daisy Chains*, etc., at all." A later generation might see, in the classing of these works together, a high compliment to the second named.

Boys and girls of all ages delighted in Miss Yonge's stories. John Godley (afterwards Lord Kilbracken) gives her as one of his favourite authors before he went to school at the age of nine years and ten months. Lucy Lyttelton said that *The Heir of Redclyffe* and *Heartsease* occupied special thrones in her memory because they were the first modern novels she was allowed to read. She says also that she read *Dynevor Terrace* with Princess Helena during the time she spent at Windsor as maid-in-waiting to Queen Victoria in 1864, and next year, after she was married, she read *The Clever Woman of the Family*, which she thought "a sad failure of a book and mostly very dull." Lady Rose Fane, who was nineteen years old when *The Heir of Redclyffe* was published, said that she read all Miss Yonge's novels and all Miss Sewell's, and was delighted to find that other girls of her own age were equally keen about the social subjects with which the books dealt. Hester Cholmondley, in spite of her scornful attitude towards Miss Yonge's works, seems to have read them all, for she sums up her opinion of them thus—

All Miss Yonge's stories are very young-lady-like, too good, too dull and too High Church. They are all so exclusively written for schoolroom girls. I hate them.

The popularity of Miss Yonge and Miss Sewell quickly brought many followers and imitators. Authors and publishers realized that there was a demand for fiction with a bias towards High or Low Church, and a literature to meet the demand soon came into existence. Frank Smedley gave an amusing account of the beginnings of this literature in *Lewis Arundel*, written in 1852. When Rose Arundel took her poems to a London publisher, he assured her that there was no market for such works, and advised her to try her hand at a book something like *Amy Herbert*.

Clever book, *Amy Herbert*, very. So much tenderness in it, ma'am; nothing pays better than judicious tenderness; the mothers of England like it to read about—the daughters of England like it—the little girls of England like it—and so the husbands of England are forced to pay for it. If you recollect, ma'am, there's a pathetic governess in *Amy Herbert* who calls the children "dearest"; well-imagined character, that. She's sold many copies, has that governess.

He went on to tell her of other so-called religious novels which had had a wonderful success, such as *Ambrosius; or the Curate Confessed*, which turned on the wearing of a surplice by a curate of High Church tendencies while preaching to a Low Church congregation; and *Loyaliana; or the Jesuit in the Chimney Corner*, which was about an Anglican clergyman who went over to Rome. There were, actually, novels of this somewhat lurid type which were inspired by the religious dissensions of the day, but there were others, less extravagant, which were more obvious attempts to follow in the road where Miss Sewell had first adventured. Emma Jane Worboise, who was a very popular writer on the Low Church side, makes one of her heroines (herself an author) say—

If I wrote a red-hot Puseyite story, I knew exactly to whose care it ought to be confided; if a Low Church novel, where it would receive a hearty welcome.

Even in novels which had, as a whole, no definite religious tendency, glimpses of the world of Miss Charlotte Yonge were to be obtained. Those "two sweet Puseyites," Eleanor Hilton and blind Lord Edward Barty, of whom Henry Kingsley tells in *Austin Elliot*, were certainly denizens of that world; while Miss Braddon deftly added to the mixture of sentiment and melodrama that composed her novels a sufficient tincture of religion to produce an occasional hero who was "that *rara avis* among modern scholars and young laymen," being "honestly and unaffectedly religious, a staunch Anglican of the school of Pusey, and not ashamed to confess his faith at all times and seasons."

When, in 1855, Anthony Trollope published *The Warden*, it seemed to many readers that here was a greater than Charlotte Yonge, come to invade her territory and make it his own. When *Barchester Towers* followed two years later, these readers saw that they had been right as to the author's powers, but wrong as to his intentions. He was, it appeared, bent on creating a new world rather than on annexing one already in existence. Here was a picture of an Anglican community as seen by a man of the world, who stood apart and looked on with detachment, though with keen insight. The picture differed in many respects from the intimate, sympathetic presentment of Charlotte Yonge. Trollope's bishops and archdeacons, deans and vicars, true and lifelike as they were, would scarcely have been acceptable as spiritual guides to girls who, like Theodora Martindale of *Heartsease*, were burning to live a life of renunciation and service, or to poor Leonard Ward in his condemned cell. Mr. Arabin, Newman's ardent disciple, would have been at home in Miss Yonge's world, and so would the Reverend Septimus Harding, the Warden, but Barchester society in general would have found its atmosphere uncomfortably bracing.

Perhaps the one of Trollope's books that approaches most nearly to those of Miss Yonge is *Framley Parsonage*. Lady Lufton, we are told, had High Church tendencies, though she did not carry her principles so far as to advocate celibacy of the clergy.

She liked cheerful, quiet, well-to-do people, who loved their Church, their country and their Queen, and who were not too anxious to make a noise in the world.

Miss Yonge would certainly have agreed, though she might have added something to the description. Yet even *Framley Parsonage*, judged by the standards of her world, did not tend entirely to edification. The elders read it, but hesitated to put it into the hands of the young. Mr. Clare, the delightful blind rector of *The Clever Woman of the Family*, had been much attracted by some extracts from it that his niece had read to him, but had refused her offer to lend him the book, since he had to employ a pupil teacher from his school to read aloud to him, and "it would not edify Will Walker."

High Church people who had reached years of discretion did not confine their reading to their own special literature. They read what other people were reading. The works of Dickens and Thackeray, Tennyson and Browning, and the other great Victorians they received with enthusiasm. When in the late 'fifties and the 'sixties new scientific theories were being put forward and controversies founded upon them were agitating the country, the Anglicans—most of them—read the books dealing with these exciting matters, though sometimes they shuddered as they read. They read, too, the more frivolous literature of the day. Mary Gladstone's diary mentions dozens of novels, not only by the great writers, but also by such lesser lights as Rhoda Broughton, Julia Kavanagh, Marion Crawford, and Matilda Betham-Edwards, and these seem to have been read and discussed by the entire family. There is a story of Mr. Gladstone being seen sitting in the library of his Club absorbed in a book which a curious fellow-member, looking over his shoulder, discovered to be Miss Broughton's *Red as a Rose is She*. "Papa deep in *The Woman in White*," wrote Lucy Lyttelton in June 1861, soon after this "thriller" by Wilkie Collins had been published. Arthur Martindale, of *Heartsease*, read Mrs. Marsh's immensely popular *Emilia Wyndham*, which had been recommended to him by his sister Theodora, the most uncompromising of High Churchwomen. Even the heir of Redclyffe read the notorious *Ten Thousand a Year*, and Ethel May had great faith in the cheering properties of *Frank Fairlegh*.

The reading of the young people was strictly supervised. When Mrs. Kendal, of *The Young Stepmother*, found that her stepson, Guy, was reading *The Three Musketeers*, "one of the worst and most fascinating of Dumas' romances," she was terribly shocked, and gently suggested that he should give her the book and allow her to read to him the less obnoxious parts. It is to this incident, obviously, that Robert Louis Stevenson referred when he said that, meeting at the age of thirteen the name of D'Artagnan on certain illustrated dessert plates at a hotel in Nice, he greeted it like an old friend, seeing that he had met it in a work by Miss Yonge, "who introduced me to the name of D'Artagnan only to dissuade me from a nearer knowledge of the man." Even Shakespeare these young Anglicans read in Bowdler's edition. Sir Edmund Gosse shows us Algernon Swinburne as a small boy of twelve, with a large head and a flaming halo of red hair, arriving at Eton with a big volume of Bowdler's Shakespeare under his arm. The Swinburnes were a devout Anglican family, and Algernon's parents watched carefully over his reading. Lucy Lyttelton also made acquaintance with Shakespeare by the help of Mr. Bowdler. George Eliot, too, was held to require expurgation. "Granny began yesterday to spout to us the new novel about which the world raves, *Adam Bede*, to be duly bowdlerized for our young minds," Lucy recorded in her diary in April 1859, when she was eighteen years old. In most families George Eliot's works were absolutely forbidden to the young. Mr. Maurice Baring says that his sisters were not allowed to read them, and Mrs. Benson was by many people considered reprehensibly lax because she read some of them aloud to her children.

Miss Yonge, however, was always open to them, and of her they did not tire. Throughout the 'eighties she kept a large circle of readers, though the days of her greatest popularity were past. Miss Lilian Faithful says that she and her contemporaries loved Miss Yonge's novels.

How many of us would have to confess to weeping over the death of Guy in *The Heir of Redclyffe*. . . . The boys and girls of Miss Yonge's huge families were indeed ourselves . . . and we were as intimate with every detail of their lives as with the lives of our sisters, cousins, and aunts.

Mr. Baring's sisters were brought up on Miss Yonge's "domestic epics," though he himself read only the historical stories, *The Little Duke*, *The Lances of Lynwood*, and *The Chaplet of Pearls*, which last he thought "thrilling."

Lady Frederick Cavendish remained faithful to the author who had charmed her youth. In June 1881 she recorded in her diary that she had

made great acquaintance with the dear little body, Ethel Fane, aged fourteen, Henry Cowper's niece. We had no end of topics in common, being equal lovers of Miss Yonge, and I did enjoy the little body's intense enthusiasm and discernment, coupled with very pretty modesty. She is a loving little Churchwoman.

The world of Miss Charlotte Yonge may seem to-day to any who read her novels narrow, tame, and uninteresting. But its inhabitants were not as closely shut in as might appear. They lived in the familiar contemplation of great mysteries. They had a real consciousness of unseen realms which were as truly theirs as their actual home on earth. Their keen historic sense opened to them the world of the past. They acknowledged duties and obligations towards their neighbours and towards the nation the fulfilment of which freed them from the bounds of their own personal concerns. Many of them were eminent public servants. To claim such men as William Gladstone and Lord John Manners, Edward Burne-Jones, and Lord Frederick Cavendish as denizens of Miss Yonge's world may appear to some unwarranted; yet in a vital sense they were. Their characters were formed by the same training and the same books that she gave to her creations, and they would have been proud to have been classed as the fellows and equals of Guy Morville.

CHAPTER IV

THE CHAPEL FOLKS

"Dissent in any of its forms was a crime in our house," said James Anthony Froude; and most Church people, except those belonging to the extreme Evangelical party, would have agreed that it was both natural and right for Nonconformity to be so regarded. The curates of the Reverend Patrick Brontë—immortalized in *Shirley*—held that faith and held it firmly. "Dissent was schism, and schism was condemned in the Bible. In default of turbaned Saracens, they entered on a crusade against Methodists in broadcloth," says Mrs. Gaskell. Schism was a terrible word to the High Churchman. "If she will persist in going to chapel I cannot overlook the sin of schism," said Frank Headley, the saintly young curate of Kingsley's *Two Years Ago*, upholding his decree of dismissal against the no less saintly young village schoolmistress, Grace Harvey. Frank fought against dissent not as against turbaned Turks, but as against the devil himself, and there were hundreds of high-minded and devoted clergymen in the country who were engaged in the same (as they honestly conceived it to be) holy warfare.

Some of these clergymen were narrow-minded and self-righteous, and made the warfare appear spiteful and ridiculous instead of high and holy. Mary Cholmondley, in her novel, *Red Pottage*, has shown us one of these, the Reverend James Gresley, and has allowed us to listen to one of his sermons, by means of the comments of his adoring wife.

James is simply surpassing himself. "Worms!" What a splendid comparison. The Churchman the full-grown man after the stature of Christ, and the Dissenter invertebrate like a worm cleaving to the earth. But possibly God in His mercy may let them slip in by a back door to heaven! How like him to say that, so generous, so wide-minded, taking the hopeful view of everything. How noble he looks. These are days in which we should stick to our colours. I wonder how he can think of such beautiful things.

We hear also something of what Mr. Gresley's more intelligent sister thought of the same sermon—

Dear James! How good he is; how much in earnest. But worms don't go in at back doors. Why are not clergymen taught a few elementary rules of composition before they are ordained? But perhaps no one will notice it except myself. James is certainly a saint. He has the courage of his opinions. I believe he loves God and the Church with his whole heart and would go to the stake for them, or would send me there if he thought it was for the good of my soul.

The laity, since it could not preach against the Dissenters, contented itself with maintaining a lofty attitude of superiority, which was not in the least assumed. Most Churchmen really did look down upon the Dissenters as their inferiors, not only in spiritual enlightenment, but also in education and breeding and social position. To a certain extent they were justified. The congregations that gathered in the Bethels and Ebenezers and Salems and obscure meeting-houses all over the country were, for the most part, made up of the less educated and less polished classes; and their ministers were often little above their own level. Lower still came those companies of the absolutely illiterate and ignorant who were attracted by the Stigginses and Chadbands and Moses Barracloughs, who preached a form of unctuous yet hysterical piety nauseating to the ordinary sensible and self-respecting man.

Yet those Churchmen who allowed the term Dissenter to stand only for this predominating element made a very serious mistake. They took no account of the minority—a large one—made up of highly cultured and intellectual people who were proud to be called Nonconformists. They forgot James Martineau and Thomas Erskine, William Howitt and Mrs. Gaskell. They forgot those families in which for generations a sturdy Nonconformist faith and a vigorous intellectual life had existed side by side. Such were the Presbyterian Taylors of Norwich, in whose "old-fashioned parlour in St. George's, Colegate, might be heard the most brilliant conversation as eminent people of every opinion gathered round the hospitable, unpretentious fireside, and Mrs. John Taylor darned her boys' grey worsted stockings while holding her own with Southey, Brougham, or Mackintosh." Such, too, were the Dobells of Cranbrook in Kent, who founded a sect on the model of the Primitive Christians, and who produced the cultured and intellectual poet, Sydney Dobell; the Methodist Smethams, of Pately Bridge, Yorkshire, where the love of literature and learning amounted to a passion; and the Unitarian Chamberlains of Highgate, who trained statesmen for their country's service. Some of the most brilliant students and daring thinkers of the 'fifties and 'sixties, when a new era was opening in science, came from Dissenting homes.

In households such as these the reading habits of the family were those of the ordinary educated Englishman; yet even among them there lingered a trace of the old Puritan characteristic—a distrust of fictional literature, or, indeed, of any literature whose main purpose was to interest or amuse. This does not mean that the Dissenters never read novels. Some, probably many, of them did, but usually with a sense of doing something not entirely praiseworthy. Few Dissenting ministers would have gone as far as the Reverend Dismal Horror, of Samuel Warren's *Ten Thousand a Year*, who held up to his congregation the awful example of Miss Snooks, who kept a circulating library and, plunging still deeper into sin, went on one unhappy Thursday to a theatre. She was taken ill on Friday, and "was a lifeless corpse when the next Sabbath dawned"; at which terrible climax the women in Mr. Dismal Horror's congregation sobbed hysterically, and vowed that they would never again read a novel or enter a theatre. There were many ministers, however, who fulminated vigorously against both these abominations, and among them was the Reverend William Stead, Congregational minister in the little Yorkshire village of Addingham. His son, William T. Stead, who afterwards became such a conspicuous figure in London journalism, said—

I was born and brought up in a home where life was regarded as the vestibule of Eternity, and where everything that tended to waste time, which is life in instalments, was regarded as an evil thing. . . . Hence in our north country manse a severe interdict was laid on all time-wasting amusements. . . . Among them in my youth three stood conspicuous from the subtlety of their allurements and the deadly results which followed yielding to their seductions. The first was the Theatre, which was the Devil's Chapel; the second was Cards, which were the Devil's Prayer Book; and the third was the Novel, which was regarded as a kind of Devil's Bible, whose meretricious attractions waged an unholy competition against the reading of God's word. Where novel-reading comes in Bible-reading goes out was a belief which, after all, has much to justify it in the experience of mankind.

Yet poetry was freely admitted to the manse, and William learnt to read from the works of Byron and of Scott. The same inconsistency is seen in other denouncers of novels. The Reverend Robert Brown, Vicar of St. Matthew's, Douglas, Isle of Man, would not allow any novels—not even those of Scott, in whose favour an exception was often made—to come into the house. Yet he loved Scott's poems, and he loved still more those of Byron. He would not read *Waverley*, yet he read and re-read *Don Juan*. It is true that Mr. Brown was not a Dissenter, but he was an Evangelical, and the views of the Dissenters and the Evangelicals on the subject of reading were in most cases identical. In him, as in Mr. Stead, an urgent literary instinct found a means of satisfying itself in spite of the limitations imposed by a narrow religious creed.

By the true Dissenter poetry was valued for its religious content, not for its beauty or its music. This is clearly illustrated in the case of Miss Emma Tatham. She was the daughter of an upholsterer of High Holborn, and known among the congregation of Great Queen Street Chapel, which she attended, for her piety, the sweetness of her disposition, and her talents. She wrote poetry, she drew and painted, and she died at the age of twenty-six. Her reading was much wider than that of most of her fellow Dissenters. She had read, we are told, Watts' *World to Come*, *The Vicar of Wakefield*, *The Turkish Spy*, *Tales of the Wars*, Thomas Moore's *Epicurean*, and some of Scott's novels; and she took in *Chambers's* and *Eliza Cook's Journals*. She read and studied the poems of Byron, Wordsworth, Moore, Campbell, and Shelley, but her favourite poet was Robert Pollok, who wrote *The Course of Time*. He, she said—

like the royal eagle, soars in the very path of descending light, towards the eternal sun. He is erect and triumphant, yet withal so pure and tender that he is the very poet of my heart.

Pollok was very highly esteemed in Dissenting circles. George Cubitt, the editor of *Chambers's Journal*, wrote to Emma Tatham in 1846, when she was seventeen years old, holding up Pollok to her as an example of a poet who prepared for his work by prayer and devotion.

Robert Pollok, who wrote *The Course of Time*, thus prepared for the work which though he died as soon as it was completed has made his name immortal.

Emma Tatham was eager to follow such an example. Matthew Arnold, who read her poems, compared her Protestantism to the town in which she spent the last years of her short life—"Margate, that brick-and-mortar image of English Protestantism, representing it in all its prose, all its uncomeliness—let me add, all its salubrity." Emma Tatham, however, desired no higher aesthetic satisfaction than poems imbued with this Protestantism could give. In 1854 she wrote—

While I was at Barnes Common I read Longfellow's *Evangeline*. He is a fine poet, but too much inclined to Puseyism—the outward form and rite, I think. *The Arsenal* is one of my favourites. At the same place also I saw Gerald Massey's poems; they are fine, eloquent, sparkling, but will not stand the *Scripture test*. I would love *no poetry* but such as Christ can smile on. Oh, may I *write no other*!

The more rigid sects, such as the Calvinists, doubted whether Christ would smile on any poetry. They were very certain He would not smile on Byron's. The poor boy-tailor of Kingsley's *Alton Locke* knew that in the sight of his stern Calvinistic mother he was committing a deadly sin when day by day he stopped stealthily outside a second-hand bookshop, and, taking up one of the volumes set out for sale, snatched at some passages from *Childe Harold*, or *Lara*, or *The Corsair*. When his mother saw him with a volume of Virgil in his hand, it seemed to the anxious, unlettered woman that her son was going straight to perdition, and even Milton's name held for her no reassurance. "Will poetry, will Latin save an immortal soul?" groaned the hard, grim minister from the chapel, whom she had called in to reprove the erring boy. Here was a tragedy that had its counterpart in many of the homes of the chapel folks, when the young refused to remain within the narrow walls their elders had built up round them, and broke away, with pain to themselves, and leaving desolation behind them.

Sir Edmund Gosse, in the story of his own life told in *Father and Son*, sets forward one of the most poignant of these tragedies. Both his parents belonged to the extreme Calvinistic sect known as the Plymouth Brethren. His father, though he was a man of great gifts and fine intellectual ability, prided himself upon never having read a page of Shakespeare, and having entered a theatre only once. His mother refused to read Scott's novels because they were "not true."

"Never in all my early childhood," said Sir Edmund, "did anyone address to me the affecting preamble, 'Once upon a time.' I was told about missionaries, but never about pirates. I was familiar with humming birds, but I had never heard of fairies."

The boy grew up in an atmosphere overcharged with religious emotion, and became that unhappy being, a young prodigy of piety. Before he was eight years old he had read aloud to his parents a book on prophecy by a writer named Jukes, and Newton's *Thoughts on the Apocalypse.* His mother died before his eighth birthday, and he and his father left London and went to live in Devonshire. Up to this time he had read no story-books except a few pages of a sensational novel, which, by a wonderful chance, he had found lining the lid of a trunk in the garret of his home. After some years his father married again, and his stepmother, who had more liberal ideas on the subject of reading, tried hard to obtain permission for him to read the Waverley novels. But Mr. Gosse refused, though with some inconsistency he allowed the boy to read *Tom Cringle's Log* and several of the works of Dickens. By *Pickwick* Sir Edmund says he was "gloriously enslaved." "I suppose no child will ever again enjoy that rapture of unresisting, humorous appreciation of *Pickwick.*" At thirteen he went to school, and here he read some of the Waverley novels, some plays of Shakespeare, and a little poetry by other writers. When the time came for him to go to London to earn his own living, his father took him up, and they attended a religious conference together at which the seventeen-year-old boy heard with horror one of the speakers say—

At this very moment there is proceeding unreproved a blasphemous celebration of the birth of Shakespeare, a lost soul now suffering for his sins in hell.

When the son settled in London the anxious father wrote every few days long letters of exhortation, warnings, questionings. The son, resentful and tormented, answered as best he could; until the tension grew too great and there came the breach which to one, at least, meant tragedy.

But the Victorian Churchman when he thought of the "Chapel

folk," did not see them as tragic, aspiring figures. To him the Dissenter was a self-satisfied, smug, and sanctimonious person, a fellow, to use Hurrell Froude's phrase, "who turned up the whites of his eyes and said *Lawd*." He was of no importance socially, and he and his chapel and his minister were all a trifle ridiculous as well as schismatic.

It is this view of the Dissenter that Mrs. Oliphant gave in the series of stories that make up her *Chronicles of Carlingford*. She showed her readers a pleasant country town in the 'fifties, and described the different religious parties into which its inhabitants were divided with a nice regard for the social rather than the spiritual standing of each. The Low Church party was the largest, and it attended the parish church, and was ministered to by the Evangelical rector, Mr. Bury. It included most of the professional and business men and their families, who lived in large, comfortable houses in the best part of the town. They had been brought up "in the old-fashioned orthodox way of having a great respect for religion and as little to do with it as possible."

It was the custom of good society in Carlingford to give a respectful assent to Mr. Bury's extreme Low Churchism—as if it were profane, as it certainly was not respectable to differ from the Rector—and to give him as wide a field as possible for his missionary operations by keeping out of the way.

These people sent their daughters to expensive boarding schools from which the young ladies returned with a strong taste for social pleasures and a mild respect for literature. They and their mammas read, mostly in private, a good many novels—thus demonstrating the laxity of their Low Church principles. On Sunday afternoons, and in solemn seasons of affliction, they read "good books" and sermons. The gentlemen read little besides the newspapers and the literature belonging to their professions.

There was a High Church party, led by Mr. Wentworth, the enthusiastic and well-born young Perpetual Curate of St. Roqué's. His congregation was made up of a few of the "best families" in Carlingford, a small number of respectable working men, and as many of the rough bargemen from the wharfside as he and his band of Sisters of Mercy could bring in. There was no Broad Church party in Carlingford, but something was known of the views of that section through Archdeacon Beverley, who paid the town a long visit. The Archdeacon was liberal in his ideas, read all the new works on science and religion that were coming out, and shocked the Low Church rector and his following by the freedom with which he discussed all sorts of questions, social, moral, and theological.

It was against this background that Mrs. Oliphant set her company of Dissenters. They were Congregationalists, and worshipped in a red-brick building known as Salem Chapel, that stood on the shabby side of one of the meaner streets of the town.

Greengrocers, dealers in cheese and bacon, milkmen, with some dressmakers of inferior pretensions and teachers of day schools of similar humble character formed the *élite* of the congregation. . . . The names which figured highest in the benevolent lists of Salem Chapel were known to society only as appearing in gold letters on the backs of those mystic tradesmen's books which were deposited every Monday in little heaps at every house in Grange Lane. The Dissenters, on their part, aspired to no conquests in the unattainable territory of high life as it existed in Carlingford. They were content to keep their privileges among themselves, and to enjoy their superior preaching and purity with a compassionate complaisance.

The deacons of Salem Chapel were Mr. Tozer, the butterman, Mr. Pigeon, the poulterer, and Mr. Brown of the Devonshire Dairy. They were well-meaning, kindly men, ignorant of everything that lay beyond their business, very proud of their chapel and generous in supporting it. They lived snugly in their comfortable though stuffy back parlours, where there was always something hot for supper, at which meal the minister was heartily welcome "if he comes in familiar and takes us as we are." There were few books in those back parlours except Bibles and ledgers. Mr. Tozer had sent his daughter Phœbe—pink, plump, and pretty—to boarding school, and she had come back able to write little pink notes of invitation to her mother's tea-parties, and to play several "pieces" on the piano; but her education was "finished," and any further reading would obviously have been waste of time.

All the Salemites delighted in tea-parties, held either in the best room above the shop or in the room beneath the chapel, where

dark-complexioned cake and heavy buns were handed round, and the atmosphere grew hot and steamy as the big urns emptied; and the faces that were turned towards the platform when tea was over, and the minister stood up to make his speech, were flushed and shining with heat and with good humour.

The kind of speech which this audience most appreciated was one which was pious and at the same time jocular, filled with personalities and quite free from any taint of learning or intellectual appeal—which things these worthy people were apt to look upon as worldly, and unbecoming in a minister. They were never quite at their ease with young Mr. Vincent, who had come to them after their old minister, Mr. Tufton, had been disabled by a paralytic stroke. Mr. Tufton was a harmless old man, little superior to his flock in intelligence or education, who had offered them Sunday by Sunday a "pious palaver" by way of a sermon, and whose reading was almost entirely confined to the *Carlingford Gazette*. Mr. Vincent was a student fresh from Homerton Theological Training College, filled with all sorts of new ideas and enthusiasms. He took in the *Nonconformist* and the *Eclectic Review*, and was a reader of many books, especially those on the history of Nonconformity. He was not very happy at Carlingford, where he felt himself shut out from all society save that of his illiterate, kindly, vulgar flock, and he resented their claims to control his actions and engross his time. He looked at Mr. Wentworth, the Perpetual Curate, who was about the same age as himself, no better looking, possessed of about the same means, and dressed in the same correct clerical fashion; and he wondered how it was that, socially, "so vast a world of separation and difference lay between them." The High Churchman would have said that much of the difference came from the fact that the Anglican priest claimed a high and sacred authority, holding, as he did, the doctrine of the Apostolic Succession; while the Dissenting minister was, as Newman had reminded those who read the first of the *Tracts*, "the creature of the people"—or as Mrs. Pigeon put it, a man who was "getting his livin' off you all the time." The rift between Mr. Vincent and his congregation grew wider as time went on, and although the people of Salem were proud of their pastor's brilliance and considered that it shed great distinction on the "connection," they became more and more uncomfortable under his sway. All of them—except a small party headed by the faithful and admiring Mr. Tozer—felt it a relief when Mr. Vincent resigned, and they were free to decline upon the more ordinary type of minister in Mr. Beecher, who—

if he was not quite equal to Mr. Vincent in the pulpit, was much more complaisant at all the tea-parties; and after a year's experience was fully acknowledged, both by himself and others, to have made an 'it.

From *Salem Chapel* we turn to the *Autobiography of Mark Rutherford*, and find there a picture of life in a Dissenting community more intimate and poignant than that of Mrs. Oliphant, but agreeing with it in all essential particulars. "Mark Rutherford" was the pen-name of Mr. William Hale White, who as a young man had been a Dissenting minister. He was trained at a Theological College, and from there went as pastor to a small Independent chapel in one of the eastern counties. The circle in which he found himself was as illiterate as that which welcomed Mr. Vincent to Carlingford, and much more dreary. One of his deacons was an old farmer—a plain, honest man, very kind, but very ignorant, who never read any book except the Bible, and of that he knew only a few favourite chapters, or any newspaper except *Bell's Weekly Messenger*. The second deacon was an undertaker and carpenter, "a mere shadow of a man, of whom nothing could be said, good or evil. The third was a Mr. Snale, who kept the principal draper's shop in the town, and was considered very genteel.

It was the custom of the chapel that monthly Dorcas meetings should be held at the houses of each of these deacons in turn. When it was Mr. Snale's turn, the company assembled in the drawing-room over the shop. There was a round table in the middle of the room, on which a heavy tea was served, and after all had eaten heartily, the ladies worked on garments for the poor while one of the gentlemen read aloud, usually from the denominational magazine. When it came to the minister's turn to read, he brought *The Vicar of Wakefield*. No objection was raised at the time, but afterwards the unctuous Mr. Snale came to him, with a request that the book might not be read again—

Because, you know, Mr. Rutherford, the company is mixed; there are young ladies present, and perhaps, Mr. Rutherford, a book with a more requisite tone might be more suitable on such an occasion.

Next time the minister tried a selection from *George Fox's Journal*, but to this also Mr. Snale objected—

It was "hardly of a character adapted for social intercourse," he thought; and furthermore, "although Mr. Fox might be a very good man, and was a converted character, yet he did not, you know, Mr. Rutherford, belong to us."

The discouraged minister was obliged to resume the vapid religious literature he detested, but to which his hearers listened with complete satisfaction. The only people he could find among his congregation who had any literary tastes at all were two maiden ladies, who greatly admired Cowper, and who read a few other books by obscure authors.

After a period of spiritual doubt and depression Mark Rutherford became a Unitarian, and had charge of a small Unitarian chapel in a large, straggling village. Here his regular congregation was made up of about five families. They were, he said, "a petrified set."

They plumed themselves greatly on their intellectual superiority over the Wesleyans and Baptists round them; and so far as I could make out, the only topics they delighted in were demonstrations of the unity of God from texts in the Bible, and polemics against tri-theism. Sympathy with the great problems then beginning to agitate men they had none.

This searching for texts simply for the purpose of proving themselves in the right and everybody else in the wrong did not lead to that loving familiarity with the Bible which, to many people, has proved in itself a means of culture. "I am bound to say," said Mark Rutherford, "that so far as my experience goes, the character so frequently drawn in romances of intense Bible students in Dissenting congregations is very rare."

Mark Rutherford's novels are largely founded upon his experiences as a Dissenting minister. In *The Revolution in Tanner's Lane* he gives a picture of Cowfold, a small country town about fifty miles from London, in the early 'forties. There were three chapels in Cowfold—the Wesleyan, whose chief supporter was a wealthy brewer; the Baptist, which was called Zoar, and which had a congregation of "about fifty sullen, half-stupid, wholly ignorant people who found in the Zoar services something sleepier and requiring less mental effort than they met with elsewhere"; and the Independent Meeting House in Tanner's Lane, where the Reverend John Broad ministered to about seven hundred and fifty people, drawn not from Cowfold only, but also from the surrounding district. Mr. Broad was a "big, gross, heavy-feeding person, with heavy ox-face and large mouth," and was "probably as sincere as his build of soul and body allowed him to be. Certainly no doubt of the truth of what he preached had ever crossed his mind." He read his Bible, and rarely spoke without quoting or misquoting several texts. Among the members of his congregation there were three—Mr. Allen, an ironmonger in Cowfold, his wife, and his son—who were intelligent and open-minded, and lovers of books. Here again it was Scott and Byron who gave the greatest delight, and afforded those three alert minds an escape beyond the dreary limits imposed by their narrow creed. By the rest of the flock, including the pastor, the Allens were regarded with suspicion, and by some with positive dislike. This interest in books and ideas which had nothing to do with the scheme of salvation was obviously a sign of a carnal and worldly nature.

In the more important chapels of London and other large towns the Dissenting communities were doubtless more intelligent and enlightened. Some of the ministers of these chapels were men of high ability, and broad-minded enough to examine with eager interest the scientific theories put forward in the 'fifties and 'sixties, which many of their brethren denounced as emanating from the Evil One, and scarcely to be mentioned in the hearing of a Christian. There were brilliant preachers among them, but these did not attract the ordinary chapel-going public; that desired something more unctuous and sensational. Fortunately, provision was made for it also. There were many Little Bethels such as the one Dickens shows us in *The Old Curiosity Shop*, where poor women like Mrs. Nubbles "sat under" a loud-voiced preacher who thrilled and terrified them by lurid pictures of the punishment of those sinners who went to the play, or wore bows in their bonnets. There was the famous Dr. Cumming, of the Scotch Church in Crown Court, Covent Garden, whose great subject was the End of the World, which he held to be imminent. It was a favourite exercise with him, said George Eliot—

to form conjectures of the process by which the earth is to be burned up, and to picture Dr. Chalmers and Mr. Wilberforce being caught up to meet Christ in the air, while Romanists, Puseyites, and infidels are given over to gnashing of teeth.

Dr. Cumming's congregation was a very large and a very fashionable one. His sermons and his prophetic interpretations of the Book of the Revelation were published under such titles as *Voices of the Night, Voices of the Dead, Apocalyptic Sketches,* and all of them sold by thousands. They were highly praised in certain Evangelical newspapers, but won no recognition from serious thinkers or theologians. George Eliot, in a long and scathing notice of Dr. Cumming's works published in the *Westminster Review* in 1857, gave an example of his method of interpreting Scripture.

The serpent, he informs us, said to Eve, "Can it be so? Surely you are mistaken, that God hath said you shall die, a creature so fair, so lovely, so beautiful. It is impossible. The laws of nature and physical science tell you that my interpretation is correct. You shall not die. I can tell you by my own experience as an angel that you shall be as gods, knowing good and evil."

Even more famous than Dr. Cumming was Mr. Spurgeon. Charles Haddon Spurgeon came to the Baptist Chapel at New Park Street, Southwark, in 1853, when he was nineteen years old. He had already been for two years pastor of a small chapel at Waterbeach, and had become known as the Boy Preacher. He was not illiterate, like some of the Dissenting ministers, but he had had only an ordinary school education, and had left school when he was fifteen. He had read little except the ordinary Nonconformist literature. "I have to bless God," he said, "for many good books—Doddridge's *Rise and Progress of Religion,* Baxter's *Call to the Unconverted,* Allen's *Alarm to Sinners,* James' *Anxious Inquirer.*" His appeal to his hearers was entirely emotional, and his power came from his remarkable personality. Later, when he preached each Sunday at the Surrey Music Hall, thousands came to hear him. Charles Greville went on February 8, 1857, and recorded in his diary—

I am just come from hearing the celebrated Mr. Spurgeon preach in the Music Hall of the Surrey Gardens. It was quite full, he told us from the pulpit that nine thousand people were present.

. . . He is certainly very remarkable and a very fine character, not remarkable in person, in face rather resembling a smaller Macaulay, a very clear and powerful voice which was heard through the whole hall, a manner natural, impassioned, and without affectation or extravagance, wonderful fluency and command of language, abounding in illustration and very often of a familiar kind, but without anything either ridiculous or irreverent, without book or notes.

He spoke, Greville says, for three-quarters of an hour on the text, "Cleanse me from my secret sins," while handkerchiefs were taken out, and sobs resounded through the building. Greville seemed rather surprised that he could find in Spurgeon nothing either ridiculous or irreverent. So much fun had been made of the preacher that it was natural to expect an exhibition in the worst possible taste of Dissenting sensationalism. Spurgeon had been frequently attacked in the newspapers, and his sermons had been called melodramatic, bombastic, vulgar, and hypocritical. *Punch* had "calculated that on an average the reverend teacher uses in every sermon no less than three tons of coal, and all red-hot." There were caricatures of him in the windows of the print-sellers' shops, representing him in all sorts of absurd and undignified positions; one was called "Catch-'em-alive-O," and showed him with a fly-paper round his head to which were adhering, or towards which were fluttering, a variety of winged figures, from the Lord Chancellor to Mrs. Gamp. It is certain that to a great many people his sermons and his services were painfully offensive; but this did not hinder his having an immense following. John Morley admired him for his "taking gift of unction," and compared him in this respect to Bishop Wilberforce. His sermons were printed week by week in the Baptist paper, the *Record*, and sold by thousands. Mrs. Fawcett said that her mother took it in regularly when the family lived at Aldeburgh during her girlhood; Surtees in his *Ask Mamma* shows us Mrs. Pringle gloating over it.

Yet sermons—even Spurgeon's sermons—could not entirely satisfy the literary needs of the Dissenting community. In them, as in all people in all ages, there existed the desire which the child puts into words when he says, "Tell me a story." They wanted their stories, more stories than the Bible or the anecdotes of their preachers could give them; yet the restrictions that their creed imposed upon them made these very difficult to obtain, and this goes far towards explaining the immense popularity of the tract. Tracts had been originally the special property of the Evangelical party in the English Church, and they had been intended for the conversion of sinners and the instruction of the ignorant. The evidence seems to show that from these the tract received but scant appreciation. Their attitude towards the zealous ladies and gentlemen who pressed this literature upon them too often approached that of the old woman in Besant's *Golden Butterfly*— "Gimme brandy and you shall read me a track." But soon the tracts caught the eye of the elect—the regular chapel-goers—who needed neither to be converted nor instructed, but who did need to be interested and thrilled. Both these things the leaflets sent out by "Spurgeon and Co." (as one of Miss Rhoda Broughton's heroines irreverently puts it) could do. Their crudity did not offend those who listened, week by week, to sermons equally crude. Their snow-white saints and inky sinners, their edifying death-beds and awful judgments, were received with tearful or shuddering interest; while their avowed religious purpose gave their readers a gratifying sense of having joined in an act of pious devotion. Here, certainly, were works that Christ could smile upon. In Dissenting and Evangelical households tracts had a place among the literature suitable for Sunday reading. There was doubtless a pile of them in Mr. Tozer's comfortable back parlour, though Mrs. Oliphant neglects to mention them; and there were almost certainly some in the home in which Edmund Gosse was brought up, for his mother wrote one called *The Guardsman of the Alma* (founded on the spiritual experiences of a Guardsman who, through her ministrations, had been converted shortly before he was killed at the battle of the Alma), of which more than half a million copies were circulated. There were tracts in that dismal house by the Thames-side which Dickens shows us in *Little Dorrit*, and little Arthur Clennam for his Sunday reading was given one which commenced business with the poor child by asking him in the title why he was going to Perdition?—a piece of curiosity that he really, in a frock and drawers, was not in a position to satisfy.

Mrs. Tag-rag, in *Ten Thousand a Year*, read a tract by Mr. Dismal Horror, called *Groans from the Bottomless Pit to Awaken Sleeping Sinners*, and groaned over it herself with immense satisfaction. "I do *love* a track," said Mrs. Humphry Ward's pious

Mrs. Jervis, as she laid down *A Pennorth of Grace or a Pound of Works.*

That's why I don't like these buildings as well as them others. Here you never get no tracks; and there, what with one person and another, there was a new one most weeks.

Next to the tracts came the religious stories, which were really only tracts enlarged. One of the most popular of these was *The Dairyman's Daughter*, which had been written by an Evangelical clergyman, Mr. Legh Richmond, and had become at once enormously popular. Its popularity lasted for at least fifty years. Sir James Crichton Browne says it was one of the books put into his hands when he was a boy; and in *Christopher Kirkland*, which is in many respects the autobiography of its writer, Mrs. Lynn Linton who was born in 1822, it is also mentioned. George Borrow, in his *Lavengro*, published in 1851, tells how he offered to a publisher some old ballads and a romance in the German style, and was told that such things had no chance of success with the readers of that day.

"Don't you think you could write a series of Evangelical tales?" said the publisher.

"Evangelical tales, sir?"

"Yes, sir, Evangelical novels. . . . Something in the style of *The Dairyman's Daughter.*"

"I never heard of the work till the present moment."

"Then, sir, procure it by all means. Sir, I could afford as much as ten pounds for a well-written tale in the style of *The Dairyman's Daughter*; that is the kind of literature, sir, that sells at the present day."

Another very popular writer of religious stories was Hesba Stretton. Of her *Jessica's First Prayer*, which appeared first in the *Sunday at Home*, and was published as a book in 1866, one and a half million copies were sold. It was highly commended by the Earl of Shaftesbury, and it quickly became one of the standard books for children in Dissenting and Evangelical households. Miss Lilian Faithful says she read it with other books of "a morbid and sentimental kind" that abounded during her childhood. "We loved the sentiment," she says, "but disliked the children." Grown-ups also read *Jessica's First Prayer*, and were deeply affected by it. Edith Nesbit, who was a woman of robust intellect and neither a Dissenter nor an Evangelical, said that she read it to her maid, and felt her eyes smart and her throat grow lumpy towards the end. "Pathetic simplicity is a grand gift in writing," she concluded. Whether Miss Stretton possessed this gift might appear to some readers doubtful, but she touched the hearts of thousands of her own generation. Her *Little Meg's Children*, 1868, and *Alone in London*, 1869, were not quite as popular as her first work, although they reached together a sale of three-quarters of a million.

Dickens made fun of the over-righteous children who figured in these stories when he wrote in *Our Mutual Friend* about a

good child's book, *The Adventures of Little Margery*, who resided in the village cottage by the mill; severely reproved and morally squashed the miller when she was five and he was fifty; divided her porridge with singing-birds; denied herself a new nankeen bonnet on the ground that the turnips did not wear nankeen bonnets, neither did the sheep who ate them; who plaited straw and delivered the dreariest orations to all comers at all sorts of unseasonable times.

There were also stories of naughty children who came to terrible ends, and for whom there waited eternal punishment in a material, flaming, torturing hell. The *Peep of Day*, denounced by Lady Frederick Cavendish for its "irreverent familiarity," but in high favour with most Dissenters and Evangelicals, presented its readers with many stories of this kind. Lord Frederick Hamilton says that in the 'sixties his nurse used to read to him every Sunday out of this book which, he remembers, had most terrifying pictures. One Sunday his mother came in during the reading, and asked how he liked the story. "Is it about Heaven?" she said, and the little boy replied with gleeful relish, "No, it's about 'ell."

As the years of Queen Victoria's reign went on the difference between the reading habits of the chapel folks and those of the general public became less marked. Especially was this the case with the younger members. How far the advanced guard had progressed by the time the late 'seventies were reached we may see if, by the help of Mrs. Oliphant's *Phoebe Junior*, we look in upon the household of the Reverend Mr. Beecher of Regent's Park, late of Salem Chapel, Carlingford. It is the same Mr.

Beecher who followed Mr. Vincent and made an 'it; and the 'it was such a decisive one that it carried him from Carlingford to a fashionable chapel at Regent's Park. Here he and his wife—who had once been Miss Phoebe Tozer—found themselves gradually adopting a good many new ideas and practices; and when their daughter, Phoebe junior, grew up, they found themselves carried forward at a rate that sometimes confused and even troubled them. Phoebe was pretty like her mother, but not quite so plump or so pink. She was a self-possessed and elegant young lady, and was determined, in spite of her Dissenting parentage, to be very modern and up-to-date. She took her reluctant mother to evening parties at the houses of the richer members of her father's congregation, and managed to attract more attention than it was becoming—so many people thought—for a minister's daughter to receive.

She was very well got up on the subject of education for women, and lamented often and pathetically the difficulty they lay under of acquiring the highest instruction; but at the same time she patronized Mr. Ruskin's theory that dancing, drawing, and cooking were three of the higher arts that ought to be studied by girls.

In the morning Phoebe read serious books such as the works of Mr. John Stuart Mill, and she even attempted Virgil. Later in the day, in the hours dedicated to amusement, she read novels and other light literature, claiming for herself the freedom allowed to well-brought-up young ladies outside the Dissenting pale. She paid regular visits to her grandparents at the comfortable house on the outskirts of Carlingford to which they had gone when they had retired from business, and was very sweet and dutiful to them; and old Mr. and Mrs. Tozer were fond and proud of her, though they stood a little in awe of her elegance, and did not entirely approve of her education. On one of these visits Phoebe became acquainted with a clergyman—a Mr. May—and his family who lived near by, and visited them on terms of equality; which seemed strange to those who remembered how great had been the social gulf between the Dissenters and the Church people of Carlingford in earlier days. It was impossible to imagine Phoebe Tozer from the butter shop conversing freely with Mr. Wentworth or Mr. Bury as his daughter conversed with Mr. May. The two had a common acquaintance, one Clarence Copperhead.

"He's not the fascinating pupil of a Church novel," said Phoebe. "There's nothing the least like the heir of Redclyffe about him." "You seem very well up in Miss Yonge's novels, Miss Beecham," said Mr. May. "Yes. One reads Scott for Scotland (and a few other things) and one reads Miss Yonge for the Church. Mr. Trollope is good for that too, but not so good. All that I know of clergymen's families I have got from her. I can recognize you quite well, and your sister, but the young ones puzzle me. They are not in Miss Yonge."

But not every Salemite family produced a Miss Phoebe Beecham in the third generation. Not every provincial butterman saw his grandchildren pass so lightly by the warnings and danger signals set up by their forefathers. Old ideas and habits took long to die out. They lingered in the country places and smaller towns where the Zoars and Bethels still held their own; and they survived through at least another generation in the form of a vague prejudice against reading, and especially against the reading of fiction, as a frivolous and mischievous wasting of time that had been given for more useful purposes.

CHAPTER V

SCIENCE AND RELIGION

To this Victorian England, with its thousands of men and women intensely, even fiercely, preoccupied with questions of religion, there came, in 1844, a book which startled High Church, Low Church, and Dissenters alike. It was called *Vestiges of the Natural History of Creation*, and was published anonymously; and it caused such an outcry that, in the second edition, the author tried to explain the real purpose of his work, and to set right those who had formed mistaken ideas concerning it. The book, he said,

is not primarily designed, as many have intimated, and as the Title might be thought partly to imply, to establish a new theory respecting the origin of animated Nature; . . . the purpose is to show that the revelation of the works of God presented to our senses and reason, is a system based on what we are compelled for want of a better term to call Law; by which is not meant a system independent or exclusive of Deity, but one which only proposes a certain mode of His working.

In spite of this declaration, however, most of the readers of *Vestiges* continued to hold the opinion that it did proclaim a new theory of creation, and one which was in direct opposition to the account given in the Word of God. The great majority of Englishmen and Englishwomen, not only the ignorant but also the educated and the devout, believed firmly in the verbal inspiration of the Bible. All that it contained was literally true, and it contained the whole truth necessary to salvation. The Reverend Theobald Pontifex, of Samuel Butler's *The Way of All Flesh*, was in this respect typical of both the clergy and the laity of his day.

It had never so much as crossed Theobald's mind to doubt the literal accuracy of any syllable in the Bible. He had never seen any book in which this was disputed, nor met with anyone who doubted it.

The advancement of any theory of creation which differed in a single respect from the story as told in Genesis was regarded as atheistical and blasphemous; and as an atheist and a blasphemer the unknown author of *Vestiges* was by many people condemned. When the book appeared *Tract 90* was still being hotly discussed, and the year that followed its publication was the year of Newman's secession to Rome. Yet *Vestiges* had its share, and that a large one, of public attention. It was denounced from the pulpit, abused in the Press, laughed at by superior persons anxious to exhibit their own scientific knowledge; it was the theme of conversation in fashionable drawing-rooms and in devout religious assemblies; so that even those who had not read it knew something of its theory and purpose.

But neither denunciation nor ridicule could kill the book, for it was founded on a truth towards which men of real scientific knowledge and ability had long been travelling. These men upheld the main conclusions of *Vestiges*, although they were inclined to laugh at the unscientific nature of the reasoning by which these conclusions were reached. Sir J. D. Hooker, the botanist, read it, and wrote to Charles Darwin ridiculing some of its statements. Darwin, who had for years been working with unflagging enthusiasm on the problems which *Vestiges* touched so lightly, replied—

I have been somewhat less amused at it than you appear to have been; the writing and arrangement are certainly admirable, but his geology strikes me as bad, and his zoology far worse.

A few months later Darwin wrote to his friend William Fox—

Have you read that strange, unphilosophical, but capitally written book, the *Vestiges*? It has made more talk than any work of late, and has been by some attributed to me—at which I ought to be much flattered and unflattered.

Darwin was one of many who were credited with—or accused of—the authorship of *Vestiges*. A large and indignant section of the reading public searched busily for the culprit, and few men known to be interested in science escaped suspicion. Some readers followed Henry Sedgwick, Dean of Westminster and a noted geologist, who in reviewing the book for the *Edinburgh* declared his belief that the author was a woman, "partly from the fair dress and agreeable exterior of the *Vestiges*; and partly from the utter ignorance the book displays of all sound physical logic." Some went further, and identified Lady Lovelace, daughter of Lord Byron and a noted mathematician, as the offending female. It was not very long, however, before the name of the rightful author, known to a few, spread from one to another until it became general property. It was Robert Chambers, the younger of the two brothers who, in 1832, had begun the publication of *Chambers's Journal,* a valuable educational periodical for working men. He maintained earnestly that his object in writing *Vestiges* was to uphold, not to attack religion, by trying to remove some of the difficulties felt by the most intelligent among the readers of the *Journal* in reconciling science and revelation.

But the general public continued to regard it as atheistical and dangerous. Fanny Kemble's attitude towards it represents perhaps that of the more open-minded section.

The book is extremely disagreeable to me, though my ignorance and desire for knowledge combined give it, when treating of facts, a thousand times more interest than the best of novels for me; but its conclusions are utterly revolting to me—nevertheless they may be true.

Later she declared herself "more reconciled to the theory it presents towards the close of the book for obvious reasons—it is impossible to limit future progress."

The clergy, as a whole, were against it. Some attacked it violently, others believed that the best way to kill the book was to take no notice of it; others, again, stood firm in the faith, and held that any inquiry into the truths of religion should be welcomed, since such inquiry could only establish those truths more surely. Edward FitzGerald said that he asked John Allen, the saintly young chaplain to the Bishop of Chichester, whether he thought *Vestiges* atheistical, and Allen laughed and replied, "No inquiry can be atheistical." Richard Church found time, even during that last stormy year of the Oxford Movement, to read the book about which everyone was talking. He was much interested in it, and thought the arguments used against it unphilosophical and unsatisfactory; people, he said, "wrote about it in much too great a fright as to the consequences of the theory, and answered him often more like old ladies than philosophers." Jowett wrote from Balliol—

The *Vestiges of Creation* I have read. The way in which it was attacked by Sedgwick disgusted me. . . . I daresay it is all wrong, but cannot see there is any religious interest against it any more than against science in general.

Some of the attacks made upon the book showed such flagrant ignorance of the subject under discussion that they amused as well as disgusted all sensible readers. Dr. Cumming said that

the idea of the author of *Vestiges* is that man is the development of a monkey, that the monkey is the embryo man; so that if you keep a baboon long enough it will develop itself into a man.

Those readers who had, either secretly or openly, allowed themselves to speculate as to whether there could be another and a more scientific explanation of the origin of the universe than that generally accepted received *Vestiges* with eagerness. Many, though not all these daring inquirers, were young people of strong and restless intellect; some were in revolt against a too rigid religious creed that had ruled their upbringing. Froude said that the book introduced science to him under an unexpected aspect and opened new avenues of thought. Frances Cobbe, best remembered as one of the leaders in the "Woman's Rights" movement, declared that, at eighteen, she pinned her faith to *Vestiges*. Alfred Tennyson, now thirty-five years old, but still a poor and struggling poet, wrote to his publishers asking them to send him a copy of the book.

It seems to contain many speculations with which I have been familiar for years, and on which I have written more than one poem.

FitzGerald was also eager to read the book. He wrote from London to Bernard Barton, the Quaker poet, who lived near his own home at Woodbridge in Suffolk—

You did not tell me how you and Miss Barton got on with the *Vestiges*. I found people talking about it here, and one laudatory critique in the *Examiner* sold an edition in a few days. I long to finish it.

Some of the young people were unimpressed and critical. Thomas Huxley, who was nineteen when the book appeared, was "simply irritated by the prodigious ignorance and thoroughly unscientific habit of mind manifested by the writer of *Vestiges*." Another youth six years older than Huxley, and of an equally powerful and inquiring intellect, rejected the theories of the book and exposed the weakness of its arguments. This was Herbert Spencer, who had lately given up the calling of engineer for which he had been preparing in order to devote himself to the scientific and philosophical subjects in which lay his deepest interests. He first heard of *Vestiges* through the praise of "a gentleman at Liverpool who was evidently a good judge"; and he wrote to his friend, Charles Lott, recommending the book for his reading, and suggesting that it might be suitable for the library of a Mechanics' Institute in which Lott was interested. But when he came to read the book his opinion changed; and when, in 1850, he met and talked with G. H. Lewes, he surprised that versatile man of letters by his uncompromising rejection of the arguments advanced in *Vestiges*. Lewes, like others who were prepared to give up the first chapter of Genesis, but whose knowledge of science was superficial, had supposed Robert Chambers' theory to be the only alternative.

In drawing-rooms where the religious implications of the book were not taken very seriously, clever people found in it an intellectual stimulus, and delighted in the speculations and flights of imagination that it suggested. Florence Nightingale tells how at Sir William Heathcote's, where Lord and Lady Ashburton were among the guests, the company began to talk about mesmerism and such speculative subjects, and at length got so high up into *Vestiges* that she could not get down again. Unfortunately, other drawing-room circles, of distinctly weaker intellectual power, attempted similar flights. Disraeli's satirical version, in *Tancred*, of the conversation of these muddled aspirants is delightful. Tancred, Marquis of Montacute, young, rich, handsome, clever, and devout, is inclined to fall in love with Lady Constance Rawleigh, and calls on her at her mother's house.

After making herself very agreeable Lady Constance took up a book which was at hand, and said, "Do you know this?" And Tancred, opening a volume which he had never seen, and turning to its title-page, found it was *The Revelations of Chaos*, a startling work just published, and of which a rumour had reached him.

"No," he replied, "I have not seen it."

"I will lend it you if you like: it is one of those books one must read. It explains everything, and is written in a very agreeable style."

"It explains everything!" said Tancred; "it must, indeed, be a very remarkable book!"

"I think it will just suit you," said Lady Constance. "Do you know I thought so several times while I was reading it."

"To judge from the title, the subject is rather obscure," said Tancred.

"No longer so," said Lady Constance. "It is treated scientifically; everything is explained by geology and astronomy, and in that way. It shows you exactly how a star is formed; nothing can be so pretty! A cluster of vapour, the cream of the milky way, a sort of celestial cheese churned into light. You must read it, 'tis charming."

"Nobody ever saw a star formed," said Tancred.

"Perhaps not. You must read the *Revelations*; it is all explained. But what is most interesting is the way in which man has been developed. You know, all is development. The principle is perpetually going on. First, there was nothing, then there was something; then, I forget the next, I think there were shells, then fishes; then we came, let me see, did we come next? Never mind that, we came at last. And the next change there will be something very superior to us, something with wings. Ah! that's it; we were fishes, and I believe we shall be crows. But you must read it."

"I don't believe I ever was a fish," said Tancred.

"Oh! but it is all proved; you must not argue on my rapid sketch; read the book. It is impossible to contradict anything in it. You understand, it is all science; it is not like those books in which one says one thing and another the contrary, and both may be wrong. Everything is proved; by geology, you know. You see exactly how everything is made; how many worlds there have been; how long they lasted; what went before, what comes next. We are a link in the chain, as inferior animals were that preceded us; we in turn shall be inferior. All that will remain of us will be some relics in a new red sandstone. This is development. We had fins; we may have wings."

Tancred grew silent and thoughtful; . . . He bowed very low, and then bade farewell to Lady Constance, who said, "We shall meet to-night."

"I was a fish and I shall be a crow," said Tancred to himself as the hall door closed on him. "What a spiritual mistress!" And that was the end of his courtship of Lady Constance.

It was largely through *Tancred* that the memory of *Vestiges* was kept alive after the first excitement caused by its appearance had died down, and it survived chiefly as a jest. Frank Smedley,

in *Harry Coverdale's Courtship*, written in 1858, described a dinner
at Blackwall—

First appears a course of fish, enough to constitute a dinner in
itself; . . . and then the fishes are ignored, and develop, according
to the *Vestiges of Creation* theory, into the higher forms of animal,
into which the highest form of all—man—pitches cannibal-like,
until the culinary cosmos is resolved into its pristine chaotic elements.

As late as 1869 Shirley Brooks, editor of *Punch*, wrote, "We
shall be crows, see *Vestiges of Creation* as explained by *Tancred*."

The *Vestiges*, inexact and even absurd as were some of its
statements, yet holds an important place in the history of the
literature that deals with the conflict between science and religion.
It prepared the way for greater books that were to come. Darwin
himself said that it had "done excellent service in this country in
calling attention to the subject and removing prejudice." The hero
of Mrs. Lynn Linton's autobiographical novel, *Christopher Kirkland*, declared that it "takes rank as one of the advanced guard in
the forces of knowledge as they stand arrayed against those of
ignorance"; it marks, he said, "the coming of dawn that heralds
the full day."

Full day was, or seemed to be, long delayed. Fifteen years
passed before another book rousing the public to a startled interest
in that burning question, the relation between science and religion,
was published. They were years during which all the religious
bodies in the country were striving to reconstitute themselves
according to the ideas which, directly or indirectly, had been the
outcome of the Oxford Movement. While they were thus occupied
they had no time for the consideration of scientific theories. The
scientists, for their part, were not yet prepared to issue their
challenge. Darwin was working with persevering devotion at the
research which was to result in his first great book. Herbert Spencer
was travelling by a somewhat different road towards similar conclusions, and there were others whose work was tending in the
same direction.

Samuel Butler chose these years as the period during which his
hero, Ernest Pontifex, grew from a boy into a man. There was
not, he says, a single book published during this time

that caused a serious commotion within the bosom of the Church.
Perhaps Buckle's *History of Civilization* and Mill's *Liberty* were

the most alarming, but they neither of them reached the substratum of the English public, and Ernest and his friends were ignorant of their very existence.

Butler might also have mentioned George Eliot's translation of Strauss's *Leben Jesu*, which was widely read and had great influence, especially among working men; and *Letters on the Laws of Man's Social Nature and Development*, by Harriet Martineau and Henry Atkinson, published in 1851. This was not a work of genuine and lasting importance. Scientists for the most part put it contemptuously aside as a piece of quackery, but it raised a storm which was fierce though brief, and it helped to make those people who loved and revered the truths of their religion look with an added suspicion and bitterness on any who, in the name of science, laid hands on sacred things. The *Letters* set forth the principles of a faith which denied the operation of God in the world, and made man's fate depend solely on the right direction of his own will-power upon his physical constitution.

"You can have no idea what an excitement Harriet Martineau's book is making," wrote Mary Howitt to her daughter. "It is always out when we send to the London Library for it." A little later she wrote—

We have read Miss Martineau's book. It is to my mind the most awful book that was ever written by a woman. It made me sick and ill to hear them talk of Jesus as a mere clever mesmerist.

She recounted some of the remarks she had heard made about the book, ending with Douglas Jerrold's "There is no God, and Harriet Martineau is His Prophet."

Dr. Robertson of Brighton considered it the most offensive book he had read for a long time. He could conceive, he said, "a mind loyal to truth driven to atheism," but he had no patience with a self-complacent smirk which says, "Shut up the prophets; read Martineau and Atkinson." According to them—

Friendship and Patriotism are mesmerized brain; Faith a mistake of the stomach; Love a titillatory movement occurring in the upper part of the nape of the neck; Immortality the craving of dyspepsia; God a fancy produced by a certain pressure upon the grey parts of the hasty pudding within the skull; Shakespeare, Plato, and Hannibal and all they did and wrote weighed by an extra ounce or so of said pudding.

Few people found anything in the book to be praised, or even tolerated. Charlotte Brontë and Mrs. Gaskell, who liked and respected Harriet Martineau, agreed that its courage and sincerity entitled it to something better than the harsh, contemptuous treatment it had received from most of the critics. But even they were outraged by the opinions expressed in the *Letters*.

"It is the first exposition of avowed atheism and materialism I have ever read," wrote Charlotte Brontë to her publisher, Mr. Smith, "the first unequivocal declaration of disbelief in the existence of God or a future life I have ever seen. In judging of such exposition and declaration one would wish entirely to put aside the sort of instinctive horror they awaken, and to consider them in an impartial spirit and collected mood. This I find it difficult to do. The strangest thing is we are called upon to rejoice over this hopeless blank—to receive this bitter bereavement as a great gain—to welcome this unutterable desolation as a state of pleasant freedom. Who *could* do this if he would? Who *would* do it if he could?"

Kingsley believed that the authors of the *Letters* were better than their creed, but he feared that only evil could result from the setting forward of such doctrines. "Humanity and common sense are too mighty even for H. Martineau and Atkinson," he said, "but they will not be so for their disciples," who will "formulize, systematize, carry out—persecute"; and the end will be "a fetish worship, out-poperying Popery itself." George Eliot was noncommittal. "Whatever else one may think of the book," she said, "it is certainly the boldest I have seen in the English language." The sensation caused by Miss Martineau's book did not last long and it left behind it, if we may judge by chance references in biographies and novels of the next ten years, a feeling of slightly contemptuous distaste for the author and her doctrine. The *Letters* were not accepted as helping in any way to solve the problems that were troubling men's minds. Spiritual and intellectual restlessness increased. Matthew Arnold, in the introduction to the 1853 edition of his poems, spoke of "the bewildering confusion of our times" and the deep unrest experienced by many who could not see their way plainly before them. Men were waiting for a new revelation that would clear away the doubts and perplexities that the discoveries of science and the controversies concerning religion had raised. Some went to the poets for help and found in them sympathy and consolation and soul refreshment. But the poets themselves had but a clouded vision; they too were troubled and anxious. The light that was to show the way past stumbling-blocks and dark places into a larger, freer air was not lit by one of them. It was lit by a man, of genius as rare as theirs, who had worked patiently, steadily, hopefully, year after year, until at last he was able to give his fellow-men the guidance for which they had been waiting. In October 1859 Charles Darwin published his *Origin of Species*, and a new era in the history of science and religion was begun.

The book, at first, did not arouse general interest. It was not written in a popular manner, and its reasoning required close and earnest attention on the part of the reader. George Eliot, who began to read it with G. H. Lewes on November 23rd, wrote in her Journal, "Though full of interesting matter it is not impressive, from want of luminous and orderly presentation." It did not attract the public that had been thrilled by *Vestiges*. Of the 1,250 copies that were sold on the day of publication most were probably bought by scientists who were already interested in the line of research followed by Darwin, or by theologians who were eager to see how the new theories bore upon the truths of Scripture.

Of the scientists some enthusiastically agreed with the book and some attacked it violently. Sir J. D. Hooker, and Sir Charles Lyell, whose *Principles of Geology*, published in 1831, had tended in the same direction as *The Origin of Species*, were Darwin's ardent supporters. Huxley, who in the fifteen years since *Vestiges* had been working hard at natural history and had become famous as a writer and a speaker, was so impressed by the greatness of Darwin's work that he set himself to do what Darwin had no power of doing. He took upon himself the task of popularizing the book, speaking and lecturing and writing about it whenever there was an opportunity. His style had the graces that Darwin lacked, and it was largely through him that *The Origin of Species* became known to the general public. The sale of the book increased. On January 14, 1860, Darwin wrote to Sir Charles Lyell—

In a letter to-day from a lady to E. she says she heard a man inquiring for it at the Railway Station!! at Waterloo Bridge, and the bookseller said he had none until the new edition was out.

The bookseller said he had not read it, but had heard it was a very remarkable book!!!

The violence of the scientists and theologians who were opposed to Darwin also helped to spread the fame of the book. Professor Owen hotly denounced its teaching, and Professor Sedgwick wrote a savage review of it in the *Spectator*. Dr. Whewell, Master of Trinity College, Cambridge, who, as scientist and theologian, spoke with double authority, was perhaps its most formidable opponent. He refused to admit a copy of the work to the library of his College, and did all he could to prevent its being read in the University. But his efforts failed almost completely, and as fruitless were the attempts of Bishop Wilberforce to ban the book at Oxford. The undergraduates of both Universities could not be prevented from reading it.

At a meeting of the British Association in 1860 Bishop Wilberforce made a vehement attack on *The Origin of Species*; but he was no scientist, and was unable to meet Huxley's learned and eloquent arguments in its defence. It was at this meeting that Huxley made the retort which has become famous. Wilberforce declared that he refused, for himself, to regard monkeys as his ancestors, and turning to Huxley asked whether it was through his grandfather or his grandmother that he claimed descent from "a venerable ape." There are various versions of Huxley's reply. Dr. Vernon Harcourt, his biographer, gives it—

"If I am asked whether I would choose to be descended from the poor animal of low intelligence and stooping gait who grins and chatters as we pass, or from a man endowed with great ability and a splendid position who should use these gifts to discredit and crush humble seekers after truth, I hesitate what answer to make."

In the bishop's biography the version runs, "I would rather be descended from an ape than from a bishop."

The Origin of Species travelled down to Devonshire and was read by that convinced Plymouth Brother, Mr. Gosse, who was himself a scientist with a wide practical knowledge of natural history. His reception of it is described by his son—

Every instinct in his intelligence went out at first to meet the new light. It had hardly done so when a recollection of the opening chapter of Genesis checked it at the outset. He consulted Carpenter

... and both determined on various grounds to have nothing to do with the terrible theory, but to hold steadily to the law of fixity of species.

Mr. Gosse could not rest until he had worked out to his own satisfaction a complete refutation of Darwin's arguments, and this he published under the title of *Omphalos*. He confidently expected a great and conclusive triumph for his theory, but to his bitter disappointment the book was hardly noticed. A few newspapers reviewed it briefly, and one of these summed up its arguments in the words, "God hid the fossils in the rocks in order to tempt geologists into infidelity."

To convinced opponents such as these the light which Darwin was holding up showed only the obstacles in the way and the gigantic shadows which they cast. Others, who saw the obstacles no less plainly, saw also the path leading past them, and had courage and faith to adventure on it. "If you be right," Charles Kingsley wrote to Darwin, "I must give up much that I have believed and written. In that I care little. Let God be true and every man a liar." Richard Church remained calm and steadfast as he had remained through earlier storms. He did not believe that any revelation of science could affect the vital truths of the Christian religion. He compared the reception of *The Origin of Species* with that of *Vestiges*.

Mr. Darwin's book, partly from the greater power and gravity of the writer, and partly from, I think, a little more wisdom in the public, has not made such an outcry. Perhaps it is not so popular in style and so widely read; but I should think that it is *the* book of science which has produced most impression here of any that has appeared in many years.

Church wrote this in March 1860, when the popular outcry had not become very loud; but it rose higher as the book became more widely known, and if it was not quite as general as the outcry against *Vestiges* it was certainly more serious and more bitter. There were many deeply religious men and women to whom Darwin's theories appeared a wanton attack upon the most sacred and most treasured spiritual truths. The Roman Catholics as a body agreed with Cardinal Manning when he denounced them as "a brutal philosophy—to wit, there is no God, and the ape is our Adam." Carlyle put his great influence in the scale against Darwin, although he owned he had not read *The Origin of Species*. He never could read a page of it, he said, nor waste the least thought on it; the popularity of the book was a wonder to him, and indicated the capricious stupidity of mankind. Many of those who clamoured loudest, like Carlyle, had never read the book. Their whole idea of its contents was gained from the constantly repeated cry that it declared man to be descended from a monkey. This became a catch phrase, and gave to ignorant people openings for cheap wit and coarse ridicule.

In the autumn of 1864 Disraeli supplied the public with another catch phrase which was even more telling. At a meeting at Oxford, with Bishop Wilberforce in the chair, *The Origin of Species* became the subject of discussion.

"What is the question now being placed before society with glib assurance the most astounding?" asked Disraeli. "The question is this. Is man an ape or an angel? My lord, I am on the side of the angels."

Henceforward the opponents of Darwin's theory delighted to declare that they were "on the side of the angels." The phrase seemed to give authority, if not sanctity, to their pronouncements.

There was, however, a body of readers, large though not clamorous, by whom Darwin's book was recognized as a revelation. The doubts and speculations, the aspirations and questionings that had been working in men's minds changed from torments to joys now that there was hope of answer and fulfilment. More especially was this felt by the young. No one, we have been told over and over again, who was not on the threshold of full manhood or full womanhood in this *annus mirabilis* of 1859 and the years that followed, can realize what Darwin and Huxley meant to the quick, eager brain and boundless curiosity of youth. At last, said Christopher Kirkland, full day had come. "Darwin first, and then the spectroscope, opened a new world to me." Edward Clodd, the son of an Aldeburgh brig-owner, came up to London in 1855, and he tells how he found himself in the midst of an intellectual movement that thrilled and excited him, and how, when *The Origin of Species* appeared, it roused all his faculties to a state of joyous activity. He went to Huxley's lectures, and he discussed endlessly with his fellows the wonders of evolution and the destiny of man's soul. Lord Balfour, whose time at Eton and Oxford fell within these stirring 'sixties, bore witness to the intense interest which his contemporaries felt in the Darwinian theories. The intellectual excitement reached young men of humbler rank also, as some of the older generation who had not advanced with the times indignantly noted. "I went the other morning to have my hair cut," said an old gentleman in Justin McCarthy's *Dear Lady Disdain.*

The fellow who cut my hair—a fine, strapping young fellow, too, nearly six feet high, and with the air of a soldier about him—I found out he was a Volunteer—what do you think he discoursed about while he was cutting my hair? The doctrine of evolution, sir, Darwin and Huxley and the lot of them—hashed up somehow with the good time coming and the universal brotherhood, and I don't know what else.

Even humble girl students in the London educational institutes, like Wilhelmina Galbraith of *Windyhaugh*, felt themselves enrolled in a great army that was going out to fight for Truth.

Solitary souls—groups of two or three—have gone forth in all ages; but here was a whole army with its enthusiasts, its raw recruits, its mercenaries, its troop of mere camp followers. Well that the army had leaders so noble.

Darwin and Huxley shared the leadership of the troops that fought in the name of science. It was Huxley's part to sound the call to battle and lead the army into the field. His lecture on *The Physical Basis of Life* had made a recruit of Wilhelmina, as it had made recruits of many other eager young students. His address to the Royal Society in 1860 gave to his army its marching orders, and they were remembered and quoted in the days when victory seemed very far off.

The Origin of Species is not the first and it will not be the last of the great questions born of science which will demand settlement from this generation. The general mind is seething strangely, and to those who watch the signs of the times it seems plain that this nineteenth century will see revolutions of thought and practice as great as those which the sixteenth witnessed. . . . But I verily believe that come what will the part which England may play in the battle is a great and noble one. . . . That depends on how you, the public, deal with science. Cherish her, venerate her, follow her methods faithfully and implicitly in their application to all branches of human thought, and the future of this people will be greater than the past. Listen to those who would silence and crush her, and I fear our children will see the glory of England vanishing like Arthur in the mist; they will cry too late the woeful cry of Guinevere—

> It was my duty to have loved the highest:
> It surely was my profit had I known:
> It would have been my pleasure had I seen.

The Church, however, was not minded to resign its leadership in this battle for truth, and under the Church banners, too, an army went forward. The Broad Church party, accepting the principle that free criticism and inquiry *must* have beneficial consequences, applied this principle to the study of Scripture and theology. As a result, there appeared early in 1860 a book of *Essays and Reviews*, by seven writers—six clergymen and one layman. The editor was Henry Bristow Wilson, a country rector, who wrote on *The National Church*. Mark Pattison, now Rector of Exeter College, wrote on *Tendencies of Religious Thought in England, 1688–1750*; Judge Charles Wycliffe Goodwin—the layman— on *Mosaic Cosmogony*. Benjamin Jowett, Professor of Greek at Oxford, in an essay on *The Interpretation of the Scriptures*, maintained that "Scripture has an inner life or soul; it has also an outward body or form." This outward form, he urged, should be dealt with critically as all other books were dealt with; the soul would remain untouched. Frederick Temple, Headmaster of Rugby, wrote on *The Education of the World*. None of these five essays contained anything to which orthodox Churchmen could find just ground for objection, except that they all pleaded strongly for freedom of criticism in matters theological. "He is guilty of high treason against the faith," said Temple, "who fears the result of any investigation, whether philosophical, or scientific, or historical."

It was the two remaining essays that caused the book to be condemned. One was by Baden Powell, Professor of Geometry at Oxford, *On the Study and Evidences of Christianity*. He argued against the credibility of miracles, and referred to the "masterly volume on the *Origin of Species*," which, he said, "must soon bring about an entire revolution of opinion in favour of the grand principles of the self-evolving powers of Nature." The seventh essay was by Rowland Williams, and was a review of Bunsen's *Biblical Researches*, upholding the German philosopher's views, and speaking of the "half ideal, half traditional notices of the beginnings of our race compiled in Genesis."

Essays and Reviews was at first read chiefly by the clergy, and for a time attracted little general notice. Then came the shocked discovery by the few that this book, issued by clergymen of the Church of England, contained views as opposed to Scripture as it was generally interpreted as the obnoxious *Origin of Species* itself. Soon the alarm spread. Wilberforce reviewed the book in the *Quarterly*, and declared that it tended "towards infidelity if not to atheism" and that the writers were "guilty of criminal levity."

"Of all books in any language that I ever laid my hands on," passionately declared Archdeacon Denison, "this is incomparably the worst. It contains all the poison that is contained in Tom Paine's *Age of Reason*, while it has the additional disadvantage of having been written by clergymen."

Bishop Whately denounced it in the House of Lords. Walter Farquhar Hook, on the High Church side, regarded the publication of the book as a breach of faith on the part of its authors, as ordained ministers of the English Church.

"If the writers had resigned their preferments," he said, "they would have at least proved their sincerity, but what we object to is their obtaining an extensive hearing for their opinions from the circumstance of their being English clergymen."

Even by Broad Churchmen *Essays and Reviews* was received with disapproval and distress. Frederick Denison Maurice declared himself pained and puzzled by the book; the writers aimed at pulling down man's belief, but made no attempt at building up anything to take the place of what had been destroyed. Stanley made a similar criticism. Kingsley said—

I confess to having thrust the book away in disgust as saying once again, very weakly, what I had long put out of sight and mind in the practical realities of parish work.

He advised his newly ordained curate not to read it, and he wrote to Stanley in February 1861 telling him that at Cambridge (where he was then lecturing, as Regius Professor of Modern History) the book was making little stir. There was little or nothing in it that the University had not already faced.

Church, as usual, advocated reasonableness and toleration. "It seems to me, with many good and true things in it, to be a reckless book," he said. ". . . But there has been a great deal of unwise panic, and unjust and hasty abuse." There was little chance that his moderate counsel would be listened to while passion ran so high. Almost the whole body of the clergy was outraged at what was held to be a treacherous and disloyal attack on the Christian faith. The laymen at first took little part in the controversy.

"I called on Robert Chambers at his very nice house in St. John's Wood," wrote Darwin to Hooker on April 23, 1861. "He made one good remark and chuckled over it, that the laymen universally had treated the controversy on *Essays and Reviews* as a merely professional subject, and had not joined in it, but had left it to the clergy."

But this did not mean that the laymen took no interest in the matter, only that the book took longer in reaching them. When they did read it there was no lack of response. It was talked about everywhere, and edition after edition was sold. The general feeling aroused was shocked indignation, but there were some who approved. William Hardman, a young barrister of rather advanced opinions, was one of them. Writing, in November 1860, to a friend, Edward Holroyd, who had settled in Australia, he said—

Considerable scandal has been caused in the religious world by the publication of a book called *Essays and Reviews*. It is highly gratifying to me to find men of talent and position in the Church coming forward and giving in their adhesion (with some reservation, nevertheless) to opinions which I have now held for twelve years.

The Lyttelton family thought the book pernicious. "Albert wrote to John saying that Edward's tutor seems bitten with those horrible *Essays and Reviews*, which some sound theologian ought to answer," Lucy Lyttelton wrote in her diary on January 19, 1861. In country houses all over England the book was received with something of the same horror as Trollope tells us it aroused at Aylmer Park, the Yorkshire mansion of Sir Anthony Aylmer, where the daughter of the house firmly believed that it "came direct from the Evil One." It penetrated even into country kitchens, for Mary Howitt says that when she visited Pen-y-bryn in 1862 she found that the cook at the house where she stayed had read *Essays and Reviews* and been shocked by it.

Pious, God-fearing parents in quiet provincial homes read it with dismay, and shuddered to think of the son or daughter away in some great town in the midst of those who approved such wickedness; and the sons and daughters read it with eager excitement, and joined with zest in the discussions it aroused. Edward Clodd saved part of his lunch money each day until he could buy it; and Sophia Jex Blake, the twenty-one-year-old daughter of a strictly Evangelical proctor of Doctors' Commons, wrote home from Edinburgh saying that she was reading with immense interest various books on religious subjects, and must get *Essays and Reviews*. Christopher Kirkland received the book with enthusiasm, and exulted when, as he said, it "brought on its authors the honour of ecclesiastical condemnation."

This "honour" was bestowed in 1862 when the editor and Dr. Williams (Baden Powell had died soon after the publication of the book) were brought before the Court of Arches, condemned for heresy, and sentenced to suspension from their offices for one year. The excitement was intense, and rose higher when notice was given of an appeal to the Privy Council. Before the appeal could be heard there came another book which stirred the religious agitation of the country almost to passion. Dr. Colenso, Bishop of Natal, had been induced, as he explained, by questions asked him by his converts, to make a close study of the Old Testament. He had a strong mathematical bias, and was chiefly known in England through an arithmetical textbook he had written, which was widely used in schools; and in making his examination of the Pentateuch he used arithmetical methods wherever it was possible to do so. In this way he discovered, he said, that many of the statements, such as those relating to time, distance, and numbers of people, were demonstrably incorrect. From this he proceeded to the discovery of other discrepancies in the Scripture narrative which convinced him that the books of the Pentateuch, although they contained much valuable historical matter, contained also much that was mythical and legendary.

In 1862 Colenso published the first volume of his work, *The Pentateuch and the Book of Joshua Critically Examined*, in which he set forward the conclusions at which he had arrived. For this he was condemned by the Synod of South Africa, and excommunicated by Bishop Gray of Capetown. Colenso appealed to the authorities of the English Church, and both bishops came to England, where Colenso was cited before the Ecclesiastical Court and charged with heresy.

Religious England was stirred to its depths. Very few, even of the Broad Church party, supported Colenso. His specific denials and detailed mishandling of stories with which all Bible readers were reverently familiar shocked the public even more than the enunciation of general theories and principles had done. Charles Kingsley was repelled by it; it seemed to him to be "possessed by the fanaticism of disbelief." So dangerous did he consider it that he preached a course of sermons to his people at Eversley warning them against its errors. In the preface to the published edition of these sermons he said that Colenso's book was especially dangerous "to the hundreds of thousands . . . who, being no scholars, must take on trust the historic truths of the Bible. . . . It was picking the body of Scripture to pieces so earnestly that it seemed to forget that Scripture had a spirit as well as a body."

Matthew Arnold was scornful of the "jejune and technical way" in which the book dealt with the controversy; F. D. Maurice said that Colenso's idea of history seemed to be that it was a branch of arithmetic. To many devout believers the bishop's arithmetical calculations were inexpressibly shocking and painful; for others, as for eighteen-year-old Philip Wicksteed, later to be famous as the translator of Dante, they had a strong fascination. Some found in them simply a subject for ridicule; as Sophia Jex Blake severely remarked, "It is so very easy to get up a laugh . . . against opinions you don't agree with by such a jest as that Colenso 'wants to turn the Bible into Rule of Three sums'—so much more easy than justifiable or Christian." Sophia herself read *The Pentateuch*, and so, to her great surprise, did her father. "Only fancy, Daddy has been reading Colenso's book," she wrote. Everybody read it. Ruskin, lecturing to an audience of working men at Camberwell, could refer to it, confident that his reference would be understood.

> You quarrel with Bishop Colenso, forsooth, as if he denied the Bible and you believed it! though every deliberate act of your lives is a deliberate defiance of its primary orders,

said this denunciatory prophet. And if we are to believe Cuthbert

Bede, the author of *Verdant Green*, the rustic population was equally familiar with the religious controversial literature of the day. In *Muttons and Mattins*, which, during the 'sixties, was almost as popular as *Verdant Green*, he reports, with comments, a conversation between the parish clerk of a Sussex village and Mr. Dibbles, a farm bailiff—

"I never did flatter them innowations," said the bailiff. "They be dangerous, Mr. Dibbles," said the parish clerk, ". . . you may take my word for it that they be all of a piece with them *Essays and Reviews* and posturings and monkeries and going dead against the Scriptures." Dibble had considered that he had done his best to put down these alarming novelties by signing his name to a petition carried round by the clerk for the annihilation of the *Essays and Reviews* and Bishop Colenso. It seemed, however, as if Colenso and the *Essays* declined to be put down.

Stanley, now Dean of Westminster, and one of the few clergymen who supported Colenso, summed up the arguments reasonably and without heat when he said—

The case of Colenso's book appears to me to be in a nutshell—perfectly decisive against those who make the exactness of numbers in the Old Testament and the Mosaic authorship of the Pentateuch essential to revelation, but almost entirely ineffectual to any wider conclusion. In fact, it only suggests this curious question: How far does the Oriental tendency to exaggerate numbers invalidate the narrative in which they occur?

The Bishop had some friends who were as enthusiastic as his enemies were violent. Edward Lear, author of *The Book of Nonsense*, was immensely interested in the contest, and inveighed against the "silly bishops" who, instead of trusting that truth would prevail, were persecuting the man who was trying, even if mistakenly, to search truth out. In a letter written to Lady Waldegrave in March 1863, Lear said—

Not those who believe that God the Creator is greater than a Book, and that millions unborn are to look up to higher thoughts than those stereotyped by ancient legends, gross ignorance and hideous bigotry—not those are the Infidels—but these same screaming ganders of the Church who put darkness forward and insist that it is light.

Christopher Kirkland considered that the fact of Colenso's book having been condemned by Convocation as "full of errors of the gravest and most dangerous kind" was equivalent to its being "stamped in gold." Frances Cobbe sought the writer out in London, and visited him at his house in Sussex Place. William Hardman was his staunch supporter, and could not refrain, he said, from writing a letter congratulating the bishop on having set

the greatest example in our times of an effort to rescue our religion from the weeds which in these days of advancing knowledge threatened, if not to destroy it, at least so to choke it as to render it effete or useless.

The Headmaster of Harrow was also his champion and invited him and Mrs. Colenso to Speech Day at the school in 1863, and here, the bishop says, he had an enthusiastic reception.

It is usual for the school to take note of their *friends* when they come out of the recitation by calling out their names for cheers. And it may show how the tide has turned to mention . . . that the lads gave me a hearty double set of cheers in presence of my arch opponents Dr. Wordsworth and Dean Trench.

The tide had, possibly, begun to turn, but there was little sign of a general reaction in Dr. Colenso's favour. "The great Colenso controversy still rages and grows hotter and hotter," William Hardman had written to Edward Holroyd in the April of that same year; and it continued to rage while men discussed the chances of a decision in the bishop's favour when the appeal should be tried. Some people thought it would grow hotter still, with serious consequences to the Church. Henry Sidgwick wrote to his mother—

As to Colenso, I seriously think a crisis is coming on again in the Church of England—much like that of the Tractarians. Colenso's book is simply interesting as the spark that fires the straw. Its conclusions have long been familiar to scholars.

There were a few people who did not take one side or other in the controversy, and these, it would appear, included the family of W. P. Frith, the artist. His daughter tells how Dr. Colenso called at their house one day while Mrs. Frith was entertaining Bishop Gray and his nephew in the drawing-room. The young lady had to sit and talk to "the heretic bishop" in the dining-room, until, from the window, they saw the other visitors depart; whereupon Colenso made his young hostess a courtly bow, declaring that he had "never thought to be obliged to Bishop Gray."

In February 1864 the case of *Essays and Reviews* came before the Privy Council, and the judgment of the Church Court was reversed.

"There is violent excitement at the Privy Council having passed a judgment in favour of Wilson and Williams, two writers in the *Essays and Reviews*," wrote Lucy Lyttelton in her diary, ". . . Some people think the decision of terrible consequence, and likely to compromise the Church, but Papa and others take the more reasonable line of viewing it as what it is—a mere legal acquittal of men whose opinions the Church has disavowed and protested against as strongly as she is capable of doing. And the Judgment carefully disclaims any intention of expressing approval of the horrid book."

The decision raised a storm in the Church, and a declaration protesting against it, which every clergyman was entreated to sign "for the love of God," was sent round; and eleven thousand did sign it. For weeks the newspapers were full of the case, and when at length there were some signs of a lull, the success of Dr. Colenso's appeal caused the storm to break out again. All through the 'sixties the conflict between science and religion continued acute. Mrs. Fawcett tells how, towards the end of the decade, Dr. Williams and his wife were still frowned upon by the "county" and the cathedral dignitaries of Salisbury. A stream of books bearing upon different aspects of the controversy poured from the press. Most of these were read mainly by scientists and theologians, but occasionally there came one, such as *Ecce Homo*, by Robert Seeley, Professor of Latin at University College, London, that made a strong appeal to the general public.

Meantime the scientists were steadily and laboriously pursuing the line of research which would lead them, they believed, to a truth they saw in the distance. They were advancing more rapidly now, for many eager and enthusiastic workers had joined the early pioneers. "Darwin is conquering everywhere," said Kingsley in 1863, "and rushing in like a flood by the mere force of truth and

fact." Kingsley was, as it proved, too optimistic in his generaliza-
tion. Darwin was conquering, but his victory was as yet neither
widespread nor spectacular. When his second great book, *The
Descent of Man*, appeared in 1871, the clamour was as loud, the
scorn as bitter, as that which had greeted *The Origin of Species*.
Yet it seems probable that the crowd which clamoured was not
as large. Scientific education had advanced, and there were more
who understood something of the principles underlying Darwin's
work, and did not see him simply as a charlatan and a blasphemer.
Moreover, the novelty of the idea had faded, and there was, as
always, a large company of men and women who were content
to shrug their shoulders and say, let the scientists and the theologians fight it out between them. The convinced opponents
maintained their old positions. The Anglicans and Roman Catholics
were saddened and outraged by this fresh attack on beliefs that
they held precious and divine. Dr. Pusey and Vincent Coles both
spoke and wrote strongly against the book. Mr. Gladstone attacked
it almost fiercely. Carlyle continued to denounce Darwin as "the
apostle of dirt worship." Whitwell Elwin declared Darwinism to
be "a wild and discredited hypothesis." Yet among both clergy
and laity there were many who were ready to see, with Dr.
Temple—

Something more majestic, more befitting Him to whom a
thousand years are as one day thus to impress His will once for all
on His creation and provide for all the countless varieties by this
one original impress, than by special acts of creation to be
perpetually modifying what he had previously made.

In *The Descent of Man* the theory of evolution which had been
set forward in *The Origin of Species* was applied especially to man,
and this seemed to some of Darwin's opponents to make the old
cry, "Man descended from a monkey," specially appropriate. It
was raised everywhere, and taken by the ignorant to summarize
the whole teaching of the book. All who held, or were supposed
to hold, Darwin's views were, by his bigoted opponents, classed
as equally pestiferous with himself. Herbert Spencer, although his
works were not widely read by the general public, was known as
a Darwinian.

"A story is in circulation," he wrote in 1881, "which originally
made its appearance in one of the personal journals, *The World*,

that a place which I visited has been exorcised in consequence of my presence. It was at Braemar, where I had been staying for some days, and a Free Church clergyman saw my name in the visitors' book. He was seen to shudder, and being asked what was the matter, in tremulous accents said that Anti-Christ was living under the same roof, and straightway convened a prayer-meeting in the billiard-room as a fumigatory measure."

When Darwin died in 1882 he was given a place in Westminster Abbey among those who had rendered great services to their country. The feeling of one section of the public was expressed by Dr. Laing, who declared that the fact of such a man being buried in the Abbey was a proof that England was no longer a Christian country. The feeling of another section was expressed by Dean Farrar, who preached the funeral sermon.

This man, on whom for years bigotry and ignorance poured out their scorn, has been called a materialist. I do not see in all his writings one trace of materialism. I read in every line the healthy, noble, well-balanced wonder of a spirit profoundly reverent, kindled into deepest admiration for the works of God.

CHAPTER VI

PREACHERS AND THEIR HEARERS

THE Victorian age was the age of the preacher, and although the sermon was not the only form his preaching took, it was the most obvious and the most widely popular. No right-minded Victorian thought his Sunday properly spent unless he heard at least one sermon. Many made a practice of hearing two, and there were some who often heard three. When Lucy Lyttelton was on duty at Osborne as Maid-of-Honour in January 1864, she recorded sadly in her diary for Sunday, January 10th, that after morning service no one went to church again.

I was glad I brought Arnold's sermons and Archbishop Leighton with me; but, O dear, it doesn't feel much like Sunday.

Nor was this hearing of sermons looked upon merely as a duty. It was to many men and women a keen pleasure, for which they were willing to pay in time and trouble. Lady Frances Balfour says that her father would go to any Christian church to hear one of the great preachers of the day, and would "study the sermon on its theological merits and on the method of delivery. It was his Sunday pleasure, I had almost said his pastime." He was ready to listen to clergymen of every denomination and every shade of opinion—the Broad Church Dean Stanley, the Low Church Bishop Wilberforce, the Free Church Dr. Guthrie, the Presbyterian Dr. Oswald Dykes, Dr. Caird of the Established Church of Scotland, or Père Hyacinthe of the Church of Rome. For any of these he would "go a Sabbath day's journey and sit under them with the true ear of a hearer of the word." In those days, Lady Frances says, "the sermon was as important as the Sacraments, and had a place of honour in divine worship." Long sermons were preferred to short ones. Some clergymen, like Trollope's decorously orthodox divines, confined themselves to the minimum half-hour; but this with congregations more ardent than those of Barsetshire, was regarded as stinted and ungenerous measure. Sermons lasting an hour and even more were common. Edward Burne-Jones wrote from Oxford in October 1853, saying—

I heard Pusey on Sunday, a magnificent sermon, profound and exhaustive, on Justification. He came out now and then gloriously, full of liberality. It lasted close on two hours.

Dr. Pusey had taken Newman's place at Oxford as the leader of the Tractarian movement, and although he never stirred the University as Newman had stirred it, he upheld worthily the great traditions of the pulpit of St. Mary's. He was, apparently, given to long sermons. Mrs. Jeune, wife of the Master of Pembroke, recorded in her diary on a Sunday in 1862 that she and her family went to church and heard Dr. Pusey preach a sermon "full of piety and without controversy." "As it was of great length," she said, "and brought us to a late hour, we did not go again in the afternoon but walked instead."

Sara Coleridge perhaps explains the length of Dr. Pusey's discourses when she says of a sermon she heard that it was "a rhapsody describing with infinite repetition the wickedness of sin, the worthlessness of earth and the blessedness of heaven." He had, in her opinion, "not one of the graces of oratory"; but Mrs. Humphry Ward describes him as wielding a spell which is worth much oratory—the spell of a soul dwelling spiritually on the heights. When Mrs. Ward knew Pusey at Oxford in the early 'seventies he was an old man and preached but seldom; when he did it made her think, she says, "of some modern Elijah returning after long silence and exile to protest against an unbelieving world."

The sermons of the Evangelical clergy were as lengthy as those of the Anglicans. General Gordon, we are told, remembered in his manhood the "dreadful sermons" he had been obliged to listen to when he was a boy, and shuddered at the recollection. They lasted for an hour, and were too long even for his elder sister Augusta, who was the most devoted of Evangelicals. Nevertheless, she must be regarded as falling short of the standard set up by true sermon lovers, for with them a discourse was scarcely worthy to be called a sermon unless it lasted for at least an hour. Morley, in his *Life of Gladstone*, says—

I remember dining at Sir Robert Peel's with the Scotch deputation. It included Collins, a Church bookseller of note, who told me that no sermon ought ever to fall short of an hour, for in less time than that it was not possible to explain any text of Holy Scripture.

In one of its phases the Victorian sermon became a definitely intellectual as well as a spiritual and emotional exercise. When Edward Clodd came up to London in 1855 he exchanged the strict, repressive atmosphere of his Baptist home in Norfolk for a freer, larger air, where daring speculation and bold theorizing clashed with an almost fierce attachment to old principles and loyalties. The different causes which men were called upon to support were set forward in the books on science and religion that were appearing then and during the years that followed; and the champions of these causes were the preachers. Everywhere they were urged on by eager congregations. Edward Clodd tells how he went to hear one noted divine after another, and found every time the church or chapel crowded to the doors. He was only a boy of nineteen, but he had his share of the ardent curiosity and zest for new experiences which made life thrilling and wonderful for the youth of that day. For the next ten years or more, while he worked as a bank clerk in London, religion and science were his great absorbing interests. He heard Newman Hall's persuasive eloquence at Rowland Hill's Chapel in Blackfriars Road, and Thomas Binney's thunders against the Church of England at the Weigh House, Eastcheap. He went to the chapel in Great Portland Street where James Martineau brought learning and piety and a keen logical faculty to the expounding of the doctrines of Unitarianism. He heard Canon Liddon at St. Paul's and Dean Stanley at Westminster, Frederick Denison Maurice at Lincoln's Inn Chapel, and Sheridan Knowles, whom he had previously admired as an actor, at Cross Street Chapel, Islington. He heard doctrines and beliefs attacked and defended from every point of vantage and with all sorts of weapons. The "scientific and quasi-religious lectures" which Nathaniel Cramp, the advanced young barber of *Dear Lady Disdain*, attended on Sundays differed very little from some of the sermons that were to be heard in places of worship.

Frederick Denison Maurice had a large following, and Lincoln's Inn Chapel was nearly always crowded, but opinions concerning his sermons were strangely divided. Kingsley, who was his devoted disciple, thought him a marvellous preacher, "inspired—gigantic." Young people were usually much impressed by him. Alfred Ainger, when he was a boy at boarding school, went every Sunday with the other pupils to Maurice's chapel, and he long remembered the sermons he heard there.

There is one among them, on the raising of Lazarus, simpler I think than his wont and presenting fewer of his peculiar difficulties of thought and style. It is sixteen years since that balmy summer afternoon when I heard him deliver it in the solemn, quiet chapel of Lincoln's Inn; and even as I write I see the "prophets blazoned on the panes" of the ancient windows, and look up to that living prophet face which no one who ever saw it could forget and hear once more "The trembling fervency of prayer" with which he led our souls the prayerful way.

Millicent Garrett (afterwards Mrs. Fawcett) heard him when she was a girl of about seventeen, staying with her elder sister in London. She thought herself fortunate, she said, to have had this opportunity while her mind was in process of formation.

He had the voice, the look, the inspiration of a prophet; and spiritual things were to him the greatest realities of the universe. . . . He awakened in me new thoughts, and, I hope, partially at all events, new reverences.

Lord Frederick Cavendish went to Lincoln's Inn Chapel in 1864, and was very much struck with the sermon, of which he remembered some "beautiful bits" to repeat to Lucy Lyttelton. On the other hand, Matthew Arnold described Maurice as "always beating the bush with great emotion but never starting the hare"; and Lord Mountstuart Duff says that he had heard Maurice preach thirty or forty times and had "never carried away one clear idea, or even the impression that he had more than the faintest conception of what he himself meant." He quotes Aubrey de Vere as saying that listening to Maurice was like eating pea-soup with a fork, and says that Jowett, when asked what a sermon preached by Maurice before the University was about, replied, "Well, all that I could make out was that to-day was yesterday and this world the same as the next."

"The fact that he should have exerted a stimulating influence on so many more or less remarkable people," says Lord Mountstuart Duff, "is sufficiently strange; but it must be remembered that he was a noble fellow, with immense power of sympathy, and an ardent, passionate nature, which often led him to right conclusions, in spite of his hopelessly confused reasoning. To listen to him was like drinking spiritual champagne."

The eager interest in sermons that dealt with science and doctrine lasted on well into the 'seventies. Dr. Margaret Todd gives, in her novel, *Windyhaugh*, a picture of student life in London, and shows us a girl coming up from her country home for the Matriculation Examination of the London University, and regarding as the most thrilling experience of that eventful week the hearing of a stirring Methodist sermon at the Tabernacle. She shows us also an elderly grocer from a small village in Scotland paying a visit to another girl student, and going with her to hear so many noted preachers that the week became "a sheer spiritual debauch." The grocer, we are told, showed "a partiality for heretics," but his catholic taste included the saints and the seers.

In most of the large towns there was as fervent an energy among the preachers, and as lively an interest among the hearers as there was in London. In the country districts, where stimulus was lacking, energy and interest were apt to flag. The minor Victorian novelists are fond of painting the Sunday morning service at a village church—the rustics, bovine and vacuous, the restless, shuffling schoolchildren in the gallery, the yawning squire with his family—usually large and exuberant—in the pew of state, the dull clergyman droning out his discourse with its firstly and secondly, and even sometimes, we are asked to believe, its sixthly and seventhly. Helen Mathers' description, in *Comin' Thro' the Rye*, of the Reverend Mr. Skipworth, who, having given out his text—

walks up to it, it is true, and looks at us over the other side, ambles at it, makes dashes at it, repeats it over and over again, but never really grasps its meaning and brings it home to us,

is typical. It is probable that in many country churches sermons were preached as crude and as insipid as these writers report them to have been, but to this dismal rule there were many and striking exceptions. In the church that served the Hampshire parish of Eversley—a parish made up of three tiny hamlets, surrounded by great stretches of moorland and forests of fir-trees—a young man of twenty-five, Charles Kingsley, began in 1842 to preach sermons that made him famous. His congregation consisted chiefly of sturdy rustics, most of whom were of gipsy stock and many of whom were poachers, yet, as their pastor said, thorough good fellows nevertheless. They were not habitual churchgoers, but had been brought in by the power of those same sermons, which drew also hearers from the other parishes round about. Later, when Kingsley became Canon, first of Chester and afterwards of Westminster, crowds of men and women, including the foremost in the country for intellect and attainments, gathered in the great cathedrals where he preached. "But," said his friend and curate, Mr. Harrison—

to my mind he was never heard to greater advantage than in his own village pulpit. I have sometimes been so moved by what he then said that I could scarcely restrain myself from calling out, as he poured forth words, now exquisitely sad and tender, now grand and heroic; with an insight into character, a knowledge of the world, and a sustained eloquence which, each in its own way, was matchless.

Ten years after Charles Kingsley had begun his ministry at Eversley, there came as rector to the little Somersetshire parish of Whatley, with its two hundred inhabitants, a man who, though he had not the fire and passion of Kingsley, was a preacher of the highest order. This was Richard Church, the friend of Newman, the famous Oxford scholar and writer, who was content to use his great abilities in serving this remote parish, and preaching to a tiny congregation of farmers and farm labourers with their wives and children. Yet the sermons that he preached were full of such thought and wisdom as would have delighted an assembly of theologians, though they were simple and direct enough to appeal to the uneducated folks of Whatley. It was only long afterwards, through the earnest representations of friends, that he unwillingly consented to publish these sermons, and then their quiet beauty gained for them many enthusiastic readers.

In 1871 Church left Whatley to become Dean of St. Paul's. Dr. Barnet, President of the Congregational Union, says that he heard him preach there one Whit-Sunday on the text "Grieve not the Spirit," and he describes

the spare figure, almost insignificant in its stature, standing in the pulpit, the upward look, then the quiet reading of the text, and then the whole vast congregation subdued into breathless attention, not by the spell of a great orator, but by the wonderful spiritual power of the man, as the first sentence of the sermon fell on their ears: "Grieve not—pain not—pain not the Spirit of God. Then we may pain God."

Another great village priest was John Keble. He remained working and preaching at Hursley until his death in 1866. Mark Rutherford says that he made a pilgrimage to Hursley one harvest time to hear Keble preach, and was deeply impressed by the way in which, after dealing in practical fashion with the relationship between masters and men at that season, the preacher lifted the thoughts of his hearers towards the perfect example of their Master in heaven. "It was noble Christian doctrine," said Mark Rutherford, "such as I have not often heard since."

Mrs. Twistleton, wife of the American ambassador, also paid a visit to Hursley church one Sunday morning in 1854, and noted especially the congregation gathered there.

It was a regular country congregation, farmers in their white smock frocks, old women and young maidens their daughters, two bands of Sunday School children with their teachers, and just a few of the "gentry"—as decorous and attentive a one as I ever saw.

The scientific controversy which formed the subject of so many sermons in the large towns was seldom more than touched upon in country pulpits; but the battle between Church and Dissent raged fiercely even in the remote villages. Charlotte Brontë, writing in 1840 to her friend, Ellen Nussey, described how her father's two curates, whom she called Mr. W. and Mr. C., announced that on a certain Sunday they would preach—the one in the morning, the other in the evening—in support of High Church doctrines. The Dissenters were invited to be present, and they shut up their chapels and came in a body.

Mr. W. delivered a noble, eloquent, High Church, Apostolic Succession discourse, in which he banged the Dissenters most fearlessly and unflinchingly. I thought they had got enough for one while, but it was nothing to the dose that was thrust down their throats in the evening. A keener, cleverer, bolder, and more heart-stirring harangue than that which Mr. C. delivered from Haworth pulpit last Sunday evening I never heard. He did not rant; he did not cant; he did not whine; he did not sniggle; he just got up and spoke with the boldness of the man who was impressed with the truth of what he was saying, who has no fear of his enemies, and no dread of consequences. His sermon lasted an hour, yet I was sorry when it was done. I do not say that I agree either with him, or with Mr. W., either in all or in half of their opinions. I consider them bigoted, intolerant, and wholly unjustifiable on the ground of common sense.

It is not recorded that either of these sermons was printed, but they became known to fame in the pages of Mrs. Gaskell's *Life of Charlotte Brontë*. Their effect on the intellectual and religious life of Haworth must have been, in little, like the effect of *Tracts for the Times* on the country at large. They must have stirred the religious pugnacity of the Yorkshireman to its depths; and the discussion and argument that followed must have shaken his mental powers into healthy activity.

The Dissenters were not without their champions even in the Salems and Zions and Ebenezers of the villages and small towns. Young Mr. Vincent, who came to Carlingford fresh from Homerton Theological College, upheld their cause with fervid eloquence—

With fiery zeal he flew to the question of Church and State, and set forth the wrongs which Christianity sustained from endowment, and the heinous evils of rich livings, episcopal palaces, and spiritual lords. . . . These men had joined God and mammon— they were in the pay of the State. Mr. Vincent thundered forth the lofty censures of an evangelist whom the State did not recognize, and with whom mammon had little enough to do. He brought forth all the weapons out of the Homerton armoury, new, bright, and dazzling.

Mr. Vincent's sermons and lectures on Church and State "shook society in Carlingford to its very foundations." He could preach in another vein also, and his last discourse in Salem Chapel raised an excitement that was almost terror.

Faces grew pale, long sobs of emotion burst here and there from the half-terrified, excited audience, who seemed to see around them instead of the everyday familiar world a throng of those souls whom the preacher disrobed of everything but passion, and consciousness, and immortality.

The type of sermon that thrilled and horrified was common among some bodies of Dissenters. Mr. Vincent's terrors were of the finer and more spiritual kind; more usual were the "red-hot coals" of Mr. Spurgeon. Many sects used methods of an even more lurid nature than those which he employed. Kingsley, in

Two Years Ago, tells of the Brianite preachers of Cornwall, who, during a cholera visitation, preached the village folk of Aberalva into a state of wild hysteria.

The great preachers published their sermons almost as a matter of course, and many who were not great, but had attained a certain amount of popularity with their own congregations and could depend upon even a moderate local sale, were ambitious to see their discourses in print. A congregation could offer no higher compliment to its pastor than a request that his sermon or sermons should be published. We remember the Reverend John Jenkyns of *Cranford*, whose sermon, preached before "My Lord Judge" at the assize, was published "by request"; and how he found it necessary to go up to London to see it through the press, and afterwards had his portrait painted, with his hand upon a copy of the wonderful completed product. Less ambitious preachers were contented with a small leaflet locally printed, or even with a column in the religious periodical of their denomination. To achieve a volume of sermons was the vision of a soaring ambition.

The output was enormous, yet buyers and readers were found to absorb it. Sermons, we are told, held, in Victorian days, the place that is now held by novels. Everybody read them; some with the drowsy attention that came with the consciousness of a Sunday afternoon duty carefully performed, many with keen enjoyment and spiritual satisfaction. There were many households like that of Squire Hamley of *Wives and Daughters*, where the unwritten laws for the regulation of conduct on Sundays included "cold meat, sermon reading, and no smoking until after evening prayers"; and Mrs. Gaskell's description of the poor squire trying to pass a Sunday afternoon with the aid of a volume of Blair's sermons might apply to many readers in many houses, both in town and country. In houses where only half a dozen books were to be found one of them was almost sure to be a volume of sermons. Such a volume was, indeed, a necessity, for even in those lax families where sermons were not read on Sundays there was an immediate call for them in times of bereavement or on specially solemn occasions. Mrs. Oliphant's exemplary heroine, Miss Lucilla Marjoribanks, devoted herself to a volume of sermons in the sad days that followed her father's death, sitting quietly in a corner of the sofa, and getting through fifty pages in a day. Lucilla was not of a religious temperament, but neither was she a hypocrite. She grieved deeply and genuinely for the death of her father, and the reading of sermons presented itself to her, as it presented itself to all those around her, as a fitting and decorous tribute to his memory.

There was a type of sermon that was very popular among a certain class of readers, because, while its perusal could be regarded as a pious exercise, it gave the same sort of entertainment as could be obtained from a third-rate novel. It was this type of sermon which George Eliot attacked in her article on Dr. Cumming. In enumerating the means by which an Evangelical preacher might become popular, she said—

Above all, let him set up as an interpreter of prophecy, and rival Moore's Almanack in the prediction of political events, tickling the interest of hearers who are but moderately spiritual by showing how the Holy Spirit has dictated problems and charades for their benefit, and how if they are ingenious enough to solve them, they may have their Christian graces nourished by learning precisely to whom they may point as "the horn that had eyes," "the lying prophet," and "the unclean spirit." . . . In this way he may gain a metropolitan pulpit; the avenues to his church will be crowded as passages to the opera; he has but to print his prophetic sermons and bind them in lilac and gold, and they will adorn the drawing-room of all Evangelical ladies, who will regard as a sort of pious "light reading" the demonstration that the prophecy of the locusts whose sting is in their tail is fulfilled in the fact of the Turkish commander's having taken a horse's tail for his standard, and that the French are the very frogs predicted in the Revelation.

The higher type of sermon, however, held its own, even against the ingeniously contrived entertainment presented by Dr. Cumming and his fellows. Newman, as has been said, took the first place, and next to him came Dr. Arnold. Most of Arnold's sermons were preached in the College chapel at Rugby, and Thomas Hughes, who listened to many of them there, has told us, in *Tom Brown's Schooldays*, something about their effect on their hearers. Sara Coleridge was a great admirer of Arnold's sermons. She read them herself, and she warmly thanked a clergyman friend who gave a volume of them to her schoolboy son, Herbert. Mr. Gladstone, who was a great lover of sermons, and was in the habit of reading them aloud to his family, preferred Arnold's to any others.

Mary Gladstone followed her father in her fondness for sermon reading. She read many by a great variety of preachers, and described herself as "gloating over" one preached by Canon Scott Holland at Winchester on a Good Friday. Walter Bagehot took a volume of sermons with him on his honeymoon, and read a discourse by F. D. Maurice aloud to his wife. Lord and Lady Frederick Cavendish read sermons together both before and after their marriage. "After dinner Fred read aloud two fine sermons on *The Subjection of the Creature to Vanity*," wrote Lady Cavendish in June 1864, and in October of the same year, "Fred read to me a powerful and earnest sermon of Liddon's." Digby Mackworth Dolben, the poet, was a great admirer of Liddon. "I have been reading Liddon's sermons. They are most wonderful and beautiful," he wrote to his friend, Robert Bridges, in 1864, when he was sixteen years old.

Charles Kingsley probably came next in popularity to Arnold. In 1849 he published a volume of *Twenty-five Village Sermons* which he had preached in the church at Eversley, and it had a large, immediate sale. What pleased the author most was that it was read by the Chartist working men with whom he was in such strong sympathy.

"My *Village Sermons* are being read from man to man among the South London Chartists," he wrote to his wife during a visit he paid to London in June 1849, "at such a pace that C. can't get them back again."

An officer of the Royal Artillery suggested that a few of Kingsley's sermons and extracts from his works should be printed for soldiers' libraries; and from all over the country came letters from people of every class telling him how some particular sermon had been helpful to each in his difficulties.

Frederick Robertson of Brighton was another favourite. John Bright and Bishop Thirlwall both read his sermons with keen interest. Sophia Jex Blake read them over and over again. "Her volumes of Robertson are falling to pieces with sheer honest, careful, lifelong use," said her biographer.

Dean Stanley's sermons were extremely popular with some readers. "I am reading with great delight Stanley's *Sermons*," wrote Sara Coleridge in 1849, "which, strange to say, I never read through till now." To others the Dean's Broad Church principles were unacceptable. "Stanley's sermons are excellent, but they seem to me curiously unorthodox," said Fanny Kemble. Lady Frederick Cavendish took this unorthodoxy very seriously. In January 1864 she wrote in her diary—

I read Stanley's farewell sermon at Oxford. It grieved and shocked me, in spite of great eloquence, earnestness, and feeling; for I cannot help seeing that the aims and standards he puts forward are not distinctly Christian, but more like those of some refined philosophy; and one asks oneself, where are the old paths? the Bible rules, the humble obedience, and, above all, the following of the simple but Perfect Pattern. These dangerous days are full of teaching that wanders from all these and bewilders one with false liberality and confused belief. God keep us in the strait and narrow way.

Sometimes a single sermon, published as a separate pamphlet, aroused special interest. Everybody rushed to read it and there was as much talk and discussion about it as about a new novel or a new poem. In 1838 Walter Farquhar Hook preached before Queen Victoria and her Court a sermon which became known as the "Hear the Church" sermon. It was not new, but was slightly altered from one which he had preached some years before at his church at Leeds. He chose it, he said, because he thought it would serve to "lay before the young sovereign the claims, character, and privileges of the Church of which, in the providence of God, she had been called to be temporal head." To his surprise the sermon made a great commotion in the political and fashionable worlds. It was rumoured that the Queen had been affronted by his words, and various meanings which he had not intended were read into them. This rumour, as it turned out, was quite unfounded, but it served to make the general public eager to read the sermon. It quickly ran through twenty-eight editions; a hundred thousand copies were sold, while from all over the country letters poured in thanking the preacher for his brave, outspoken discourse.

The reading of sermons gradually declined as the Queen's reign went on. Sarah Tytler, in her novel, *Buried Diamonds*, which tells of the early 'eighties, shows one of her characters reading "novels by the hundred and sermons by the score." Twenty years earlier the numbers would have been reversed.

CHAPTER VII

THE TWO NATIONS

In 1845 Disraeli published his second political novel, which he called *Sybil: or the Two Nations*. The story opened in 1837, and it attempted to give a picture of the English people during the early years of the Queen's reign. Two nations, said Disraeli, then dwelt in the country. They were of the same blood, yet they differed as widely as did men of different races. Very seldom did the members of one nation come into contact with the members of the other, and when they did meet it was as strangers, almost as enemies. They scarcely understood one another's language, they knew almost nothing of one another's beliefs or ideals or habits. Their dwellings, their clothes, their food were all different; only the fact that there were some men in each nation who worshipped the same God made a slight bond between them.

The two nations were the Rich and the Poor. The first lived in comfort and luxury, having all things that could make life pleasant. They had full opportunity for self-development and for happy social intercourse. The second lived hardly and painfully, toiling for long hours with no leisure and with scant sleep, and, even so, earning only just enough to keep their bodies alive. They were untaught, brutalized, miserable, cold, and hungry.

In making this division Disraeli took little count of that vast section of the population that lay between the two extremes. He considered mainly the very rich and the very poor. His Rich were the wealthy landowners and manufacturers, whose fortunes, in many cases, came through the misery of those who worked for them. His Poor consisted largely of those absolutely sunk in ignorance, vice, and want, though it included also the underpaid and struggling working men whose longing for something that would feed their minds and delight their imaginations was almost as painful as their longing for some relief from their bodily misery.

Of the lowest section of this nation of the Poor we need here say little. Most of them could not read, and books were strange, almost unknown things to them. There were boys like Disraeli's Devil's Dust, who at two years old was sent out to pick up his living in the streets, and at five was set to work in a factory. There were miserable lads like poor crossing-sweeper Jo of *Bleak House*, and hideous "baby-devils" like the "manservant up at the Travellers' Twopenny" of *Edwin Drood*. There were whole communities of heathen, almost savage men and women, like the squatters of Woodgate, where, said Disraeli—

swarming thousands were lodged in the most miserable tenements in the most hideous borough in the ugliest country in the world. . . It is not that the people are immoral, for immorality implies some forethought; or ignorant, for ignorance is relative; but they are animals; unconscious; their minds a blank; and their worst actions only the impulse of a gross, savage instinct. There are many in the town who are ignorant of their very names; very few who can spell them. It is rare that you meet with a young person who knows his own age; rarer to find the boy who has seen a book or the girl who has seen a flower. Ask them the name of their sovereign, and they will give you an unmeaning stare; ask them the name of their religion, and they will laugh; who rules them on earth, or who can save them in heaven, are alike mysteries to them.

We might be inclined to say that these were the creatures of the novelist's imagination were it not that the Blue Books of the day and the reports of Parliamentary debates show that their counterparts were to be found in all the industrial districts of England. It is true that some of these unfortunate children managed to struggle into a state higher than that into which they were born. Disraeli's Devil's Dust learnt to read in the factory school, and, being ambitious and discontented, seized on books as a means of escape from his degradation. Dickens' George Silverman, whose infant home was a cellar in Preston, lived to be a scholar and the vicar of a country parish. But for the most part they lived and died in ignorance.

We must mount a good many steps above these miserable and degraded creatures before we find, in any numbers, our first readers among the nation of the poor. Even when we reach the decent working man we shall discover only here and there a reader. Thirty years or so before the time of which Disraeli wrote, when the full effects of the religious revival that began with the preaching of the Wesleys was being felt throughout England, the Bible and a few tracts were to be found in many—probably most—working-class homes. When Victoria came to the throne this was not so commonly the case, yet even then it is probable that more copies of the Bible than of any other book could have been collected from such homes. There were, as we have seen, many Nonconformist sects that regarded the Scriptures with fanatical reverence, and the Tractarian movement was quickening the zeal of the Church of England. But there were strong forces at work tending to push the Bible from the place that it had held among the nation of the Poor. John Hungerford Pollen, who from 1837 to 1842 was one of a small band of High Church clergymen working under Hook at Leeds, in the midst of a crowded factory population, tells of the efforts made to destroy such faith as existed among his ignorant parishioners.

"After dark," he says, "a crowd of young persons of both sexes return to their homes in narrow lanes. . . . In a back street is a large upper room, with lights; a place for balls. Further is the great hall of the Socialists; their band in summer months parades the streets to lure the young to attractive haunts where 'the restraints of society' have no hold. . . . Follow a youth . . . the youngest of whose sisters, thirteen years old, has been for the last half hour wandering in the dark streets. He is perhaps not attracted to the dancing room. He has gone to hear an old man lecturing to many listeners."

When the youth comes out of the building he has a printed paper in his hand, a leaflet issued by the Society of Rational Pioneers, Leeds. It is headed, *Twenty-five Reasons for being an Atheist*, and the boy spends the rest of his evening in puzzling over arguments such as this—

The idea of God originated when man was in a savage state, unable to comprehend Nature's laws, and is perpetuated by crafty and tyrannical priests who live by raising the hopes and exciting the fears of their followers.

Much of it is beyond his understanding, but the words of the lecturer have given him a clue to its general meaning, and there are plenty of his fellows ready to discuss it with him, to his further enlightenment. It is no wonder that the clergy of St. Saviour's found their task a hard one, and that there were not many Bible readers among the factory hands of Leeds.

In the other great manufacturing centres rationalistic influences were equally active. Florence Nightingale, whose deep interest in the poor led her to an investigation, as complete as she could make it, of the conditions of their lives, stated, in 1852, the conclusions to which she had been led on this subject of atheism among working men. She had read widely, she had talked to statesmen and writers and clergymen, and to the men themselves; and, as a result, "The most thinking and conscientious of the artisans have no religion at all," she declared. They had read Locke and Hume and Voltaire, and they met any attempts to convince them of the truth of the Christian faith with arguments drawn from these books. They would read books against the Bible, but nothing on the other side, except sometimes one of the new scientific works, which upheld the main facts of the Scriptures while treating them as matter for argument and logical proof. In Halifax, Huddersfield, Leeds, Bradford, and Manchester only about three per cent of the working men ever went to church. This was partly because there were not nearly enough churches and clergymen to reach the enormous populations that had gathered in these industrial centres. Even in Leeds, said Miss Nightingale, where Dr. Hook was so active, many men had told her they had never spoken to an Anglican in their lives. As for the lower type of working man, he was entirely vicious and degraded, and had nothing that could be called either active belief or disbelief.

Mrs. Gaskell, who had lived among the working people of Manchester, gave a picture of the cotton operatives in the early 'forties that was more intimate and personal and so even more convincing than that of Miss Nightingale. In her novel, *Mary Barton*, the father of the heroine is a weaver, shrewd, capable, sober, industrious, and with a great store of humanity and loving-kindness. Life treated this poor John Barton very hardly, forcing him to deeds that were contrary to his nature, and cutting him off from the means of satisfying his intellectual and spiritual needs. "I've so often been hankering after the right way," he said, when the end of his sad and toilsome life was very near,

and it's a hard one for the poor man to find. At least it's been so to me. No one learnt me and no one told me. When I was a little chap they taught me to read, and then they ne'er gave me no books; only I heard say the Bible was a good book. . . . So when I grew thoughtful and puzzled, I took to it.

But reading the Bible made him more puzzled than ever, for he could not reconcile its teaching with the ways of the world round about him. "They all spoke up for it, and went and did clean contrary." So he left off reading it, and at the end of his life was still puzzled and despairing; like that other brave and thoughtful worker, Stephen Blackpool, of whom Dickens tells us in *Hard Times*. Stephen was one of the "hands" in Mr. Bounderby's factory at Coketown, who read his Bible, but could not find there an answer to the problems that perplexed him. "It's aw a muddle," he said, as he lay dying. "Fro' first to last a muddle."

There arose, however, soon after the Queen's accession, a class of readers whose numbers increased rapidly throughout the 'forties. Education was spreading, and most of the young people, except those belonging to the very lowest stratum of the population, were learning to read with sufficient ease to make reading a pleasure. These were not satisfied either with the Bible or with rationalistic literature. They wanted stories, and they yearned for romance, for something to take them outside the dullness and monotony of their lives; and the cheap newspapers that came with the 'forties endeavoured to give them what they wanted. There was the *Family Herald*, which started in 1842, and in a few years reached a circulation of a hundred and twenty-five thousand weekly. It was read largely by working girls, like the "young ladies" in Miss Simmonds' workroom, where Mary Barton, of Mrs. Gaskell's story, was apprenticed to the dressmaking, and it filled their heads with visions of handsome lovers and romantic marriages, such as brought poor Mary to sorrow. Thomas Burt, the son of a Northumberland coal-hewer, and afterwards Member of Parliament, got his romance from a few stray numbers of the *London Journal* lent to him by one of his boy friends, a highly spiced periodical, he says, which he read with much gusto.

It was full of adventures, of wild romantic stories depicting duels and battles, deeds of daring, hair-breadth escapes by land or sea, the heroes being banditti, pirates, robbers, and outlaws.

Thomas's father gently rebuked him for wasting his time on such rubbish, but to the boy this scanty draught of romance, which to more fastidious palates might have seemed over-flavoured and a little stale, brought real delight and refreshment.

The *Police Gazette*, which was very popular, contained highly sensational accounts of the week's crimes, with illustrations, coarse both in subject and execution. To accompany this came *Lloyd's Companion to the Penny Sunday Times and People's Police Gazette,* which was full of stories, suggested largely by the most lurid of these crimes, and embellished with the most horrible details that the writers' imagination could suggest. *Lloyd's Penny Weekly Miscellany,* which came from the same office—that of Edward Lloyd, in Salisbury Square—claimed to be highly moral in character. Its aim, so its editor said, was to "rescue cheap literature from the puerilities and from what may deserve a worse title with which it was beset in the London markets." In so far as in its stories virtue was always triumphant and the wicked duly punished (or, as the editor more eloquently put it, "the innocent, although environed by snares, and nearly brought to destruction by the wicked and designing, ultimately triumphed, and proved the goodness of right over might") the claim was justified. All the sentiments were most correct, and expressed in language of extreme elegance. "My Septimus," said the lovely girl-heroine of *A Flaw in the Diamond: a Romance of the Affections,* "the angel Hope will lend us some beauty from the lustre of its wings until fortune smiles upon us." Yet it cannot be denied that the villain was the most interesting person in the story, and that his dark and evil machinations took up most of the space, as well as providing all the thrills.

Thomas Frost, who was during the 'forties a young and struggling journalist, tells us a good deal about these stories, for he studied them closely in order that he might find out something about the public taste to guide him in his own writing. There was one called *Varney the Vampire* which he said was morbid and unreal, and another, *Ada the Betrayed,* which was full of sickly sentimentality. There was *The Lady in Black,* founded upon the story, well known at the time, of a beautiful girl who went out of her mind when her brother, a clerk in the Bank of England, was hanged for forgery, and who was to be seen day after day, pale and wasted and dressed in black, walking up and down before the bank waiting for her lost brother. As time went on Thomas Frost became very successful in producing this type of story—the Salisbury Square school of fiction, as it was called. His younger readers, he said, preferred stories of highwaymen, robbers, and pirates to any others, and he told of a letter he received while he was editing the *Family Paper* which came from a little company of boys who bought and shared the paper between them.

Mr. Editor, If you don't give us a good highwayman story we shan't take your pub any longer. So take notis.

The letter was signed with the names Jack Sheppard, Dick Turpin, Claude Duval, and those of other notable highwaymen; which showed the kind of literature these young gentlemen were in the habit of reading. Sixpenny paper-covered books containing the lives of notorious characters—mostly criminals—were issued in large numbers from Salisbury Square and had a ready sale; as did stories of the same type as the serials contained in the newspapers. Thomas Frost mentions *The Gipsy Mother* and *The Ruined Cottage* by Anna Maria Jones, *Melinda the Murderess* by Stephen Hunt, and *Tyburn Tree* by James Lindridge.

Cuthbert Bede's description in his *Muttons and Mattins* of the periodical which formed the literary sustenance of the domestic servant population of Brighton is sufficiently close to fact. It was called *The Hair Lifter*, and it guaranteed at least one sensation in every chapter. Its stories told of pages who had been changed in the cradle, and who were really heirs to large estates and princely fortunes; of footmen who won the hearts of their masters' rich and lovely daughters; of lady's maids who were their mistress's rivals, and triumphantly bore off noble and wealthy lovers whom high-born damsels sought in vain to allure. Anthony Trollope knew something of these fascinating periodicals, and made fun of them in *The Three Clerks*, where he described Charlie Tudor as writing a serial for *The Daily Delight*. The serial was to be called *Sir Anthony Allan-a-dale and the Baron of Ballyporeen*. The writer was to supply ten paragraphs for each number, and was expected to have an incident for every other paragraph in the first four instalments. The story was to be thrilling—"in the first paragraph Sir Anthony Allan-a-dale is lying dead, and the Baron of Ballyporeen is standing over him with a bloody sword." It was to be up-to-date —in the last instalment Sir Anthony (who, of course, is not dead) turns Puseyite, reads the *Tracts*, and finally goes over to Rome. It was to be instructive—a digression was to be made to enable the writer to bring in "a succinct little account of the Conquest, which will be beneficial to the lower classes." It was to deal with social questions—the editor gave the author the choice of four, adulteration of food, need of education for the poor, street music, and the miscellaneous sale of poisons. Such is Trollope's description of the serial which editors of cheap periodicals were prepared to accept, and it sums up with admirable completeness the tendencies of the Salisbury Square school of fiction.

Literature of a more solid and elevating character was also in demand. That remarkable body of readers which had been formed during the industrial revolution of the eighteenth century had persisted through the early nineteenth, though the increase in the number of operatives that had come through the extended use of machinery had swamped and almost hidden it. Its members struggled grimly against the obstacles that poverty and lack of leisure put in the way of their attaining their desires. They realized intensely that knowledge is power, and that it could bring con-solation and joy into hard, weary lives; and they pursued know-ledge with an ardour that could not be quenched. Mrs. Gaskell tells of a class of men to be found in the manufacturing districts of Lancashire, common hand-loom weavers "who throw the shuttle with unceasing sound, though Newton's *Principia* lies open on the loom, to be snatched at in work hours, but revelled over in meal-times or at night." Kingsley says that Watts' *Logic* and Locke's *On the Use of the Understanding* were well known to reading artisans; and he shows us Jim Crossthwaite, the Chartist tailor, who knew something about Alexander and Caesar and Attila and Ariosto as well as of the great men of his own nation. Samuel Bamford, the Manchester cotton spinner who wrote *Passages in the Life of a Radical*, read widely, especially history and poetry, and he delighted in the poetry of Milton.

O! John Milton! John Milton! of all the poetry ever read or heard recited by me, none has spoke out the whole feelings of my heart as have certain passages of thy divine minstrelsy.

Nearly all the most intelligent of the working men read Shelley. "The poetry of Coleridge and Shelley was stirring within me and making me a Chartist and more," said Thomas Frost. Most of them were interested in history. When Carlyle's *French Revolution* was published in 1837, a poor Paisley weaver wrote to the author thanking him for the enlightenment the book had brought to him and his friends; and a tribute to his *History* that delighted Macaulay came from a company of working men to whom the book had been read aloud, in the form of a vote of thanks to the author "for having written a history that working men can understand."

Often these men must pay for their books with the price of a meal or a fire, and read them under conditions of cold and weariness, such as less fervent seekers after knowledge would have held to make reading impossible. The sickly, sweated boy tailor, Alton Locke, read in his miserable, unventilated garret bedroom with aching eyes and limbs numbed with cold, forcing himself to wake in time to have several hours of study before rising at six to go to his work. Alton Locke is the typical book-hungry city worker, whose sedentary occupation joins with semi-starvation to produce a diseased body. Thomas Burt, the future Labour leader, is an example of the sturdier, more virile class whose work demanded bodily strength and vigour, and whose conditions were somewhat less deplorable. Like Alton Locke, Burt was brought up in a strictly religious home. His father was an earnest, though not a fanatical Primitive Methodist, and in the two-roomed cottage in the unlovely mining village where the family lived there was firm yet kindly discipline and a good deal of happiness amidst great poverty. Thomas went to work in the mine when he was nine years old. Fortunately for him, there were among the putters a few young men who were ardent members of the Primitive Methodist chapel. "In place of the frivolous, trivial, or worse still the foul and ribald conversation common among the miners," says Thomas, "these young men discussed the merits of their favourite preachers and books." Most of them had read Paley's *Natural Theology*, the works of Dr. Dick, and the Reverend William Cook's *Theology*. Burt's father had a library of religious books such as very few working men of that day possessed. There was a set of Albert Barnes' *Notes on the New Testament and the Book of Job*, which filled a whole shelf. He had *Hamilton on Rewards and Punishments*, *The Homilist*, *The Christian Witness*, and several volumes of the *Primitive Methodist Magazine*.

As Thomas Burt grew up his love of reading became a passion. He tells how he walked nine miles to Newcastle to buy a second-hand copy of Cowper's poems which he had seen in a shop window, marked one-and-sixpence, and with what a light heart he covered the nine miles back, reading as he fared along. That was the first book he bought for himself. Afterwards he bought many others— odd volumes of Channing's works and of Milton's, and Gibbon's

Decline and Fall, which his father looked at doubtfully, as tending to infidelity.

Vividly do I remember bringing the first volume home. With youthful glee I read to a late hour. I slept but little that night. The book haunted my dreams. I awoke about four on the bright summer Sunday morning, and went into the fields to read till breakfast time.

This was better than a lean-to bedroom in a close city alley, but the self-denial that had gone to the buying of the books gave Burt a place among heroic working-men readers. Shakespeare he read in Dicks' penny edition "by the side of the murmuring Warsbeck," and ever afterwards the plays were associated in his mind with the soft flowing of the stream. He was fortunate in having friends of his own age with tastes similar to his own, with whom he read and discussed such books as Alison's *History of Europe,* Humboldt's *Cosmos,* and Bailey's *Festus.* To Ruskin, he said, he owed more than he could ever tell; and he delighted in the poetry of Longfellow, Pope, Milton, and Wordsworth.

For working men of this higher type there were periodicals differing widely, from *Lloyd's Weekly Miscellany* and the *Family Herald.* In 1832 the brothers William and Robert Chambers issued the first number of *Chambers's Edinburgh Journal.* The aim of this *Journal* was "to present knowledge under its most cheering and captivating aspect." Each weekly number contained simple, interesting articles on scientific, historical, or literary subjects, and one short story—"no ordinary trash about Italian castles and daggers and ghosts in the blue chamber, and similar nonsense, but something really good." For all this the charge was only three-halfpence. Thoughtful working men welcomed the *Journal* with delight. It gave them just what they wanted. Walter Farquhar Hook testified to the good work that William Chambers was doing, "I live among the class which reads his works, the working people, and I know them." Mark Rutherford, who also lived among them, said, "Blessings on the brothers Chambers for that magazine, and for the *Miscellany* that came afterwards." In a few weeks the *Journal* had a circulation of thirty thousand, which rose steadily until it reached eighty thousand.

Chambers's Journal was quickly followed by the *Penny Magazine,* published by the Society for the Diffusion of Useful Knowledge, which had been founded chiefly through the efforts of Lord Brougham. A little later came the *Saturday Magazine*, published by the S.P.C.K., but neither of these had the circulation or the length of life of *Chambers's Journal*; and the same may be said of other and less notable periodicals of a similar class that appeared and vanished during the 'forties and 'fifties.

All these, except the short-lived *Saturday Magazine*, were entirely secular in character. As Florence Nightingale said, the most intelligent among the working men would not look at a book that treated of religion from any but the scientific or rationalistic point of view. They believed that the Church was the enemy of education. The parsons, so John Crossthwaite told Alton Locke, held the monopoly of education, and they served out to the poor man just a

miserable smattering of general information—just enough to serve as sauce for their great first and last lesson of "Obey the powers that be—whatever they be; leave us alone in our comforts and starve patiently; do, like good boys, for it's God will."

These men hated the Church because it was part of the established order under which they suffered injustice and oppression. They were firmly convinced that all their miseries were due to misgovernment. Their fathers had had visions of a perfect State, and had believed that if once the Reform Bill were passed their visions would become reality. The Reform Bill had been passed, and the working men were worse rather than better off than they had been before. Yet still they saw the Promised Land in the distance, and still they believed that the road to it lay through Parliamentary reform. Now it was the People's Charter that was to bring them to their goal. Once let them get the Charter and all would be well.

Chartist newspapers appeared all over the country; scarcely a working man who could read that did not see at least one of them each week. Fergus O'Connor's *Northern Star* was the most popular; then there were *The Voice of the People, The Poor Man's Advocate, The Working Man's Friend,* and many others. The more violent were their denunciations of the Rich, the more acceptable they were to men who believed that they were being robbed of what was theirs by right and that only through the Charter could they force their tyrants to make restitution.

Nor was it only material benefits that the working man hoped to obtain from the Charter; he looked to it as the bestower of all delights, social, intellectual, and spiritual. Kingsley shows us old Sandy Mackaye, the Scottish bookseller of *Alton Locke*, passing the door of the Victoria Theatre just as "a herd of ragged boys, vomiting forth filth and blasphemy," were going in. "Look there," he said—

look at the amusements, the training, the civilization which the Government permits to the children of the people!—these licensed pits of darkness, traps of temptation, profligacy, and ruin, triumphantly yawning night after night—and then tell me that the people who see their children thus kidnapped into hell are represented by a Government who licenses such things. Would a change in the franchise cure that? Household suffrage mightn't, but give us the Charter, and we'll see about it. Give us the Charter, and we'll send workmen into Parliament that shall soon find out whether something better can't be put in the way of the ten thousand boys and girls in London who live by theft and prostitution than the tender mercies of the Victoria—a pretty name. They say the Queen's a good woman—and I don't doubt it. I wonder often if she knows what her precious namesake here is like.

The Charter therefore they must have, and if the Government refused to give it them, might must help right. So there grew up a great body of Chartists, fierce, eager, determined. They were untaught and ignorant, but many were making desperate efforts to improve, and each year saw an advance. Mechanics' Institutes were being established in various parts of the country, and though these did not really meet the needs of the class for which they were intended, they did help some of its most earnest and intelligent members to educate themselves; and these men rapidly rose to be leaders in the movement.

Such a leader was Thomas Cooper. He was brought up in the Christian faith and held ardently to his religion until he was nearly forty. His father died when he was a small boy, and his mother had a terrible struggle to keep him and herself until he was old enough to earn money by shoemaking. He was clever and fiercely ambitious, and he contrived to educate himself sufficiently to take a post as a schoolmaster. Afterwards he became a Wesleyan preacher, and in 1836 he came to London to try his fortune as a journalist. There followed a time of terrible privation, until at length he managed to get an ill-paid position on the staff of a newspaper. By this time he had become a Chartist, and the fact becoming known to the proprietors of the newspaper, they dismissed him. Then, with the help of some friends, he managed to establish a Chartist newspaper. He opened a bookshop which became a meeting-place where working men gathered to discuss political and religious questions. When Cooper found how ignorant many of these men were, he established an adult Sunday School, where the Bible was read and explained, and where moral questions were earnestly discussed. A large number of men were drawn to this Sunday School, in spite of the prevailing rationalistic tendencies, and Cooper taught religion as earnestly as he taught Chartism. He lectured to his pupils on Milton, Shakespeare, and Burns, and on geology and history. A special Chartist hymn-book was used, and most of the hymns it contained were learned by heart. A favourite one began—

> All men are equal in His sight,
> The bond, the free, the black, the white;
> He made them all—then freedom gave,
> God made the man—man made the slave.

By this time England had entered on the "hungry 'forties" and the suffering among the nation of the Poor was growing more and more terrible. Thomas Cooper wrote and taught and lectured with ever-increasing fervour. On fine summer evenings the Chartists paraded the streets five abreast, singing to the tune of "Rule, Britannia!"—

> Spread—spread the Charter—
> Spread the Charter through the land;
> Let Britons brave and bold join heart and hand.

Turn now to the other nation, the nation of the Rich; and in this we will include not only Disraeli's wealthy landowners and factory-owners, but all the educated, leisured class that lived in comfort and moderate affluence. Among them was slowly spreading some conception of what these poor unfortunates, who were Englishmen like themselves, were suffering. Industrialism had grown at so tremendous a rate that this vast, needy company had been formed before the country as a whole had realized what was going on; before the law, or the consciences of men, or the resources of the country could fit themselves to the new conditions. There were men of the baser sort, greedy and hard and narrow, who were ready to make profit out of their brothers' helplessness; there were more who were careless and indifferent; more still who were really ignorant of the truth. But the nobler spirits, who knew and realized the sufferings of their fellows, were on fire to help. Yet it was difficult to decide how help could best be given. To support those who relied on violence could only make the men's case worse; but if the national conscience could be aroused and the Rich made to realize the sufferings of the Poor, justice and compassion might give what force could not extort.

Dr. Arnold tried to form a society "to collect information as to every point in the condition of the poor throughout the kingdom, and to call public attention to it by every possible means." He wrote to Carlyle about this plan in January 1840, but Carlyle was already trying to attain the same object in his own way. He had written a little book which he called *Chartism*. Carlyle had by this time attained a position of influence in the country; in *Chartism* he came forward for the first time as a writer definitely concerned with the political questions of the day. He was ardently on the side of the working men, but the remedy he advocated was not that of the Charter. It was a remedy founded on the idea that he was to put forward more strongly the following year in his lectures on *Heroes*—the rule of the fittest, of the just, strong man whom his fellows could revere and trust.

"What is an Aristocracy?" Carlyle asked. "A corporation of the Best, of the Bravest. To this joyfully, with heart loyalty, do men pay the half of their substance, to equip and decorate their best, to lodge them in palaces, set them high over all."

The root of England's trouble was that her Aristocracy had failed her. They were no longer the Best and the Bravest. The people had lost their natural leaders, and so had gone astray.

Chartism was denounced by many as foolish and unpractical, but it served its purpose of turning men's attention to the ills from which the country was suffering, and Carlyle's next book, *Past and Present*, which came three years later, carried on the work. In this he told the story of a certain Abbot Sampson of St. Edmundsbury, who lived in the twelfth century, and alongside of this he gave a picture of England as she was and England as she might be if the right remedies were applied to her ills. The remedies were the same as those which he had advocated in his previous books—righteousness, justice, the putting aside of shams; faith in the true, strong man as a leader; and work. "The latest Gospel in this world is, Know thy work and do it." "Love not Pleasure; love God."

The book was widely read, and was denounced, as *Chartism* had been, for advocating a policy which was impracticable and almost mad. But to many, especially to the young and ardent who were borne down by a sense of the country's miseries and their own helplessness, it brought light and hope and stimulus. John Ruskin, fresh from Oxford, and just beginning his life's work, was deeply touched by it. Charles Kingsley, lately settled in his first curacy, and looking forward hopefully to marriage, said that Carlyle seemed to him like

an old Hebrew prophet, who goes to prince and beggar, and says, "If you do this or that you shall go to Hell!—not the hell that priests talk of, but a hell on this earth."

Frederick Robertson, working as a curate at Cheltenham, declared that he had gained "good and energy" from the book; and twenty-three-year-old Florence Nightingale wrote to her cousin—

Carlyle's new *Past and Present* is a beautiful book. There are bits about work which how I should like to read with you!

Tom Brown, of *Tom Brown at Oxford*, is shown by his creator as one of a company of quite unremarkable young men, neither specially talented nor specially devout, who, all over the country, were waking up to an uneasy consciousness that something was wrong. All through his first year at Oxford Tom had puzzled over questions of religion and conduct. He had thought over the difference between the lot of the Poor and the lot of the Rich, and had been unable to devise a means of redress for what seemed to him the monstrous injustice of that inequality. He studied Bentham and Malthus, but found that they gave him little help. Then, when he was in his second year, his friend Hardy discovered *Past and Present*, and triumphantly put it into Tom's hands. He read it eagerly, and found in it just what he wanted.

He had scarcely ever in his life been so moved by a book before. He laughed over it, and cried over it, and began half a dozen letters to the author to thank him, which he fortunately tore up.

Here was the call for which he had been waiting, the call

to men as men, to every man as a man—to the weakest and meanest as well as to the strongest and most noble—telling them that the world is God's world, that everyone of them has a work in it, and bidding them find their work and set about it.

Tom joined himself to a set of young men in the University who called themselves the party of progress, and who took Carlyle as their guide and inspiration. They did many things that were wild and some that were foolish, for their master was often extreme in his teaching and had no tolerance for the conventions and shams which, as he believed, kept men from true brotherhood. Tom Brown, after he had read *Past and Present*, had "a head filled with a set of contradictory notions and beliefs which were destined to astonish and perplex the mind of that worthy J.P. for the county of Berks, Brown the elder." Doubtless other young men astonished their fathers in the same way. They were on fire to preach their new gospel to willing or unwilling ears, and felt a real joy in pouring out such denunciations of the Rich as Tom, in the fullness of conviction, sent to the local paper, the *Wessex Freeman*.

One would think, to hear these landlords, our rulers, talk, that the glorious green fields, the deep woods, the everlasting hills, and the rivers that run among them were made for the sole purpose of ministering to their greedy lusts and ambitions; that they may roll out amongst realities their pitiful mock lives, from their silk and lace cradles to their spangled coffins, studded with silver knots and lying coats of arms; reaping where they have not sowed, and gathering where they have not strawed,

and so on. The indignation was sincere, and the desire to help real and unselfish; though Tom owned later that the articles were too strong and distinctly one-sided. They were read with much approval in the bar of the village public-house at Englebourne, where the constable and the blacksmith were in revolt against the almost universal Toryism of the place. Katie, the Vicar's daughter and Tom's cousin, was horrified at them, and begged him to send

her no more copies of the paper. She dared not keep them in the
house lest her father or one of the servants should get hold of
them. Englebourne was, in its attitude towards politics, a typical
village of the time. The movement that was so active in the towns
had scarcely reached the rural districts, and the rural "gentry"
were among those who were least affected by it. Neither they, nor
any other members of the nation of the Rich, took much notice
of such Chartist newspaper eloquence—which was often fully as
wild as this effort of Tom's, and much more violent—as they
happened to read. It aroused in them amusement, contempt, or
horror, according to their several dispositions, but their views on
"the condition of England" question remained unchanged.

It was different when *Blackwood's* began to plead the same cause.
The landowners and country squires, the clergymen, doctors, and
lawyers, and all the other educated and well-to-do folk who made
up the list of subscribers to that staunch Tory magazine, opened
the August number of 1843, and read the poignant lines in which
Mrs. Browning told of the woes of the children of the Poor—

> "For oh," say the children, "we are weary
>   And we cannot run or leap;
> If we cared for any meadows it were merely
>   To drop down in them and sleep;
> Our knees tremble sorely in the stooping,
>   We fall upon our faces, trying to go;
> And underneath our heavy eyelids drooping,
>   The reddest flower would look as pale as snow.
> For all day we drag our burden tiring
>   Through the coal-dark underground;
> Or all day we drive the wheels of iron
>   In the factories round and round."

Everyone knew, vaguely, that hundreds of English children,
some of them only five or six years old, worked in the mines and
the factories, and that their lot was a hard one; but few had really
seen these tortured little ones, until Mrs. Browning's genius set
them in the light. The sight filled even the most indifferent with
horror and pity. Here were clear, plain statements of terrible facts,
not windy talk about the rights of one class and the iniquities of
another. Here was something to touch the conscience, and make
the sight of one's own happy and well-cared-for children a reproach
instead of a pleasure. An uneasy feeling of pity and shame grew in
the country. All was not well in free, enlightened England.

Then Christmas came; and the readers of the new but already highly popular periodical, *Punch*, opened their Christmas number, prepared to laugh and make merry over its pages. There, among seasonable jokes and mirth-provoking pictures, they found a song that was as completely out of harmony with the goodwill and the good cheer of Christmas as a song could well be. It came from a poor shirtmaker sitting in her miserable garret, and toiling at her never-ending task—

> With fingers weary and worn,
> With eyelids heavy and red,
> A woman sat in unwomanly rags
> Plying her needle and thread.
> Stitch, stitch, stitch!
> In poverty, hunger, and dirt,
> And still with a voice of dolorous pitch,
> She sang this song of a shirt.

It was a song that haunted many people all through the Christmas festivities. True, they had known in a dim, general fashion that the women who sewed the shirts—"seam and gusset and band"—which they bought with no great pangs of conscience, were underpaid. But they had not before been forced to look at their victims, and to note each detail of their sufferings. The children and the women—here were two sets of unhappy workers for whom something must be done.

The *Song of the Shirt* had an enormous popularity. It is said to have trebled the circulation of *Punch*. It was printed as a broadsheet and sold in the streets for a penny. It was printed on cheap pocket handkerchiefs. The poorest class, even those who could not read, knew it by heart. Within a week of its publication a beggar-woman came singing it down the street where its author, Thomas Hood, though sick and suffering, still worked on; and the tears of joy come into his eyes at this recognition of his effort by one as unfortunate as those for whom he had pleaded.

Charles Dickens, too, was working vigorously to bring home to the consciences of the Rich the woes of the Poor, and to draw the two nations together in a spirit of brotherly kindliness. In *Oliver Twist*, published in 1838, he told of the miseries of workhouse inmates, and the pitfalls in the way of neglected lads in great cities. Sir Francis Burdett praised the book in a speech he made at Birmingham while the story was coming out in monthly parts, and this gave Dickens great pleasure. There were some people who thought, with Lord Melbourne, that the book was spoilt by the introduction of unpleasant subjects. It was all about workhouses and coffin-makers and pickpockets, said his lordship; "I don't like that low, debasing style: it's just like the *Beggars' Opera*. I shouldn't think it would tend to raise morals."

But the voices of such fastidious gentlemen and ladies were lost in the burst of generous sympathy and appreciation that the book aroused, and Dickens went on his way encouraged. In 1839 came *Nicholas Nickleby*, which pleaded the cause of the miserable, unwanted children who were sent to cheap and infamous York- shire boarding schools. So terrible was the description of Dotheboys Hall that young readers could not believe it to be true. George Hughes (brother of Thomas, and seventeen years old) read *Nicholas Nickleby* at his own happy school—Dr. Arnold's Rugby— and wrote to his mother, "I liked it very much, though I thought some parts of it are very exaggerated and unnatural; particularly that about the school." The people who knew anything of these schools did not charge Dickens with exaggeration; and the effects of his blow, seen in the rapid decrease of such establishments, showed that it had been struck with accuracy as well as with force.

The Old Curiosity Shop (1840–41) brought all classes together to weep at the grave of a girl, poor, ignorant, an outcast, and almost a beggar. The appeal that it made may seem to us to-day intolerably sentimental and unreal, but it served a great purpose; and *Martin Chuzzlewit* (1843–44) carried on the good work largely by means of a call for sympathy for those unhappy people who must, in sickness, be cared for by drunken and callous nurses like Sairey Gamp and Betsy Prig.

Thus books were helping the nation of the Rich to form some acquaintance with the nation of the Poor—were enabling it to see here one toiling company and there another, borne down by almost intolerable ills. The feeling that was aroused strengthened the hands of those who, in Parliament, were fighting for social reform. A Bill for the regulation of factory labour was brought in, and, against bitter opposition, was at length passed.

It was at this time that Disraeli began in haste to write *Sybil: or the Two Nations*. He used the information gathered by the Commission appointed to inquire into the condition of the working classes in connection with the Factory Bill, and he tried to give, not an isolated view of this or that evil, but a comprehensive survey of England in the condition to which the unhappy and unnatural division into two nations had brought her. The book was published in June 1845, and before the summer ended it had gone through three editions. "We dare not predict for *Sybil* so wide a popularity as *Coningsby*," said the *Athenaeum*, but it hailed the book as "a sign that the relations of rich and poor—the enlargement of the former's sympathies and the amelioration of the latter's misery—are becoming matters of interest."

The narrower and more selfish among the landlords, colliery-owners, and factory proprietors read *Sybil* with disgust. They recognized with something near to fury the portrait of Lord Marny, and writhed to hear a travesty of the arguments they had so often used put into his mouth.

I wish the people were as well off all over the country as they are on my estate. They get here their eight shillings a week, always at least seven shillings, and every hand is at this moment in employment, except a parcel of scoundrels who would prefer wood-stealing and poaching if you gave them double the wages. The rate of wages is nothing; certainty is the thing; and every man in Marny may be sure of his seven shillings a week for at least nine months in the year; and for the other three they can go to the House, and a very proper place for them; it is heated with hot air and has every comfort. . . . The poor are well off, at least the agricultural poor, very well off indeed. Their incomes are certain, that is a great point, and they have no cares, no anxieties; they always have a resource, they always have the House. People without cares do not require so much food as those whose life entails anxieties.

The Benthamites, or Philosophic Radicals as they liked to call themselves, who were able to see something beautiful in the thought of children of five or six contributing to the prosperity of the country, considered *Sybil* a bad and dangerous book. It advocated an interference with the working of economic law, and economic law was to them almost a sacred thing governing inexorably the fate of the nation.

But to those whose hearts were not hardened by custom or self-interest or pedantry, *Sybil* came, as *Past and Present* had come, as a stirring call to be up and doing that England's reproach might be wiped away. It was addressed to youth—to the young Queen and to her young subjects. "Will it," asked Disraeli, in the somewhat high-flown style that his enemies derided——

be her [the Queen's] proud destiny at length to bear relief to suffering millions, and with that soft hand that might inspire troubadours and guerdon knights, break the last links in the chain of Saxon thraldom?

At the end of the book came an eloquent appeal to the youth of the country—

We live in an age when to be young and to be indifferent can be no longer synonymous. We must prepare for the coming hour. The claims of the Future are represented by suffering millions; and the Youth of a Nation are the Trustees of Posterity.

Youth was quick to answer the appeal. The enthusiastic band known as the Young England party, which was working under Disraeli's leadership towards the revival of old ideals in Church and State, took *Sybil* as their textbook. As long ago as 1838 John Manners and George Smythe had resolved on a great Crusade.

"We have now virtually pledged ourselves," wrote John Manners in his Journal, "to attempt to restore what? I hardly know, but still it is a glorious attempt, and he is really well qualified to take the lead in it; but what rebuffs, sneers, and opposition must we expect; however, I think a change is working for the better, and all, or nearly all, the enthusiasm of the young spirits of Britain is with us."

By 1845 the two young men knew more clearly what it was they wanted to restore, and in *Sybil* they found their aims set forward with force and passion. They wanted a return to the times when the Church, the King, and the Nobility took their rightful part in governing and serving the country. "From a beneficent aristocracy and a reawakened Church a continual stream of blessings should flow."

The nucleus of the Young England party was the group of students who had been brought into the Oxford Movement chiefly through Frederick Faber. To some people it seemed strange that these young High Churchmen should put themselves under the leadership of Disraeli; but, as Mr. Moneypenny in his *Life of Disraeli* suggests, it was easy for followers of Newman to become followers of the Jewish statesman.

"Newman, Carlyle, and Disraeli," he says, "were far different figures; but little as they may have known it, they were in a sense spiritual brethren, working in their several ways with a common purpose. Beneath a thousand superficial differences they had all three the same romantic temperament; all three had in them something of the artist; and all three were deeply imbued with that historical sentiment which is the fatal enemy of Benthamism, as of every kind of system-mongering."

So the ardent band of Young Englanders read Newman's sermons and the *Tracts*, Carlyle's *Past and Present*, and Disraeli's *Sybil*, and drew much the same lessons from each. But the book which came even closer to them than any of these was not one that bore directly on the social and religious questions of the day. It had been written in 1822 by Kenelm Digby, and was called *The Broadstone of Honour; or Rules for the Gentlemen of England*. It had been read and honoured by their fathers, and they had inherited it with the traditional code that governed the conduct of their class.

"You are born a Gentleman," said the author. "This is a high privilege, but are you aware of its obligations? It has pleased God to place you in a post of honour; but are you conscious that it is one which demands high and peculiar qualities? Such, however, is the fact. The rank which you have to support requires not so much an inheritance, or the acquisition of wealth and property, as of elevated virtue and spotless fame."

To Kenelm Digby the Golden Age of England was the Age of Chivalry; and he exhorted his readers to revive the ideals and practices of that age, and so make their country noble, virtuous, and happy. The high romantic tone of the book captured the imaginations of these young idealists, and they were as eager, at its bidding, to restore medievalism in the State as they had been, at the call of Newman, to restore medievalism in the Church. *Sybil* pictured a country where the great monasteries and the great feudal lords held their old high places, while the Crown was supreme over all. For this ideal they would work.

They were young and they were ardent, and even the wise leadership of Disraeli could not save them from some foolish excesses. Disraeli himself was inclined to extravagance, and had none of the ordinary Englishman's dread of appearing ridiculous.

His party was laughed at in Parliament and out, and a great many jokes were made about it in *Punch* and elsewhere. "They're always writing about battleaxes and shivolry, these young chaps," said Thackeray's Jeames de la Pluche. Monckton Milnes wrote a poem which he called, *Lines to a Judge, by a culprit actuated by Young England sentiments*.

> Oh, flog me at the old cart's tail,
>   I surely should enjoy
> That fine old English punishment
>   I witnessed when a boy!
> I should not heed the mocking crowd,
>   I should not feel the pain,
> If *one* old English custom
>   Could be brought back again.

Young England was perhaps stung, but it was certainly not disheartened, and it went on adding its efforts to those of other men and parties who were striving to bring about a better understanding between the two nations. But the nation of the Poor was too bitterly conscious of its wrongs and too firmly convinced that there was only one effective remedy to pay much heed to what the nation of the Rich might say. Chartism was spreading everywhere. Thomas Cooper and men like him were lecturing all over the country, forming Chartist societies and editing Chartist newspapers, insisting that if working men could only get the Charter all would be well with them.

A great change had come over Thomas Cooper since he had begun his career as a Chartist leader. He had been imprisoned for seditious speeches, and in prison he had read a good deal of cheap rationalistic literature, as well as George Eliot's translation of Strauss's *Leben Jesu*; and he had become an atheist. After his release he had written a long poem called *The Purgatory of Suicides*, which Kingsley thought "brilliant," and which was widely read among his followers. His influence with working men was tremendous, and he used it to urge them on in their fight for the Charter.

Then came April 1848, with the Chartist monster petition and bands of Chartists marching in from all parts of the country to a great gathering on Kennington Common. All London went in fear of what might happen if the temper of the mob should be roused and rioting should break out. Charles Kingsley hurried up

to London to consult with his friends—Frederick Denison
Maurice, John Ludlow, Thomas Hughes, and others—whose
work among the London poor had given them a sympathetic
understanding of the situation. "The storm has blown over until
to-morrow," Kingsley wrote to his wife on the morning of
April 11th—

but all are under arms—specials, police, and military. Maurice is
in great excitement. He has sent me to Ludlow, and we are getting
out a placard for the walls to speak a word for God with.

On April 12th the first placard was posted. It was headed "Workmen of England," and it went on—

You say you are wronged. Many of you are wronged, and
many besides yourselves know it; above all, the working clergy
know it. . . . You have more friends than you think for. . . . You
think the Charter would make you free—would to God it would.
The Charter is not bad—*if the men who use it are not bad.* But
will the Charter make you *free?* Will it free you from slavery to
ten-pound bribes? Slavery to beer and gin? Slavery to every spouter
who flatters your self-conceit and stirs up bitterness and endless
rage in you?

The placard went on to show that violence could never gain the
rights that working men claimed, and it ended, "Workers of
England! Be wise and then you *must* be free, for you will be *fit*
to be free." It was signed, "A Working Parson."

How much these placards had to do with the quiet dispersion
of the Chartists cannot be told. Maurice and his friends believed
firmly in their usefulness, and planned to carry on their work by
means of a new set of "real *Tracts for the Times.*" "If the Oxford
Tracts did wonders, why should not we," they said. On May 16th
the first number of the new series appeared. It was called *Politics
for the People,* consisted of sixteen pages, and was sold for a penny.

Through the difficult months that followed, while heavy
sentences were being passed on the Chartist leaders, and the men
they had led were enduring the bitterness of humiliation and
defeat, Maurice and his helpers worked on. A plea for the
unhappy offenders came also from another quarter. Mrs. Gaskell's
Mary Barton was published in the early autumn; and it gave such
a poignant picture of the terrible conditions under which these

men lived, and the way in which they were driven, step by step, towards the desperation that saw no help save in violence, that the hearts of most of those who read it were wrung with pity. The blame, it was felt, lay more with the system that made such things possible than with its unhappy victims. There were, as in the case of *Sybil*, some who took the other view. The political economists reproved Mrs. Gaskell severely for attempting to interfere with the unalterable and almost sacred laws that governed labour and production. There were harsh reviews in many of the magazines. Selfish factory owners feared that these humanitarian ideas would tend to lower their profits. Mary Howitt, writing to her daughter, said—

Last evening a rich silk manufacturer of Macclesfield called, with his wife, upon us. He is a fat, jolly Conservative, whose people are emphatically *hands*, and who thinks *Mary Barton* a dangerous, bad book.

Fairer-minded readers recognized the book's great qualities, though doubtless some agreed with Herbert Spencer when he said—

I cannot say it is at all an agreeable book to read. It is, on the contrary, a very painful one. In fact, in one part of it I got quite angry with the authoress . . . for torturing my feelings so needlessly. However, it is a very instructive book, and one that everyone should read.

Carlyle thought it

a beautiful, cheerfully pious, social, clear, and observant book; character is everywhere recognizable in the writer, which sense is the welcomest sight any writer can show in his books.

Readers who belonged to the class for which the book pleaded recognized its truth, its courage, and its humanity. Mrs. Gaskell lent a copy to a family of zealous Chartists—poor, but respectable and hard-working; they were so enthralled by it that they sat up far into the night reading it, and cried over it heartily. An Oldham weaver regularly brought his children to gaze upon the house in Plymouth Grove where the authoress of *Mary Barton* had lived; and Samuel Bamford called it "a sorrowfully beautiful production which few could contemplate with tearless eyes."

Meantime Maurice and Kingsley were going on with their

Politics for the People, and trying very hard to give the working men something that would be really helpful to them in their hard daily struggle. They invited small parties of Chartists to meet them and talk over what could be done, and they held public meetings at which they were often fiercely attacked by free-thinking working men who could not believe that "parsons" could be the true friends of the poorer classes. But they did not lose patience or heart, and in time they gained a considerable following, who read *Politics for the People*, and when that series was discontinued read *The Christian Socialist* and *The People's Friend*, which followed on the same lines. The writers in these papers did not flatter their readers, but showed the working men that reform among themselves must come first if reform of the law was to do them any good. One of Kingsley's articles in *Politics for the People* throws considerable light upon the reading of Chartist working men. It describes a visit he paid to a London bookseller's, where a Chartist newspaper was published, and Chartist books were on sale.

Now, as a book as well as a man may be known by his companions I looked round the shop to see what was the general sort of stock there, and behold, there was hardly anything but *Flash Songsters* and the *Swell's Guide* and *Tales of Horror* and dirty, milksop French novels.

He found also that

almost the only books puffed in the advertising columns of the paper itself were the same French dirt that lay on the counter: Voltaire's *Tales*, Tom Paine, and by way of a finish, *The Devil's Pulpit*.

The spread of infidelity among working men weighed heavily on Kingsley's heart. When, in 1850, Thomas Cooper sent him the first number of *Cooper's Journal*, he wrote in distress to Mr. Ludlow—

Here is a man of immense influence openly preaching Straussism to the workmen, and in a fair, honest, manly way that must tell. Who will answer him? Who will answer Strauss?

He decided that he himself must attempt to do so, and he wrote several articles in *The Christian Socialist*, but his real effort to meet the arguments of those who opposed Christianity was made in his next novel, *Alton Locke, Tailor and Poet.* "We are reading a wonderful book, *Alton Locke,*" wrote Mary Howitt, "an extraordinary production. It will make a great stir." It did make a great stir. Shirley Brooke wrote to the publishers, Chapman and Hall, saying—

> I have not been so struck with any work I have taken up for years. . . . It is a gratifying thing to see that a publisher *dares* to publish such a work. . . . *Alton Locke* must make a strange sensation.

Courage had indeed been needed to publish a book that made such grave and definite charges against the employers in a specified industry. Most of the leading journals reviewed it very severely, but it did not shock the public in the way that most of those who had seen the manuscript had feared it would. Kingsley said that he was surprised at the number of "steady-going, respectable people" who approved of *Alton Locke.* These included "one of the safest Whig traditionists in England," "both the Marshals," and Lord Ashburton, besides, "strange to say, more than one respectable High-Tory Squire." "So," reflected Kingsley, "goes the world. If you do anything above party, the true-hearted ones of all parties sympathize with you."

Florence Nightingale was deeply impressed by the book, and so was Tennyson. Lewis Carroll thought that if it were only "a little more definite it might stir up many fellow-workers in the same good field of social improvement." Alfred Ainger, after reading it for the second time while he was an undergraduate at Cambridge, wrote—

> I have been reading again that grand Epic, *Alton Locke,* which I find I have been rather under-rating. It is most fine in parts. The chapters about Cambridge have a fresh interest for me now. . . . *Alton Locke* appears to me the most searching and the most earnest application of the laws of Christ to the present condition of society that I have ever read in fiction.

Mrs. Carlyle "waded to the end of it," and wrote to her husband, who was away in Scotland—

> To-morrow I shall lay out two sixpences in forwarding *Alton Locke.* (The Devil among the Tailors would have been the best name for it.) It will surely be gratifying to you to find your own name in almost every second page. But for *that,* I am ashamed to

say, I should have broken down in it a great way this side the end. It seems to me . . . a mere—not very well boiled—broth of Morning Chronicleism, in which *you* play the part of the tasting-bone of Poverty Row. An oppressive, painful book. But the old Scotchman (Saunders Mackaye) is capital, except that there never was nor ever will be *such* an old Scotchman.

Carlyle's opinion of the book was more favourable than his wife's, though he found in it many faults. "I am bound to say," he wrote to Kingsley, "that the book is *crude*; by no manner of means the best we expect of you—if you will resolutely temper your fire."

Kingsley probably did not mind being called crude, since Carlyle recognized the book as "a salvo of red-hot shot against the Devil's Dung-heap," which was what the author had meant it to be.

In *Yeast*, which came out first in *Frazer's Magazine*, Kingsley drew a terrible picture of the lot of the agricultural labourer. It was severely criticized by a certain section of the Anglican Church, but the author received many letters from readers of various classes —undergraduates, fashionable London gentlemen, Wesleyan ministers, artisans, and labourers among them—telling him how they had been impressed and influenced by his work.

The stream of social novels continued throughout the 'fifties, and helped to keep the national conscience active. Real efforts were made to bring about a better state of things. Many abuses were reformed. Factory Acts and other legislation improved the condition of the workers. That much of this was due to the influence of books was owned by everybody. Dickens' public was an enormous one, and his popularity with all classes was, in itself, a means of bringing rich and poor into sympathy. *Hard Times*, which is perhaps the most purely social in intention of all his novels, appeared in 1854. Its plea was not so much for improvement in the material conditions of the working man as for a recognition of the fact that "man does not live by bread alone." It pictured the unlovely manufacturing centre of Coketown. There was little actual want among the people, but they were starved of beauty and romance and joy, and they pined and deteriorated for lack of them. They rebelled, too, and snatched at any specimens of the forbidden fruit that came within their reach. There was a public library at Coketown, furnished for the most part with books filled with "facts"; but the "hands" persisted in ignoring these, and trying to find something that would supply food for their imaginations.

They sometimes after fifteen hours' work sat down to read mere fables about men and women more or less like themselves, and about children more or less like their own. They took De Foe to their bosoms instead of Euclid, and seemed to be on the whole more comforted by Goldsmith than by Cocker.

Ruskin entered the field at the end of the 'fifties. Since 1843, when he published the first volume of *Modern Painters*, he had been writing on aesthetic subjects, and had dwelt insistently on the need for beauty in the everyday lives of men. This had led him to the consideration of the industrial world, so bare of beauty and of joy, and with the same enthusiasm that he had given to the study of art he turned to economic problems. In 1857 he delivered two lectures at Manchester, which were afterwards published as *The Political Economy of Art*, and in 1860 four essays on the first principles of Political Economy appeared in the *Cornhill Magazine*. The ideas they set forward were so startling, and, as the readers of the *Cornhill* thought, so revolutionary, that a great outcry was raised, and the editor refused to continue the series. The essays were published in book form in 1862, with the title, *Unto This Last*, and then they found many readers, who found in them something that supplemented and gave graciousness to the teaching of Carlyle. Ruskin, like Carlyle, preached the gospel of work, but he showed also that, to true living, beauty and joy were as essential as industry.

As the art of life is learned, it will be found at last that all lovely things are also necessary—the wild flower by the wayside as well as the tended corn; and the wild birds and creatures of the forest as well as the tended cattle; because man doth not live by bread only, but also by the desert manna, by every wondrous word and unknowable work of God.

Thomas Burt said that he owed more to Ruskin than he could ever tell, and he declared that *Unto This Last* made a great impression upon the reading working man, and became a landmark in the Labour movement. Other books followed in which economics and aesthetics were mingled, sometimes a little strangely, and Ruskin took his place among the Social Prophets.

When, in 1869, Ruskin was appointed Slade Professor of Fine Art at Oxford, he attempted to put some of his social ideas into practice, and set the devoted band of students that speedily gathered round him to road-making and street-sweeping. One undergraduate, a young man of twenty, by name Cecil Rhodes, who came up to Oxford in 1873, after some years of busy commercial life in South Africa, never forgot some of the words he heard as he sat among his fellows at Ruskin's lectures. There was, said the Professor,

a destiny now possible to us, the highest ever set before a nation to be accepted or refused. Will you youths of England make your country again a royal throne of kings, a sceptred isle, for all the world a source of light, a centre of peace?

But high as Ruskin stood as a prophet, Carlyle stood still higher, and not all the disapproval of those who thought his theories wild and even destructive could move him from his place. Mrs. Austin thought him "one of the dissolvents of the age—as mischievous as his extravagances will let him be," and Dr. Whewell agreed with her. Frances Cobbe thought his influence harmful to the country. Henry Sidgwick, writing to H. G. Dakyns, said, "I am sorry you are in so nightmarish a state. Have you been reading Carlyle or any such poison?" FitzGerald said he never read any of Carlyle's books—

for though divers persons profess to understand and admire them, the few passages I have looked at seem always such absurd and unintelligible rant that I feel no desire to go further.

When the *Latter-Day Pamphlets* were published in 1850, FitzGerald wrote to John Allen—

Do you see Carlyle's *Latter-Day Pamphlets?* They make the world laugh, and his friends rather sorry for him. But that is because people will still look for practical measures from him. One must be content with him as a great satirist who can make us feel when we are wrong, though he cannot set us right. There is a bottom of truth in Carlyle's wildest rhapsodies.

Anthony Trollope agreed with FitzGerald. In *The Warden*, published in 1855, he dealt with Carlyle at length under the name

of Dr. Pessimist Anticant. In Trollope's opinion it was popularity
that had spoilt Dr. Anticant.

"While, with some diffidence, he confined his objurgations to
the occasional follies or shortcomings of mankind . . . it was all
well." When he "began the great task of reprobating everything
and everybody . . . this was not so well."

His theories were all beautiful, and the code of morals that he
taught was certainly an improvement on the practice of the age.
We all of us could, and many of us did, learn much from the
doctor while he chose to remain vague, mysterious, and cloudy.
But when he became practical the charm was gone.

But for those who in their youth had been Carlyle's ardent
disciples the charm remained to the end. One of these was William
Hale White, the "Mark Rutherford" of the *Autobiography*. When
the *Latter-Day Pamphlets* were published he was not yet twenty
years old, and looking back on that time many years later he
recalled how Carlyle's books were read by himself and the young
men of his generation with excitement and tears of joy, and how
the readers "were thankful that it was their privilege to live when
he also was alive." Walt Whitman, who was ten years older than
William Hale White, has written—

As a representative author, a literary figure, no man else will
bequeath to the future more significant hints of our stormy era,
its fierce paradoxes, its din, and its struggling parturition periods,
than Carlyle. . . . Rugged, mountainous, volcanic, he was himself
more of a French revolution than any of his volumes.

The influence of Carlyle and Ruskin scarcely began to wane
until the 'eighties had set in, and by that time there had been
many changes in the social condition of the country. The people
were no longer as sharply divided into two nations as they had
been at the beginning of the Queen's reign. Chartism had collapsed
and the working classes were prosperous. The spread of education
and the establishment of free libraries had made a great difference
in their reading habits. The relation between the Rich and the
Poor had entered on a new phase.

CHAPTER VIII

DICKENS

NOBODY, it is to be presumed, awoke on the morning of the last day of March 1836 with the feeling that here was dawning a great day in the history of England, and, indeed, of all nations. Mr. Charles Dickens, then a young man of twenty-four, living with his father and mother in Bentinck Street, probably remembered with excitement as he opened his eyes that it was the day on which was to be published the first number of the story he had been commissioned to write for Messrs. Chapman and Hall, *The Posthumous Papers of the Pickwick Club, containing a faithful record of the Perambulations, Perils, Travels, Adventures, and Sporting Transactions of the Corresponding Members.* The rest of the population rose, had its breakfast, and departed to its daily work as calmly as usual. A few—a very few, comparatively— noticed in the windows of the booksellers' shops a thin, paperbound volume with a pale green cover on which were depicted various rather remarkable-looking gentlemen, some fat and some thin, who were fishing, shooting, riding, skating, and indulging in other active pastimes; and, reading the title as above and the name of the author, remembered that Charles Dickens had lately written a series of *Sketches*, which showed a diverting humour, in the *Old Monthly Magazine*. Some were sufficiently intrigued to pay their shilling and go off with the number, but there was no rush for it, and the publisher found the four hundred copies that had been printed quite enough to supply the demand. Nobody suspected the modest little volume of being other than it seemed, and a good many months were to pass before realization of its full significance began.

Meantime *Pickwick* quickly showed signs of growing popularity. In May came another number, and this time there was a bigger sale; and, month by month, as further instalments appeared, the tale of buyers increased. When the fifth number arrived, and with it the great Mr. Samuel Weller, the sales went up with a tremendous leap. People began to count the days to the next issue. Mr. Augustus de Morgan, Professor of Mathematics at University College, London, and father of William de Morgan, the future novelist, used to say to his wife as a certain morning in each month came round, "We shall have a *Pickwick* to-morrow." Lady Georgina Peel says that in her family the numbers were awaited with the utmost eagerness. We are told, too, on the authority of an archdeacon, who told Carlyle, who told John Forster, of the shock received by an extremely serious clergyman, who, standing outside a sick room where he had just paid a pastoral visit, heard the patient exclaim, "Well, thank God, *Pickwick* will be out in ten days, anyway."

Impecunious people who could not put down a shilling and carry away the treasure contrived other means of reading the delectable pages. Walter Frith, then nineteen years old, had lately come from his home at Harrogate to study art in London. He bought the numbers when he could, and when the necessary shilling failed, he went about from one bookshop to another, where there were copies lying open, until he had managed to read the whole. Two of the copies he had bought he sent home to his mother, at the Dragon Inn, Harrogate, of which his father was the proprietor, but Mrs. Frith happened to be one of the few unlucky people who could not appreciate *Pickwick*, and she wrote huffily to her son—

I never read such nonsense in my life. Pray don't send any more such stuff to me, and I do hope you don't buy these things. What good can they do you?

There were some ladies, whose taste had been spoilt by a continuous diet of Minerva novels, who thought the book coarse, and hesitated to admit it to their drawing-rooms; and their view had the support of that high literary authority, Mr. John Lockhart, editor of the *Quarterly Review*, who pronounced *Pickwick*, "All very well but damned low." But these formed a small minority. That omnivorous reader, Mary Russell Mitford—now a highly esteemed spinster nearing fifty—spoke for the majority when she said, "A lady may read it aloud." She herself read it aloud to her father and they both enjoyed it keenly. Miss Deborah Jenkyns, of *Cranford*, guardian of propriety as she was, objected to it only on the ground that it was not equal to Dr. Johnson. We all remember how Captain Brown read aloud in Miss Deborah's drawing-room the account of the "swarry" attended by Mr. Samuel Weller, while his hostess listened with patient gravity, and only two or three of the company were courageous enough to laugh; and how Miss Deborah followed with a passage from *Rasselas*, which she offered with kindly condescension as a model for young Mr. Dickens.

Captain Brown, alas! did not live to read the end of *Pickwick*, but died with one of the beloved monthly numbers open in his hand when he leapt to the rescue of a little girl who had strayed on to the railway line in front of an oncoming train. But month by month the list of those who followed him in his enthusiasm for *Pickwick* grew longer. Sir Benjamin Brodie took it to read in his carriage between patient and patient, and Lord Denman studied it on the bench while the jury were deliberating. Miss Emily Eden, who had gone to India with her brother, Lord Auckland, the Governor-General, received the first numbers in May 1837. She, and the whole English colony at Calcutta, read and delighted in them, and were anxious to know how this story was being received in England. "I wish you would say more about the *Pickwicks*," wrote Miss Eden to her sister. "We are all so fond of them. Are we wrong?" Her sister might have answered by simply stating that when the fifteenth number of *Pickwick* came out forty thousand instead of four hundred were issued, and these were not enough to supply the demand.

Schoolboys and schoolgirls loved Dickens. "All the boys and girls talk his fun," said Miss Mitford, and Mr. Monicure Conway, speaking for himself and his brothers and sisters, said—

Our neighbour, Douglas Gordon, broke a small blood-vessel laughing over *Pickwick*, and we pitied him, not for the lesion, but because his doctor forbade him to read *Pickwick*.

Dr. Arnold complained that his pupils showed to an increasing extent the fault of childishness, and this he severely attributed to their reading "a great number of exciting books as *Pickwick* and *Nickleby*" (the first number of which appeared early in 1838), which satisfied their intellectual appetites and left them with no taste for "good literature of all sorts, even for History and Poetry." Thomas Hughes, in *Tom Brown's Schooldays*, exhibits one of these offending Rugby boys stretched on the sofa in his study and chuckling over the manœuvres of Mr. Winkle and his horse. This young gentleman, Harry East, was certainly open to the reproach of having no taste for History or Poetry, but no such charge could be brought against Sara Coleridge's precociously clever and well-read son, Herbert, who also enjoyed with his school friends the "never-to-be-exhausted fun of *Pickwick*." Dean Hole says that when he was a boy at school "with an infinite appreciation of cheesecakes," he nevertheless saved half his income of sixpence a week to buy the monthly numbers as they came out.

Charles Kingsley, like Dr. Arnold, believed that the influence of Dickens on his less mature and less thoughtful readers was not in all respects a good one. The books, he complained, supported "a false ethical theorem," namely—

The man is not responsible for his faults. They are to be imputed to his circumstances. But he is responsible for, and therefore to be valued solely by, his virtues. They are to be imputed to himself.

In this way, said Kingsley, Dickens exercised an unfavourable influence on the efforts of those who were working to bring about "a just and rational treatment of crime" in England.

Most readers did not trouble themselves about Dickens' moral influence, but simply enjoyed the stories. If they noticed the tendency of which Kingsley complained they took it simply as a part of the atmosphere of goodwill and kindliness that pervaded the novels. To a nation divided as England then was by religious strife and industrial conditions the works of Dickens did succeed in bringing some small sense of union. An enjoyment in common must prove a bond, and *Pickwick* and *Nickleby* and *Oliver Twist* (which had come between the other two) went not to one sect or class only, but everywhere, except to those to whom all fiction was anathema.

The High Church party read them, though Gladstone complained of *Nickleby* that "there is no Church in the book, and the motives are not those of religion." Yet he allowed that "the tone is very human, and it is most happy in touches of natural pathos." Miss Yonge shows us the heir of Redclyffe enjoying *Pickwick* with Charles and Amy Edmondstone, having been condescendingly authorized to read Dickens by the superior cousin Philip, who held that "those books open field for thought; and as their principles are negative, they are not likely to hurt a person well armed with the truth."

Pickwick and its successors went regularly month by month to the house of the Unitarian Chamberlains at Camberwell, where, later, "young Joe" read them and became one of Dickens' most fervent admirers. They went also to the house of the orthodox Low Church stockbroker, Mr. Burnand, who lived at Stoke Newington, and whose young son, Francis, the future editor of *Punch*, read them until he almost knew them by heart. Where they went they (with, it must be acknowledged, a few exceptions) conquered. They conquered Lord Kew of *The Newcomes*, and his charming and devout Evangelical mother, Lady Walham. Lord Kew was recovering from a wound received in a duel, and his mother

was for improving the shining hour by reading amusing extracts from her favourite volumes, gentle anecdotes of Chinese and Hottentot converts, and incidents from missionary travel. George Barnes, a wily young diplomatist . . . hinted that Kew might like a novel; and a profane work called *Oliver Twist* having appeared about this time, which George read out to his family with admirable emphasis, it is a fact that Lady Walham became so interested in the parish boy's progress that she took his history into her bedroom (where it was discovered under Blatherwick's *Voice from Mesopotamia* by her ladyship's maid), and that Kew laughed so immensely at Mr. Bumble, the Beadle, as to endanger the reopening of his wound.

The nation of the Poor loved Dickens. They could not afford to buy the numbers, but they were sometimes able to borrow them; and when *Cleave's Gazette*, which circulated among the lowest classes in London, published long extracts from *Nicholas Nickleby*, these were rapturously received by its readers. As for his reception by the Rich, we may take the testimony of the Honourable Mrs. Twistleton, wife of the American ambassador, who said that she found *Pickwick* a favourite subject of conversation at fashionable evening parties. She induced her husband to take a course of *Pickwick* "as he had been roused to sense of his deplorable ignorance of that fount of wisdom." "I read to him," she said, "half an hour between dinner and Hume" (they were taking a course of that historian also) "as a sort of fancy work before the regular duty begins." This was in 1854, when the serial publication of *Pickwick* had long been completed, and handsome bound volumes of the work had been given a place in every gentleman's library.

Mary Gladstone has recorded that Mr. Hamilton declared *Pickwick* to be "one of the Scriptures for our learning"; and

Harriet Martineau gave it as her opinion that "in humour, he (Dickens) will hardly surpass *Pickwick* simply because *Pickwick* is scarcely surpassable in humour." If any further testimony is required as to the unique place which *Pickwick* held in the estimation of well-qualified critics, it may be found in the proceedings of the Cambridge don, Charles Stuart Calverley—scholar, wit, parodist—as recorded by Sir Walter Besant, who went up to Cambridge in 1855—

In my second year Calverley announced an examination for a prize in the study of *Pickwick Papers*. The examination was held in the evening in his own room. If I remember aright there were about ten candidates, most of whom had no chance whatever. . . . We were allowed, I think, two hours, or perhaps three. When the papers were handed in we refreshed ourselves after our labours with a supper of oysters, beer, milk punch, etc.

This truly Pickwickian banquet formed a fitting climax to an evening that had been spent in wrestling with thirty questions, such as

(1) Mention any occasion on which it was specified that the Fat Boy was *not* asleep; and that (1) Mr. Pickwick and (2) Mr. Weller, Senior, ran. Deduce, from expressions used on one occasion, Mr. Pickwick's maximum of speed.

(4) What operation was performed on Tom Smart's chair? Who little thinks that in which pocket of what garment, in where, he has left what entreating him to return to whom with how many what and all how big?

(19) What is a red-faced Nixon?

(26) Give some account of the word "fanteeg," and hazard any conjecture explanatory of the expression "My Prooshan Blue" applied to Mr. Samuel Weller by Mr. Tony Weller.

The first prize was won by Walter Besant, and next to him came Walter Skeat (later Professor of Anglo-Saxon). "There was a good deal of talk about the examination," said Besant, "copies of the paper were in great request all over the University, and for a whole day Skeat and I were famous."

All this time works from Dickens' pen had been coming almost without intermission from the press. It is not necessary to give a list of them, because everybody knows at least their names; and to attempt to follow even such a small proportion of the copies sold as it is possible to trace would be too large an undertaking.

We will take one of these works as a sample of what was going on in connection with each book.

Dombey and Son came out between October 1846 and April 1848. The sale of the first number exceeded thirty thousand, and although there was some falling off later, the average sale was over twenty-five thousand. One number travelled down regularly to the home of Admiral Swinburne, at Bonchurch, and was read by the members of that staunchly Anglican household. We may believe that it was approved, for it was given to the Admiral's eleven-year-old son, Algernon, and the precocious little boy fell upon it with ardour. It was the first work of fiction he had been allowed to read, but before he went to Eton in 1849 he had read several other works by Dickens, and his schoolfellows remembered long afterwards how freely and aptly he would quote from them.

Another copy went to the Yonges at Otterbourne. Charlotte read it, and remembered it when she wrote *The Heir of Redclyffe* a few years later, for we find the serial numbers, in the familiar green cover, among the books that littered the table by Charles Edmondstone's sofa. Sir Guy read it on Amy's recommendation. The May family of *The Daisy Chain* read it, and so did most of the High Church families in real life, including the Lytteltons and the Gladstones.

Frank Smedley, the crippled author of *Frank Fairlegh* and other books famous in their day, shows us that *Dombey* was well known also in another circle. His heroes were mostly wealthy, dashing young gentlemen, who found their chief pleasure in country sports, and were seldom within-doors. Yet they found time to read *Dombey* as the numbers came out, and were ready with quotations from it. Frank Fairlegh borrowed the language of the "redoubtable Chicken" to describe an encounter in which a fair lady was rescued from villains who were trying to carry her off; and in *Harry Coverdale* we read how the hero's wife "did what the unfortunate first Mrs. Dombey failed to effect—she made an effort."

Men and women of cultivated taste read *Dombey* eagerly, and although they criticized, also admired. Macaulay, home from India and comfortably settled in luxurious chambers in the Albany, wrote to his sister—

Have you seen the first number of *Dombey*? There is not much in it, but there is one passage which made me cry as if my heart would break. It is the description of a little girl, who has lost an affectionate mother, and is unkindly treated by everybody.

Miss Eden said that the fourth number gave her infinite pleasure. But the great sensation came with the fifth number in February 1847. It told of little Paul Dombey's death, and from all over the country came loud though tearful cries of admiration. Thackeray (the first number of whose *Vanity Fair* had lately appeared, and been very well received) was quite overcome by it. He rushed round to the office of *Punch*, where the editor, Mark Lemon, sat at work. Flinging the number on the table, he exclaimed, "There's no writing against this; one hasn't an atom of chance. It's stupendous!"

Soon after the sixth number appeared, Dickens, who had hurried home from Paris on hearing that his eldest son was ill with scarlet fever, was allowed to visit the boy at the lodging in Albany Street where he was being nursed by his grandmother, Mrs. Hogarth. "Mr. Charles Dickens, the writer, whom you may have heard of, is coming to see his son this afternoon," said Mrs. Hogarth, to an elderly charwoman who was employed about the house. The charwoman's eyes opened in amazement. "Lawk, ma'am," she said, "is the young gentleman upstairs the son of the man who put together *Dombey*?" As Mrs. Hogarth knew the woman could not read, she inquired how she came to have any knowledge of Dickens' story; and a new circle of admirers was revealed. She lodged, the woman said, in the house of a man who kept a snuff shop, and on the first Monday in each month she, with such of the other lodgers in the house as could pay a small sum for the entertainment, took tea with the landlord. After tea he read aloud the month's instalment of *Dombey*, and to this reading all lodgers were admitted, without payment. The impression made on these unlettered hearers can be judged by the charwoman's concluding compliment, "Lawk, ma'am, I thought that three or four men must have put together *Dombey*."

Edward FitzGerald reserved his criticism until the story was finished, then wrote to John Allen, "Dickens has fallen off in his last novel, *Dombey*, but there are wonderful things in it, too." A few such notes of disapproval were to be heard among the chorus of praise, and from the Rev. W. H. Brookfield—the friend of Tennyson, Thackeray, and FitzGerald—came a harsher judgment. "*Dombey* viler than ever," he had said of the fifth number, and for him it grew viler and viler to the end.

But it is time now to turn back to notice the phenomenon

which, it has been suggested, made March 31, 1836, such a notable day in the annals of England and which began to be apparent after the first few numbers of *Pickwick*. The characters were stepping out of the books into the real world, and were taking their places among the men and women there. You could curtsey to them all, declared Miss Mitford, if you met them in the streets. They were talking and acting and working just as other people did, and accommodating themselves so well to the material conditions of the country to which they had migrated that their shadowy extraction was soon forgotten and they became as natives of the land. Moreover, they had a frank, revealing method of presenting themselves that brought them into quick and close intimacy; so that very soon it was not a matter of having read *Pickwick Papers* or *Oliver Twist* or *Nicholas Nickleby*, but of having made the acquaintance of Mr. Pickwick and Sam Weller, Bill Sikes and Nancy, delightful, exasperating Mrs. Nickleby, and poor unfortunate Smike, and the host of others who came, brimming over with life and individuality, to join the company that was being added to the population of England. It was plain, though perhaps the readers of that day did not see it as clearly as we, looking back, can see it, that here was no mere writing of books, but an act of creation.

This act of creation was, as it proved, to go on for years, with men and women appearing in quick succession, each ready to take up a part and live it with a fullness and vigour that put ordinary, lackadaisical mortals to shame. Nor did their vitality fail as the years went by. Age could not wither them; the passage of time only brought them into more affectionate intimacy with their first acquaintances, while the new generation growing up greeted them as family friends who were yet their own contemporaries.

Plump little Mr. Pickwick went everywhere. His neat legs in their drab tights and black gaiters carried him into all sorts of society, and in most places he was well received. Many people laughed at him, some with lofty condescension, regarding him as an amusing but rather foolish old gentleman. But the laughter was usually kindly, and by and by, he became a "dear old gentleman" and was looked upon with something of the indulgent affection with which young people are apt to regard a soft-hearted and generous uncle. Thackeray declared that he loved him. Henry Kingsley claimed him as a friend; and various young ladies, we are told, proclaimed themselves ready to follow the example of black-eyed Miss Arabella Allen, should he perchance be found a second time under the mistletoe.

Behind the plump figure of Mr. Pickwick appeared the lanky one of Mr. Samuel Weller, in "a grey coat with the Pickwick Club button, a black hat with a cockade to it, a pink striped waistcoat, light breeches, and gaiters." "Samivel, that prince of heroes," young Charles Darwin called him, and as such he was greeted far and wide. Not to know him and his master was esteemed a misfortune. "Consekens is, as Mr. Sam Weller says," began Fanny Kemble in a letter to an American friend, and then, checking herself, went on compassionately, "But alas for you! You don't know *Pickwick*." Sam had a sprightly cockney tongue and a ready wit, and his retorts were adopted and repeated by many of his admirers. "Then, as Sam Weller says, you may take down the bill, for I'm let to a single gentleman," was Harry Coverdale's method of accepting an invitation from a friend to spend a few days at his country house. "Like Sam Weller I am an 'Inkred'lous Turnip,' " said William Hardman; and, "My wision and remarks are limited, as Sam Weller has it," declared Francis Burnand. Sam's love-letter to Mary, the pretty house-maid, was regarded as a masterpiece of that species of composition from its beginning, "Lovely creetur," to its masterly "pull up," "Except of me Mary my dear as your walentine . . . Your love-sick, Pickwick." Mr. Joseph Chamberlain when, in the late 'fifties, he read it, as he frequently did, at Penny Readings, found it always received with ecstatic applause.

Sam was welcome in almost any society; only in circles of extreme Evangelicalism was there no relish for his wit. One of Walter Frith's first sitters was a jolly, portly man—"like Pick-wick," said the artist—who had a serious Low Church wife of depressing piety. This lady undertook to read *Pickwick* aloud to her husband during the sittings; the choice, we may be sure, was his. "If you know'd who was near, sir, I rayther think you'd change your note. As the hawk remarked to himself with a cheerful laugh, ven he heerd the robin redbreast a-singin' round the corner," she read, in exactly the same tone as that in which she recited morning and evening prayers; and Mr. Frith was not surprised to hear his sitter respond with an ironical "Amen."

By the time Mr. Pickwick left the Fleet Prison readers were

inclined to agree with Mr. Weller that he was "a reg'lar thorough-bred angel," in spite of his tights and gaiters. The elderly gentleman, who had been at first something of a figure of fun, had won their respect as well as their affection. Sam, too, had risen in the estimation of all who knew him. Mortimer Collins compared the master and man to Don Quixote and Sancho Panza—with the contours of their figures reversed. Before the last number of *Pickwick* appeared the two were on terms of cordial intimacy with many hundreds of their fellow-countrymen. So close did this intimacy become that Englishmen travelling abroad held them in cherished remembrance as dear and absent friends. Mrs. Wood, great-niece of Fanny Burney, relates how one evening in June 1841—

a young man, lately returned from an extended foreign tour, told a ridiculous anecdote of a young English nobleman, who was last year travelling in Egypt. Seeing some written characters on one of the Pyramids, he exclaimed with delight that he had found some hieroglyphics. Imagine his disgust to find upon a nearer view "Pickwick and Weller" cut upon the stone.

These two were certainly the favourites, but there were many other characters from *Pickwick* who won friends in the world they had so confidently entered. Macaulay's first intimacy was with a tall, thin young man in a green coat, who came to Mr. Pickwick's assistance in an encounter with a cabman, and who, later, announced himself as Alfred Jingle, Esq., of No Hall, Nowhere. His conversation so enchanted Macaulay that he eagerly pursued the acquaintance of the other *Pickwick* characters, and they became his lifelong friends. Twenty years later, when he sat in the House of Lords, waiting for an attack (which never came) from Lord Ellenborough, his thoughts went back to two of them, and he wrote that night in his journal—

They say that he (the noble lord) has far less pluck than his warm and somewhat petulant manner indicates. I can only say that I was quite as much afraid of him as he could be of me. I thought of Winkle and Dowler in the *Pickwick Papers*.

Familiarity grew, and soon these people from *Pickwick*, even the less conspicuous ones, were recognized as the common acquaintances of a large reading circle.

There was, indeed, no statesman or writer, no clergyman of any denomination, no lady of fashion, no popular actor, no noted beauty or famous wit who had a circle of acquaintances as large and as appreciative as had the members of this motley company from *Pickwick*.

Sydney Smith was not very strongly attracted to this company. He confessed to Sir George Philips that he stood out against Mr. Dickens as long as he could. Then one day he met, walking from Cavendish Square towards Tottenham Court Road, three ladies, arm-in-arm. In the middle was a short, over-dressed, old-young spinster, who regarded her companions on either side with beaming condescension. One of these was a buxom lady of middle age, the other a beautiful girl of seventeen. Sydney Smith listened to the conversation with delight.

"I have taken such a fancy to your daughter, Mrs. Nickleby, you can't think," said the lady in the middle; and the delighted matron, fully believing in the genuineness of the compliment, began to pour out reminiscences of Kate in her childhood. "She always was clever," said the proud mother—

always, from a baby. I recollect when she was only two years and a half old, that a gentleman who used to visit very much at our house—Mr. Watkins, you know, Kate my dear, that your poor papa went bail for, who afterwards ran away to the United States, and sent us a pair of snow-shoes, with such an affectionate letter it made your poor dear father cry for a week. . . . He wasn't any relation, Miss Knag will understand, to the Watkins who kept the Old Boar in the village; bye-the-bye, I don't remember whether it was the Old Boar or the George the Third, but it was one of the two, I know, and it's much the same. That Mr. Watkins said, when you were only two and a half years old, that you were one of the most astonishing children he ever saw. He did, indeed, Miss Knag, and he wasn't at all fond of children, and couldn't have had the slightest motive for doing it. I know it was he who said so, because I recollect as if it was only yesterday his borrowing twenty pounds of her poor dear papa the very moment afterwards.

It needed no more. Sydney Smith's heart was won. Henceforward he was among the most ardent of Mrs. Nickleby's admirers, and through her he entered into a closer and more appreciative intimacy with the whole Dickens company. He found that most of his acquaintances had been before him in this matter, and that some were ambitious of themselves becoming members of Mrs. Nickleby's circle.

"My friends," he wrote to Dickens, "have not the smallest objection to being put into a number, but on the contrary would be proud of the distinction; and Lady Charlotte, in particular, you may marry to Newman Noggs."

Cheeryble Brothers had countless admirers, Henry Kingsley among them, and letters poured in to Dickens begging him to introduce the writers to these rich and benevolent merchants. Impecunious and selfish Mr. Mantalini charmed by his engaging impudence. Miss Broughton's penniless Nell L'Estrange endeavoured, when a butcher's bill for £34 5s. 4½d. was presented to her, to emulate the coolness of this much dunned gentleman; "The halfpenny be demned," she quoted. Even those figures of Mr. Mantalini's lively imagination, the countess and the dowager, took life and substance; so that Swinburne, comparing two poems of the day, said that one was like the dowager, who had a demd outline, and the other like the countess, who had no outline at all.

Then there was the Crummles family and their acting company who entertained the whole country, as no acting company has done before or since; and the Squeers family, whom everybody hated, but everybody delighted to know, rejoicing especially in Miss Fanny and her flowers of speech. "My sensibilities, like Miss Squeers', came late into blow," said Walter Frith, and Miss Matilda Betham-Edwards loved to sign her postcards to her friends, "base and degrading 'Tilda." Mrs. Squeers was best known as administering nauseous concoctions to the unhappy boys under her charge. Mrs. Panton said that her mother

every year in the early spring . . . made a jorum of brimstone and treacle . . . and for about a fortnight she enacted the part of Mrs. Squeers on her unfortunate offspring.

But not the benevolent Cheerybles nor the talented Crummles nor the brutal Squeers could rival Mrs. Nickleby in the public favour. She outshone her daughter, though Kate, too, had her admirers. One of them was Walter Frith, now an extremely popular artist. His daughter tells of his delight when he first conceived the idea of asking this beautiful young lady to sit for him, and of his enjoyment as the painting of the picture proceeded.

There were few people, however, who were not ready to leave the charming girl to join the circle that gathered round her mother. Mrs. Nickleby's conversational powers enchanted her hearers. Many people tried to imitate her, but with no great success. Miss Braddon made an attempt by the mouth of one of her characters, Roger Wendover, who, remarking on his cousin Bessie's style of letter-writing, said that it always recalled

our dear Mrs. Nickleby. "Aunt Bessie was asking after you the other day, and that reminds me that the last litter of black Hampshires was sixteen—the largest number father ever remembers having. The vicar and his wife are coming to dinner on Tuesday, and do tell me if this new picture everybody is talking about is really better than *The Derby Day*.

This is poor stuff, the mere coupling of the unrelated. It has none of the subtle, inconsequent suggestiveness for which Mrs. Nickleby's hearers loved her.

After Mrs. Nickleby, poor ill-starred Smike excited the most interest. It was a real personal and tender feeling that prompted the shower of letters which came to Dickens imploring him to spare the life of Mr. Squeers' unhappy victim. Nothing like it had been known since the days when the eighteenth-century public pleaded with Richardson for Clarissa. But Smike was foredoomed to an early death, and not all the tears of his sympathizers could save him.

Scarcely had the public dried its eyes after his pathetic end when another figure appeared—a childish, beautiful figure, yet with a sad and wistful grace, that caused the tenderness with which it was watched by thousands of enchanted readers to be touched with apprehension. Everybody loved Little Nell. Dickens' treatment of her has been condemned as sentimental and unnatural, but the Victorians were sentimental, and were proud rather than ashamed of being so. The few who, like W. H. Brookfield, were unmoved by the little girl's sorrows were, in the eyes of the majority, the people who ought to feel shame. As to the charge of unnaturalness, Little Nell was to them the most natural figure possible, for she was the embodiment of their ideal of what a child should be. It is true that Swinburne, staunch admirer of Dickens as he was, declared that she was as inhuman as a baby with two heads, but even he was not entirely proof against her.

Sara Coleridge admired her enthusiastically. Francis Jeffrey—now Lord Jeffrey, Judge of the Court of Sessions—rode about Edinburgh declaring that there had been nothing like Nell since Cordelia. Mary Howitt and her family delighted in Little Nell, and Walter Savage Landor adored her. He intended, he said, to buy the house, 35, St. James's Square, which was Dickens' Old Curiosity Shop and Nell's birthplace, that it might never be desecrated by any meaner associations.

All through the year 1841 these and many others watched the child as she wandered with her grandfather on her weary and painful way. Charles Ravenshoe remembered pitifully how she had tried to earn a few pence by selling nosegays on a racecourse, and how a lady sitting alone in a carriage had bought the poor flowers and bidden her for God's sake go home. Bret Harte has told how Englishmen very far from home followed the child in her wanderings. He showed a group of rough men seated round the fire in a western camp, while one of their number read aloud the story of Little Nell—

> The fir-trees gathering closer in the shadows,
> Listened in every spray,
> While the whole camp with "Nell" on English meadows,
> Wandered and lost their way.

As the year drew towards its close those who watched the child began to perceive a dark presence drawing nearer and nearer to that pure, bright little figure. Some, and among them was Dickens' friend, John Forster, had recognized from the first that this must be so. For such as Nell there could be no ordinary, happy woman's life. She must remain always a child. Yet many efforts were made to avert her doom. W. C. Macready, the actor, entreated Dickens to spare her life, telling him that he was cruel to think of killing such a gentle, loving creature. Dickens himself hated the deed that he must do. "I shan't recover it for a long time," he wrote to Forster. "Nobody will miss her like I shall. It is such a very painful thing to me, that I really cannot express my sorrow." But he knew that nothing could save Little Nell, and in November she died.

It is scarcely too much to say that all England mourned for her. Macready said that he opened the November number and

saw one print in it of the dear, dead child that gave a dead chill to my blood. I dread to read it, but I must get it over.

Later he wrote—

> I have read the two numbers. I never have read printed words that gave me so much pain. I could not weep for some time.

Daniel O'Connell, the famous Irish agitator, was travelling with a friend when the November number of *The Old Curiosity Shop* came out. He bought a copy, and as he read it his eyes filled with tears, and he began to sob aloud. "He should not have killed her! —he should not have killed her!—she was too good!" he exclaimed; and in grief and indignation he threw the book out of the window.

Jeffrey felt the blow still more keenly. Mrs. Henry Siddons, a friend who lived near him, said that she opened his library door one day and saw him sitting in his chair with his head bowed upon the table before him. She turned, meaning to go quietly away, but he looked up and signed to her to remain. She saw that his eyes were full of tears.

> "Don't go, my dear friend," he said. "I shall be all right again in another minute." "I had no idea you had had any bad news or cause for grief," said the lady, "or I would not have come in. Is anyone dead?" "Yes, indeed," was the reply. "I'm a great goose to have given way so, but I couldn't help it. You'll be sorry to hear that little Nelly, Boz's little Nelly, is dead."

Nearly six years later Jeffrey's heart was again lacerated by the death of little Paul Dombey.

> "Oh, my dear, dear Dickens!" he wrote. "What a No. 5 you have now given us. I have sobbed and cried over it last night and again this morning. . . . Since the divine Nelly was found dead on her humble couch, beneath the snow and ivy, there has been nothing like the actual dying of that sweet Paul, in the summer sunshine of that lofty room."

Almost as many tears were shed for Paul as for Little Nell. Laura Edmondstone found Amy weeping bitterly in the greenhouse, and was relieved to find that the cause of her grief was nothing more personal than the death of Paul Dombey. Macready, when he saw Dickens for the first time after Paul's death, could not speak for sobs, and Thackeray was almost as much affected. Ada, Lady Lovelace, had been strangely fascinated by the little boy:—

"I was sent for to have a very solemn interview with Ada when she was dying," said Dickens. "She had wished for it in consequence of her having thought much during her illness of the death of the child in *Dombey*."

This was five years later, in 1852, but little Paul was still loved and remembered by a large public. The many young ladies who sang "What are the Wild Waves Saying?", the pathetic song written by Henry Carpenter, and founded on a conversation between Florence and Paul Dombey, still sang it with a quaver in their voices, and the audiences still paid a tribute of tears to the memory of the little boy and his sister.

But if tears were plentiful in the company of these creations of Dickens', laughter was more plentiful still. Between Little Nell and Paul there appeared one who, wherever she came, brought hilarity. She was a most unpleasant old woman, really. If the Victorians had known anyone at all resembling her among their flesh-and-blood acquaintances they would have disliked her extremely, and, moreover, been shocked at her moral delinquencies. She was dirty, lazy, dishonest, cruel, ignorant, and given to drink. Yet thousands of upright and kindly English people took Mrs. Sarah Gamp to their hearts and delighted in her company. They did not love her qualities; indeed, they learned to hate them so much that they bestirred themselves to clear the hospitals and other institutions of the country of such of her professional sisters as bore any likeness to her. Part of her charm undoubtedly lay in her conversation. Her subject was herself, and she treated it with a fullness and an ingenuity which was as revealing as it was fascinating. She invented Mrs. Harris to serve as an invisible Chorus, and this lady became as familiar to the reading public as was Sarah herself. Betsy Prig also, Mrs. Gamp's fellow-nurse and rival, had for her chief function the acting as a foil to that remarkable woman. Sara Coleridge tells how she, with her son Herbert and his boy friends, laughed over the "thrice notable Sairey Gamp, with Betsy Prig to show her off." How successfully Mrs. Prig played her part is seen on that great occasion when the two ladies took tea together in Mrs. Gamp's apartment in Kingsgate Street, High Holborn—that apartment which, as his wife tells us, fascinated Edward Burne-Jones. The description of it, she said, "was read over and over again, until I, but not he, was wearied for a time." Here the professional sisters partook of tea and pickled salmon, with a "cowcumber," and afterwards of liquid refreshment which, although it came out of a black teapot, was stronger than tea, and it was Mrs. Prig's action in stretching out her hand for the second time, in counterfeit absence of mind, towards this receptacle, which drew from Mrs. Gamp the retort that has since served so many other people in like circumstances, "Drink fair, wotever you do!" "Whatever you do, drink fair, so saith the immortal Gamp," said Guy Livingstone.

This was not the only saying of Mrs. Gamp's that passed into common speech. She was quoted widely and constantly. "She is a young lady free from what Mrs. Gamp would call bragian boldness," said Edgar, of *Muttons and Mattins,* and "Perhaps it may be as well not to proticipate, to use Mrs. Gamp's expression," said Sara Coleridge. Swinburne was never tired of quoting her, and Thomas Hughes tried to do so, but to his shame attributed one of her unmistakable utterances to two other members of the Dickens company whose eloquence was of a definitely different order. "One of the great moralists whom we sat under in my youth," he said, "was it the great Richard Swiveller or Mr. Stiggins?—says, 'We are born in a vale and must take the consequences of being found in such a situation.'" Whereas it was, of course, the great Sarah who put the thought into her unique vernacular.

"He was born in a wale," she said, with reference to that aforetime ornament of Todgers' boarding-house, Bailey Junior, "and he lived in a wale; and he must take the consequencés of sech a sitiwation." Even Mr. William de Morgan was not quite fair to Mrs. Gamp in this matter. "Mr. and Mrs. Demorgannéepickering," he wrote to Burne-Jones, soon after his marriage to Miss Evelyn Pickering, "are going to reside in a wale, where, indeed, Mr. Mould told Mrs. Gamp we all reside." The "wale" in this case was the Vale of Chelsea.

Yet William de Morgan was on very familiar terms with Mrs. Gamp, and so were the other members of his circle, including Burne-Jones and William Morris. He tells how, in the summer of 1881, a party of them made an excursion down the Thames, and stopped for a night at an hotel in Henley. In the evening they played the game of "Twenty Questions." De Morgan was sent out of the room, and the others chose as their subject Mrs.

Harris. On being recalled his first question was, "Is it abstract or concrete?" Then there arose a hubbub, and he was sent out of the room again while the rest argued hotly as to what the answer should be. Charles Faulkner maintained that Mrs. Harris was just as concrete as any other character in fiction. William Morris vigorously opposed this view; Mrs. Harris, he said, was simply a creature of Mrs. Gamp's imagination and did not appear in the story at all. Everyone got wildly excited, and the waiter came up with a message from the people beneath to know if anything was the matter. In the end the question remained unsettled, but it continued to interest de Morgan and Morris for some time afterwards.

But whatever might be said of Mrs. Harris, Mrs. Gamp was certainly concrete and living, with a personality large and forceful enough to spread itself over all the members of her caste. Soon every monthly nurse became a Mrs. Gamp. Anthony Trollope, in *The Three Clerks*, showed Charlie Tudor writing a story, *Crinoline and Macassar*, the last chapter of which told of the marriage of the lovers and the birth of their son. For this occasion Crinoline engaged the services of Mrs. Gamp, who, as the doctor certified, was all that could be desired. Trollope, wisely, gave only one sample of her conversational powers, and the success of that is due rather to imitation than to inspiration—

It's just half-past heleven this wery moment as is and the finest boy babby as my heyes, which has seen a many, has ever sat upon.

There was another member of this amazing Dickens company who was as popular as Mrs. Gamp and much more agreeable. He was to be met with in the neighbourhood of Windsor Terrace, walking jauntily with his cane and his dangling eye-glass, and he had an air of such extreme gentility that one felt almost ashamed of noticing the shabbiness of his brown surtout, black tights, and carefully polished shoes. This gentleman, Mr. Wilkins Micawber, had evolved a scheme of life which rested mainly upon two, or perhaps, more correctly, three maxims. The first two of these he set forward feelingly to his young friend, David Copperfield—

Annual income twenty pounds, annual expenditure nineteen-nine-six, result happiness. Annual income twenty pounds, annual expenditure twenty pounds ought and six, result misery. The blossom is blighted, the leaf is withered, the god of day goes down upon the dreary scene, and—and, in short, you are for ever floored. As I am.

But he did not remain floored for long. The third maxim "Something will turn up presently," quickly restored him to an upright, jaunty attitude, in which he looked cheerfully towards a rosy future.

"I have known him," said David, "come home to supper with a flood of tears and a declaration that nothing was now left but a jail; and go to bed making a calculation of the expense of putting bow-windows to the house 'in case anything turned up.'"

These maxims endeared him greatly to the Victorians. The first two tickled their sense of prudence, the third their high optimism. Mary Kingsley declared, "I am determined to have my finance under my own hand, and have twenty shillings for every fifteen shillings I owe, remembering the immortal words of Mr. Micawber." "I am like Mr. Micawber," professed Mrs. Hungerford's heroine, Molly Bawn, "I have an almost religious belief in the power things have of turning up." To James Smetham he was an "awful example."

Mr. Micawber fills me with wholesome terror; not that, like him, I ever expected in his sense anything to "turn up," but because I see that all "being behind hand" has a fatal quality in it.

Henry Sidgwick wrote to his sister, "I have been . . . hoping, like Mr. Micawber, that something would turn up." Mr. Edmund Yates, describing a certain Mr. Stone, remarked, "He was the bright side of Micawber in the constant anticipation of something good about to turn up."

But as a whole-hearted follower of Mr. Wilkins Micawber and Emma his wife Jerome K. Jerome stands pre-eminent.

"How often," he says, "has the example of your philosophy saved me when I likewise have suffered under the temporary pressure of pecuniary liabilities. I have asked myself what would the Micawbers have done in my place. And I have answered myself. They would have sat down to a dish of lamb's fry, cooked and breaded by the deft hands of Emma, followed by a brew of punch concocted by the beaming Wilkins, and have forgotten their troubles for the time being."

This fine example Mr. Jerome decided to follow as closely as possible. He sought the nearest restaurant and ordered the best dinner his remaining small change would buy; and emerging, refreshed and comforted, was aware of the sun of prosperity peeping through the clouds as if to say, "Cheer up, I am only round the corner."

Most of Dickens' readers had their particular friends among his creations. Henry Kingsley loved best Mr. Pickwick, the Cheeryble brothers, Tom Pinch, and Captain Cuttle. William Morris specially favoured Joe Gargery and Mr. Boffin. "Wot larks!" he would say, imitating the childlike enjoyment of Dickens' large-hearted blacksmith, and "Morning, morning!" with the genial nod of the Golden Dustman. He delighted, too, in that remarkable old lady, Mr. F.'s aunt. "Bring him forard and I'll chuck him out o' winder," was his manner of expressing anger against any offender. Thackeray had a weakness for Mrs. Steerforth. Emily Eden declared herself "so fond" of Dick Swiveller and the Marchioness. Trollope's sympathies went out to Bill Sikes. "Poor Bill, I have a sort of love for him as he walks about with that dog of his, though I know it is necessary to hang him." Even Agnes Wickfield, who might seem too immaculate to inspire any warm feeling, had, it is said, at least one adorer. A certain middle-aged gentleman fell deeply in love with her, and set out resolutely to find her counterpart that he might win her for his wife. Far and wide he sought, and many ladies he hopefully approached, but all in vain. Even advertisements failed to produce an acceptable candidate. At length, giving up the search, he settled down to celibacy, and solaced himself by writing long letters—which were found after his death—addressed to Miss Agnes Wickfield.

Some of the younger Victorians grew up in such close familiarity with the Dickens people that these became their intimate life companions, meeting them at every turn of the road. Thus Francis Burnand says that his nursery governess was a Cornelia Blimber, and that at his first school one of the masters was "a Professor of Turveydropian deportment." When he was eight years old he fell ill, and then he "acted Paul Dombey to the life," with a touch of Smike. At his next school there was a Toots, a Traddles, and a Mr. Mell, and when he went to Eton he felt, as a new boy, "like one of Squeers' queer collection at Dotheboys Hall"; and so the story goes on. Edmund Yates, Canon Ainger, Dean Hole, and Sir Edward Parry enjoyed a similar lifelong intimacy. Dickens tells how once, in York, a lady stopped him in the street and said, "Mr. Dickens, will you let me touch the hand that has filled my house with many friends," and there were readers all over the country ready to offer a similar tribute.

But although these Dickens people went in and out many houses and up and down many streets, they were no mere floating and detached population. They had their homes and their haunts, where they established themselves so securely that ordinary mortal inmates taking up subsequent quarters there could not dislodge them. George Richmond, when he was a boy in the 'sixties, used to go down to Holborn "to walk the walks of Fagin." Helen Melladew, of *Muttons and Mattins*, walked about Brighton speculating as to which was the house where Cornelia Blimber "brought on" little Dombey. Du Maurier's boy-hero, Peter Ibbetson, coming, in the 'seventies, from his beloved Paris to London, said—

Not, indeed, but what London had its merits. Sam Weller lived there, and Charley Bates, and the irresistible Artful Dodger—and Dick Swiveller and his adorable Marchioness, who divided my allegiance with Rebecca of York and sweet Diana Vernon.

For George Gissing, also, London was the London of Dickens. He said that when he first came to the great city—

What I chiefly thought of was that now I could go hither and thither in London's immensity seeking for the places that had been made known to me by Dickens. At times when walking with other thoughts I would come upon a discovery, the name at a street corner would catch my eye and thrill me. Thus one day in the City I found myself at the entrance to Bevis Marks. Here dwelt Mr. Brass and Sally and the Marchioness. Up and down the little street, this side and that, I went, gazing and dreaming. . . . I am not sure that I had any dinner that day, but if not, I daresay I did not mind very much.

With *David Copperfield* (1850) Dickens reached the height of his popularity, and many years were to pass before it showed any signs of serious decline. During these years Dickens was taking his place beside Scott as a national possession. Sir Sidney Colvin, recalling memories of Burne-Jones, says that his favourite books were, "as they are the favourites of every wise man," Scott and Dickens. Ellen Terry told of a visit she paid to Paris in the early 'sixties—

What was the thing that made me homesick for London? *Household Words.* The excitement in the 'sixties over each new Dickens can be understood only by people who experienced it at the time. Boys used to sell *Household Words* in the streets, and they were often pursued by an eager crowd, for all the world as if they were carrying news of the latest winner.

There were, naturally, a few readers who did not share the general enthusiasm. W. H. Brookfield remained implacable. "I detest *Humphrey's Clock* more than I can tell you," he wrote. "I really find no genius in it. Except Swiveller and Mrs. Jarley I have not found a natural character in the story." Miss Beale, Principal of Cheltenham Ladies' College, gained little pleasure from any of Dickens' writings except *A Tale of Two Cities.* Mrs. Oliphant wrote in 1862, "Dickens is not a favourite of mine. I think it would go against the grain to applaud him highly in his present phase." This was a reference to the lately published *Great Expectations,* which some people thought was in many ways the finest of his books.

Leslie Stephen said rather unkindly—

If literary fame could be safely measured by popularity with the half-educated, he must claim the highest position among English novelists.

This was scarcely fair, for it was certainly not only with the half-educated that Dickens was popular. Trollope, though he laughed at Dickens as Mr. Sentiment, and made fun of his heroes and heroines, yet took a juster view of his claim to immortality.

Perhaps, however, Mr. Sentiment's great attraction is his second-rate characters. If his heroes and heroines walk upon stilts, as heroes and heroines, I fear, ever must, their attendant satellites are as natural as though one met them in the street. They walk and talk like men and women, and live among our friends a rattling, lively life; yes, live, and will live, till the names of their calling shall be forgotten in their own, and Bucket and Mrs. Gamp will be the only words left to us to signify a detective police officer and a monthly nurse.

CHAPTER IX

READERS OF POETRY

WHEN Queen Victoria came to the throne, the Byron fever, that had raged so violently during the Regency, had abated, but had by no means died out. The young gentlemen who had imitated the poet and the young ladies who had adored him in those earlier days were now approaching middle age, yet most of them looked back on their youthful extravagances with pride rather than with shame; and when they spoke or wrote, as many of them did, of their young raptures it was in the tone of one who recounts treasured and happy memories.

Nor did the succession of his worshippers fail as the years went on; a new generation arose which was as ardent, if not as demonstrative, as the first. The Tennyson brothers—Frederick, Charles, and Alfred—looked on him as the king of poets. "He lorded it over us with an immitigable tyranny," wrote Frederick many years afterwards. Lord John Manners and other members of the Young England group fell completely under his spell. John Bright, son of the Quaker mill-owner of Rochdale, loved Byron's poems all his life long. Young Robert Browning told Miss Barrett that he would gladly have made a journey to see a curl of his hair or one of his gloves, while he "could not get up enthusiasm enough to cross the room if, at the other end of it, all Wordsworth, Coleridge, and Shelley were condensed into the little china bottle yonder." Charles Darwin and Charles Kingsley were among those who eagerly read Byron in those early days, and a little later came Walter Bagehot, who was admiring, though critical. "What a command of language and illustration is shown in *Childe Harold*," he said. "What a pity he had nothing better to say than what an uncomfortable place the world is."

The fiction of the day introduces us to many Byron worshippers. Kingsley shows Alton Locke standing day after day in front of a second-hand bookshop, reading, in defiance of his Calvinistic mother's stern teaching, snatches of *Childe Harold*, *Lara*, and *The Corsair*, and finding in them something that opened to him a new world of wonders. Thackeray tells us that *Don Juan* was the fashionable reading of young men about town, and of aspiring members of the commercial world, such as young Mr. Sackville Maine, the coal-merchant. Smedley's heroes, though they were not great readers, sometimes read Byron. Nathaniel Mullins of *Frank Fairlegh* took a copy of the poet's works with him to his private tutor's, and Harry Oaklands, one of his fellow-pupils, borrowed the book and read it, apparently with interest. Harry Coverdale, when he felt the pangs of love-sickness overtaking him, was moved to take a volume of Byron from his host's library shelves, and for the space of a sunny summer afternoon lay under a tree reading *The Bride of Abydos*. Miss Braddon's works abound in sentimental young ladies and dashing young gentlemen who adored Byron, especially *Don Juan*; Guy Livingstone loved *Childe Harold*. Ouida's magnificent heroes, too, delighted in Byron, and she sentimentalizes over the

thousands of young fellows who have dropped down under the trees bordering the Cam, dreaming over *Don Juan* or the *Lotos-Eaters*.

Even Miss Yonge's immaculate Philip Morville read and admired the works of the noble poet, though the heir of Redclyffe himself shunned them as being dangerous and untrue; and it is clear that this is Miss Yonge's own view, for she says—

Who could have told where the mastery might have been in the period of fearful conflict with his passions, if he had been feeding his imagination with the contemplation of revenge, dark hatred, and malice, and identifying himself with Byron's brooding, lowering heroes?

She would have agreed with Mark Rutherford, when he said—

When the boy becomes a man he may read Byron without danger. To a youth he is fatal.

Yet it was true, as Philip Morville said, that many of the passages from his works had by that time become classics. Within twenty years or so of the Queen's accession, some of these passages even found their way into books of selections intended for the Victorian schoolroom. Lucy Lyttelton used such a book, and so did Miss Jane Harrison, who tells us, in her *Reminiscences of a Student's Life*, that she learnt by heart *The Prisoner of Chillon*, with a good many other poems, lying on the backboard to which she was condemned for some hours each day. Cynthia Kirkpatrick, of Mrs. Gaskell's *Wives and Daughters*, learnt at her boarding-school, as her mother boasted, to repeat the same melancholy poem, though the young lady herself declared that she preferred Johnnie Gilpin. Thus, some works of the poet whose very name, uttered in the presence of their charges, had caused mothers and governesses to shudder, were opened to the young; although even as late as the early 'seventies, Marie Corelli, as a precocious child of eight or nine, found that she could seriously alarm what she called the prudery of her governess by declaiming passages from *Don Juan*.

Wordsworth, in these early Victorian days, had as many and as enthusiastic readers as Byron. There were still some left of the staunch little band that had held so loyally to him through the long years of ridicule and neglect which had followed the publication of his earlier poems, among them Dr. Arnold, Keble, Crabb Robinson, Mrs. Clarkson, Harriet Martineau, Thomas Poole, and John Stuart Mill. There was a larger following that had been drawn to him later by the discovery that his poems possessed, as Matthew Arnold said, a "healing power" for the man sick at heart with doubts and perplexities. "To me he is not only poet, but preacher and prophet of God's new and divine philosophy, a man raised up as light in a dark time," wrote Charles Kingsley in 1844. Thomas Burt said that although his first feeling with regard to Wordsworth had been disappointing, yet later the poet had become "part of my moral and intellectual being." Men and women of high intellectual powers found help and comfort in the simple poems of nature that earlier critics had denounced as silly, childish, and worse. Charles Darwin, who at the beginning of Queen Victoria's reign, was a young man of twenty-eight, took much delight in reading Wordsworth. "I can boast," he said, "that I read *The Excursion* twice through." Walter Bagehot loved Wordsworth, and hastened to make Miss Eliza Wilson, his future wife, a sharer in his delight. The day after they were engaged he brought to her a book of selections from Wordsworth, and read aloud *Lord Clifford*; and a little later, on her birthday, he gave her in eight volumes the works of Wordsworth, Shelley, and Keats. George Eliot read Wordsworth as a girl, and continued to find pleasure in his works to the end of her life. Newman spoke of him as a master of "philosophic meditation." Young men as far apart in temperament as James Clerk Maxwell and Algernon

Swinburne found pleasure in his works. It is true that a good
many people—including some really devout Wordsworthians—
made fun of some of the poems, as a good many people do to this
day. Charlotte Yonge's father loved to turn *Peter Bell* and *The
Pet Lamb* into ridicule. *We are Seven* was constantly quoted and
misquoted with derision. *Alice Fell* was regarded as a theme for
the parodist, and *Lucy Gray* as a poem suitable for little girls to
recite at children's parties.

It is true also that there was still, as there had been from the
beginning, a more serious anti-Wordsworthian party. William
Morris disliked Wordsworth's works; Charles Dickens thought
little of them. Benjamin Jowett, then a young Oxford don, could
not be induced by all the enthusiasm of John Duke Coleridge,
William Shairp, and other friends to acknowledge that they
possessed any great merit. Macaulay continued to decry him.

"I brought home and read *The Prelude*," he wrote in his
Journal in July 1850. "It is a poorer *Excursion*, the same sort of
faults and beauties; but the

faults greater, and the beauties fainter, both in themselves and
because faults are always made more offensive and beauties less
pleasing by repetition. The story is the old story. There are the
old raptures about mountains and cataracts; the old flimsy philosophy about the effect of scenery upon the mind; the old crazy,
mystical metaphysics; the endless wilderness of dull, flat, prosaic
twaddle; and here and there fine descriptions and energetic
declamations interspersed."

But those who were for Wordsworth were now many more
than those who were against him. His poems were becoming the
ordinary, universal possession of English readers. Not all of them
became enthusiasts, but most learned to see some real poetic value
in the works. There were probably a good many who could have
said with Alice Meynell—

In quite early childhood I lived upon Wordsworth. I don't know
that I particularly enjoyed him, but he was put into my hands,
and, to me, Wordsworth's poetry was the normal poetry, *par
excellence.*

There were also at this time, as at all other times, a certain number
of real poetry lovers who read eagerly the works of all the great

poets, old and new. Shakespeare and Milton, Dryden and Pope, Shelley, Keats, and Coleridge are names that occur frequently in the records of this small, elect band. But these readers must be taken for granted. They were not distinctive of the age they lived in, and therefore have no special interest as Victorian readers.

Yet, in spite of their great heritage from the past, the Victorians wanted, as all people at all times have wanted, a poet of their own. They felt that their age had many things to say that had not been said before, and they wanted these things said clearly and beautifully, as only a poet could say them. And although they loved the old tunes, their ears pined for new melodies and fresh delights of sound. They were, perhaps, not very conscious that they wanted these things, but nevertheless the desire was real and strong; and in their eagerness to satisfy it, some people mistook the little for the great, the tinsel for the gold, and acclaimed as the poet of the age some minor versifier. Felicia Hemans, who had died in 1835, was so acclaimed. All through the early years of Victoria's reign she was read and praised and almost reverenced. Every young lady had a copy of her poems, and in every schoolroom they were read and learnt by heart. Florence Nightingale loved *The Better Land*, and copied it out to send to her cousin. Mary Ann Evans wrote in 1840 to Miss Lewis—

I am reading eclectically Mrs. Hemans' poems, and venture to recommend to your perusal, if unknown to you, one of the longest ones—*The Forest Sanctuary*. I can give it my pet adjective—exquisite.

Emily Eden wrote from India, "Dear Mrs. Hemans! I dote on that book. She just said the things I was thinking."

Not only young ladies, but older people too, of cultivated tastes, praised Mrs. Hemans. Dr. Whewell was enthusiastic about her *Greek Exile*, which showed, he said, a "perfectness of sound to sense"; and Wordsworth lamented her death with high eulogy—

> Mourn rather for that holy Spirit,
>   Sweet as the spring, as ocean deep,
> For Her, who, ere her summer faded
>   Has sunk into a breathless sleep.

In 1838 came another claimant for immortality—Martin Farquhar Tupper, with his *Proverbial Philosophy*; and the amazing popularity of this most unpoetical and platitudinous work is a

measure of the eagerness with which the general public awaited
an authentic voice from its own times. For nearly fifty years
Tupper kept his place with a certain section of English readers,
although long before that period ended he had become to the
majority an object of derision. His works sold in thousands and
tens of thousands. His name was blessed, and his words were
quoted as containing the essence of moral and spiritual wisdom.
One reviewer said—

There is more novelty in the sentiments, a greater sweep of
subject, and a finer sense of moral beauty in this poem than in
any other work we have read—excepting, of course, the *Proverbs
of Solomon.*

Meredith contemptuously referred to it as "a cold hash of Solomon,"
which was much nearer the truth; but the public accepted the
flowery tribute of the reviewer as sound criticism. One reader
claimed to have read the work sixty times. It became, Tupper
boasted, a common gift book for marriages, and more than once
appeared at royal weddings. "Small wonder," he said, "that I have
often been greeted by old and young married couples as having
been a sort of spiritual Cupid on such occasions."

Proverbial Philosophy had no music to recommend it. It was
written in rough, halting hexameters, which sounded unpleasantly
on the ear. The following lines are chosen at random—

O books, ye monuments of mind, concrete wisdom of the wisest,
Sweet solace of daily life; proofs and results of immortality;
Trees yielding all fruits whose leaves are for the healing of the nation;
Groves of knowledge where all may eat, nor fear a flaming sword.

Tupper wrote ballads, too, which ran somewhat more easily—

Never give up! it is wiser and better
  Always to hope than once to despair;
Fling off the load of Doubt's heavy fetter,
  And break the dark spell of tyrannical care.

The critics lauded his works, and proclaimed that he had "won
for himself the vacant throne waiting for him amidst the
immortals"; and thousands of readers believed that here was the
great Victorian poet for whom the nation had waited.

Another false start was made when the Victorians ran after
Philip James Bailey, whose *Festus* was published in 1839. It was

a long poem, and told, with many variations and digressions, the old story of Dr. Faustus. *Festus* was not, like *Proverbial Philosophy*, a negligible piece of work. It had thought and learning and some beauty, but only a small part of it was poetry. It was read by thoughtful, intelligent people who were interested in philosophical and theological subjects, and of these there must have been a goodly number, for twelve large editions of it were sold in England and thirty in America. Tennyson was one of its readers—one, too, who overestimated its qualities, for he said that while he was himself like a wren beating about a hedgerow, the author of *Festus* was like an eagle soaring to the sun.

James Clerk-Maxwell, the future great scientist, read *Festus* when he was nineteen, and wrote to his friend, Lewis Campbell—

Did you finish *Festus*? I had only two days to read it, so that I skipped part of the long speech and a good deal of the jollification, which I think the dullest part of the book.

He went on to write two pages of criticism, most of which was enthusiastic eulogy. Thomas Burt borrowed a paper-covered copy of *Festus* from one of his Primitive Methodist friends, William Ritson, and read it with great delight. Mrs. Craik was an enthusiastic admirer of *Festus*, and quoted from it freely in her books. The poem had no long popularity; and it is an ironical comment on such a thoughtful, philosophical piece of work that it is largely kept in memory by Swinburne's Dickensian comparison. Bailey, said Swinburne, had no ear and no metrical power, and his work, like the dowager, had a demd outline; Sydney Dobell (author of *Balder*, another poem that had some vogue about this time) never wrote a bad verse, but his work, like the countess, had no outline. In 1868 James Smetham wrote to a friend—

Don't you remember that just when you were shedding your mere youth and entering on the golden age . . . there appeared what was considered a starry group of poets, soon and most unfairly obscured as the spasmodic school, Alexander Smith, Sydney Dobell, Philip Bailey. I can't say I was ever carried off my feet by them. . . . I used to dislike the *Festus* and *Balder* tone considerably, and the only book I ever flung to the other side of the room was *Festus*.

While these and other lesser writers were attracting an undue share of public notice, the two poets who were to be the special possession and glory of the Victorian age were slowly gathering a small band of followers. These were drawn chiefly from a party of readers belonging to the new generation, which was in revolt against the poetic dictums of its elders. Colonel Newcome, listening with puzzled deference to the talk of his son's literary friends, learnt that Byron was no great poet; that Pope had been unjustly decried and must be restored to his high place; that Sir Walter was a poet of the second order; that Dr. Johnson, though he talked admirably, did not write English; that young Keats was a genius; and that "a young gentleman of Cambridge, who had lately published two volumes of verses, might take rank with the greatest poets of all." This seemed to the old-fashioned Colonel pure blasphemy. He tried to read the "young gentleman from Cambridge's" *Œnone*, but could make nothing of it. *Ulysses* he understood, but thought it not worth the "prodigious laudations" bestowed upon it. He felt that he was sadly behind the times, as indeed he was; but it might have consoled him to know that most of his own generation were lagging with him, and that, of the younger ones, only a few had advanced far enough to hear clearly the wonderful harmonies and new and captivating measures of Mr. Tennyson's verse.

Tennyson's earliest admirers were to be found among the group of friends who had known him at Cambridge. As early as June 1832 James Spedding, afterwards the famous editor of Bacon's works, had written to W. H. Thompson (another of the Cambridge group, later Master of Trinity)—

I have no copy of the *Palace of Art*, but shall be happy to repeat it to you when you come—no copy of *The Legend of Fair Women*, but can repeat a dozen stanzas, which are the finest.

John Mitchell Kemble, still another college friend, raved about the great Alfred and his poems. "My brother John gave me the first copy of the poems I ever possessed," said Fanny Kemble, who was then about twenty-one and the idol of theatregoers—

"with a prophecy of his future fame and excellence written on the fly-leaf. I have never ceased to exult in my possession of that copy of the first edition of those poems which became the songs of our every day and every hour almost. We delighted in them and knew them by heart, and read and said them over and over again incessantly; they were our pictures, our music, and infinite was the scorn and indignation with which we received the slightest word of adverse criticism upon them."

Of adverse criticism there was no lack. The Young England group would have nothing to do with the new poet. It was intolerable, they said, that Cambridge, the mother of such poets as Dryden and Milton, should encourage "all this humbug" about this young versifier. Lord John Manners was shaken with indignation when he remembered the "wordy trash" he had heard quoted at Union debates and in private conversations to prove that Alfred Tennyson was a poet. A few people shared his indignation, but a much larger number remained unmoved, because they cared nothing at all about Alfred Tennyson, and did not intend to read his poetry. Not many copies of the 1833 volume were sold. Fanny Kemble had one; and Sir John Simeon said he recalled the day when—

both being undergraduates at Christchurch, his friend, Charles Wynne, brought him the first published volume, saying to him "There is something new to you who love poetry."

A few reviews of the poems appeared—none very favourable, some adverse, some even derisive; and then, as far as the general public was concerned, they disappeared from notice.

Mr. Robert Browning, the second of the two poets who were to take a high place among the Victorians, had even fewer readers than Mr. Tennyson. He published two poems, *Pauline* and *Paracelsus*, before Queen Victoria came to the throne, and a drama, *Strafford*, in the year of her accession. Of these no notice at all was taken except by a few discerning reviewers, such as John Forster, who said, "Without the slightest hesitation we name Mr. Robert Browning with Shelley, Coleridge, and Wordsworth"; and a few equally discerning writers of eminence—Dickens, Carlyle, and Landor among them—who thought so well of the poems that they sought out the young author and encouraged him with hearty praise.

Browning was not disheartened, but went on writing with unflagging enthusiasm. In 1840 he published *Sordello*, a poem telling the story of the Guelphs and Ghibellines in the thirteenth century. It was received with a bewilderment that soon passed into ridicule. None of those who read it—they were not a large company—could understand it, and it became a byword for unintelligibility. We are told that Carlyle wrote to Browning, saying that Mrs. Carlyle had read the poem with great interest and would be glad to know whether Sordello was a man, a city, or a book. Another reader declared that there were only two intelligible lines in the poem, the first, "Who will, may hear Sordello's story told," and the last, "Who would has heard Sordello's story told," and that each of these contained a lie.

In 1841 appeared a small, paper-covered book which was announced as the first of a series to be called *Bells and Pomegranates*. It contained a poem by Robert Browning entitled *Pippa Passes*. Only a very few people bought the book, although it was sold at the modest price of sixpence. Readers remembered *Sordello*; and then there was the strange title—nobody could imagine what could possibly be meant by *Bells and Pomegranates*. But the few who did read *Pippa Passes* found it a beautiful and moving story put into fine, and in some parts captivatingly lovely, verse, of a day in the life of a girl silk weaver of Asolo. Even those few do not seem to have found in it the help and inspiration for which they were seeking. Perhaps Browning's optimism, which reached its supreme expression in Pippa's song, "God's in His heaven, All's right with the world," offered too severe a trial of faith in those dark times when, to most thinking people, it seemed that all was very far from right in their own particular corner of God's world. The good times which were to encourage the growth of a sturdy Victorian optimism were as yet not in sight.

There were other new works coming out which offered more attractive reading than did *Sordello* or *Pippa*. In 1841 came Macaulay's *Lays of Ancient Rome*, of which the *Athenaeum*, after quoting several stanzas, said—

If the foregoing fragments fail to attract the reader's curiosity to the work . . . we shall feel that our age is deeper sunk in apathy than the most melancholy of our bewailers have asserted.

If the apathy existed, the *Lays* undoubtedly did something towards dispelling it. Florence Nightingale, it is true, did not like them. They were not, she said, worthy to be placed beside the real primitive ballads, and she declared she hated the "wizened politician" who had thus degraded the poetry she loved best. But to most readers the *Lays* recalled the delight that they and their fathers before them had felt in some of the spirited, heart-stirring passages of Scott. Charles Greville read them the day they came out, and pronounced them admirable. Guy Livingstone found that they stirred his blood like a trumpet. Soon a copy lay on every drawing-room table, and boys and girls all over the country were declaiming with vigour "How Horatius kept the bridge In the brave days of old." Edmund Yates says they were "favourite spouting pieces at Highgate" where, at the time of their publication, he was at school. Charles Dodgson read them, and a few years later wrote a parody of *Horatius* for *The Rectory Umbrella*, which was a magazine run by the rectory inhabitants. The parody commemorated an escapade with a refractory donkey, on which Charles's brother valiantly mounted, while Charles and his sister prevented the animal from going back into his stable. It concluded—

> They gave him bread and butter,
>   That was of public right,
> As much as four strong rabbits
>   Could munch from morn to night,
> For he'd done a deed of daring,
>   And faced that savage steed,
> And therefore cups of coffee sweet,
> And everything that was a treat
>   Were but his right and meed.

So for the first five years or so of Queen Victoria's reign the public treasured its older poets, rushed to buy copies of *Proverbial Philosophy* and *Festus*, recited Mr. Macaulay's *Lays*, and, when they were not laughing at Mr. Tennyson and Mr. Browning, ignored them. But a change was coming, although the indications of it were so slight as to give to the admirers of the young poets little encouragement.

Tennyson's turn came first. In 1842 he published a new and enlarged edition of his poems, and this had a somewhat better sale than the previous edition. Young Charles Kingsley read it, and wrote to Miss Fanny Grenfell, who was later to be his wife, "I have a book called *Tennyson's Poems*, the most beautiful poetry of the last fifteen years." The reason that Kingsley delighted in these poems was probably that which he expressed by the mouth of his poet-tailor, Alton Locke, who found in them "the embodiment of thoughts about the world around me which I had concealed because I fancied them peculiar to myself." Here is Tennyson acknowledged, by one man at least, as spokesman and interpreter, the poet for whom the age had been waiting. To the poor tailor, whose chief delight had been to watch the sunset from Battersea Bridge, Tennyson's descriptions came as an overwhelming revelation. He read the passages that describe the fen country, with its long, level sweeps, its desolate creeks and pools, its silver-green poplars and marsh mosses.

I had always known there was something beautiful, wonderful, sublime in those flowery dykes of Battersea Fields; in the long gravelly sweeps of that lone tidal shore, and here was a man who had put them into words for me. . . . And what specially endeared Tennyson to me, the working man, was the altogether democratic tendency of his poems. . . . Not his political opinions, of which I know nothing, but his handling of the everyday simple sights and sounds of nature. . . . That is what I call democratic art, the revelation of the poetry that lies in common things.

Not only to those shut up in cities did Tennyson give a new sense of Nature's loveliness. He opened the eyes of country dwellers to beauties and wonders they had looked on before but never really seen. Mr. Holbrook, the gentleman farmer of *Cranford*, read a review of the 1842 edition of Tennyson's poems in *Blackwood*, and at once set off, walking to the nearest town seven miles away, and ordered a copy of them. Here, in the author of the poems, he found a man who loved the beauties of Nature as well as he did, and who could help him to a fuller knowledge and appreciation of them. "The cedar spreads his dark green layers of shade," quoted Mr. Holbrook, from *The Gardener's Daughter*. "Capital term!— layers—wonderful man!" "What colour are ash-buds in March?" he asked suddenly of a visitor who was accompanying him in a walk round his fields. "I am sure I don't know, sir," replied the young lady, with the meekness of conscious ignorance.

I knew you didn't. No more did I—an old fool that I am!— till that young man comes and tells me. "Black as ash-buds in March." And I've lived all my life in the country: more shame for me not to know. Black: they are jet-black, madam.

There were those, also, for whom Tennyson's poems opened not only the bodily eye, but the eye of the imagination, so that they saw things which lay outside ordinary human vision. Charles Dickens read two of the poems, *The Merman* and *The Mermaid*, on a sunny summer morning, sitting by the sea at Broadstairs.

"Among other things," he wrote to John Forster, "the waters have dried up as they did of old, and shown me all the mermaids and mermen at the bottom of the ocean; together with millions of queer creatures, half fish and half fungus, looking down into all manner of coral caves and seaweed conservatories; and staring in with dull eyes at every open nook and loophole."

He turned over the pages until he came to *The Dream of Fair Women*, and again he saw visions, one wonderful picture following another. He wrote to Tennyson, sending him a set of his own works, and saying, "For the love I bear you as a man whose writings enlist my whole heart and nature in admiration of their Truth and Beauty, set these books upon your shelves."

Some people sneered at the simpler poems in the collection, as they had sneered at the "babyish" poems of Wordsworth. Lockhart derided them in the *Quarterly*. Others who, like Colonel Newcome, were puzzled by the higher flights of *Œnone* welcomed them eagerly. W. G. Ward, who was "almost barbarously indifferent to poetry," shed many tears over *The Children's Hospital*. The young undergraduate of Clough's *Bothie*, Hewson, "the Chartist, the poet, the eloquent speaker," read *The Miller's Daughter* with keen appreciation. Sara Coleridge specially admired *The Gardener's Daughter*. On the other hand, Mr. Maurice Baring says that, for his father, Tennyson was spoilt by the very existence of *The May Queen*. *Dora* was ridiculed by many; though Carlyle wrote to Tennyson, "Your *Dora* reminds me of the Book of Ruth," and Wordsworth declared that it was just the poem he himself had been trying to write for years.

But there was between Tennyson and his readers a deeper sympathy than that which came from his power of revealing to them new beauties in common things. He could voice their doubts and their difficulties; he could put into words the thoughts on man's duty and man's destiny that perplexed so many earnest, troubled souls. The 'forties, as we have seen, were years of both material and spiritual distress. There was poverty and want and bitter feeling between man and man; and science was, as it seemed, undermining the old religion and taking away the consolations that faith in God might give. Men looked for a prophet; and Carlyle and Ruskin gave them high and noble teaching. But they wanted something more. They wanted that swifter, more poignant penetration of the spirit which comes only through poetry; and this Tennyson gave them.

"The best and bravest of my own contemporaries," said J A. Froude, speaking of the period between 1842 and 1850, "determined to have done with insincerity, to find ground under their feet, to let the uncertain remain uncertain, but to learn how much and what we could honestly regard as true, and to believe that and live by it. Tennyson became the voice of this feeling in poetry, Carlyle in what was called prose. . . . Tennyson's Poems, the group of Poems which closed with *In Memoriam*, became to many of us what *The Christian Year* was to orthodox Churchmen. We read them, and they became part of our minds, the expression, in exquisite language, of the feelings which were working in ourselves."

Robert Browning, too, had things to say vital to his generation, but he had not yet been able to gain a hearing. *Bells and Pomegranates* went on until 1840, eight numbers in all being issued, but the general public took little notice of them. Only the few discerning admirers who from the first had recognized Browning's powers showed any satisfying appreciation. Of the number which contained a play called *A Blot in the 'Scutcheon*, Dickens wrote—

Browning's play has thrown me into a perfect passion of sorrow. To say that there is anything in its subject save what is lovely, true, deeply affecting, full of the best emotion, the most earnest feeling, and the most true and tender sort of interest, is to say that there is no light in the sun and no heat in the blood.

In 1844 came two small volumes of poetry by Miss Elizabeth Barrett. Miss Barrett was known to be an invalid, and to have published previously some philosophical poems and translations from the Greek. She was regarded as being rather uncomfortably learned, and had only a very small and select circle of readers which included Florence Nightingale and her cousin Hilary. When, in September 1846, it was announced that she had married Robert Browning and that they had gone to Italy together, there was a great deal of surprise and a little amusement. "Let us hope they will at least be intelligible to one another," said a reader who had failed to understand either of them.

For a time nothing more was heard concerning the Brownings, and soon a new poem by Tennyson engrossed the attention of the poetry-reading public. It was called *The Princess,* and in it Tennyson expressed his views on a subject in which a large number of people were keenly interested—the relative positions of man and woman in the scheme of life. By this time Tennyson's opinion carried considerable weight, and when he pronounced—

> Woman is not undevelopt man
> But diverse; could we make her as the man,
> Sweet Love were slain; his dearest bond is this
> Not like to like, but like in difference.
> Yet in the long years liker must they grow; . . .
> Till at the last she set herself to man
> Like perfect music unto noble words,

the question, with many people, was regarded as settled.

Sir William Rowan Hamilton, the mathematician, said, "It deeply presses on my reflection how much wiser a book is Tennyson's *Princess* than my *Quaternions.*" Edward White Benson, then a young man of nineteen, read the poem to his twelve-year-old cousin, Minnie Sidgwick, calling her attention especially to the passage quoted above. Smedley tells how Harry Coverdale read the poem to the ladies in Mrs. Hazlehurst's drawing-room "in a deep, rich voice, with so much feeling that surprise turned to admiration." FitzGerald did not like *The Princess.* He did not think much of anything that Tennyson wrote after 1842—with one exception. But, as he says himself, he was considered a great heretic for abusing it. In 1849 he wrote to Bernard Barton—

I heard from Miss Barton you were reading, and even liking, *The Princess.* I believe it is greatly admired in London coteries. I remain in the same mind about it.

True poetry lovers held that the best parts of *The Princess* were the exquisite songs scattered through it. "Read songs in *The Princess,*" wrote John Millais in his diary in 1851. "Have greater (if possible) veneration for Tennyson." George Lawrence liked particularly "Tears, idle tears," and so did the heroine of Mrs. Craik's *Agatha's Husband*; while Du Maurier shows Peter Ibbetson in his lonely London life mentally reciting for his "solace and delectation some beloved lyric like . . . 'Tears, idle tears,' or 'Break, break, break.' "

It was about two years after the publication of *The Princess* that Mrs. Gaskell wrote to John Forster telling him about the old handloom weaver, Samuel Bamford. He was a self-educated man who had always loved books. He had written a book himself, called *The Adventures of a Radical*, telling of the part he had taken in trying to get better conditions for working people, and he had written several poems. Now he was nearly seventy, "a great, gaunt, stalwart Lancashire man" living in decent poverty with his "neat little apple-faced wife." "Bamford is the most hearty (it's saying a good deal) admirer of Tennyson I know," wrote Mrs. Gaskell. He knew many of the poems by heart, because whenever he went into a house where a copy of them was to be found he learnt as many as he could. "Thank God, I have a good memory," he said. He would repeat these with intense enjoyment, not caring whether people liked to hear him or not. When the memory of past troubles kept him awake at night, he would find comfort in saying over the poems he had learned. More than anything else he desired a copy of his own, but he could not afford the fourteen or sixteen shillings that it cost. Would Mr. Forster, Mrs. Gaskell begged, ask Tennyson to give him one.

When Tennyson heard of the request he at once sent a copy of his poems, and Mrs. Gaskell took it to the old man's house. He had gone into the town for the market, and she went to find him. She saw him coming out of a little public-house, which was a meeting-place for farmers of the district, and she put the book into his hands. He was so overcome with delight that at first he could hardly speak. "Well, I am a proud man this day," he said at length, and opening the book began at once to read *The Sleeping Beauty*. "We left him," said Mrs. Gaskell, "in a sort of sleep-walking state, and only hope he will not be run over."

Another year, and Tennyson's fame with discerning poetry lovers reached almost its highest point. In 1850 he published *In Memoriam*, the poem commemorating his college friend, Arthur Hallam, upon which he had been at work for seventeen years. Its poignant human sadness, with the homely touches which made that sadness the more heart-rending; the wide questionings, the unflinching yet not hopeless expression of doubts and fears which many were feeling, gave it a deep, almost a painful interest. Its marvellous rhythms and harmonies, which had taxed Tennyson's most loving skill, entranced the ear. It was read with a feeling that was near to reverence.

"When I was little more than a boy," said Sir James Knowles, the architect who designed Tennyson's home at Aldworth, "I came by chance upon a copy of *In Memoriam*, then just published anonymously. I was quite entirely ignorant and indifferent in those days about all poetry, and did not in the least know or guess who had written it, but opening it at haphazard at the Geological Stanzas, was so impressed—for I was a student of Geology at the time—that I could not put the book down until I had read it all through and from end to end. I was caught up and enthralled by its spirit, and my eyes seemed suddenly opened on a whole new world. It made an epoch in my life and an ineffaceable impression. I soon came to know my Tennyson almost by heart, and was taunted by my friends for my worship of the 'divine Alfred,' as I reverently called him."

Alfred Ainger read the poem when he was about sixteen years old, and the effect that it had upon him was similar to that which it had upon Sir James Knowles.

"It was in the early 'fifties," says Miss Edith Sichel, his biographer, "that he came across *In Memoriam*, and felt he had discovered a world. He and his friend Richard Brown, together with two others, would take the book out on spring afternoons to the terrace of Somerset House and read it together there, 'sitting by the stone lions and looking across the river to the Surrey hills.' And after that some volume of Tennyson was never far from Alfred's hands."

Charlotte Brontë, with her grief for the loss of her two sisters still fresh and keen, could not take the poem to her heart, though she acknowledged its beauty.

"I have read Tennyson's *In Memoriam*," she wrote to Mrs. Gaskell, "or rather part of it. I closed the book when I got about half-way. It is beautiful; it is mournful; it is monotonous. Many of the feelings bear in their utterance the stamp of truth; yet if Arthur Hallam had been somewhat nearer Alfred Tennyson—his brother instead of his friend—I should have distrusted this rhymed and measured and printed monument of grief. What change the lapse of years may work I do not know; but it seems to me that bitter sorrow, while recent, does not flow out in verse."

But the strongest appeal of the poem was to the troubled and earnest young people—"the best and bravest," as Froude called them—who were perplexed by what seemed the contradictions between the new teaching and the old faith. Tennyson offered them no easy and final solution of their difficulties; he showed them how those difficulties could be made the means of greater and loftier attainment. Scholars like Arthur Sidgwick and scientists like Tyndall acknowledged gratefully the help they had gained from *In Memoriam*. Frederick Robertson declared, "To my mind and heart the most satisfactory things that have been said about the future state are contained in *In Memoriam*."

By this time Tennyson was recognized, not only by the select circle of poetry lovers, but also by a large section of the general public as the greatest poet of the age. When Wordsworth died in 1853 the question arose as to who should succeed him in the Laureateship. Some people suggested Mrs. Browning. Lord John Russell, who knew little about poetry, said there were "three or four authors of nearly equal merit—Henry Taylor, Sheridan Knowles, Professor Wilson, and Mr. Tennyson." But there could be no doubt about the nation's choice; and Tennyson became Poet Laureate.

It was a different England now from that in which Tennyson's early poems had made their appearance. The "hungry 'forties" were over; the prosperous 'fifties had begun. The Chartist agitation had died out. Science was making great steps forward and was helping to increase the material prosperity of the country. Religious dissensions were, for a time, in abeyance. The period of national prosperity, which the critics of the Victorian age have labelled as one of materialism and smug self-satisfaction, had set in. The chief trouble of the decade was the Crimean War, and that only touched England through her sympathy with the sufferings of her soldiers. Yet, in spite of all this, there was a large company of thinking people among whom mental unrest was, year by year, rising higher and becoming more painful. Problems of religion remained unsolved; doubts and perplexities still blocked the way; men still felt the need of a guide and a prophet.

"It is difficult for the present generation to understand," says Professor Mackail in his *Life of William Morris*, "the Tennysonian enthusiasm that then prevailed both in Oxford and in the world. All reading men were Tennysonians; all sets of reading men talked poetry." The enthusiasm for the poet does not seem, however, to have penetrated to the senior members of the University. Holman Hunt tells of a visit he paid to Oxford in 1852, when he was a young man of twenty-five. At a College breakfast he quoted some lines from Tennyson's *Golden Year*—

> . . . the fair new forms
> That float about the threshold of an age,
> Like truths of Science waiting to be caught—
> Catch me who can, and make the catcher crown'd.

"Stop, pray," said a don; "please tell us whom you quote."

"I was quoting a passage from Tennyson's *Golden Year*, which expresses my meaning better than anything I can say." "Tennyson!" was the chorus from several voices. "You don't regard Tennyson as a poet"; and some lines from the *May Queen* were quoted to settle the question. I gave up that poem as poor, but justified my admiration by quoting others, but with no effect.

Hunt held several other arguments with the College dons, but found only one who agreed with him in his estimate of Tennyson; *In Memoriam*, he says, "my courteous and learned hosts were indisposed even to consider. . . . But

I have reason to believe that had the name of the author of *Ulysses*, *In Memoriam*, and *Sir Galahad* been uttered in a company of the undergraduates of the University, its reception would have been very different from that which their elders, either in the University or outside it, gave it."

If Hunt had gone to Oxford during the next year, and talked to a newly arrived freshman, named William Fulford, he would have assured himself of this. Fulford belonged to the set which included Morris, Burne-Jones, Dixon, Faulkner, and Harry Macdonald, and he was "absolutely devoured" with admiration of Tennyson. He read the poet's works aloud to his fellows, and helped them to an appreciative understanding of what he himself loved so much. "I have listened entranced to his reading of *In Memoriam*," said William Morris. Morris was not as whole-hearted as Fulford in his Tennyson worship. Sir Galahad he thought "a rather mild youth"; there was a bullying element in *Locksley Hall*; and as for *The Princess* and *Lady Clare*, they could not be called poetry. But Fulford would hear of no flaw in his idol, and most of the little group agreed with him. Burne-Jones wrote to his Birmingham friend, Cornell Price, who did not come up to Oxford until a year later than the others—

If Tennyson affords you as many hours of unmitigated happiness as he has to me, you will look with gratitude to any who helped you to appreciate him.

Price, in reply, testified to the enjoyment he had gained from the poet's works—

I think one song in *The Princess* remarkable: "Tears, idle tears." In some hot, dreamy afternoons I have thought upon it for hours, until I have been exquisitely miserable.

Not content with lauding his hero at Oxford, Fulford aspired to gain more worshippers for him among his Birmingham friends. Frequent meetings were held during the vacations, chiefly at the house of Cornell Price. The young people sat round a small oak table and listened while Fulford read to them the poems he loved. One evening it is recorded that he read *The Palace of Art*, *The Vision of Sin*, and *Œnone*. After the reading there was much lively discussion and argument. Occasionally works by other writers were admitted, but Tennyson's poems formed the staple provision, and enthusiasm for him rose high.

At Cambridge things were much the same as at Oxford. Walter Besant says that while he was there, from 1855–58, Tennyson was in everybody's hands. Boyd Carpenter, afterwards Bishop of Ripon, who went up in 1860, says that Tennyson was then the oracle among the younger men, but the older ones were critical, and charged him with being obscure and sometimes meaningless. He remembered a friendly dispute between the Senior and a Junior Fellow of his own College, in which the younger failed to explain with precision what was the meaning of a passage from *In Memoriam* quoted by the elder.

It was a typical conflict; the older generation could not understand; the younger was under the spell of the poet, and though unable to interpret everything, believed in Tennyson's message to his own age.

The Crimean War began in 1854; and in 1855 came *Maud*, which owed some of its inspiration to the struggle. It was received with tremendous enthusiasm. Even FitzGerald, who since *The Princess* had despaired of Tennyson, admitted that here was real poetry. Five thousand copies were sold on the day of publication. Walter Besant, then a boy of nineteen, read it on the beach at Freshwater. "I had seen the splendid fleets of which he spoke go forth to war," he said. "Heaven! how the lines at the end of *Maud* rang in my brain." Mark Rutherford read it as he walked along Holborn at six o'clock in the morning towards Paternoster Row, where (having given up the ministry) he worked as a publisher's assistant. Swinburne was enchanted with it. He had a great love for Tennyson, "into whose church," he said, "I and all my generation were baptized." While he was an undergraduate at Oxford he went to stay at St. Peter's College, Radley, a boys' school, of which William Sewell, a friend of the Swinburnes, was warden. He joined the boys in their play hours, and all went well until he attended a meeting of the School Debating Society, where the resolution for discussion was "That *Maud* detracts from the poet's reputation." In spite of Swinburne's indignant opposition the motion was carried, and he rushed from the room, crying angrily, "You're a lot of Philistines!"

One of the most beautiful tributes to *Maud* came from James Smetham. "Read *Maud*," he noted in his Journal, "a very complete story, told with flying hints and musical echoes; as though Ariel had piped it in the little wild island of *The Tempest*."

Another Tennysonian poem inspired by the war was *The Charge of the Light Brigade*. A chaplain to the forces in the Crimea wrote to a friend at home—

The greatest service you can do just now is to send out on printed slips Mr. Alfred Tennyson's *Charge of Balaclava*. It is the greatest favourite with the soldiers; half are singing it, and all want to have it in black and white so as to read what has so taken them.

The request was made known to Tennyson, and he at once arranged for slips to be sent out, and they were distributed among the troops. One man who had taken part in the charge was still in hospital, ill and depressed. The poem was read to him while leeches were being applied. His eyes kindled and his depression vanished; in a few days he was discharged. Whether the cure was effected by the leeches or the poem it is impossible to say, but the doctor on giving him his discharge-card murmured, "Well done, Mr. Tennyson."

All through the 'fifties Tennyson's popularity was spreading. Dean Farrar, Lewis Carroll, Sophia Jex Blake, and Frederick Myers are representative of various sections of his many admirers. He became the fashion. Novelists made their characters quote Tennyson instead of Byron. *Harry Coverdale* shows "blue" young ladies, with red noses and sharp tongues, discoursing earnestly on obscure passages in Tennyson's poems, mixed up with Ruskin and Carlyle and pre-Raphaelitism and the "dark Brownings"; while Horace D'Almayne, "the greatest dandy and most incorrigible male flirt about town," rhapsodized on

that charming soul creation of Tennyson, *Locksley Hall*. What an unrivalled picture does it not present of the spirit torture of a proud despair.

And even the schoolboy, Tom Hazlehurst, knew enough of "that stunning poet, Tennyson" to misquote him.

Meanwhile the "dark Brownings" were living happily in Italy, paying only short and infrequent visits to England. Mrs. Browning's *Sonnets from the Portuguese* were published, with some other poems, in 1850, and raised her name so high that she was, as has been said, mentioned with Tennyson as a possible successor to the Laureateship. When Charlotte Brontë came to London in February 1850, she found that at all the fashionable assemblies to which she was taken Mrs. Browning was a favourite subject of conversation. Charlotte wrote to her old schoolmistress, Miss Wooler—

It seems now very much the custom to admire a certain wordy, intricate, obscure style of poetry, such as Elizabeth Barrett Browning writes. Some pieces were referred to about which Currer Bell was expected to be very rapturous, and, failing this, he disappointed.

In 1855 came a poem from each of the Brownings, *Men and Women* by Robert, and *Aurora Leigh* by Mrs. Browning. The first attracted little notice, the second made a great sensation. Some people admired it immensely, some declared it unfit for the reading of pure-minded persons. There were elderly ladies, we are told, who complained that they had never felt pure since reading the work. Young ladies, if they read it at all, did so surreptitiously, under fear of shocked displeasure if discovered.

FitzGerald hated the book. Coventry Patmore wrote to George Allingham—

> Have you read *Aurora Leigh*? Is it not strange that writers—and still more strange that readers—should prefer shrieking G or F to singing E or D? . . .
> *Aurora Leigh* is a strange book for a modest, sensible little woman like Mrs. Browning to have written.

Clerk Maxwell, however, read the poem and liked it; and in 1857 George Eliot wrote to Miss Sara Hennell—

> We are reading *Aurora Leigh* for the third time with more enjoyment than ever. I know no book that gives me a deeper sense of communion with a large as well as a beautiful mind. It is in process of appearing in a third edition, and no wonder.

Sydney Dobell read the poem for the first time in 1857, and wrote a rapturous eulogy of it to one of his friends beginning—

> I am reading it with great admiration. It contains some of the finest poetry written in the century; poetry such as Shakespeare's sister might have written if he had had a twin. The same voice with the female difference in it. . . . But it is no poem. No woman can write a poem.

Both praise and blame helped to sell the book, but Mrs. Browning was more outraged by the neglect of her husband's work than pleased by the recognition given to her own.

"I set it down as infamy of that public—no other word," she wrote indignantly to a friend. "I don't complain myself of an unappreciating public—*I have no reason*. . . . To you I may say that the blindness, deafness, and stupidity of the English public to Robert are amazing. . . . Nobody there, except a small knot of pre-Raffaelite men, pretends to do him justice."

Browning, for his part, was overjoyed at his wife's success, whole-heartedly believing her poetry to be better than his own. He was not entirely despondent with regard to himself. If his admirers were few, they included some of the finest intellects in the country. Carlyle and Dickens had been among them from the first, and now some younger men were coming in. Rossetti had written to him saying that he had come across a copy of *Pauline* in the British Museum Reading Room, and had been so struck with it that he had copied out the whole poem; and Mr. Quillinan, Wordsworth's son-in-law, was an ardent disciple.

At Oxford Browning's voice was only just beginning to be heard. Many of the undergraduates did not know even the name of the poet who had been writing as long as their idol, Tennyson. Lord Bryce tells of a meeting held in Swinburne's rooms in 1858, at which the host repeated *The Statue and the Bust, The Heretic's Tragedy,* and *Bishop Blougram's Apology.* In the discussion that followed it was revealed that only one of those present had read any work by Browning. There were a few undergraduates, however, who were more enlightened. By 1856 William Morris's group had got hold of *Men and Women,* and were eagerly discussing *Bishop Blougram's Apology,* and in the same year Burne-Jones wrote to a Birmingham friend, Miss Charlotte Salt, urging her to read Browning's poems.

You won't at first like him much, perhaps, he is too different from anyone else to be liked at first sight by most, but he is the deepest and intensest of all poets—writes lower down in the deep heart of things—rises up to the seemingly clear surface less often. Oh, how ten lines of him help one!

At Cambridge no one, says Walter Besant, seemed to have heard of Robert Browning. Besant himself read none of the poet's works until after going down. The poems in the 1850 volume, although they were less obscure than *Sordello,* yet required closer attention and study than most readers were willing to give. Edward Lushington, who had married Tennyson's sister, found them very hard reading.

"I have been trying to construe them," he said, "and no gold had ever to be digged out through more stubborn rocks. But he is a poet as well as a good fellow."

With such small meed of recognition Browning had to be content; and he soon became absorbed in writing a new work, more ambitious than any he had attempted before. Tennyson also had embarked on his largest, most comprehensive poetical undertaking. In 1859 he published a volume containing the first four of the *Idylls of the King*, and with this volume he became a really popular poet. Professor Bradley says that it "opened to him the heart of the public and began that immense popularity which he never saw diminished." The succeeding *Idylls*, which came within the next ten years, extended and strengthened this popularity. To the ordinary mid-Victorian reader they contained the essence of poetry as well as the highest spiritual teaching. Macaulay read them in his quiet retirement at Holly Lodge.

"I like it extremely," he said of *Guinevere*, "notwithstanding some faults, extremely. The parting of Lancelot and Guinevere, her penitence, and Arthur's farewell are all very affecting. I cried over some passages."

William Ayton wrote to John Blackwood, "About Tennyson, I have as yet read only the first of the stories, *Enid*, which I sipped like cream. It is *very good*."

Tennyson's more severely critical readers saw in the *Idylls* much to deplore. FitzGerald, Swinburne, and Carlyle looked upon them as a terrible falling-off from the heights that had been reached in 1842. As time went on more and more readers took up this critical attitude. Some were ready to attribute their lack of appreciation to a deficiency in themselves. Robert Bridges, who was a boy at Eton while the early *Idylls* were appearing, said that although he had loved and learnt by heart some of Tennyson's lyrics—

Yet when I heard the *Idylls of the King* praised as if they were the final attainment of all poetry, then I drew into my shell, contented to think that I might be too stupid to understand, but that I could never expect as good a pleasure from following another's taste as I got from my own I remember how I submissively concluded that it must be my own dullness that prevented my admiring Tennyson as much as William Johnson did.

Many, like George Eliot, criticized tenderly and with reluctance.

"I was a little uneasy on Sunday," George Eliot wrote to Mr. Cross, "because I had seemed in the unmanageable current of talk to echo a too slight way of speaking about a great poet. I did not mean to say Amen when the *Idylls of the King* seemed to be judged *de haut en bas*. I only meant that I should value for my own mind *In Memoriam* as the chief of the larger works; and that while I feel exquisite beauty in passages scattered through the *Idylls*, I must judge some smaller wholes among the lyrics as the works most decisive of Tennyson's high place among the immortals."

Others threw all allegiance to the winds and mocked freely and openly. Meredith called Arthur a "crowned curate," and said that his answer to Guinevere should have been "Get up!" Swinburne went so far as to write, for the amusement of his friends, a burlesque in which Queen Victoria figured as Guinevere and Lord John Russell as Lancelot. One of the devoutest Tennyson worshippers, James Smetham, discerned, as early as 1864, some slight change in the attitude of the public towards the popular poet—

Took down *Tennyson*. That book has a charm for me that no other book but the Bible has. It is like moonlight and music and the shores of old romance and "the light that never was on sea or land." . . . The *rabies* for Tennyson has passed with the public, but he has taken his immortal seat among the poets.

Four years later John Addington Symonds wrote to Mrs. Clough—

Have you observed that we are going to have an insurrection against Tennyson? . . . I have sympathized with this revolt, having been a slave as a boy, and spoilt my taste and style by absurd reverence for the faults of our great poet.

That robust critic, Mortimer Collins, brother of the more famous Wilkie, summed up the talk that was going round in a malicious verse—

> Is Tennyson no poet? Yes, indeed,
> "Miss Alfred's" are delicious books to read. . . .
> Ethics of Dr. Watts; Colenso's creed,
> Those nice green volumes give you all you need.

Of the Brownings little was heard until, in 1861, came the news of Mrs. Browning's death at Florence. Soon afterwards Robert Browning came back to England and settled in London; and now at last recognition came to him. His little band of admirers grew rapidly. "In the early 'sixties Browning was very much in the air," said Miss Elizabeth Wordsworth, who was at school at Brighton at this time, and an eager reader of the poet's works. "Do you ever read Browning's poems?" wrote Henry Sidgwick to his friend, H. C. Dakyns, in 1862; "they form my light reading at present." Robert Francillon, who had lately left Oxford, and was living with his brother in chambers in Mitre Court, recalls how they two, with a friend, George Stott, read the poems together. "Browning had no more thorough devotees," he says.

Dramatis Personæ was published in 1864, and was eagerly read, in spite of the *Edinburgh Review,* which found it "a subject of amazement that poems of so obscure and uninviting a character should find numerous readers." A new edition was called for within the year. In 1868 appeared *The Ring and the Book,* the great poem on which Browning had been working for some years, and with this came his full triumph. Enthusiasm for him rose as high, though it was not as universal, as enthusiasm for Tennyson. He, in his turn, had become the fashion. To admire his works was regarded as the test of a fine literary taste. His obscurities were regarded by his followers with pride as distinctions which put his poetry out of reach of the vulgar. In all places where intellectuals or would-be intellectuals met, he was the subject of conversation, and there was the inevitable comparison between his work and that of Tennyson. "Browning and Tennyson were being worked as hard as cab-horses, and used up pretty much as those quadrupeds," said Ouida, describing the conversation at one of these functions.

Soon Browning's works made their appearance in schoolrooms, both public and private, and the generation that was growing up studied his works with almost reverent earnestness. Mrs. Fawcett tells how her younger sisters vied with each other in learning his poems by heart. Mrs. Benson—the Minnie of *The Princess* days, who had married her cousin Edward in 1859—was his fervent admirer, and brought up her children in his worship. Miss Beale of Cheltenham College gave him the highest place among poets and quoted him often in her talks to her pupils. For the elder girls she had regular readings of his works, and they caught something of her enthusiasm.

The earlier works shared in the popularity that the later ones had gained. Mark Rutherford tells how he read *Pippa Passes* with delight, late at night in his dark little lodging in Serle Street. Swinburne wrote to his Oxford friend, Hutch, who was then curate of an East End parish, "I long to be with you by firelight, between the sunset and the sea, to have talk of *Sordello.* It is one of my canonical Scriptures."

On the other side were the readers who disapproved and mocked. Carlyle, though he allowed *The Ring and the Book* some merits said that it was "among the absurdest books written by a gifted man." Frederick Tennyson could not find courage to attempt it. Browning, he said, was one of his great friends. "But it does not follow that I should put up with obsolete horrors and unrhythmical composition." Henry Arthur Jones tried two or three of Browning's poems—

but he is a dreadful heavy dumpling, the toughest and hardest baked I ever stuck my jaws into.

James Smetham read three volumes of *The Ring and the Book*

with a curious mixture of impatience and admiration. To find every character thinking and talking Browning is like drinking strong coffee that swells the nerves and causes a dull ache over the eyes.

Mrs. Panton (Walter Frith's daughter) confessed that she still much preferred Mrs. Browning's works to her husband's, although after very severe struggles she had learnt to appreciate *The Ring and the Book*. Walter Besant was a harsher critic—

It is considered rather a mark of distinction, a separating seal upon the brow, by that poet's admirers to reverence his later works. Their creed is that because a poem is rough, harsh, ungrammatical, and dark, it must have a meaning as deep as its black obscurity.

In his *Golden Butterfly* (1873) Besant showed a reader—an American visiting England—wrestling with Browning's *Red Cotton Nightcap Country* published in 1872—

When the clock struck six he was sitting among the volumes on the table, with *Red Cotton Nightcap Country* still in his hand. His eyes were bloodshot, his hair was pushed in disorder about his head, his hands were trembling, the nerves in his face were twitching. He looked about him wildly and tried to collect his faculties. Then he arose and solemnly cursed Robert Browning. He cursed him eating, drinking, and sleeping. And then he took all his volumes, and disposing them carefully in the fireplace, he set light to them. "I wish," he said, "that I could put the poet there too." I think he would have done it, this mild and gentle-hearted stranger, so strongly was his spirit moved to wrath.

All through the 'sixties and the 'seventies Browning's fame grew, and the tradition of his obscurity grew with it. The tendency of a certain type of Browningite to look down with contemptuous satisfaction on those who said they could not understand *Sordello,* or could not get through *The Ring and the Book,* became more and more marked. When, in 1881, Dr. Furnivall proposed to establish a London Browning Society, for the purpose of studying the poet's works, most of the worshippers felt that this was not only a fitting tribute to a great genius, but also a means of distinguishing between readers of cultivated taste and intelligence and the crowd of common men. "They praise Browning's poetry chiefly because they believe that they alone understand it," wrote Andrew Lang. About two hundred people joined the Society, mostly ordinary middle-class men and women, but including some—Bishop Westcott, G. B. Shaw, J. T. Nettleship, Mrs. Orr, and Dr. Berdoe—who were more distinguished. Lady Eastlake says that she was asked to join, but she pleaded too great stupidity, and was excused. Ridicule was poured upon the Society from every side, but it kept bravely on. "Imagine a man abetting all this," said FitzGerald contemptuously.

Soon Dr. Furnivall's example was being followed all over the country, and Browning Societies were rising in the Universities, in the London suburbs, and in provincial towns. These shared the ridicule bestowed upon the parent organization. Ellen Terry said she believed that most people would have taken Browning's poetry straightforwardly and read it with a fair amount of ease

if certain enthusiasts had not founded societies for making his crooked places plain, and (to me) his plain places very crooked. These societies have terrorized the ordinary reader into letting Browning alone.

It might be thought that with all this Browning worship Tennyson would be forgotten. But he still kept his place with the great body of English readers as *the* poet of the age, though he was no longer set so high as to be unapproachable.

The attitude of the general public towards the poets of the day is indicated by Austin Dobson in his poem *Incognita,* where the writer tells how he met on a train journey a charming young lady, who chattered prettily about the popular novelists and poets—·

> "Like Browning?" But so-so. His proof lay
>   Too deep for her frivolous mood,
> That preferred your more metrical soufflé
>   To the stronger poetical food;
> Yet at times he was good—as a tonic,
>   Was Tennyson writing just now?
> And was this new poet Byronic
>   And clever and naughty or how?

Mr. W. L. Courtney, writing of his college days (the late 'sixties) shows in much the same way as the young lady in the train how the honours were divided—

In the days when I was at Oxford masterpieces used to appear in regular order. To a new enigma of Browning would succeed a poem by Tennyson. Then came the grave, philosophic muse of Matthew Arnold, and last but by no means least, the rich, emotional picturesque of Algernon Swinburne.

Concerning the readers of these two latter poets something will be said in another connection. Neither Arnold nor Swinburne ever attained to anything like the popularity of Tennyson. To him the mid-Victorians remained faithful, even when the inevitable reaction against him came.

"I have always loved his poetry, as a true mid-Victorian should do," said Lady Battersea in her *Recollections*, "and am annoyed with some critics of the present day for belittling his genius."

But Miss Jane Harrison chose the more excellent way: "When I hear young reactionaries say he is no poet at all, I think them simply silly."

CHAPTER X

THE BROWNS OF ENGLAND

No Englishman or Englishwoman needs an introduction to the Browns. Many of us can boast with Thomas Hughes of being "nearly connected with an eminently respectable branch of the great Brown family," or at least of having been brought up with several worthy Browns as our neighbours and companions. For to quote Thomas Hughes once more—

For centuries, in their quiet, dogged, homespun way, they have been subduing the earth in most English counties, and leaving their mark in American forests and Australian uplands.

They have been toiling and fighting in the armies which the men belonging to more brilliant families have led—

getting hard knocks and hard work in plenty, which was on the whole what they looked for, and the best thing for them; and little praise or pudding, which indeed they, and most of us, are better without.

In the early years of the reign of Queen Victoria the Browns were as prolific, as obstinate, as staunch, and as active a family as they have always been. They had settled themselves in quiet corners all over the country on the broad acres that their fathers' toil, or their own, had won, and there they tilled the land and kept law and order in their boundaries, and hunted and shot and fished and kept up the old customs of their fathers, and reared large families of sons and daughters, some to stay at home and reign in their turn, some to go out and spread the Brown tradition in crowded cities and in new lands across the seas. In whatever district of England a stranger came to settle the chances were that one of his first acquaintances would be a Brown. If there was not a clan headed by the squire, there would be a farmer, a doctor, a lawyer, a parson, a retired army officer, or an Anglo-Indian come to end his days in the old familiar English country that he and all his brother Browns rated far above the glories of the East.

It was easy to recognize a Brown in those Victorian days, even when, as often happened, the branch of the family to which he belonged no longer bore the family name. The Browns, said Thomas Hughes, were a fighting stock, and were to be found "wherever hard knocks, visible or invisible," were going. They were quixotic, and could never leave "the most disreputable lame dog on the other side of the stile," and so obstinate that they would never listen to the advice of sensible people and mind their own business.

It must always be a matter of regret that the authentic annals of the Brown family should be as scanty as they unfortunately are; but it is clear that we could not reasonably expect this to be otherwise. Few of the Browns pushed themselves sufficiently into public notice to be deemed worthy of a *Life*; and as for writing his autobiography, a Brown would as soon have thought of showing himself at church on Sunday in his shirt-sleeves. It has happened sometimes, however, that the sons of the family have, through sheer force of character, and sticking to their job, found themselves, to their own surprise, eminent public figures; or they have developed an un-Brownlike brilliance which has had a similar result. Of these, biographies have been written which have contained a few details concerning their fathers and the habits of their clan. Outstanding examples of such are Robert Evans, father of George Eliot, Archdeacon Froude, who had two brilliant sons, Charles Kingsley the elder, and Thomas Stevenson. Occasionally, too, there are references to the Browns in the memoirs of more distinguished people, and such scanty gleanings here and there make up the store of information that our authentic annals can afford of this prolific and widespread family.

Yet the history of the Brown family under Victoria has been written, and written with sympathy and understanding. The squires of England and their progeny seem to have had an irresistible fascination for the novelists of the period—which proves them to have been an interesting as well as a worthy and a lovable race. In novel after novel Mr. Brown and his household appear under varying names, but easily recognizable as of the same kin. Scarcely one of the Victorian novelists, major or minor, but presents to our notice some of these hardy English growths.

Some of the country squires thus presented are of the stolid, stupid, coarse species—like the gross clown of Tennyson's *Locksley Hall*, who cared little for anything except his horse, his dog, and his wine. But these are not true Browns, and need not be considered here. They held no rank among the readers of the nation.

From authentic records, then, aided by fiction, we are able to make out something concerning the reading habits of the Browns. From a first study emerge certain facts applying generally to the tribe. The Browns were not great readers. They read the fine old solid books their fathers had read, and they had nearly always a few special favourites of their own—often out-of-the-way and little-read works chosen to satisfy a strong individual taste. They were slow in taking up new ideas, and their reading was little influenced by popular movements or fashionable crazes. The Browns, at least the older members of the family, were distrustful of the Oxford Movement as tending to Popery, and read little of its literature except the *Christian Year*. The Dissenters, as a body, they held in greater disfavour than the Tractarians, and would have scorned to be bound by such restrictions on their reading as were imposed by the creed of the "Chapel folks." They were, for the most part, sturdy Church and Queen men, loyal to the core, but holding that in matters private and personal a Brown knew best what it befitted a Brown to do. They were soft-hearted and deeply moved by such appeals as *The Cry of the Children* and *The Song of the Shirt*, but on the whole the books dealing with social matters did not much trouble the older generation, though they touched the consciences of the sons. The Browns had long ago solved their own social problem by accepting responsibility for their immediate dependants and poorer neighbours, and working hard—with many grumbles usually, and some harsh words—in their service. As for current poetry and fiction, they left it, a little contemptuously, alone; except when some truly national writer appealed to their deep-rooted sympathies and convictions, and then their response was ready. Tennyson, in some of his moods, made this appeal, and Dickens never failed.

Most Brown households possessed a library. It contained a collection of English classics gathered through several generations, and added to by the reigning Brown of the day. When one of these gentlemen felt that his library was inadequate, he made a journey to London and called on one of those old-fashioned booksellers, "a man of fine taste and fastidious choice," of whom Mr. Arthur Waugh has told us in *A Hundred Years of Publishing*. The bookseller gave his advice carefully and conscientiously, and presently copies of those books without reading which "no gentleman's education is complete" travelled down to the corner of England inhabited by that particular Brown, and took their places on his library shelves beside the older English classics and the Latin and Greek works that he and his fathers before him had brought down from Oxford or Cambridge.

It has often been said that these books were never taken from the shelves, and that Squire Brown when he retired to his library seated himself in a comfortable chair before the fire and went to sleep. This may sometimes have happened, for after many hours spent in the open air slumber is apt to overcome the desire for intellectual enjoyment. But that many of the Browns did read, with intelligence and appreciation, we have the testimony of the authorities before-cited, the Victorian novelists, who were privileged to accompany these gentlemen into their libraries and watch their doings there. Anthony Trollope, in *Barchester Towers*, testifies to the industry of that staunch and delightful Brown, Squire Thorne of Ullathorne.

He was a man of considerable literary attainments in a certain way and on certain subjects. His favourite authors were Montaigne and Burton, and he knew more perhaps than any other man in his own county, and the next to it, of the English essayists of the last two centuries. He possessed complete sets of *The Idler*, *The Spectator*, *The Tatler*, *The Guardian*, and *The Rambler*; and would discourse by hours together on the superiority of such publications to anything which has since been produced in our *Edinburghs* and *Quarterlies*.

His sister, Miss Thorne—a pretty old lady, who wore always a rich silk dress and a dainty white lace cap on her short, crisp, grey curls—also possessed the Brown traits in a high state of development.

She would not open a modern quarterly, did not choose to see a magazine in her drawing-room, and would not have polluted her fingers with a shred of *The Times* for any consideration. She spoke of Addison, Swift, and Steele as though they were still living, regarded De Foe as the best known novelist of his country and thought of Fielding as a young but meritorious novice in the fields of romance. In poetry, she was familiar with names as late as Dryden, and had once been seduced into reading *The Rape of the Lock*, but she regarded Spenser as the purest type of her country's literature in this line.

"Such," said Trollope, after having given a detailed account of their home, characters, tastes, and habits, "a year or two since were the Thornes of Ullathorne. Such, we believe, are the inhabitants of many an English country home. May it be long before their number diminishes." In some of his other novels he takes us into several of these homes, and shows us various members of the great Brown family leading the active, wholesome lives natural to them. There is Dr. Thorne, second cousin of the Thornes of Ullathorne. There is stern Squire Dale of *The Small House at Allington*, chivalrous Sir Peregrine Cleeve of *Orley Farm*, and loyal, downright Will Belton of *The Belton Estate*. Unfortunately, Trollope does not, in the case of any of these, give us those full details concerning their reading which he supplied in the case of the Thornes of Ullathorne. Dr. Thorne, we are told, possessed a collection of standard works, and superintended the reading of his niece, Mary, so that by the time she reached young ladyhood she was familiar with all the best English authors; Will Belton, on his own confession, read little. The other two had fine libraries, but what use they made of them is not revealed.

There was a fine library, too, at Glossop Grange, in the county of York, where—as Mortimer Collins tell us in his *Two Plunges for a Pearl*—for many generations the Glossops had lived in true Brown fashion, ruling their small estate with beneficent, autocratic hand. They were a bookish race, and they had always sought out those rare books whose names, even, are scarcely known to the common reader.

Few are the writers who are popular, and whose works are easily obtainable, by reason of actual greatness. Numerous enough are the popular authors whose popularity is due to their being thoroughly bad. Between the serene sphere of Shakespeare and Homer, kings of thought, and the slime of—well, never mind whom—there is a mediate region where dwell those to whom is given audience fit though few. Quaint are their rhyme and prose, of delicate flavour, conveying tortuous thoughts and capricious fancies. How often is a *rare book* of rare intrinsic qualities.

It was books such as these that were to be found on the shelves of the Glossop library, where

Blake's *Marriage of Heaven and Hell* jostled Collins' *Scripscrapologia*; where *The Land of Sinai*, and *The Bravo of Bohemia* had impudently inserted themselves amid a royal row of Baskerville classics.

When the direct line of the Glossops died out, as it did towards the middle of the reign of Queen Victoria, the succession passed to a distant member of the family, one Launcelot Lydiard. Fortunately, he was a true Brown, and loved the library as much as his predecessors had done. Especially he revelled in the rare periodicals it contained—Sylvanus Urban's *Gentleman's Magazine*, *The Town and Country Magazine*, *The Ladies' Diary*, *The Spectator*, *The Tatler*, Coleridge's *Friend*, Canning's *Microcosm*, Praed's *Etonian*. Over these he spent many delightful hours.

Mr. Holbrook, of *Cranford*, that "tall, thin, Don Quixote-looking old man," who was one of Tennyson's early admirers, was almost as much attached to old customs and old ideas as was Miss Thorne herself. He refused to be called squire, saying that his property was not large enough to entitle him to rank higher than a yeoman.

He rejected all domestic innovations; he would have the house door stand open in summer and shut in winter without knocker or bell to summon a servant. The closed fist or the knob of a stick did this office for him if he found the door locked. He despised every refinement which had not its root deep down in humanity.

He dined in a fine, oak-lined kitchen, and supplied his guests—much to their embarrassment—with two-pronged, black-handled forks with which to eat his delicious green peas. Yet Mr. Holbrook was a great reader. His own special sitting-room was filled to overflowing with books of all sorts, poetry and wild, weird tales prevailing. He quoted freely and naturally from Shakespeare and George Herbert, Byron and Goethe, as well as from the poets of his own day; and he had that mark of a true Brown, he "chose his books in accordance with his own tastes, not because such and such were classical or established favourites." Mr. Holbrook lived only four or five miles out of Cranford, yet he never seems to have met that other delightful member of his clan, gallant Captain Brown. They would perhaps have disagreed, as Browns often did when they met, and they might have had great arguments concerning the merits of their favourite books; but they would certainly have fraternized over *Pickwick*.

Charles and Henry Kingsley, who themselves only escape being classed as Browns because their genius places them in a higher category, had a sympathetic understanding of the family's faults as well as of its virtues. Dr. Tom Thurnall, of *Two Years Ago*, is perhaps the finest representative the novelists have shown us of the wandering Brown, who, having sought his fortune in the wild and remote places of the earth, comes home at last to end his days in his native village. In his youth Tom despised poetry, and derided his fellow-apprentice, a budding poet, for hanging entranced over *Percy's Reliques* when he ought to have been making up draughts and pills; but he seems to have managed, in spite of his adventurous life, to read widely, if not very deeply, for he shows some acquaintance with Elizabethan poetry generally, and especially with Ben Jonson's *Alchemist*, he can quote from Rochester and Dibdin, Byron and Shelley, talks familiarly of the novels of Charlotte Brontë and of Dickens, and acknowledges that one of his favourite books is "old Darwin's *Loves of the Plants*; bosh as it is in a scientific point of view, it amuses one's fancy without making one lose one's temper." A good deal of Tom's familiarity with books was doubtless due to his father, the quiet, devoted village doctor, a true Brown, whose allegiance was divided between the botanists and the poets.

Henry Kingsley also shows a father and son of the authentic Brown stock. Squire Densil Ravenshoe, of *Ravenshoe* was, unlike most of the family, of the Roman Catholic faith. He was not a great reader, although there was a fine library at his beautiful home on the Devonshire coast. It contained some rare books—a copy of *Bewick's Birds* dated 1799, and the works of the Fathers of the Church, as well as those of the poets old and new, and the novels of Dickens.

Lord Lytton, in his later novels, introduces us to some very attractive Victorian Browns. Captain Roland Caxton, of *The Caxtons*, is a splendid specimen of the brave and upright soldiers that the family gave, in large numbers, to their country. In his youth he read all the poetry and books of chivalry to be found in his father's library, which was rich in such works; and when he retired from active service and went to live in his ancestral tower in Cumberland, he arranged his library on some stout oaken shelves in his own room, where his sword hung over the chimney-piece.

There they were, Froissart, Barante, Joinville, the *Morte d'Arthur*, Amadis of Gaul, Spenser's *Faery Queen*, a noble copy of Strutt's *Horda*, Mallet's *Northern Antiquities*, *Percy's Reliques*, Pope's *Homer*, books on gunnery, archery, hawking, fortification— old chivalry and modern war, together cheek by jowl.

Sir Peter Chillingly, of *Kenelm Chillingly*, was also an authentic member of the widespread Brown family.

Although belonging to that class of country gentlemen to whom certain political reasoners deny the intelligence vouchsafed to other members of the community, Sir Peter was not without a considerable degree of book-learning, and a great taste for speculative philosophy.

We gather that Sir Peter's library contained John Locke's *On the Human Understanding*, the works of Sir Kenelm Digby and those of Voltaire, *Tristram Shandy*, and many philosophical works. Sir Peter's cousin, the Reverend John Stalworth Chillingly, was "a decided adherent to the creed of what is called muscular Christianity, and a very fine specimen of it too." A good many of the Browns inclined to muscular Christianity, of which Charles Kingsley was held to be the great exponent. The Reverend John was

a great reader of poetry, but he disliked Scott and Byron, whom he considered flashy and noisy; he maintained that Pope was only a versifier, and that the greatest poet in the language was Wordsworth; he did not care much for the ancient classics.

Dickens was not very well acquainted with the country Browns, and his second-hand impressions only served to produce Mr. Wardle, who, with a good many Brown traits, is scarcely up to the family level of intelligence. With city Browns he was happier. Traddles, of *David Copperfield*, bears all the authentic marks, from the days when, as a poor law-student living in a bed-sitting-room, he arranged his few books neatly on a shelf, with his boot-brushes and blacking hidden behind a dictionary, until, having become a famous barrister, he is possessed of a spacious family residence, complete with a fine library. Then there is Canon Crisparkle, of *Edwin Drood*, whose modest book-room is well stored with college prizes and Greek and Latin and English classics, all constantly and lovingly read. Tom Pinch, had he been a little more robust and a little harder headed, would have been a model Brown. He had the true Brown taste in books, though he possessed few of his own; he would stand outside the bookshops gazing at the wealth within, and coveting, beyond all the "spick-and-span new works," those volumes with "many a grave portrait and time-honoured name, whose matter he knew well." Mr. Pickwick himself, by virtue of a simplicity of character, an amiable obstinacy, and an active stirring on behalf of his fellow-men, may claim to be at least a connection of the family. We hear of no books that he took with him in the expeditions that he made as head of the Corresponding Society of the Pickwick Club, but when he settled down in a house of his own he stocked it with "books out of number," which Sam Weller read aloud "with such remarks as suggested themselves to his mind which never failed to afford Mr. Pickwick great amusement." They would doubtless afford us great amusement too, if only we could hear them; but they, with the names of the books that were read, remain unrecorded.

Smedley's books contain portraits of many Browns. Sir John Oaklands, of *Frank Fairlegh*, is one; his library contained a fine collection of books, including such legal works as *Blackstone*, *Coke upon Lyttelton*, and *De Lolme*; and Squire Hazlehurst, of *Harry Coverdale*, had a poetic section which contained Rogers' *Pleasures of Memory* and the works of Byron and Tennyson. The large company of squires assembled by Miss Braddon are either of the completely unintellectual type, like Squire Tempest of *Vixen*, who read nothing except the *Sporting Magazine*, *Nimrod*, and *Assheton Smith's Memoirs*, or they are would-be Browns, somewhat spoiled by more luxurious living than the family tradition authorized. Their libraries were magnificent apartments, adorned with rare treasures of art; and although some of the shelves held soberly bound editions of classic works, dating from the sixteenth century or earlier, there was usually a preponderance of handsome volumes in bindings of scarlet and gold, representing the fashionable literature of the day. The same falling away from the severe simplicity of the unspoiled Browns is shown in the squirearchy of Rhoda Broughton and Helen Mathers; but most of its members read the old books, with Dickens and Tennyson—if they read anything at all. As to the immensely popular Mrs. Henry Wood, she contributes nothing to our knowledge of the clan. Her squires are too wooden and conventional to deserve consideration; and when, in *East Lynne*, she tried to create a really superior Brown, in the person of the country lawyer, Mr. Carlyle, she produced only an incredibly unattractive puppet.

To Thackeray belongs the honour of having shown to the world a Brown in his highest development—a Brown true and unspoiled, with all the honourable family marks upon him. That simple-hearted, gallant gentleman, Colonel Newcome, is the head of the clan. He sets such a lofty standard that it would be unreasonable to expect many of the family to approach it very nearly; yet all who claim to be his kinsmen must show proofs of affinity to him. This is the infallible Brown test.

The Colonel set an example—which, most regrettably, the other Browns did not follow—of stating, fully and clearly, his tastes in literature. We know which were his favourite books, and why he liked them. During the years he had spent as a soldier he had taken with him upon all his journeys Boswell's *Life of Johnson*, Caesar, Tacitus, *The Spectator*, *Don Quixote*, and *Sir Charles Grandison*. "I read these, sir," he used to say, "because I like to be in the company of gentlemen; and Sir Roger de Coverley, and Sir Charles Grandison, and Don Quixote are the finest gentlemen in the world." He did not appreciate Fielding, although many of the Browns read this writer's works with great enjoyment.

"*Tom Jones*, sir; *Joseph Andrews*, sir," he cried, twirling his mustachios. "I read them when I was a boy, when I kept other bad company, and did other low and disgraceful things of which I am ashamed now. Sir, in my father's library I happened to fall in with those books; and I read them in secret, just as I used to go in private and drink beer, and fight cocks, and smoke pipes with Jack and Tom, the grooms in the stables. . . . A book, sir, that tells the story of a parcel of servants, of a pack of footmen and ladies'-maids fuddling in ale-houses! Do you suppose I want to know what my kitmutgars and consomahs are doing? I am as little proud as any man in the world; but there must be distinction, sir; and as it is my lot, and Clive's lot, to be a gentleman, I won't sit in the kitchen and booze in the servants' hall. As for that Tom Jones—that fellow that sells himself, sir—by heavens, my blood boils when I think of him! I wouldn't sit down in that same room with such a fellow, sir. If he came in at that door I would say, 'How dare you, you hireling ruffian, to sully with your presence an apartment where my young friend and I are conversing together? Where two gentlemen, I say, are taking their wine after dinner? How dare you, you degraded villain?"

The Colonel tried hard to like the new books that his son liked, and did, as we have seen, succeed in cultivating some appreciation for certain works of Tennyson. He could not understand the enthusiasm for Wordsworth shown by these young people.

Had he not written *Peter Bell* and been turned into deserved ridicule? Was that dreary *Excursion* to be compared to Goldsmith's *Traveller*, or Dr. Johnson's *Imitation of the Tenth Satire of Juvenal*?

Admiration for the writers of the eighteenth century was with him an article of belief, and the disparaging comparisons made between them and the new writers seemed to him rank blasphemy. "The Colonel doesn't admire Carlyle," wrote Clive Newcome, when, with his father, he was spending a short holiday in Paris, where a walk in the Tuileries had brought *The French Revolution* forcibly back to his memory. "He says Mrs. Graham's *Letters from Paris* are excellent; and we bought Scott's *Visit to Paris* and *Paris Revisited*, and read them in the diligence."

Thus far the novelists. If they had told us as much about the reading habits of the Browns as they have told us of their other activities, we should have been grateful; but even from the scanty records they have chosen to provide we are able, as has been shown, to gather some important information concerning Mr. Brown and his books. How far this information is to be relied upon may be tested by a comparison with the few available facts concerning the reading of the Browns of real life. And, first, we are rejoiced to know that among these Browns is to be found a Colonel Newcome. Mr. William Archer, writing to a friend in 1879, said, "I could never have appreciated my father's character as I do had I not studied Colonel Newcome"; which surely means that Thomas Archer, the father, may be claimed as a true and eminent member of the Brown clan. He had spent many years out of England, as the Colonel had done. In 1837, when he was fourteen years old, he went to Australia, where he was apprenticed to a grand-uncle who had settled there. He carried no travelling library, but when he went on a journey he would pray for rain to detain him at any station where there happened to be a small collection of books. He read and re-read Snorre Sturleson's *Sagas of the Kings* and any other books he could lay his hands on, and he loved to sing or recite Scottish and Norwegian ballads. When he came home to England in 1855, he kept his love of the old books, although he read, too, some works by later writers. Sir Walter Scott was held in reverence in his household, and the novels of Dickens and Thackeray were eagerly devoured.

That intrepid traveller, Mary Kingsley, daughter of George and niece of Charles and Henry Kingsley, was, as her ancestry warranted, a reader of the robust Brown type. In her girlhood her favourite books were *The Anatomy of Melancholy*, Johnson's *Robberies and Murders of the Most Notorious Pirates*, and Bayle's *Dictionary*. Once her father brought home Norman Lockyer's *Solar Physics*, which Mary seized upon and read with great delight. Before she had finished it she heard her father offering to lend it to a friend. "Not if I know it," said Mary to herself, and she hid the book, and took care that it should not be discovered until she had read it through, and then she suffered stoically the punishment she had incurred by her nefarious deed. She took in a periodical called *English Mechanics*, and read it with intense interest, learning from it how to do those mechanical jobs about the house (including plumbing) that are usually left to men— which knowledge she found extremely useful in later emergencies.

Thomas Stevenson, engineer and lighthouse builder and upright, God-fearing Scot, though he read but little, was, his son tells us, constant to his favourite books.

Latin he happily re-taught himself after he had left school. . . . Lacantius, Vossius, and Cardinal Bona were his chief authors. The first he must have read for twenty years uninterruptedly, keeping it near him in his study and carrying it in his bag on journeys. Another old theologian, Brown of Wamphray, was often in his hands. When he was indisposed he had two books, *Guy Mannering* and *The Parent's Assistant*, of which he never wearied.

The father of James Spedding was, according to the account given of him by FitzGerald, a true and delightful Brown. He was a Cumberland squire and

a wise man, who mounted his Cob after Breakfast and was at his Farm until Dinner at two; then away again until Tea; after which he sat reading by a shaded lamp; saying little, but always courteous and quite content with any company his son might bring to the house, so long as they let him go his way; which, indeed, he would have gone whether they let him or no.

It is tantalizing not to know what were those books that Mr. Spedding read during those quiet evenings. FitzGerald could so easily have told us, for it is impossible to believe that such a curious and fastidious reader was not sufficiently interested to find out at least their titles. They were probably not poetical works, for, says FitzGerald—

he had seen enough of poets not to like them or their Trade: Shelley for a time living among the Lakes: Coleridge at Southey's (whom he had a respect for—Southey, I mean); and Wordsworth whom I do not think he valued.

Very likely on some of these evenings the book that Mr. Spedding read was one of the works of Sir Walter Scott, for the Browns shared to the full the national love of the author of *Waverley*. Robert Evans loved Scott, and in his long and wearying last illness found relief in having *The Fair Maid of Perth* read aloud to him. His daughter says in a letter to Charles Bray, written in May 1848, that she is just going to begin reading of Henry Gow and Fair Catharine for her father's delectation. In December of the same year she wrote to Miss Hennell—

Father's tongue has just given utterance to a thought which has been very visibly radiating from his eager eyes for some minutes, "I thought you were going on with the book."

The name of the book is in this case not mentioned. It may well have been another of Scott's. Robert Evans had never been a reading man; probably, like Caleb Garth, in *Middlemarch* (who is in many respects drawn from him), he was too much absorbed in "business," for he had, said his daughter, "raised himself from being an artisan to be a man whose extensive knowledge in very varied practical departments made his services valued through several counties." We have only negative information concerning his taste in literature; he thought "the noisy teachers of revolutionary doctrine were, to speak mildly, a variable mixture of the fool and the scoundrel," and he had "not exactly a dislike to innovators and dissenters, but a slight opinion of them as persons of ill-founded confidence."

The young Browns were given the ordinary education of the English upper middle class. The sons were sent to a public school and university, but this was done mainly for the sake of keeping to the family tradition and turning each boy into a complete and satisfactory Brown. He was not expected, or indeed desired, to acquire any prodigious amount of book-learning. So the Squire, of *Tom Brown's Schooldays*, considering what parting words he should say to his son when the lad went to begin his school life at Rugby, communed thus with himself—

Shall I tell him to mind his work, and say he is sent to school to make himself a good scholar? Well, but he isn't sent to school for that—at any rate, not for that mainly. I don't care a straw for Greek particles or the digamma; no more does his mother. What is he sent to school for? Well, partly because he wanted to go. If he'll only turn out a brave, helpful, truth-telling Englishman and a gentleman and a Christian, that's all I want.

As for the girls, they were put in charge of a governess, and the intellectual demands made upon that lady were not very great, if we may judge by the charge given by Dr. Gibson, of *Wives and Daughters*, to Miss Eyre, whom he had engaged to teach his daughter Molly.

Now, Miss Eyre, don't teach Molly too much; she must sew and read and write and do her sums; but I want to keep her a child, and if I find more learning desirable to her, I'll see about giving it to her myself. After all, I'm not sure that reading and writing is necessary. Many a good woman gets married with only a cross instead of her name; it's rather a diluting of mother-wit to my fancy, but, however, we must yield to the prejudices of society, Miss Eyre, so you may teach the child to read.

The young Browns, however, had ideas of their own on the subject of their education, and often went far beyond their parents' designs and expectations. Tom Brown, as we have seen, read widely in the literature dealing with social subjects, and Molly either read or tried to read every book in her father's library, and worried him into letting her learn French, that she might read books in that language as well as in English. When she went to visit at Squire Hamley's, she devoured eagerly every book in the library that interested her, and embarked on a course of reading in natural science under the Squire's son, Roger.

Neither Tom nor Molly were students, or even great readers; but some of the Brown progeny became both. A long list could be made of sons and daughters of the family who attained literary fame; and although in so doing they separated themselves from the main clan they never lost its characteristics. Yet there remained a sufficient number of young Browns who went back to their old homes and led there the same kind of life that their fathers had led before them to perpetuate the race in its pure original strain. There remained houses where life was lived quietly, strenuously, unhurriedly; where the old books were read in loving and leisurely fashion, and readers consulted their own tastes, not the popular gossip of the day. One is inclined to think that the Cherrells of Condaford, in Mr. John Galsworthy's *Maid-in-Waiting*, must have been a branch of the great Brown family; for Fleur's description of them might well apply to the twentieth-century descendants of a clan that looks to Colonel Newcome as its head and exemplar.

Well, I always tell Michael that your side of his family is one of the least expressed and most interesting phenomena left in England. You're wholly unvocal, utterly out of the limelight. Too unsensational for the novelists, and yet you're there, and go on being there, and I don't quite know how. Everything's against you, from Death Duties down to gramophones. But you persist, generally at the ends of the earth, doing things that nobody knows or cares anything about. Most of your sort haven't even got Condafords now to come home to die in; and yet you still have roots and a sense of duty . . . or perhaps it's a sense of service I mean.

CHAPTER XI

THE PHILISTINES

WE have seen how Disraeli showed the English people at the beginning of the Victorian age as two nations, existing side by side—the Rich and the Poor. When the Queen had been reigning for thirty-two years, and when social reform and national prosperity had done something towards softening the most painful differences between these two nations, Matthew Arnold, in *Culture and Anarchy*, made another classification. He was not moved, as Disraeli had been, by the inequality between the lot of those who had much money and the lot of those who had little. His concern was with man's spiritual and intellectual aims and habits, and it was according to differences in these that he divided the people of England into three classes. Two of these classes, which he called the Barbarians and the Populace, corresponded roughly with Disraeli's Rich and Poor. Between them came a class which was larger, and, in the 'sixties, more influential than either of them; and to this great class, which Disraeli had almost entirely disregarded, Matthew Arnold gave the name of the "Philistines."

He borrowed the term from Germany, and in his essay on Heinrich Heine he explained exactly what it stood for—

"Philistine" must have originally meant, in the mind of those who invented the nickname, a strong, dogged, unenlightened opponent of the chosen people, of the children of the light.

Later it was more widely applied—

The enthusiast for the idea, for reason, values the reason, the idea in and for themselves; he values them irrespectively of the practical conveniences which their triumph may obtain for him; and the man who regards the possession of these practical conveniences as something sufficient in itself, something which compensates for the absence or surrender of the idea, of reason, is in his eyes a Philistine.

The Philistine, therefore, orders his life in marked variance from the precept which Matthew Arnold quoted from Bishop Wilson as expressing the ideal aim of true culture—to "make reason and the will of God prevail." From the rejection of reason, of the idea, come all his failings—his absorption in material things, his unlovely way of life, his lack of appreciation of what is highest in art and literature. On the other hand, the narrowness of his aims, and his concentration on worldly success, tend to bring him riches and, sometimes, high position; but, said Matthew Arnold—

Consider these people, then, their way of life, their habits, their manners, the very tones of their voice; look at them attentively; observe the literature they read, the things which give them pleasure, the words which come forth out of their mouth, the thoughts which make the furniture of their minds; would any amount of wealth be worth having with the condition that one was to become just like these people by having it?

In saying this Arnold was going directly against the tendency of his age, for it was an age in which the middle class was dominant and belauded. It was Arnold's keen sense of the danger of this domination that caused him to deal so severely with those whom he called Philistines. Many, indeed most, other writers of the time had given most prominence to the more admirable side of the class that he despised. They had called attention to its fundamental good sense, its capacity for steady hard work, its kindness of heart, its homely, lovable virtues. Many of the Victorian novelists took their heroes and heroines from it. The stories that were in everybody's hands were not now concerned with dukes and duchesses, with haughty young nobles and maidens of high degree. Dickens and George Eliot, Trollope and Mrs. Gaskell, were among those who had shown that the lives of the middle class could be as beautiful, as interesting, even as enthralling as the lives of those above—or below—them. When we talk of the Philistines we must remember their good qualities; must remember, too, the Englishman's incapacity for giving expression to his deeper feelings, and the possibility that some who dwelt in Philistia were really exiles from a better country. Matthew Arnold himself pointed out that there were such exiles when he said—

In each class (Barbarians, Philistines, Populace) there are born a certain number of natures with a curiosity about their best self, with a bent for seeing things as they are, for disentangling themselves from machinery, for simply concerning themselves with reason and the will of God, and doing their best to make these prevail—for the pursuit, in a word, of perfection.

The term "Philistine" attracted the attention of Matthew Arnold's readers and was recognized as one which described a class hitherto unnamed, and therefore a term that could be usefully adopted. Many who were not readers of Matthew Arnold heard it, and used it, without any clear sense of its exact meaning, so that it came in time to be loosely applied to any person who, in the speaker's opinion, did not reach a certain standard of artistic and literary taste. More especially was this the case when the aesthetic cult was at its height. The Aesthetes looked down on all those who failed to appreciate their particulat ideals in art, and threw at them the scornful epithet, "Philistines!" The Browns they unhesitatingly so designated; whereas, although there might be surface resemblances, no two classes could differ more widely in ideals and outlook than did the Browns and the Philistines.

As readers, the Philistines cannot be considered as a distinct and isolated class. Their reading was often affected by circumstances that lay outside their Philistinism. There were Philistines among all the religious parties, High Church, Low Church, Broad Church, and Dissenters, and these chose their books largely in accordance with their religious principles. There were some Philistines, also, who were interested in the social and scientific questions of the day, and the reading of these people was affected by that interest. The Philistine reader, pure and simple, was he who brought little intelligence to his reading, and made no response to an appeal to his higher perceptions; who was concerned mainly with material things, and considered abstract speculation as both tiresome and useless. Many of the Philistines, though not all, revelled in lush sentimentalism and hectic melodrama, and were —quite sincerely—moved, often to tears, by a platitudinous religiosity. It is readers such as these whose reading habits we shall try to explore. As in the case of the Browns, the task is made difficult by the lack of authentic personal records. But the scantiness of these is to some extent compensated by the Philistine habit of acting as a mass. They had no strong individual bent in literature; they were content to follow the fashion and do what was done by others of their class. Generalizations are, in their case, easier to make and of more value than in the case of readers of more varied types.

The Philistines were great readers, in quantity if not in quality. When any book had an exceptionally large sale it is safe to say that this was due to the middle class, for among the two other classes there were not nearly enough readers to provide buyers in such numbers. It was the Philistines who sent up Dickens' circulation to amazing heights; it was the Philistines who bought thousands of copies of *The Idylls of the King* and made Tennyson rich. It was the Philistines who stood in eager crowds outside the publisher's office in Wellington Street waiting for the new number of Wilkie Collins' *Moonstone*. They absorbed most of the twenty thousand copies that were sold in the year of publication of Samuel Smiles' *Self-Help*. They bought Macaulay's *History* and his *Essays* and read them, too, and formed their political opinions largely on what this Utilitarian Whig—who has himself many times been reviled as a Philistine—told them. They filled up the subscription lists of Mr. Mudie and other proprietors of circulating libraries, and scrambled for copies of Samuel Warren's *Ten Thousand a Year* and Mrs. Henry Wood's *East Lynne*. It was the Philistines who made possible the publication of the hundreds and thousands of second- and third-rate novels with which the libraries teemed. They encouraged Mr. W. H. Smith to issue his cheap editions of Railway Novels, and other publishers to follow in his steps with the Parlour Library, the Home Library, the Seaside Library, and other series of blameless sentimental stories.

They took in Eliza Cook's *Journal*, and sobbed over *The Old Arm-Chair*, indulging freely in what Carlyle called Eliza Cookery. Their daughters sang the plaintive songs of Mrs. Hemans, and moved drawing-room audiences to tears with *The Better Land*, *The Graves of a Household*, *He Never Smiled Again*, *The Child's First Grief*, *England's Dead*, and other lachrymose ditties. Every family had its store of handsomely bound books that were laid out on the drawing-room table, to be looked at rather than read. Mr. Waugh, describing his own childhood's home, says—

It was not, I suppose, an artistic home, though it was loyally true to the fashion of its time. There was a round rosewood table in the middle of the drawing-room, and, like the radii of the circle, an array of illustrated books ranged round the edge—Gray's *Elegy*, *The Parables of the Gospel*, *Bewick's Birds*, *The Life and Works of Edwin Landseer*, and *Gems of European Art*.

The favourite poet of the Philistines was Martin Tupper. Long after more enlightened readers had become ashamed of their temporary preoccupation with his works, the Philistines continued to revere him as the great teacher of the age. He was their favourite topic of conversation at social gatherings, as Tennyson and Browning were in other circles. W. S. Gilbert, in one of his *Bab Ballads, Ferdinando and Elvira*, gives a lively, mocking account of such an occasion—

> At a pleasant evening party I had taken down to supper
> One whom I will call Elvira, and we talked of love and Tupper,
> Mr. Tupper and the poets, very lightly with them dealing,
> For I've always been distinguished for a strong poetic feeling.

The lady wished to know who wrote the mottoes to be found in the bon-bons, and the gentleman attempted to obtain for her the information she required.

> Tell me, Henry Wadsworth, Alfred, Poet Close, or Mr. Tupper,
> Do you write the bon-bon mottoes my Elvira pulls at supper?
> But Henry Wadsworth smiled and said he had not had that honour,
> And Alfred, too, disclaimed the words that told so much upon her.
> Mister Martin Tupper, Poet Close, I beg of you, inform us:
> But my question seemed to throw them both into a rage enormous.
> Mr. Close expressed a wish that he could only get anigh to me,
> And Mr. Tupper sent the following reply to me:—
> "A fool is bent upon a twig, but wise men dread a bandit,"
> Which I think must have been clever, for I didn't understand it

(*Note*.—Close was a poet of the same calibre as Tupper, but without his popularity.)

Tupper was, indeed, a favourite butt for the wits; and yet edition after edition of his poetry was being sold. Said Gilbert, in another of his *Ballads*—

> Now Nelly's the prettier, p'raps, of my gals,
> But oh! she's a wayward chit;
> She dresses herself in her showy fal-lals,
> And doesn't read Tupper a bit!

> O Tupper, philosopher true,
> How do you happen to do?
> A publisher looks with respect on your books,
> For they *do* sell, philosopher true.

They *did* sell, in amazing numbers. Some people attributed Tupper's popularity to the fact that he had found favour in high

places. Queen Victoria, who, like Macaulay, has been accused of
a Philistine taste in artistic matters, had a great admiration for him.
In 1863, when the Prince of Wales married Princess Alexandra
of Denmark, Tupper wrote an *Ode of Greeting*—

> O happy heart of England,
> Shout aloud and sing, land,
>   As no land sang before;
> And let the paeans soar
> And ring from shore to shore,
> A hundred thousand welcomes,
>   And a hundred thousand more.

A number of copies of this ode were printed on white satin,
and some of these were sent to Osborne, to be placed upon the
toilet table of the bride and bridegroom to greet them on their
arrival. "The *on dit* (I can scarcely credit it)," wrote William
Hardman, "is the Queen means to knight him." The Queen did
not knight him, and as the years went on his fame gradually
declined; but he continued to write, and his *Autobiography*, which
was published in 1886, shows him still cheerful, self-satisfied, and
moralizing, and still secure of a circle of faithful and admiring
readers.

One, and perhaps the main, reason why Tupper was so extremely
popular was that he was so extremely moral. Morality—or
respectability, the two words stood for almost the same thing—
was dearer to the Philistines than any magic or music of words.
No book that was the least "improper" was allowed within their
doors. Mr. Justin MacCarthy tells how John Bright said to him,
"Make up your mind to write novels all about good people,"
which was a distinctly Philistine precept, although Bright cannot
be included in that class. Even Tennyson's *Merlin and Vivien*
was regarded as verging on the indelicate and not suitable for
reading aloud. The test that was applied in such cases was the test
of the Podsnaps of Dickens' *Our Mutual Friend*, "Would it bring
a blush into the cheek of the young person?" the young person
in this particular case being poor badgered Georgina Podsnap. If
so, though it were the highest triumph of literature, it must be
excluded.

So many and such unsuspected things caused, or were supposed
to cause, that suffusion of the cheek of the young person! It was
the young person, obviously, who caused all the trouble concerning

the edition of Sydney Smith's *Letters* which Mrs. Austin was preparing for publication.

"Now I have a case of conscience for you," she wrote to Dr. Whewell. "Lord Lyttelton has detected in our Sydney's *Letters* two oaths, or to speak more accurately (for there is no juration in the case), two d——ns. You see, Sydney is mimicking Jeffrey, and most unquestionably Jeffrey did season his discourse with that sort of condiment. I am no admirer of it, but I must say that to strike out these two innocent little d——ns seems to me absurd. Lady Holland, who is anxious to make dear old Sydney as decorous as possible, suggests, 'Hang the solar system!' If you think it better to make the alteration, I will make it."

A book in which a clergyman of the Church of England was shown as using two d——ns would have shocked all Philistia. Expurgated editions of various works were demanded in order that the young person might be protected. Mr. Cecil Torr tells how his mother's sister expurgated *The Jackdaw of Rheims* from Barham's *Ingoldsby Legends*. In the line "There's a cry and a shout and a deuce of a rout," "deuce of a" was replaced by "terrible," and "The Devil must be in that little Jackdaw" was made to read "A demon must be in that little Jackdaw," and so on.

This care for the morals of the young person, ridiculous and ill-judged as in many ways it was, had its origin in the strong attachment to home and family which was characteristic of the Victorian middle class. It was a sincere attachment, and it had in it much that was lofty and beautiful, but it was undoubtedly marred by excessive sentimentality and a too ponderous seriousness. Thackeray's summary of the lecture on *The Poetry of Womanhood and the Affections*, given (in view of a coming Parliamentary election) by Barnes Newcome, at the Newcome Athenaeum, is a very fair representation of the way in which writers and speakers of that age were used to talk of "the hearth and the home."

"The presence of this immense assembly here this evening," said Barnes, "of the industrious capitalists, of the intelligent middle class, of the pride and mainstay of England, the operatives of Newcome—these surrounded by their wives and their children show that they too have hearts to feel and homes to cherish—that they too feel the love of women, the innocence of children, the love of song!" Our lecturer then makes a distinction between man's poetry and woman's poetry, charging considerably in favour of the latter. We show that to appeal to the affections is the true office of the bard; to decorate the homely threshold, to wreathe flowers round the domestic hearth, the delightful duty of a Christian singer. We glance at Mrs. Hemans' biography and state where she was born, and under what circumstances she must have at first, etc., etc.

It is not recorded how many votes the lecture won for Barnes, but we are told that he received many compliments from the ladies and gentlemen seated on the platform. "Thank you! Delightful, I'm sure!" "I really was quite overcome!" Probably the compliments were quite genuine. An appeal to the domestic affections rarely failed. Between 1850 and 1863 Coventry Patmore published the various parts of his long poem, *The Angel in the House*, and the public bought 250,000 copies of it; not because they held, with Ruskin, that Patmore was "the only living poet who always strengthens and purifies," nor because they appreciated its philosophical subtleties and its passages of pure beauty. They bought it and read it and praised it because it glorified married love and the sanctities of wedded life. Not for them were the amorous ditties that celebrated a fleeting passion. Their approving interest was given to the faithful husband who declared—

> But truly my delight was more
> In her to whom I'm bound for aye
> Yesterday than the day before,
> And more to-day than yesterday.

They remained firm in their approval even when many of the critics made rather unkind fun of *The Angel in the House*. Quite possibly they never read or heard of these criticisms. Henry Fothergill Chorley, a journalist whose word carried weight in all literary matters, wrote in the *Athenaeum*, January 1855—

Fear not this saline Cousin Fred; He gives no tragic mischief birth; There are no tears for you to shed, unless they may be tears of mirth. From ball to bed, from field to farm, The tale flows nicely purling on; With much conceit there is no harm In the love-legend here begun. The rest will come another day, If public sympathy allows, And this is all we have to say About *The Angel in the House*.

Swinburne parodied the poem in his *Heptalogia*, introducing into his parody the Monthly Nurse, the Caudle, and the Kid. Justin MacCarthy classed the poet with Martin Tupper, which was certainly not fair. Patmore was high above Tupper, but there were certain qualities that the two writers had in common, and it was probably to these qualities that the greater of the two owed much of his popularity.

In 1828 there had been produced at Covent Garden Theatre an opera called *Clara, the Maid of Milan*, and in this opera occurred the song *Home, Sweet Home*. It is scarcely adequate to say that the song was at once immensely popular; it became the loved and familiar possession of thousands, and it may be taken as stating with admirable clearness the views of the nation as a whole and of the middle class in particular. Said Dean Hole—

No brilliant manipulation, no marvellous range has reached and troubled the fountains of your heart like that simple ballad of *Home, Sweet Home*. You admired or tried to admire or pretended to admire the more scientific music, but this melody took possession of the spirit within you.

When, in 1872, Madame Patti sang it to the Queen at Windsor, her Majesty, like her subjects, felt that the song was "touching beyond measure, and quite brought tears to one's eyes."

Thus far we have considered the reading habits of the Philistines as a whole; but there were subdivisions among them, each tending to favour a particular type of book. Each of these subdivisions had its special preoccupation which hindered its acting in accordance with the principle "to make reason and the will of God prevail," and from seeking that "sweetness and light" essential to beautiful living. For a number of people this preoccupation was with Facts, and of these Mr. Thomas Gradgrind may be taken as the type.

A man of realities. A man of facts and calculations. A man who proceeds upon the principle that two and two are four and nothing over, and who is not to be talked into allowing for anything over.

Imagination, fancy, playfulness, humour, day-dreams were all to be banished. "Facts alone are wanted in life. Plant nothing else and root out everything else." The little Gradgrinds from their earliest years were brought up upon this principle. They were told no fairy tales, they knew no nursery rhymes. The merest suspicion that an idle story-book had got into the house made their father seriously uneasy. When he caught his son and daughter peeping through the canvas of a tent where a circus was going on, he declared that he should as soon have expected to find them reading poetry—which, for Gradgrinds, would be to forfeit their birthright. They had books in plenty, all crammed with Facts; they had governesses and lecturers, and cabinets full of scientific specimens. When their mother wished to dismiss them from her presence she bade them "Go and be something-ological directly."

No little Gradgrind had ever seen a face in the moon; it was up in the moon before it could speak distinctly. No little Gradgrind had ever learnt the silly jingle, Twinkle, twinkle, little star; how I wonder what you are! No little Gradgrind had ever known wonder on the subject, each little Gradgrind having at five years old dissected the Great Bear like Professor Owen, and driven Charles's Wain like a locomotive engine-driver. No little Gradgrind had ever associated a cow in a field with that famous cow with the crumpled horn who tossed the dog who worried the cat who killed the rat that ate the malt, or with that yet more famous cow who swallowed Tom Thumb; it had never heard of those celebrities, and had only been introduced to a cow as a graminivorous ruminating quadruped with several stomachs.

Their father's library consisted mainly of Blue Books; and he never doubted that his house, with its four-and-twenty windows, and its kitchen, from whence came a scientifically planned dietary, provided all the "sweetness and light" that his family required for their highest good. Yet Mr. Gradgrind was an upright, kindhearted man, with a sincere desire to serve not only his family but his neighbours and his country. Only he lacked the gift of imagination and was wholly obsessed by Facts.

Mr. Gradgrinds, more or less true to type, existed all over the country, though they were most plentiful in the manufacturing districts. Mrs. Gaskell, who knew the Manchester factory owners as well as she knew the Manchester factory hands, had a good many Mr. Gradgrinds among her acquaintances, but with her gracious, kindly insight she was able to see in some of these hardheaded, practical men possibilities of larger intellectual growth. In *North and South* she took her readers into the home of John

Thornton, one of the leading manufacturers of the busy, ugly town of Milton, and showed them the dining-room, where not a book was to be seen except Matthew Henry's *Bible Commentaries*, six volumes of which lay in the centre of the massive sideboard, with an urn on one side and a lamp on the other; then took them into the drawing-room, where—

in the middle of the room, right under the bagged-up chandelier, was a large circular table, with smartly bound books arranged at regular intervals round the circumference of its polished surface, like gaily coloured spokes of a wheel.

There was no sign anywhere of a love of intellectual pleasures or of beauty; yet Mr. Thornton found time in his busy life to read Greek and Latin with a private tutor that he might revive old schoolboy recollections of the classics. Mr. Carson, the wealthy cotton-spinner of *Mary Barton*, was a more indulgent father than Mr. Gradgrind. He allowed his grown-up son and daughters to bring some sort of culture into the house. When an evening had to be passed at home, one of his daughters read Emerson's *Essays* —though, to be sure, she fell asleep over them—another sang Mrs. Hemans' songs, and a third copied out the music of a Spanish air. The father liked to hear the songs and listen to the conversation; nevertheless, he spent most of the evening asleep in his arm-chair.

Dickens' Mr. Podsnap was of the same family. He was as devoid of imagination as Mr. Gradgrind, and had not that gentleman's solid virtues. Mr. Podsnap's idea of literature, we are told, was

large print, respectively descriptive of getting up at eight, shaving close at a quarter past, breakfasting at nine, going to the City at ten, coming home at half-past five and dining at seven.

Painting and sculpture, to be appreciated by him, must treat of the same themes. He had no desire for beauty. "He could tolerate taste in a mushroom man who stood in need of that sort of thing, but was far above it himself."

The second type of Philistine found his great preoccupation in Money. He measured everything and valued everything by its cost. He was often a man of humble origin who had made a large fortune in trade. Having himself received but an imperfect education, he knew no other way of educating his children than by spending as much money as possible upon the process; and the children grew up in their father's faith and valued books only in their relation to Money.

Thomas Hood presents the highest development of this type in his *Miss Kilmansegg and her Precious Leg*—a poem which William Fulford read aloud one evening to his little reading circle at Birmingham, when all agreed that Hood had been underrated.

Miss Kilmansegg's father had made his money

> Through an Agricultural Interest
> In the Golden Age of Farming.

His daughter's education began early, for—

> Long before her A B C
> They had taught her by heart her L.S.D.

As she grew older—

> Instead of stories from Edgeworth's page,
> The true golden lore for our golden age,
>   Or lessons from Barbauld and Trimmer,
> Teaching the worth of Virtue and Health,
> All that she knew was the Virtue of Wealth,
>   With a Book of Leaf Gold for a Primer. . . .

> The books to teach the verbs and nouns,
> And those about countries, cities, and towns,
> Instead of their sober drabs and browns,
>   Were in crimson silk with gilt edges:
> Her Butler and Enfield and Entic—in short
> Her *Early Lessons* of every sort
>   Looked like Souvenirs, Keepsakes, and Pledges.

> Old Johnson shone out in fine array
> As he did one night when he went to the play;
> Chambaud like a beau of King Charles's day—
>   Lindley Murray in like conditions . . .

> Novels she read to amuse her mind,
> But always the affluent, matchmaking kind
>   That ends with Promessi Sposi,
> And a father-in-law so wealthy and grand,
> He could give cheque-mate to Coutts in the Strand. . . .

Plays she perused—but she liked the best
Those comedy gentlefolk always possess'd
   Of fortunes so truly romantic—
Of money so ready that right or wrong,
It always is ready to go for a song,
Throwing it, going it, pitching it strong. . . .

Then Eastern Tales she loved for the sake
Of the Purse of Oriental make,
   And the thousand pieces they put in it—
But Pastoral scenes on her heart fell cold,
For Nature with her had lost its hold,
No field but the Field of the Cloth of Gold
   Would ever have caught her foot in it.

It is no wonder that poor Miss Kilmansegg came to an unfortunate end, and all through the gold she loved.

The brass and copper founder in whose family Tom Pinch's sister was governess—"the wealthiest brass and copper founder's family known to mankind"—was certainly of the Kilmansegg clan. We are not told the titles of the books from which Miss Pinch was instructing her pupil when Mr. Pecksniff paid her his condescending visit, but doubtless they were the same as those used by Miss Kilmansegg.

Carlyle devotes a whole chapter in his *Past and Present* to these money-getting and money-worshipping Philistines, taking as his type Plugson of Undershot—"Plugson, who has indomitably spun Cotton merely to gain thousands of pounds." The chapter is full of denunciations of "Mammonism" and the Cash Gospel; yet Carlyle allows that these "indomitable" money-makers had their great qualities. "In that grim brow, in that indomitable heart which *can* conquer Cotton, do there not perhaps lie other ten-times nobler conquests?"

An even more powerful preoccupation than that of Facts or Money was Gentility. The number of Philistines who were mainly concerned with making a good appearance before the world and pushing their way upwards in society was probably more than all the Gradgrinds and the Kilmanseggs put together. Money was, of course, required for this, but money was not, of itself, the main object of desire; it was spent freely on social display. Of this class Thackeray is the special historian. His *Book of Snobs* might almost as well be called the book of the Genteel Philistines, and some of the race are to be found in almost every one of his stories. Unfortunately, against him, too, the complaint must be made that while he describes in detail their manners, their conversation, their houses, their clothes, their food, he tells us little about their reading, except by an occasional reference to the quantities of novels that they devoured.

The most complete portraits in the *Book of Snobs* (for our purposes) are those of Major Ponto and his family. Major Ponto had an income of a thousand pounds a year, and a wife who aspired to the society of lords and duchesses. He lived in "a perfect Paradise of a place . . . all over creepers and bow windows and verandahs," with lawns and flower-beds and shrubberies spread around it; yet he was miserable because his neighbour, the Marquis of Carabas, snubbed him. His children were taught by an ill-educated, pretentious governess, who professed to teach her pupils a bewildering variety of subjects, and to turn them into highly educated young ladies; but in reality most of her energies were spent (she had lived, she declared, in noble families before coming to the Pontos) in teaching them to perform upon the piano the pieces that had been "the dear Duchess's" favourites and those which Lady Jane McBeth had played when dear Lord Castle-toddy first fell in love with her. So the girls grew up without any guidance in the choice of books for their leisure hours, and with uncultivated literary tastes that led them only to large indulgence in the novels—some good, but more flimsy and poor—that they obtained from the circulating library.

The book most diligently read in Major Ponto's house was the "inevitable, abominable, maniacal, absurd, disgusting *Peerage*," as Thackeray calls it, and which he declares to be the Englishman's second Bible. We remember that the Honourable Mrs. Jameson, of *Cranford*, who was a pure Philistine, kept the *Peerage* in her drawing-room, on the "japanned table devoted to literature," alongside a Bible and Prayer-Book. The Major himself retired every morning to his study, where he remained for two hours with the door locked. "My library's small," he told his visitor, "but well selected, my boy. I've been reading the *History of England* all the morning." But the visitor, when he found an opportunity of examining his host's private apartment, could discover no books at all except *Magg's Road Book* and *The Gardener's Chronicle*.

Some of these snobbish Philistines affected a devotion to litera-

ture, reading books that they neither enjoyed nor understood, in
the hope of increasing thereby their social importance. Thus Miss
Mulock's Mrs. Lancaster, of *The Ogilvies*, became "the central
sun of a petty literary sphere," although her reading was so entirely
for show that a remark on the ordinary feminine topic of dress
set her off on "a dissertation on the costume of the middle ages,
varied by references to Froissart and the illuminated manuscripts
of monkish times." Thus, too, Mrs. Hobson Newcome protested
that she had "never admired aught but intellect" and read diligently
many "improving books."

If I can be the means—the *humble* means—to bring men of
genius together—mind to associate with mind—men of all nations
to mingle in *friendly unison*—I shall not have lived altogether in
vain,

she said, looking round at the collection of fifth-rate celebrities
assembled at one of her evening parties.

In many families this social climbing took the form of strenuous
and persevering efforts to obtain husbands for the daughters—rich
husbands if the girls were portionless, titled or important ones if
papa could supply a large dowry. Marriage being the only career
open to girls, an entrance to it was sought with feverish and often
undignified energy. Match-making papas and mammas began their
campaign betimes, and ordered their daughters' education with the
sole intent that they might make a successful appearance before a
rich and distinguished, if shadowy, company of future suitors. "I
never grudged anything to make a show," said the Philistine Sir
John Vesey to his daughter Georgina in Lord Lytton's play,
Money—

Never stuffed your head with histories and homilies; but you
draw, you sing, you dance, you walk well into a room; and that's
the way young ladies are educated nowadays, in order to become
a pride to their parents and a blessing to their husbands—that is,
when they have caught him.

In Philistine circles socially lower than that of Sir John Vesey
the daughters were equally preoccupied with the question of
marriage. Kingsley wrote, in 1858—

Who will help these young girls of the middle class who . . . are
often really less educated than the children of their parents'

workmen; sedentary, luxurious, full of petty vanity, gossip, and intrigue, without work, without purpose, except that of getting married to anyone who will ask them—bewildering brain and heart with novels which, after all, one hardly grudges them; for what other means have they of learning that there is any fairer, nobler life possible, at least on earth, than that of the sordid money-getting, often the sordid puffery and adulteration, which is the atmosphere of their home?

There were some Philistines who had no special preoccupation that kept them from "sweetness and light," but who were simply vulgar—some pardonably, almost lovably so, others in a manner both ugly and revolting. The first class lacked refinement of speech and habits, the second had tastes and aims that were inherently low and mean. Dickens gives us many examples of both classes, but as he tells us little or nothing about the books they read he is not very useful for our present purpose. Probably there was little or nothing to tell, only the old tale of cheap newspapers and poor novels.

Last of all we come to a class that we hesitate to call Philistine, or, indeed, to call by any name which carries suggestions that are not gracious and beautiful. These were the simple, quiet, happy people whose lives were governed by their hearts rather than by their heads. They had no grasp of large questions and little interest in anything outside their own small world. Most of their attention was given to small, material things—small pleasures, small economies, small annoyances; small kindnesses, too, and acts of self-denial. Ideas meant little to them, abstractions puzzled them. They read little, and that little was usually of the simplest character. Yet who would say that the lives of the ladies of *Cranford*, for example, were not lovely and fragrant? Miss Matty and Miss Deborah, Miss Pole, Miss Betty Barker, Miss Jessie Brown— how delightful were their sacrifices to gentility, their little shifts and devices, their fictions by which arrangements due to lack of means were explained as "elegant economy." They were not snobs; only the Honourable Mrs. Jamieson could possibly be classed with Mrs. Ponto. The others we are almost tempted to call Browns— but they lacked the guiding idea, the stirring activity, the intellectual grasp. Miss Deborah thought Dr. Johnson the finest of all English writers, and formed her style upon his. Miss Matty fell sound asleep while Mr. Holbrook read *Locksley Hall* aloud, and, waking, said how pretty it was, and how like a poem of Dr. Johnson's that her sister used to read. Miss Pole took advantage of the reading to count the stitches in her crochet. Miss Betty Barker's drawing-room literature consisted of three or four handsomely bound fashion books. The Aesthetes would unhesitatingly have condemned all these ladies as rank Philistines. Would Matthew Arnold have been kinder? They probably did not understand what was meant by "reason" prevailing, but they did their best to promote "peace on earth, goodwill towards men." They were deficient in "light," but of "sweetness" they had abundance.

CHAPTER XII

BOOKS FROM AMERICA

IN the early years of the nineteenth century English readers began to be aware of a great and unique gift preparing for them beyond the seas—the gift of an entirely new literature, written in their own tongue. It was not merely an extension of the literature they possessed already—fruit of a branch springing from the old stock. The seed had, it is true, been brought from England, but it had been sown in fresh soil and fostered by influences such as the mother country had never known. Its development, like the development of most things of worth, had been unhurried, and its fruits had ripened slowly; but now books were beginning to travel across the Atlantic, first in small numbers, and then in ever-growing abundance. Washington Irving's *Bracebridge Hall* and *The Sketch Book* came with the eighteen-twenties, William Cullen Bryant's poems a little later, with works by various other novelists and poets.

One of these, a young man of New England, named James Fenimore Cooper, received a specially ready and delighted welcome. When, in 1822, his novel, *The Spy*, reached England, the country thrilled at the promise it seemed to hold that here was another Scott; and during the next five years, which brought six more stories of the same type, many people declared that the promise had been fulfilled. Some were inclined to place Cooper even higher than Scott, and everyone agreed that he was better than any of Scott's many imitators. Miss Mitford said she thought his novels were as good as anything Sir Walter ever wrote, and that she liked *The Last of the Mohicans* better than any of the Waverleys except the first three and *The Heart of Midlothian*.

Much of the interest that Cooper excited in his readers was due to the new and strange scenes and characters that he presented to them. He opened to them realms which Scott had never known. He made them free of the vast prairies and forests of North America, into which, up to that time, English readers had never adventured. He gave them new friends—the Red Indians who were being driven westward by the ever-advancing tide of American civilization, and the white hunters and trappers who were that civilization's heralds. Chief among these new friends was Leather-stocking, whom readers knew first in *The Deerslayer* as a romantic, fiery-hearted youth, and from whom they parted in *The Prairie* when age had dimmed his fire, but not his courage or his integrity.

That eager reader, Mrs. Fenwick, the friend of Mary Lamb, was among the first who laid hands on the new treasure. "You must read *The Pilot* and give me your opinion of it," she wrote, as early as 1824, to a friend, Mary Hayes. "It is by James Cooper, the author of *The Spy*"; and then, with her usual strict regard for moral as well as for literary excellence, she added, "The high tone of the present race of novels is a blessing to the rising generation."

The rising generation certainly appreciated Cooper's novels though possibly more on account of their adventurous spirit than of their high tone. The books were published in England at the same time as in America, and edition after edition was quickly sold. Walter Frith, as a boy of nine or ten years old, read them at his father's inn at Harrogate, and revelled in them. Fanny Kemble said that she half killed herself with crying over *The Borderers*, and did not recover from its effects for several days; which to readers of her own generation conveyed a high recommendation of the book. Anthony Trollope tells how, about 1831, when he was a lonely, unhappy lad, living a poverty-stricken life in the "wretched, tumble-down farmhouse" near Harrow, to which his father had brought his family, he found the first two volumes of *The Prairie*—"a relic," he says, "probably a dishonest relic of Hookham's Library. I wonder how many dozen times I read those first two volumes."

Critics generally considered *The Last of the Mohicans* the best of the series, and it has had the most enduring fame. Emily Eden was one of the small minority that was not attracted by it. "I have been trying to read *The Last of the Mohicans*," she wrote to her sister, from India, "and have come to a stop at the end of the first volume. I am sure you will not like it."

By the time the Victorian age began, a generation was growing up in England that knew its *Last of the Mohicans* almost as well as it knew its *Ivanhoe* or its *Pickwick*; and this generation passed on its love of Cooper's stories to its sons and to its grandsons. To have dreamt dreams inspired by these stories was one of the common experiences of a Victorian childhood. Sir Sidney Colvin was moved by them and others of their kind to plan for himself "futures of the wildest adventure." In the early 'sixties two little boys, sons of the Duke of Abercorn, Viceroy of Ireland, had entered into Cooper's world, and were leading the thrilling and adventurous lives of Red Indian "braves." They were fortunate in having ten acres of wild woodland, which formed part of the grounds of the Viceregal Lodge, for their hunting ground, and this they speedily peopled with "two tribes of Red Indians, two bands of peculiarly bloodthirsty robbers, a sufficiency of bears, lions, and tigers, and an appalling man-eating dragon." They tried conscientiously to act the part of genuine Indian braves, but found it a little difficult, since—

according to Fenimore Cooper, our guide in these matters, it was essential to keep up an uninterrupted series of gutteral grunts of Ug! Ug! the invariable manner in which his "braves" prefaced their remarks.

A few years later Dean Church, writing to a friend in America, described the way in which his four children, a little boy and three little girls, were spending a summer afternoon.

At this moment the whole party, with the boy at the head, are in the shrubbery, showing the effect on his mind of a recent course of Cooper's novels; and energetically following his lead while he makes them "be Indians" for him—Mohawks, Delawares, and Shawnees—and they have been pursuing on the war-path, tomahawking and whooping, and displaying the scalps they have taken all the afternoon.

At King William's College, in the Isle of Man, to which Dean Farrar went as a small boy of eight in 1839, Cooper's stories, with those of Scott and Marryat, were passed round and read surreptitiously, and the boys used to lie awake at night hotly discussing their favourite heroes. William Archer was another of Cooper's enthusiastic admirers, and Sir Oliver Lodge was another. Lord Balfour, in his *Chapters of Autobiography*, says that in the library of his boyhood's home, Whittinghame, there were two long shelves filled with standard novels. A glance through these showed which were the most popular in the family, and at about what age its members began to read them; the first was indicated by the wear and tear the volume had received, the second by the number of grubby finger-marks on its pages. *The Last of the Mohicans* he instances as one of the most worn and the dirtiest.

Du Maurier shows his schoolboy Peter Ibbetson as "the friend and admirer and would-be imitator of Natty Bumpo, the Deer-slayer," and "the familiar of the last of the Mohicans and his scalp-lifting father." As for Thackeray, his boyish love of the Leatherstocking series exceeded, he says, in some ways, his love of *Waverley* and its fellows. Of Scott's heroes he says—

Much as I like those unassuming, unpretending gentlemen, I have to own I think the heroes of another writer, viz.—

LEATHERSTOCKING

UNCAS

HARDHEART

TOM COFFIN

are quite the equals of Scott's men; perhaps Leatherstocking is better than anyone in Scott's lot. La Longue Carabine is one of the great prizemen of fiction. He ranks with your Uncle Toby, Sir Roger de Coverley, Falstaff—heroic figures all—American or British, and the artist has deserved well of his country who devised them.

During the first year or two of the Victorian age the works of Cooper and of Washington Irving were the only American books widely read in England. But the Queen's accession almost coincided with the beginning of a great literary movement across the Atlantic, and soon books came pouring in—prose and poetry, history and fiction, humour and philosophy. England made her own selection, though she chose, for the most part, the works that had gained the greatest number of readers on the other side of the ocean. She acclaimed, though with a slight air of patronage, a young poet, Henry Wadsworth Longfellow. She ranked him, not exactly as a minor poet, but as belonging to an order distinctly below that in which, later, she placed Tennyson and Browning—suitable for those readers who liked what Walter Bagehot, after he had read *Voices of the Night* (the first volume of Longfellow's poems published in England), impatiently called "pretty poetry." He was, indeed, by the most severely critical readers of poetry, made over before long to the Philistines as their especial property. Mrs. Panton implied as much when, avowing that she preferred Mrs. Browning's works to those of her husband, she added, "But then

I love Longfellow's poetry and Adelaide Anne Procter's." Mrs. Henry Wood quoted him largely, and so did Mrs. Hungerford, and that popular writer of rather depressingly Evangelical novels, Emma Jane Worboise. He was the favourite poet—as far as they had favourite poets—of these ladies' characters. "His words," one of them says, "fell upon my ears like a new evangel."

John Lockhart was very severe on Longfellow, and declared him to be "a mere cleverish imitator of the versification of the day." "I have always had a special contempt for Longfellow," he said, "and lately had a single combat with the fair Norton on that field." The brilliant Mrs. Norton had no doubt been able to hold her own even against the vitriolic editor of the *Quarterly*. She would have had no difficult task in demonstrating Longfellow's immense superiority to Tupper, whom Lockhart had declared "a man of talent and a poet indeed." Tupper himself admired Longfellow, proclaiming him to be "the man of chiefest mark" among our Transatlantic friends, and in those days Tupper's praise went far towards establishing a new poet's reputation with a certain class of readers.

Longfellow was regarded also as being specially suitable for the reading of young persons who had not yet arrived at the stage when they could appreciate the highest poetry. William Fulford read a good many of his poems to the little circle at Birmingham. "He fed us with Longfellow first of all as the food suited to our years," said Miss Georgina Macdonald, "and so brought us gradually into a condition more or less fit for the revelation before introducing us to his prime hero, Tennyson."

Longfellow's poems were read with keen enjoyment by working lads like Thomas Burt, by young ladies in the schoolroom like Lucy Lyttelton and Elizabeth Wordsworth, by girls who, like Octavia Hill, were just entering upon a high and purposeful life's work. Even Ouida's heroes, magnificently scornful as they were of all that pertained to Philistia, had some acquaintance with them, for one young gentleman, in a moment of deep emotion, quoted the lines—

> Standing with reluctant feet
> Where the brook and river meet—
> Womanhood and childhood fleet.

He apologized immediately and with shame for his "lapse into Longfellow," a poet whom "no man quotes after his salad days, except in a moment of weakness," but the "lapse" serves to suggest that Louise de la Ramée, like other girls of her generation, had been brought up upon the works of the popular American poet. Austin Dobson was so brought up, and was proud of it, and he paid the poet a high tribute in a poem written a good many years later—

> Bard of the bygone days when we were young,
> Be this thy praise, that never flowered among
> Thy "Garden of Romance" aught base or mean.

Yet there were many who read and delighted in Longfellow who cannot be classed either as Philistines or as persons of immature intelligence. James Smetham wrote to his friend William Davis praising highly the *Fire of Driftwood*, "which you are to get down and read this very minute, before you go any further." Justin MacCarthy never outgrew his early love of the poems. Florence Nightingale, when she was twenty-six years old, and chafing at being held back from the career of usefulness for which she so ardently longed, declared that the feeling of all her life was summed up in the last verses of Longfellow's poem, *The Goblet of Life*.

> Let our unceasing, earnest prayer
> Be, too, for light—for strength to bear
> Our portion of the weight of care,
> That crushes into dumb despair
>   One half the human race.
>
> O suffering, sad humanity!
> O ye afflicted ones who lie
> Steeped to the lips in misery,
> Longing, and yet afraid to die,
>   Patient, though sorely tried!
>
> I pledge you in this cup of grief,
> Where floats the fennel's bitter leaf,
> The Battle of our Life is brief,
> The alarm,—the struggle,—the relief,—
>   Then sleep we side by side.

Added to these testimonies comes that of Edward FitzGerald. That captious critic, whom no one would dream of accusing of a tenderness for the second-rate or the commonplace, declared without reservation, "I love Longfellow."

When *Evangeline* appeared in 1847, it made a wider appeal to

English readers than any of Longfellow's previous poems had done. Arthur Hugh Clough read it aloud to his mother and sisters, and told Emerson later that it had been one of the influences leading to his own "outbreak into hexameters" in his poem, *The Bothie*. Samuel Smiles delighted in *Evangeline*, and hearing that Ebenezer Eliot had expressed a very strong wish to read it, he sent him a copy; which drew from the old Corn Law Rhymer the somewhat cryptic pronouncement, "When Tennyson dies he should read *Evangeline* to Homer." Aubrey de Vere, the young Catholic poet, sent a copy of *Evangeline* to Sara Coleridge, and in the letter of thanks she wrote to him she said she thought it beautiful and deeply pathetic.

This deep pathos is not the right thing in a poem. I could not take the story and the poetry together, but was obliged to skim through it and see how the misery went on and how it ended before I could *read the poem*.

With *Hiawatha*, which came in 1855, Longfellow's fame on this side of the Atlantic rose to the highest point it ever reached. Lucy Lyttelton thought it

throughout curious and interesting, and very beautiful in parts.

The two young sons of the Viceroy of Ireland, who delighted in Cooper's novels, delighted, too, in Longfellow's poem, and knew *Hiawatha's Fishing* almost by heart. Kitty Moberly said that she and her brothers and sisters knew the entire poem. Miss Broughton, who was fifteen years old when it was published, knew it well, and made one of her heroines quote from Shawondasee's "song of love and longing."

Lowell declared that, in Europe, it was of more advantage to an American writer's reputation to be known as a friend of Longfellow's than as the writer of "various immortal works." When the poet visited England in 1868 he was received everywhere with tremendous enthusiasm. He was granted an interview with Queen Victoria, who said afterwards to Sir Theodore Martin—

I wished for you this morning—the American poet, Longfellow, has been here. I noticed an unusual interest among the attendants and servants. I could scarcely credit that they so generally knew who he was. When he took leave they concealed themselves in places from which they could get a good look at him as he passed. I have since inquired among them, and am surprised and pleased to find that many of his poems are familiar to them. No other distinguished person has come here who has excited so peculiar an interest. Such poets wear a crown that is imperishable.

Long before this, in 1852, Mary Russell Mitford had given it as her opinion that Longfellow owed his success in England quite as much to his faults, his obscurity, his mysticism, and his little dash of cant "as to his merits." But at that time Miss Mitford was old and ill, an invalid who rarely left her room, and was not, perhaps, as capable of forming judgments on the literary tendencies of the day as she had once been.

The English public was not, however, left to form its opinion of American poetry solely upon the works of Longfellow. A little more than a year before the publication of *Evangeline* there had come across the ocean a poem unlike any that had been produced before either in England or America. It was called *The Raven*, and was written by Edgar Allen Poe, a writer who was known to a few among English readers chiefly by two or three weird and powerful magazine stories that had found their way to this country. Many people thought the poem weird and powerful also; others saw little in it, and declared that its effects were obtained by a cheap literary trickery. To the young and the romantic it came as the authentic, despairing cry of a lover lamenting the death of his beloved. The pre-Raphaelite group—the Rossettis, Holman Hunt, John Millais, Thomas Woolner—were enraptured with it. They read it aloud, and it helped to inspire Dante Gabriel Rossetti to write a poem that attempted to show another aspect of the separation of the lovers—the maiden in heaven leaning over the golden bar, waiting for the coming of him whom she had loved on earth. They read also other poems by Poe, *Ullalume, For Annie, The Haunted Palace,* and, later, *The Bells,* and fell completely under the spell of their wild, strange beauty.

Edward Burne-Jones was fascinated by Poe's prose stories. "One thing I am almost afraid to mention," he wrote to his father in 1854, when he was just twenty years old—

viz., the spell that man Poe throws round me. His book of horrors is by me now. I know how contrary to all rules of taste are such writings, but there is something full of delicacy and refinement in all that hideousness. The charm is only temporary, in a day or two he will be neglected, as such ephemeral works always are. . . . Read particularly that in which he exemplifies his notion of analysis and identification with another's feelings. They are *The Murders in the Rue Morgue* and *The Purloined Letter* especially. *The Gold Beetle* is a beautiful story. *A Descent into the Maelstrom*, *The Pit and the Pendulum* (especially this), and several others are marvellously startling. *The Fall of the House of Usher* is very grand and almost my favourite. Some I think very objectionable, such as *Mesmeric Effects*, *The Black Cat*, and one or two others.

From a small circle of readers—highly imaginative people with definitely poetic temperaments—Poe won for American literature a respect which Irving and Cooper and Longfellow had all failed to gain. These recognized his genius and bore with his sensationalism.

To another class of readers—the intellectual and thoughtful, who were interested in questions of philosophy and theology—America was also supplying books in generous measure. These came chiefly from a group of New England writers who were known as the Transcendentalists. The Transcendentalists were not united by a common belief in certain definite doctrines. Their bond of union was a loose one, being mainly the fact that they all found themselves unable to accept the orthodox religion of their fathers, and were earnestly seeking for a new system of theology which should give a deeper reality to their spiritual life. The conclusions at which they arrived differed widely, but they agreed in acknowledging the dignity and self-sufficiency of the individual. "Only he is religious who discovers God in himself," declared Ralph Waldo Emerson in 1839, and this flouting of authority, coming as it did before even the *Vestiges* had voiced religious questionings in England, startled and shocked many readers. Only by the more advanced thinkers was it really welcomed.

At Coventry there was to be found a group of such readers, gathered round a certain Mr. and Mrs. Bray. Mr. Bray was a well-to-do ribbon manufacturer, who lived in a beautiful house on the outskirts of the town. He was a professed free-thinker, and had written philosophical works setting forward his opinions. Mrs. Bray was the sister of Mr. Charles Hennell, who had published in 1838 a book called *An Inquiry into the Origins of Chris-*

tianity, which, although it had attracted little notice from the general public, had been favourably received by a small circle of men of science. Mr. Hennell had another sister, Sara, a brilliant and talented girl who, like the rest of the family, was a freethinker, and who later published several philosophical works. These, and the friends who gathered round them, read Emerson's *Essays* with intense appreciation; and among these friends was a young girl of twenty, Mary Anne Evans, who came with her father, in 1841, to live at Coventry. She was introduced to the Brays by a friend, and visited at their house. Soon a warm and intimate friendship, which included the two Hennells, was formed. Miss Evans had held strongly Evangelical views, but the influence of her new friends brought about, or perhaps only hastened and confirmed, a change in her opinions. She read the books that they were reading, and among these came the works of Emerson. She delighted in the *Essays* and formed a high opinion of their author. When Emerson came to England on a lecturing tour, he visited the Hennells in London in April 1848, and Miss Evans wrote to Sara, "I thoroughly enjoyed your delight in Emerson. I should have liked to see you sitting by him 'with awful eye,' for once in your life feeling all the bliss of veneration." Three months later he came to Coventry, and she had an opportunity of seeing him herself. "I have seen Emerson—the first *man* I have ever seen," she wrote.

Herbert Spencer read the *Essays* in 1844, when he was twenty-four years old, and wrote to his friend Lott, who had lent him the book, saying—

I have read Emerson and passed it on according to command. Here and there I met with a passage I was much pleased with, but as a whole the feeling was like that produced by distant thunder.

Among the most fervent adherents to the Emersonian creed was Mr. W. S. Williams, of the firm of Smith, Elder and Co. He corresponded on all sorts of literary subjects with Charlotte Brontë, whose works were published by the firm, and in July 1848 she wrote—

I never read Emerson; but the book which has had so healing an effect on your mind must be a good one. . . . Emerson, if he has cheered you, has not written in vain.

Apparently a copy of the *Essays* was contained in the next of those parcels of new books which the publishers sent regularly to the famous author of *Jane Eyre*, for in a letter to Mr. Williams of February 4, 1848, Miss Brontë gave her opinion of the book.

"Emerson's *Essays*," she wrote, "I read with much interest and often with admiration, but they are mixed gold and clay—deep and invigorating truth, dreary and depressing fallacy seem to me combined therein."

To Oxford the works of Emerson first came while the excitement of the Tractarian Movement was at its height, and they were eagerly read by those members of the University who were not in agreement with its principles, and who welcomed a book that stated the case against authority and in favour of private judgment. Matthew Arnold, in that same *Discourse* delivered in America in which he described Newman preaching at St. Mary's, said that, besides the voices of Newman and Keble and Pusey—

there came in that old Oxford time a voice also from this side of the Atlantic—a clear and pure voice, which for my ear at any rate brought a strain as new and moving and unforgettable as the strain of Newman or Carlyle or Goethe. . . . Snatches of Emerson's strain fixed themselves in my mind as imperishably as any of the eloquent words which I have been just now quoting.

In 1850 came Emerson's *Representative Men*. English readers naturally compared it with Carlyle's *Heroes and Hero Worship*, usually much to the disadvantage of the American book. Fitz-Gerald read it, and pronounced it a book "with very good scattered thoughts in it, but scarcely leaving any large impression with one, or establishing a theory." Miss Evans remained faithful to her early Emerson worship. She read *Representative Men* over and over again. In 1860, when she was living in London, and, under the name of George Eliot, had become famous, she wrote to Miss Sara Hennell—

I have been reading this morning for my spiritual good Emerson's *Man the Reformer*, which comes to me with fresh beauty and meaning. My heart goes out with venerating gratitude to that mild face which I daresay is smiling on someone as beneficently as it one day did on me, years and years ago.

Representative Men was read at Oxford, as Emerson's earlier works had been. John Morley, who went up in 1856, says that his tutor "pressed Emerson upon us, but for that wise teacher none of us were then ripe, I least of all."

James Anthony Froude represented those English readers—and there were a good many of them—who considered Emerson's teaching misdirected and harmful. When *Representative Men* was published Froude had lately lost his Fellowship at Exeter College through the publication of *The Nemesis of Faith*, a book in which he had openly recanted his early religious opinions. He was making a living by writing magazine articles, chiefly for *Frazer's Magazine* and the *Westminster Review*. One of these was a review of Emerson's book. Froude complained first of all of Emerson's choice of his representative men. All of them belonged to the Old World, and all of them, except one, were thinkers, not men of action; and it was difficult to see what claim any of them had to be considered either great or good. "Has Mr. Emerson any . . . clear idea of a great man or good?" asked Froude. "If so, where is he? What is he?"

It is not the "great man" as "man of the world" that we care for, but the "man of the world" as a "great man"—which is a very different thing. Having to live in this world, how to live greatly here is the question for us; not how, being great, we can cast our greatness in a worldly mould.

We have lost, he complained, our ideal of a good and a great man —the ideal which the Romish Church brought so clearly before its members when it bade them study the lives of the saints.

And what comes of this? Emersonianism has come, modern hagiology has come, and Ainsworth novels and Bulwer novels, and a thousand more unclean spirits. We have cast out the Catholic devil, and the Puritan has swept the house and garnished it; but as yet we do not see any symptoms showing of a healthy incoming tenant, and there may be worse states than Catholicism.

Alfred Ainger, who was at Cambridge when *Representative Men* reached England, was as opposed to Emerson's teaching as was Froude.

How can anyone rise from reading Emerson's *Conduct of Life* without feeling, if he has a human heart left within him, that if that is the whole Gospel of Humanity, it were our blessedest Fate to die and be at peace.

"Emersonianism," though it never became a real force in England, was not destroyed by these invectives. Charlotte Brontë was perhaps right when she wrote to Mr. Williams—

The world is not yet fit to receive what you and Emerson say: man, as he now is, can no more do without creeds and forms in religion than he can do without laws and rules in social intercourse. You and Emerson judge others by yourselves; all mankind are not like you, any more than every Israelite was like Nathaniel.

Yet, for a good many years Emerson's works attracted a large number of readers. Emersonianism became something of a fashionable cult, and was widely discussed in society and in the newspapers. All those people who read laboriously, as a matter of duty and self-culture, and all those who read from a desire to be considered intellectual and up-to-date, made a point of getting his books. Besides these there were the genuine admirers who found in the *Essays* and *Representative Men* both help and enjoyment. Carlyle continued to be Emerson's determined champion. "I am a lover of Ralph Emerson," declared Coventry Patmore. "I have read all his essays at least three times over." Dean Stanley was his warm admirer, and so were Henry Sidgwick and William Archer and Francis Espinasse, while FitzGerald said that he admired him, but did not feel that he knew the Philosopher as well as the Poet —by whom he meant Longfellow.

Next to Emerson among the New England writers came Nathaniel Hawthorne, the novelist. His first work, *The Scarlet Letter*, arrived in England in the same year as *Representative Men*, and was followed in 1851 by *The House of the Seven Gables*, and in 1852 by *The Blithedale Romance*. Dickens read *The Scarlet Letter* and did not very much care for it. "It falls off sadly after that fine opening scene," he said. Swinburne, who was a boy at Eton when the book came out, remembered it vividly because he was "properly flogged" for reading it when he ought to have been reading Greek. Miss Mitford was enthusiastic over the first two of Hawthorne's works—

The House with the Seven Gables is even finer in the same way than *The Scarlet Letter*—the legendary part dim, shadowy, and impressive, the living characters exquisitely true, vivid, and health-ful. The heroine, Phoebe, is almost a Shakespearian character.

Miss Mary Ann Evans read both these books, and wrote from Broadstairs, on August 19, 1852, to her friend, Mrs. Peter Taylor—

One sees no novels less than a year old at the seaside, so I am unacquainted with *The Blithedale Romance*, except through the reviews, which have whetted my curiosity more than usual. Hawthorne is a grand favourite of mine, and I shall be sorry if he do not go on surpassing himself.

Before the end of the month she was back in London, and evidently made haste to get the new book, for on September 11th she wrote to the Brays—

You may as well expect news from an old spider or bat as from me. I can only tell you what I think of *The Blithedale Romance*, of *Uncle Tom's Cabin*, and the American Fishery Dispute —all which, I am very sure, you don't want to know.

Clearly she did not think the Brays would be as interested in Hawthorne and Mrs. Stowe as they were in Emerson; which has prevented us from knowing whether she agreed with Miss Mitford, who said that she liked *The Blithedale Romance* less than the other two.

With most people *The Scarlet Letter* seems to have been the favourite. "Have you seen Hawthorne's *Scarlet Letter*?" Henry Sidgwick wrote to his sister in March 1860. "It is a wonderful work, and enchained even me who am tolerably sated of novels now." Robert Louis Stevenson cited it as an example of a high poetical romance. Henry Chorley called it—

The most powerful and most painful story of modern times— the only tale in its argument in which the purity overtops the passion. . . . It has struck me prodigiously, and I think will end in taking a remarkable place among stories of its quality.

The Scarlet Letter was read aloud in the Gladstone family, but in most families it was definitely placed among the books forbidden to the "young person." In the new generation that was growing up, however, there were many "emancipated" girls who read it eagerly and with sympathy. "I should feel like poor Hester standing in the market-place with an 'A' on her breast," said Wilhelmina of *Windyhaugh* when it was suggested that she should take the part of Beatrice in Shelley's *The Cenci*.

Frederick Robertson classed Hawthorne's novels with *Jane Eyre*, *Villette*, and *Ruth*. These, he said—

with the works of several American writers, as Hawthorne, in whom, though men, the woman movement has worked deeply, are the most remarkable of our modern novels, and characterize the commencement of an epoch.

He quoted Hawthorne's words in which the novelist declared he had

a firm belief that at some brighter period, when the world should have grown ripe for it, in heaven's own time, a new truth would be revealed in order to establish the whole relation between man and woman on a surer ground of mutual happiness.

This, Robertson said, seemed to him to coincide with "an unmistakable tendency in the present day to revive Mariolatry, as if the truth in it were not yet got out"; also with "the (sometimes frantic) efforts made for female emancipation."

But although there were many people at this time deeply interested in the woman movement, few of them took Hawthorne as seriously as did Robertson. They looked upon him as a novelist, and ignored the philosophic side of his works. He was not widely popular in England, but his great qualities were recognized by understanding readers even when they did not care for his works. "I scarce know why I could never take to that man of true genius, Hawthorne," said FitzGerald. Lord Lytton was his enthusiastic admirer. Hawthorne's genius, he said, had such a fascination for him that he found it difficult to speak of his works critically.

The first American book that made a really great sensation in England was *Uncle Tom's Cabin*, by Mrs. Beecher Stowe. The subject of the book aroused the lively and immediate interest of almost every English reader. Wilberforce and Clarkson and Zachary Macaulay were dead, but their work on behalf of the negro slaves was not forgotten, and slavery was still one of the burning questions of the day. England had followed the course of the Abolition movement in America with the closest attention; there was an Abolition and an Anti-Abolition party on this, as well as on the other side of the Atlantic. The passing of the Fugitive Slave Act in 1850 had caused intense excitement in both countries. It was this Act which inspired Mrs. Stowe to write her book; and when England saw how *Uncle Tom's Cabin* was moving the whole of America, she was eager to read it for herself. It arrived here in the spring of 1852. Twenty-seven editions were quickly sold; more than a million copies, Mary Howitt says, by the end of the year.

Mrs. Stowe sent copies to Prince Albert, Lord Shaftesbury, and other prominent English people known to be interested in the slavery questions. The Queen read the book and was much moved by it; and soon it seemed as if the whole country could think of nothing but Uncle Tom, his virtues and his woes.

"It was the year of *Uncle Tom's Cabin*," said Thomas Mozley. "All the 'ologies, all the arts and sciences, histories, travels, fictions, facts, light literature, heavy literature, everything that man can read perished in that fatal blight. Mrs. Beecher Stowe had found the Garden of Eden before her, but she left a wilderness behind. . . . I had been absorbed in the book, I had shed tears over it and devoured every line. . . . I never read it a second time, nor did I read any other work of Mrs. Beecher Stowe."

Miss Mitford, of course, had an early copy, and she wrote to her friend, Digby Starkey—

I have now on my bed (where I am writing) *Uncle Tom's Cabin*, another American book; from which, I am told, Lord Carlisle said that he could not tear himself until he had completed it. I have only just begun it, but I doubt if it will equally enthral me. Knowing many Americans and many West Indians, I have learnt to consider emancipation as a question that has two sides.

The book did not enthral her, and she was pleased to find that some of her friends agreed with her estimate of it. She wrote to Miss de Quincey giving her a message from her father—

I was also to tell you that he agreed with you in your detestation of *Uncle Tom's Cabin*, but I told him that you had not said you detested it, but that it was too painful to read, upon which he withdrew his message, but cherishes a hope that if ever you do read it you *will* detest it.

Macaulay, remembering the old days at Clapham, read Mrs. Stowe's book with close attention. On October 4th he recorded in his diary—

I finished *Uncle Tom's Cabin*; a powerful and disagreeable book; too dark and Spagnoletto-like for my taste, when considered as a work of art. But on the whole it is the most valuable addition that America has made to English literature.

A good many readers declined to go as far as Macaulay, and refused to consider Mrs. Stowe's work as a piece of literature at all. For them the purpose entirely overshadowed the story. They would have agreed with T. E. Brown, who said, "For my part, I don't care about a Tendency novel. *Uncle Tom's Cabin* is a splendid instance, but it's not a good novel." Janet Ross classed it with *Sybil* and *Alton Locke* and *Mary Barton* as one of the "party pamphlets on religious and social questions" that the novelists of the day were giving their readers in place of "pleasant stories." Perhaps there is something of the same feeling, conscious or unconscious, in Charlotte Brontë's sincere and generous praise of the book. In a letter to her publisher, written in October 1852, she said, concerning her own forthcoming book—

Villette touches on no matter of public interest. . . . Nor can I take up a philanthropic scheme, though I honour philanthropy; and voluntarily and sincerely veil my face before such a mighty subject as that handled in Mrs. Beecher Stowe's work, *Uncle Tom's Cabin*.

In 1853 Mrs. Stowe paid a visit to England, and was received with almost hysterical enthusiasm. Public meetings were held in her honour, and speeches made hailing her as the friend of the oppressed, the deliverer of those held in bondage. She was introduced to all the famous men and women of the day, was invited to all the great houses, and lionized in the most complete and flattering fashion. "The great talk now is of Mrs. Stowe and spirit-rapping," wrote Mary Howitt in May 1853, "both of which have arrived in England." A little later she wrote, "Mrs. Stowe has arrived in London. Wherever she goes a crowd gathers." Lady Priestley, daughter of Robert Chambers, of *Vestiges*, was invited to an evening party to meet the famous American authoress, who

had put "the whole world, from Queen to slavey, in a ferment."
She found her a quiet, unassuming, homely little woman, with
none of the airs of a society lion. Thomas Mozley went to a great
reception held in Mrs. Stowe's honour in Willis's rooms, and
Arthur Hugh Clough also met her. Clough's impression of the
lady can be gathered from a letter written to him a little later by
Matthew Arnold—

The woman Stowe by her picture must be a Gorgon. I can
quite believe all you tell me of her—a strong Dissenter—religious,
middle-class person—she will never go far, I think.

This was the kind of "person" with whom the author of *Culture
and Anarchy* had least sympathy, and we are prepared to hear that
when he read *Uncle Tom's Cabin* he found in it nothing worthy
of praise.

But the strictures of Matthew Arnold and Miss Mitford and
others who thought with them had no effect upon the ardour of
Mrs. Stowe's admirers. An address thanking her for the great
work she had done was presented to her by the women of England,
and Thackeray tells us that Lady Ann Newcome signed it "along
with thousands more virtuous British matrons." After Mrs. Stowe
returned to America she wrote an account of her visit to England,
and told how surprised and delighted she was to find her book so
well known to all classes of readers all over the country. The
servants at the great houses she visited were as familiar with *Uncle
Tom* as were their masters and mistresses; and in a ragged school
at Liverpool "all the little rogues were quite familiar with Topsy
and Eva, and *au fait* in the fortunes of Uncle Tom."

Children of all classes then, and for at least the next twenty
years, were brought up on Mrs. Stowe's famous anti-slavery epic.
To them it appealed chiefly as a thrilling and delightful story.
They regarded Eva with something of the reverential admiration
they felt for Little Nell; and wept bitterly at her deathbed. Topsy,
with her pranks and her grin and her " 'Specks I growed,"
enchanted them. Eliza's flight across the river, and Cassy's blood-
curdling devices in the attic of Legree's house provided thrills of
the most satisfactory character, and Uncle Tom himself became
their ideal negro, and inclined their hearts towards his race. The
book was one of the very few secular stories that Edmund Gosse
was permitted to read in his sternly repressed childhood. It was

read aloud in the Lyttelton schoolroom when Lucy Lyttelton was about twelve years old, and took, she said, a tight grip of her. Lady Frances Balfour has told how her youth was nourished upon

the copy sent by Mrs. Stowe to the Duke of Argyle. It was bound in two well-printed volumes, with illustrations. I was told not to read the second volume, but human nature cannot be denied, and of course I read it.

The little Friths, children of the artist, received *Uncle Tom* in a partisan spirit. It was dinned into their ears, said the elder sister, by both their grandmother and their governess, but when the American Civil War began—

we secretly favoured the gallant, valiant South, and thought more of their ruined plantations, dying magnolias, and beautiful houses than we cared for the rough, uncouth North.

Away up in Northumberland fifteen-year-old Thomas Burt, the coal-hewer's son, listened to it with delight—

Uncle Tom's Cabin was read aloud in our little family circle, and gave us many hours of happy, thrilling, and not unwholesome excitement.

More than twenty years later English children were still being nourished on Mrs. Stowe's masterpiece. Mrs. Huth Jackson has told us in *A Victorian Childhood* how, when she was nine-year-old Annabel Grant Duff, unruly and careless, her instinct for decoration was awakened by reading in *Uncle Tom's Cabin* the description of Eva's room, so beautiful in its exquisite purity, and how the solemn scene of St. Claire's death first made her understand the De Profundis.

When the first enthusiasm for the book waned, the number of critics who decried both its literary merits and the handling of its great theme increased. Sydney Dobell, who, although he did not admire *Uncle Tom* as a whole, yet thought that Mrs. Stowe had shown real creative power in a few passages, withdrew even this measure of praise on finding, when the *Key* was issued, that these were just the passages that had been taken from real life. Swinburne was as much antagonized by the personality of the writer as Matthew Arnold had been, and described her as a "rampant

Maenad of Massachusetts." But there was still a considerable public that delighted in *Uncle Tom* as a story, and reverenced it as an attempt to set free the prisoners and captives. Lady Frederick Cavendish wrote in 1873—

> I have been reading *Uncle Tom's Cabin* again, also its *Key* and article in the *Edinburgh* in '55 against it; . . . it has fresh gripped me now with wonderful strength.

Lady Frances Balfour, writing in 1930, said—

> I hear the criticism of to-day on its vulgar style and its melodrama; I keep silence even from good words. It did its work. A woman's pen, under divine inspiration, touched the iron fetters, the rivets fell apart, and the slave where'er he cowered went free.

Mrs. Stowe's second book, *Dred*, appeared in 1855, but although the English public bought a hundred thousand copies of it in four weeks, it had nothing like the popularity of *Uncle Tom*. The subject was again slavery, but the new book contained no characters that took the public imagination as Eva and Topsy and Tom had taken it. There was more criticism of the weaknesses of Mrs. Stowe's style, and a tendency to class her tragedy as bathos. George Trevelyan, Lord Macaulay's nephew, wrote an article making fun of it for the Cambridge magazine, *The Lion*; which article drew down upon him a reproof from his mother, and a reminder that his famous uncle had laid it down that no man should write of a woman except with respect and gentleness. Nevertheless, we are told that Macaulay himself, in the privacy of the family circle, rather enjoyed poking fun at the extravagantly belauded Mrs. Stowe.

Less sensational than the *Uncle Tom* campaign but scarcely less remarkable was the successful invasion of England by American children's stories which took place during the 'fifties and 'sixties, and which gave us some books that have become children's classics. First, in 1851, came Miss Elizabeth Wetherell's *Wide, Wide World*, of which, it is said, thirty thousand copies of the English edition were sold.

"I think I may say we have now got up a *Wide, Wide World* fever," wrote a correspondent of the firm publishing the book to Miss Wetherell, "and it is amusing to stand quietly and watch its fitful heaving. I see the book placarded about in all directions, and its pretty face exhibited in every window. . . . I am told by a correspondent that the trade in Manchester and Liverpool is simply inundated with *Wide, Wide Worlds*. Ten thousand copies were sold at one English railway station.

It is difficult to understand why the book became so popular. It was the ordinary type of children's story, following on the lines of many that had preceded it. There was a model heroine, beset on all sides by trials and temptations, which she met and surmounted with marvellous fortitude and meekness. Her occasional falls were simply opportunities for pointing the moral and adding fresh lustre to her character. The charm of the book, for young readers, perhaps lay in the abundance of homely detail with which the life on the farm where Ellen Montgomery, the heroine, lived was described. It was a book for girls; most boy readers probably agreed with Lord Frederick Hamilton, who said, "In my early youth I was given a book to read about a tiresome little girl named Ellen Montgomery, who apparently divided her time between reading her pocket Bible and indulging in paroxysms of tears." Bishop Thirlwall, who read everything that came in his way, and hated to leave unfinished a book he had begun, was conquered by the *Wide, Wide World*. "I struggled through about half of it," he said, "but at last—I could hold out no longer."

Miss Wetherell followed up this success with *Queechy*, which came in 1852. It was of the same type as the *Wide, Wide World*, and had an even more faultless heroine in Fleda Ringan, and it was almost equally popular. "Tell me if you have read *Queechy*," wrote Mrs. Browning to Miss Mitford. "I think it very clever and characteristic. Mrs. Beecher Stowe scarcely exceeds it after all her trumpets."

Next came a series, known as the Daisy books—*Melbourne House, Daisy in the Field*, and the rest—in which Miss Wetherell pursued the fortunes of a single heroine through several volumes, and these, too, were widely read and highly praised.

The *Katy* books, by Susan Coolidge, followed, and here it is easy to see why the gift from America was received by English children with exuberant gratitude. Katy began by being a tomboy and a scapegrace, and although she met with the inevitable and painful check which made of her a reformed character, yet she remained sufficiently human to hold the reader's interest. The second and most popular volume in the series, *What Katy Did at School*, began what was to be a revolution in school stories. Hitherto very few school stories had appeared in England, and these had been of the straitest and most highly moral character, modelled on the earliest example, *The Governess; or the Little Female Academy*, written by Miss Sarah Fielding in 1789, and revised by Mrs. Sherwood (of *The Fairchild Family*) in 1820. In this story all the pupils were "young ladies" and every incident carried its obvious moral. "Mischief" and "naughtiness" were terms unknown. If any young lady deviated in the least degree from the rules of conduct prescribed by Mrs. Teachum she was at once convicted of sin and mourned over as a lost sheep until with tears and penitence and due punishment she returned to the fold.

Into this correct company there came dancing merry, mischievous, charming Rose Red and her companions from across the Atlantic. Miss Fielding and Mrs. Sherwood would have regarded them with horrified disapproval, but the girls of England loved them; and they introduced into this country a class of schoolgirl heroine whose popularity has never waned.

A third series of American children's books—the *Little Women* series—came from Louisa Alcott, and these made up a gift of finer quality than that offered by either Elizabeth Wetherell or Susan Coolidge. At least one of the characters from them came to life and entered the houses of their readers and became their real friend. This was Jo March, whom English readers first met in 1868 as a harum-scarum, awkward, clever girl of fifteen, and whom they watched grow up until she became Mother Jo, with a family of boys to look after, her own and other people's.

Many other books were coming over from America during this period, and although none of them gained a very large reading public each had its appeal to a select circle. The most popular were the works of the humorists, Bret Harte, Mark Twain, and Artemus Ward. Dickens was one of the first to read and appreciate Bret Harte.

"Not many months before my friend's death," said John Forster, in his *Life of Dickens*, "he had sent me two *Overland Monthlies* containing two sketches by a young American writer far away in California, *The Luck of Roaring Camp* and *The Outcasts of Poker Flat*, in which he had found such subtle strokes of character as he had not anywhere else in late years discovered; the manner resembling himself, but the matter fresh to a degree that had surprised him; the painting in all respects masterly; and the wild, rude thing painted a quite wonderful reality. I have rarely known him more honestly moved."

The Heathen Chinee (1870), a poem in which Bret Harte burlesqued the metre of the closing passage of Swinburne's *Atalanta in Calydon*, took the fancy of the English public, and was laughed at and quoted all over the country. The poem made his name known, and obtained a reception for the stories that followed it. Lord Lytton admired Bret Harte; he thought that the American humorists represented the most thoroughly national original department of American literature, but he did not care for Mark Twain. Henry Sidgwick found Mark Twain's *Huckleberry Finn* "irresistibly laughable," and Sir Oliver Lodge says that when he was a young student at Finsbury Technical College, John Perry, the Professor of Mathematics, "greatly admired *Huckleberry Finn* and indoctrinated me with the same kind of enthusiasm for that excellent work." Thomas Burt acknowledges his obligation to his friend, Frank Bell, for introducing him to Artemus Ward, Mark Twain, and other American humorists

Oliver Wendell Holmes was not very widely read. Justin MacCarthy says that when he visited London in 1869 hardly anyone seemed to know who he was, or to attach any clear idea to *The Autocrat*. Miss Mitford read his works, and preferred him to Longfellow. FitzGerald said he loved him. Henry Sidgwick admired the *Breakfast Table* series, but found *The Poet at the Breakfast Table* a falling-off from the others, though readable. James Russell Lowell, also, had only a small, select company of readers. "His *Among my Books* is among mine," said FitzGerald, and Dean Church thought him "the most perfect exponent in poetry of the sense of national greatness of anyone that I know."

Concerning Whitman there were widely different opinions. Lytton said Whitman seemed to him "an impudent, blatant imposter, deserving of no serious consideration"; while Robert Louis Stevenson asserted that to Whitman he owed the guidance and inspiration that had helped him at a critical period in his youth. His book, said Stevenson, "should be in the hands of all parents and guardians as a specific for the distressing malady of being seventeen years old. Green-sickness yields to his treatment as to a charm of magic; and the youth after a short course of reading ceases to carry the universe on his shoulders." To John Addington Symonds, Whitman appeared as a prophet. "I find it difficult," he wrote, "to speak about *Leaves of Grass* without exaggeration," and he went on to a detailed panegyric on the work, concluding—

In short, Whitman added conviction, courage, self-reliance to my sense of the Cosmic enthusiasm. What is more, he taught me, as no enthusiasm of humanity could do, the value of fraternizing with my fellows—for their own sakes to love them, to learn from them, to teach them, to help and to be helped by them—not for any ulterior object upon either side.

So, from one source and another, all through the Queen's reign, this gift of books from America came in a never-failing though not always plenteous stream. By some readers it was highly valued, by others little accounted of. Those who valued it the most highly were those who recognized it for what it really was—an earnest of far greater things to come.

CHAPTER XIII

THE GREAT NOVELISTS AND THEIR PUBLIC

EDWARD FITZGERALD, that fastidious and whimsical literary critic, once complained that there were far too many Great Novelists of the Day; he could not read one-half of the works they sent out. But Victorian readers as a whole were not of his opinion. They greeted their Great Novelists with enthusiasm and maintained towards them an unswerving loyalty. A later age, though it has cast many gibes at the Victorians' lack of artistic perception, has never been able to convict them of a lack of appreciation of their Great Novelists. Nor has it been able to show that the Great Novelists were not worthy objects of enthusiasm. There were, naturally, a good many who were acclaimed as great who proved later to be but of very ordinary dimensions. The Victorians, like other mortals, made mistakes, and the best-seller was in their, as in every, age not necessarily the best from any other point of view. Still, after the strictest tests have been applied there remain the splendid four—Dickens, Thackeray, Charlotte Brontë, and George Eliot; and in a lower class, not of the greatest, but certainly of the great, Anthony Trollope, Charles Kingsley, and Elizabeth Gaskell. Other names might be added, but these are beyond question.

When we turn to consider the readers of these novelists' works, we are driven at once to the conclusion that the majority of them came from the hosts of the Philistines. It is clearly a question of numbers, and the records of copies sold put the fact beyond dispute, even though other evidence is scanty. The Philistines, as we have seen, rarely recorded the names of the books they read, or their impressions of them. We are forced to rely on the minority—that smaller body of readers made up of the cultivated classes, who did on occasion talk and write about the novels, and from what they said and wrote to draw our conclusions as to the way these works were received by the public.

None of the other novelists became as universally and as immediately popular as Dickens. Thackeray had to wait long for recognition, though not perhaps longer than he deserved; for as soon as he wrote what is acknowledged to be his first great work it had an enthusiastic reception. *Vanity Fair* came out in monthly parts—yellow-covered to distinguish them from the *Dombey and Son*, clad in Dickens' green, that were also making a monthly appearance—beginning in January 1847, and after two or three numbers Abraham Hayward, the popular critic and journalist, wrote to the author, "Don't get nervous, you have completely beaten Dickens out of the inner circle already." By September, Mrs. Carlyle was writing to her husband—

I brought away the last four numbers of *Vanity Fair*, and read one of them during the night. Very good indeed, beats Dickens out of the field.

The comparison with Dickens was inevitable, and judgment went sometimes one way, sometimes the other. "Dickens and Thackeray were being published in monthly parts which were awaited with the utmost eagerness," wrote Lady Georgiana Peel; "some liked Dickens best, some Thackeray. We liked Dickens." Sir Henry Sanderson says that his father loved Dickens and liked Thackeray. The chief complaint against Thackeray was that he showed only the least pleasant and least worthy side of life. "I believe *Vanity Fair* presents a true view of human life, a true view of one aspect and side of it," said Sara Coleridge. Fanny Kemble thought it very clever, but did not admire it very much. It had, she said—

one very disagreeable quality—the most prominent people in it are thorough worldlings, and though their selfishnesses and meannesses and dirtinesses and pettinesses are admirably portrayed— to the very life indeed—I do not much rejoice in their company.

Harriet Martineau went farther. "I confess to not being able to read *Vanity Fair*," she said, "from the moral disgust it occasions"; and Carlyle declared that he found a great relief in turning from the terrible cynicism of *Vanity Fair* to the cheerful geniality of Dickens.

We may perhaps allow ourselves to imagine Mr. and Mrs. Carlyle sitting one on either side of the fire in the sitting-room of Cheyne Row, he with the current yellow-covered number in his hand, she with the green, while deep growls of disgusted disapproval come from the one, and light, caustic comments from the other; until he lays down his *Vanity Fair* and she her *Dombey and Son*, and there ensues an interval during which Carlyle, with picturesque and damning invective, consigns Thackeray's book to the place where it ought to go—a place which grows the blacker and the more infamous at every spirited and witty plea for the defence made by his wife; until at length he snatches up her *Dombey and Son* to refresh his soul with the delightful ingenuousness of Captain Cuttle and Polly Toodles, and she reaches out for *Vanity Fair*, and finds the tonic properties she requires in the captivating wickedness of Becky Sharp.

Many readers were on the side of Mrs. Carlyle, and admired Thackeray whole-heartedly. "All the world admires *Vanity Fair*, and the author is courted by Dukes and Duchesses and wits of both sexes," wrote FitzGerald. Yet Thackeray's most ardent admirer was not a duke or a duchess or a fashionable wit, but a quiet, shy little lady living in a remote Yorkshire parsonage, who had never seen him and knew nothing of the world that he described. Charlotte Brontë could scarcely mention the name of the author she so revered without rhapsodizing—

The more I read Thackeray's works the more certain I am he stands alone—alone in his sagacity, alone in his truth, alone in his feeling (his feeling, though he makes no noise about it, is about the most genuine that ever lived on a printed page), alone in his power, alone in his simplicity, alone in his self-control. Thackeray is a Titan, so strong that he can afford to perform with calm the most herculean feats; there is the charm and majesty of repose in his greatest efforts; he borrows nothing from fever, his is never the energy of delirium—his energy is sane energy, deliberate energy, thoughtful energy.

Vanity Fair, said Miss Brontë, began very quietly. "It was quiet all through, but the stream as it rolled gathered a resistless volume and force." The last number was a culminating triumph.

Edward FitzGerald agreed that the book improved as it went on—

"Thackeray is progressing greatly in his line," he wrote in May 1848, "he publishes a novel in numbers—*Vanity Fair*—which began dull, I thought, but gets better every number, and has some very fine things in it."

Thackeray's daughter, Lady Ritchie, says that while the story was in course of publication her father received a letter from a young lady in the country, who declared herself weary of the faultless but insipid Amelia and the blundering, golden-hearted Dobbin, and requested the author to give his readers one or two numbers in which these prodigies did not appear; which Thackeray most willingly did. Nobody cared very much for Amelia, though they felt bound to admire her. To most readers *Vanity Fair* meant Becky Sharp. That fascinating and immoral young person managed somehow to insinuate herself into the good graces of the very moral Victorians. They did not, of course, approve of her; and some of them explained their interest as originating in a righteous satisfaction that one of the Great Novelists should have furnished such a striking example of wickedness coming to the end that it deserved. Others frankly revelled in her. The young people who made her acquaintance, which most of them did, lawfully or unlawfully, were enchanted by her. Sissy Frith said she knew *Vanity Fair* by heart and loved it long before she was pronounced old enough to read it. In the schoolroom of the six Wilson sisters— one of whom became later Mrs. Walter Bagehot—Becky Sharp was a household word. Henry Kingsley, who was seventeen when the first number of *Vanity Fair* appeared, confessed that his "first sweethearts were Julia Manning, Flora Macdonald, and even Jane Eyre, until Rebecca Sharp appeared, and then 'we loved as we had never loved before.' "

"Even Jane Eyre," said Henry Kingsley, and thus reminds us that there was another heroine competing with Becky Sharp for public favour—a heroine even less generously dowered with beauty than that green-eyed young lady. This heroine was small, plain, insignificant, and poor, and with no trace of the minx quality that in her rival had proved so attractive. *Jane Eyre* came out as a complete three-volume novel in October 1847. Nobody knew anything about the author, whose name was given as Currer Bell, not even whether the name denoted a man or a woman. But it was not long before the book began to be talked about. "There are two books that have taken the public's fancy, *Jane Eyre* and *Vanity Fair*," wrote Fanny Kemble to a friend in America. By December there was a rush for *Jane Eyre* at the libraries, and much discussion everywhere as to who Currer Bell might be. Mrs. Carlyle was convinced that the author was a woman, and so was Miss Davenport Hill. There was a rumour, believed by many, that the book was the work of a Lancashire weaver, and another, still more widely accepted, that Thackeray had written it. It was of no use applying to the publisher, for it was not until months later that he discovered the author to be Miss Charlotte Brontë.

Many readers found in the book a new, strange quality which thrilled as well as delighted them, and these praised *Jane Eyre* even to extravagance. Among the enthusiasts it is good to find Thackeray.

"How well I remember," he said, "the delight and wonder and pleasure with which I read *Jane Eyre*, sent to me by an author whose name and sex were then alike unknown to me; the strange fascination of the book; and how, with my own work pressing upon me, I could not, having taken the volumes up, lay them down until they were read through."

Charles Bray, the ribbon manufacturer of Coventry, admired the book extremely, and recommended it to Miss Mary Ann Evans. In reply, Miss Evans wrote—

I have read *Jane Eyre* and shall be glad to know what you admire in it. All self-sacrifice is good, but one would like it to be in a somewhat nobler cause than that of a diabolical law which chains a man soul and body to a putrefying carcase. However, the book *is* interesting; only I wish the characters would talk a little less like the heroes and heroines of police reports.

Many people—Mrs. Carlyle was one of them—thought the book coarse. Miss Elizabeth Sewell read it. "People said it was coarse," she said, "and I felt it was, but I felt also that the person who wrote it was not necessarily coarse-minded." Others went farther, and declared it to be dangerous and even wicked. In December, Miss Brontë wrote to her publishers—

I feel a sort of heartache when I hear the book called "godless" and "pernicious" by good and earnest-minded men.

Jane Eyre herself, upright, single-minded Jane, heroic in her selfless devotion, received far harsher treatment at the hands of the champions of morality than the unscrupulous Rebecca had done. This insignificant little woman had fire and passion, and she brought these into her love affair with Rochester; which shocked all those good Victorians who held that no modest young lady should feel for her betrothed anything stronger than a coy and decorous affection. John Lockhart called Jane "rather a brazen

Miss," although he declared that the book was worth "fifty Trollopes and Martineaus rolled into one counterpane, with fifty Dickenses and Bulwers to keep them company." Fanny Kemble, who was a champion of the book, said that she received foolish letters from a certain Lady —— about *Jane Eyre*—

then the universal theme of conversation and correspondence. She uses the expression "dished and done for and gone to the dogs," and then complains that the writer of *Jane Eyre* does not know how ladies and gentlemen talk—which I think too.

The climax of detraction came when in December 1848 an article entitled *Vanity Fair, Jane Eyre, and Governesses* appeared in the *Quarterly Review*. It was unsigned, but the writer was revealed later as Miss Rigby, afterwards Lady Eastlake. Both books received a good deal of praise, but the praise of *Jane Eyre* was neutralized by slighting remarks upon the author, whom Miss Rigby believed to be a man. She owned that the book was a very remarkable one. "We have no remembrance of another containing such undoubted power with such horrid taste." Its tone of mind and thought, she declared, was identical with that which had "overthrown authority and violated every code, human and divine, abroad, and fostered Chartism and rebellion at home." As to the author, Miss Rigby pronounced with finality that if the book was written by a woman, "she must be one who for some sufficient reason has long forfeited the society of her sex."

The authoritative voice of the *Quarterly* was felt by many to have decided the question of *Jane Eyre's* morality. A good many years were to pass before any young lady could admit that she had read and enjoyed the book without bringing down shame on her own head and on the heads of her parents. Lady Frederick Cavendish was twenty-six years old before she read *Jane Eyre* with her husband; and then her reaction to it would probably have been held by the stricter moralists to justify the ban laid upon it.

We finished *Jane Eyre*, which is, I think, the most powerful novel I ever read; the authoress turns oneself and one's opinions round her thumb. I thought my principles were pretty well established with regard to bigamy, but I might have been heard at one moment fervently wishing that circumstances had kept Jane ignorant of the first wife's existence. *N.B.*—I repented afterwards.

By this time there were other books engaging the attention of the public. *Wuthering Heights* and *Agnes Gray*, the first by Emily, the second by Anne Brontë, which appeared in 1847, had aroused only moderate interest. The strange, wild genius of *Wuthering Heights* went for a time almost unrecognized. In 1848 came Mrs. Gaskell's *Mary Barton*, which, as we have seen, was read largely for the light that it threw on the condition of the cotton operatives of Manchester. It was, besides, a powerful and a moving story, but its tragic downrightness caused some people to find it not very pleasant reading.

"For *Mary Barton* I am a little disappointed, do you know," wrote Mary Howitt to her daughter. "There is power and truth—she can shake and she can pierce, but I wish half the book away, it is so tedious every now and then; and besides, I want more beauty, more air from the universal world. . . . How could I help being disappointed when Mrs. Jameson told me that since *The Bride of Lammermoor* nothing had appeared equal to *Mary Barton*. Then the style of the book is slovenly and given to a kind of phraseology that would be vulgar even as colloquial English."

A more important event for novel readers than the publication of *Mary Barton* was the issue, in the November of the same year, of the first number of Thackeray's new story, *Pendennis*. Those readers who had hoped for another Becky Sharp were doomed to disappointment; as the numbers went on no character emerged that had anything like the fascination of that erring damsel, whom readers would gladly have recalled from the pious circles of Bath and Cheltenham to which Thackeray had consigned her. The great interest of *Pendennis* lay in its autobiographical element. Readers felt that they were learning a great deal about Thackeray, and about the life led by young writers in Bohemian London. Some liked *Pendennis* even better than *Vanity Fair*, and it roused Thackeray's fame to a height which approached, though it did not reach, that of Dickens. Edmund Yates, then a young man of eighteen, a clerk in the service of the Post Office, read the book, and declared many years later—

There is no prose story in our English language, not even the *Christmas Carol*, not even *The Newcomes*, not even the *Scenes of Clerical Life* or *Silas Marner* which interests and affects me like *Pendennis*.

FitzGerald liked the book much, and when he read it again sixteen years later he liked it much more. Shirley Brooks also read it with admiration when it first came out, and in 1863 wrote, "Last night I took up *Pendennis*, and I could not lay it down, but sat reading it till midnight." Herbert Spencer thought it had "less satire and more sympathy" than *Vanity Fair*, and Harriet Martineau said it much increased her respect and admiration for its author. Charlotte Brontë was, of course, enthusiastic. She thought the first number "rich in indication of ease, resource, promise." Fifteen months later, when the story was nearly finished, she acknowledged that "here and there we feel the pen has been guided by a tired hand . . . but Thackeray soon proves himself greater when he is weary than other writers are when they are fresh."

Miss Brontë was herself at work on another novel, but it was not published until October 1849. She, like Thackeray, had to stand the test of being judged by the high standard set up by a previous work. Like Thackeray, too, she disappointed those readers who were looking for a heroine of the same type as the former creation. Shirley Keeldar was not to the public in general nearly as intriguing as Jane Eyre, and both she and Caroline Helstone, the secondary heroine, were so irreproachable in their conduct that the stimulus which had set readers to work excitedly—and enjoyably—throwing stones at Jane was lacking. Mrs. Carlyle expressed something of this feeling when she said, "Now that the authoress has left off 'corsing and schwearing,' as my German master used to call it, one finds her neither very lively nor very original."

The part of the book to which most objection was made was that which had to do with the three curates. A good many people thought this vulgar, and some thought it irreverent and lacking in respect to the Church. Charles Kingsley began to read *Shirley*, but was disgusted with the opening chapter which shows these curates at supper together, and he gave up the author and her books, as he told Mrs. Gaskell after Charlotte Brontë was dead, "with the idea that she was a person who liked coarseness." Mrs. Gaskell's *Life of Charlotte Brontë* opened his eyes to his mistake. "How I misjudged her!" he said. "I shall now read carefully and lovingly every word she has written."

On the whole, Miss Brontë was driven to the conclusion that "*Shirley* is disparaged in comparison with *Jane Eyre*." "Mere

novel-readers, it is evident, think *Shirley* something of a failure."
Yet the book had many very sincere admirers. Mary Taylor, Miss
Brontë's school friend, writing from New Zealand, said that
Shirley was much more interesting than Jane Eyre, who "never
interests you at all until she has something to suffer." Sara Coleridge
read *Shirley*, and was delighted with it. Miss Brontë received
letters from all parts of the country telling how readers had enjoyed
the book, including one from a youth at Cambridge, who intimated
his intention of taking Jane and Shirley and Caroline for his sisters.
"You are very welcome," she replied, "and I trust they will often
speak to their adopted brother when he is solitary and soothe him
when he is sad."

Shirley, like *Jane Eyre*, was published anonymously, but the
secret of its authorship gradually became known. In Haworth and
its neighbourhood, where, by internal evidence, there had been a
fairly general identification of Miss Brontë as the writer of the
books, there was great excitement and not a little pride at the
fame that had been won for the village by the parson's daughter.

"The Haworth people have been making great fools of themselves about *Shirley*," wrote its author in January 1850; "they
have taken it in an enthusiastic light. When they got the volumes
at the Mechanics' Institute all the members wanted them. They
cast lots for the whole three, and whoever got a volume was only
allowed to keep it two days, and was to be fined a shilling *per diem*
for longer detention. It would be mere nonsense and vanity to
tell you what they say."

Pendennis was still going on, side by side with *David Copperfield*.
The first ended in December 1850, the second a month earlier.
Eighteen-fifty-one, when everyone's attention was being given to
the Great Exhibition, and there was perhaps less demand than
usual for stories, saw no important work coming from any of the
Great Novelists. Eighteen-fifty-two saw the beginning of *Bleak
House* and the publication of *The History of Henry Esmond* in
three volumes. The public, in spite of the fact that this was the
year of *Uncle Tom's Cabin*, found time to read both these stories.
The sale of the monthly numbers of *Bleak House* rose quickly
from thirty to forty thousand. Sydney Dobell called it a work of
"transcendent genius."

I am heartily glad I have been drawn into reading it, for it has given me such an estimation of Dickens as none of his former writings could justify.

Esmond, too, was in great demand. Everyone was eager to read this new book of Thackeray's which, it was said, was so very different from anything he had written before. "Have you read *Esmond*?" wrote John Millais to Mrs. Combe. "I hear from Holman Hunt that it is splendid, but it is in so much request at the library that I cannot get it."

Harriet Martineau read it, and changed her somewhat grudging appreciation of Thackeray to whole-hearted admiration. "*Esmond* appears to me the book of the century in its department," she said. Fanny Kemble called it an extraordinary literary feat. Anthony Trollope, now fulfilling conscientiously the monotonous duties of a Post Office servant, but with schemes of authorship in his head, went even farther than Miss Martineau. Before he was nineteen, he said, he had made up his mind that *Pride and Prejudice* was the best novel in the language, "a palm which I only partially withdrew after a second reading of *Ivanhoe*, and did not completely bestow elsewhere until *Esmond* was written."

So far Thackeray had every reason to be satisfied with the book's reception; but there was another side. A good many readers found *Esmond* dull, and complained that the story was too slow-moving and involved for interest to be maintained. Matthew Arnold wrote from London to his friend, Clough—

Thackeray's *Esmond* you know everyone here calls a failure, but I do not think so. It is one of the most readable books I ever met.

Miss Mitford wrote of it scathingly to her friend, Miss Jephson—

Have you ever read *Esmond*? William Harness (a friend of the author's) says, "I hate it." James Payn says, "I took it with me into the Theological Halls, and listened to the professor by preference." I dislike all the love parts exceedingly, and I feel it tiresomely long, and I dissent from much of the criticism, but bits are good, especially the mock *Spectator*.

Thackeray's most loyal admirer, Charlotte Brontë, was a little sad and disappointed. She wrote a long letter to her publisher, who had sent her an early copy of *Esmond*.

I have read, enjoyed, been interested, and, after all, felt as much ire and sorrow as gratitude and admiration. . . . As usual he is unjust to women, quite unjust. There is hardly any punishment he does not deserve for making Lady Castlewood peep through a keyhole, listen at a door, and be jealous of a boy and a milkmaid. Many other things I noticed that for my part grieved and exasperated me as I read; but then, again, came passages so true, so deeply thought, so tenderly felt, one could not help forgiving and admiring.

One more literary event of this year 1852 must be recorded. Two years before, Dickens had started a new periodical, which he called *Household Words*, and had invited Mrs. Gaskell to become one of its contributors. The first of a series of sketches written by her under the title of *Cranford* appeared in the December number of 1851. Month by month throughout 1852 and part of 1853 came a fresh and delightful paper, admitting the reader into the uniquely charming society of a small Cheshire town which, as the author said, "was in the possession of the Amazons." To spend an hour in the company of Miss Mattie and her friends was pure refreshment, and jaded readers revelled in the simplicities of the book without any fear that these might turn into stupidities. Mr. and Mrs. Burne-Jones enjoyed *Cranford* together in their early married days. Ruskin's mother, who thought very highly of Mrs. Gaskell, read it over and over again, and Ruskin began it, but flew into a passion when Captain Brown (one of the very few men in the story) was killed, and refused to go any farther; until his mother prevailed upon him to read it to her, and, coaxing him past the chapter that had so displeased him, saw him read it eagerly to the end. "I enjoyed it mightily," he confessed. "I do not know when I have read a more finished little study of human nature."

The only fault readers found with *Cranford* was that it was too short. Charlotte Brontë, when she read it aloud to her father, wished that it was twice as long; and a little later, writing to Mrs. Gaskell, she said—

Thank you for your letter; it was as pleasant as a quiet chat, as welcome as spring flowers, as reviving as a friend's visit, in short, it was very like a page of *Cranford*.

Eighteen-fifty-three was a notable year for the Great Novelists. No new work, it is true, came from Dickens, whose *Bleak House* ended in September, but Thackeray began the publication of his wonderful story, *The Newcomes*, Charlotte Brontë published *Villette*, Mrs. Gaskell *Ruth*, and Charles Kingsley *Hypatia*.

Ruth came first, at the beginning of January, and roused such a storm as left its author aghast. It was the story of a beautiful and friendless girl, a milliner's apprentice, who was seduced by a rich and dissolute young man, and befriended by a saintly Nonconformist minister, who agreed to, and took part in, an arrangement by which she was represented as a widow and her son as legitimately born. To deal with such a subject needed courage on the part of a writer, and especially of a woman writer, but Mrs. Gaskell had such a burning sense of the cruelty with which the public opinion of the time decreed that unfortunate girls should be treated, that she braved everything to put forward her plea. With a large section of the public that plea failed completely. The book was attacked on two counts—first, that the story of a fallen woman was not fit for the reading of pure and modest members of the same sex; second, that to represent a minister of God as acquiescing in a deception was to condone a grievous sin and to uphold a pernicious example before all readers.

The more enlightened among those who read the book saw its true aim, and warmly approved. Miss Haldane, in her *Mrs. Gaskell and her Friends*, gives a long list of them, which includes the names of John Forster, Monckton Milnes, Charlotte Brontë, Archdeacon and Mrs. Hare, Florence Nightingale, George Eliot, Mrs. Jameson, Frederick Denison Maurice, and the mother of Dean Stanley. Charles Kingsley, in a letter written to Mrs. Gaskell in July 1853, said—

I am told, to my great astonishment, that you have heard painful speeches on account of *Ruth*; what was told me raised all my indignation and disgust. Now I have read only a little (though of course I know the story) of the book; for the same reason that I cannot read *Uncle Tom's Cabin* or *Othello* or the *Bride of Lammermoor*. It is too painfully good, as I found before I had read half a volume. But this I can tell you, that among all my large acquaintance I never heard, or have heard, but one unanimous opinion of the beauty and righteousness of the book, and that, above all, from real *ladies* and really good women. If you could have heard the things which I heard spoken of it this evening by a thorough High Church fine lady of the world, and by her

daughter, too, as pure and pious a soul as one need see, you would
have no more doubt than I have that, whatsoever the "snobs" and
the bigots may think, English people, in general, have but one
opinion of *Ruth,* and that is, one of utter satisfaction.

Villette followed *Ruth* before the end of the month, and was
received with "one burst of acclamation." Miss Mary Ann Evans
was early with her praise. On February 15th she wrote to Mr.
Bray—

I am only just returned to a sense of the real world about me;
for I have been reading *Villette,* a still more wonderful book than
Jane Eyre. There is something almost preternatural in its power.

A little later she wrote again, ending her letter with *"Villette,*
Villette, have you read it?"

Clerk Maxwell read it in July. He was then a young man of
twenty-two, just down from Cambridge.

"I have been reading *Villette* by Currer Bell, *alias* Miss Brontë,"
he wrote to his friend, Lewis Campbell. "I think the authoress
of *Jane Eyre* has not ceased to think and acquire principles since
that work left her hands."

The ending of the book left readers in a state of excited curiosity.
Everybody wanted to know what had really happened to Paul
Emmanuel. Miss Brontë said that both Miss Mulock and Lady
Harriette St. Claire wrote to her asking for "exact and authentic
information" respecting his fate. She sent an answer "so worded
as to leave the matter pretty much as it was." Paul Emmanuel to
many people was the most interesting character in the book.
Lucy Snowe they thought colourless, and compared her unfavour-
ably with Jane and Shirley.

"You see how much the ladies think of this little man whom
none of you like," wrote Miss Brontë to Mr. Williams. "I had a
letter the other day announcing that a lady of some note, who
had always determined that whenever she married her husband
should be the counterpart of Mr. Knightley in Miss Austen's
Emma, had now changed her mind, and vowed that she would
either find the duplicate of Professor Emmanuel, or remain for
ever single."

Amid all the praise a few sounds of criticism and even of
denunciation could be heard. Janet Ross said that *Villette* belonged

to the class of novels which were not stories but "most minute and painful dissections of the least agreeable and beautiful parts of our nature." F. W. Robertson agreed with her in so far as he said that after reading one after another *Ruth* and *Villette* and several novels by Sir Walter Scott, he was

much struck by the marked difference between the fiction of his day and ours; the effect produced is very opposite. From those of Scott you rise with a vigorous, healthy tone of feeling; from the others with that sense of exhaustion and weakness which comes from feelings stirred up to end in nothing.

High Church readers objected to the book because of its contemptuous treatment of the Roman Catholic religion; and to Charlotte Brontë's great astonishment, Harriet Martineau, the mesmerist and unbeliever, found with *Villette* "nearly the same fault as the Puseyites." She accused its author of making a virulent attack on Popery, and she criticized also other points in the book with much harshness.

Matthew Arnold felt a strong personal distaste for *Villette*. "Miss Brontë has written a hideous, undelightful, convulsed, restricted novel," he wrote to Arthur Hugh Clough, and he declared, "It is one of the most utterly disagreeable books I have ever read." A little later he wrote to his sister—

Why is *Villette* disagreeable? Because the writer's mind contains nothing but hunger, rebellion, and rage, and therefore that is all she can, in fact, put into her book.

Charlotte Brontë's friend, Ellen Nussey, seems to have heard some of these unfavourable criticisms, and to have felt rather alarmed as to the fate of the book. But Charlotte reassured her, saying that only the worst notices must have come her way. "Some reports reach me of a different tendency; but no matter, time will show."

Time did show. As the years went on the comparatively small points that had excited contention in Charlotte Brontë's works sank into insignificance, and only what was fine and true claimed the reader's consideration. In 1856 James Smetham wrote that he had just finished reading *Villette* and Anne Brontë's *Tenant of Wildfell Hall*, "having been seized with a desire and determination to know the whole Brontë literature." He found in *Villette* "something pure, strong, deep, tender, reverential; something that teaches one how to live"; and he went on with a criticism which was almost a rhapsody.

Rossetti, William Morris, Edward Freeman, Lord Rayleigh, Walter Leaf, Mrs. Humphry Ward, and Mary Gladstone are among those who, during the thirty years that followed *Villette*, recorded their delight in Miss Brontë's works; Mrs. Gaskell's *Life*, published in 1857, found thousands of readers, and helped to establish that Brontë worship which has since grown into a cult.

To come back to 1853. The first part of *The Newcomes* came out in October, when the gathering tragedy of the Crimean War was beginning to cast a gloom over England. During the whole time that instalments of the story were appearing, the newspapers were telling of sufferings and disasters that wrung the hearts of English men and women far more than any woes imagined by the novelist could do. Yet Thackeray's book found many readers; and their memories of that staunch old soldier, Colonel Newcome, must have been for ever mingled with memories of other soldiers, as staunch as he, who served their country as he had served her. It was a grave, heroic, simple story, and it did not jar on minds uplifted by the thought of the heroism of the Six Hundred or the devotion of Florence Nightingale, as *Vanity Fair* or *Pickwick Papers* might possibly have done, but it touched deeply hearts that were softened by pity and unselfish pride. Herbert Spencer bought each number as it came out and took it home with him to read in the evening. "As often as I did this I got no sleep all night," he said, "or at any rate till towards morning." The dashing, turbulent George Lawrence must also have read it as it came out, or soon after, for in *Guy Livingstone*, published in 1857, he said—

We . . . feel a curious sensation in the throat—perhaps the slightest dimness of vision—when we read in *The Newcomes* how that noble old soldier crowned the chivalry of a stainless life, dying in the Grey Brother's gown.

"Everybody loves before all his [Thackeray's] other portraits the exquisite one of Colonel Newcome," said Fanny Kemble; and FitzGerald, "Oh, the Newcomes are fine." Mrs. Combe, wife of Mr. Combe of Oxford, who was the friend and patron of Holman Hunt and the other pre-Raphaelites, fell so deeply in love with Colonel Newcome that she endeavoured—vainly—to induce her staunch Tory husband to vote for Thackeray when he stood as

Whig candidate for Oxford in 1857. Miss Dorothea Beale, who did not much care for Thackeray's other novels, read *The Newcomes* with much appreciation; and Mr. Arthur Johnson was so impressed by the rare qualities of the book that he presented his well-worn copy to the newly opened College for Women, Lady Margaret Hall, Oxford.

The High Church party gave *The Newcomes* a place very near *The Heir of Redclyffe*. William Morris read it when it was issued in book form in 1855. "It is a splendid book," he said. It was one of Lady Frederick Cavendish's favourites; and as late as 1885 Burne-Jones made a pilgrimage to the Charterhouse on Founder's Day "for Colonel Newcome's sake."

Kingsley's *Hypatia*, which was published towards the end of 1853, after having run for sixteen months in *Frazer's Magazine*, aroused no great interest among the general reading public, though it was warmly praised by a small, scholarly circle. "You fire over the heads of the public . . . the pigmies of the circulating libraries," wrote Chevalier Bunsen. Edward Freeman read *Hypatia*, and so did Charlotte Brontë and Elizabeth Sewell, and it was one of the few novels enjoyed by General Gordon. Dean Stanley read it in 1862 on the ship in which he was travelling from Marseilles to Malta, but found it "too highly coloured" for his taste. Pusey considered it "a work not fit to be read by our wives and our sisters."

In 1854 Kingsley published *Westward Ho!*, his best-known and most popular work among grown-up readers as well as among children. Miss Charlotte Williams-Wynn tells how she tried for some time, in vain, to obtain it from the circulating library, until one morning, early in 1855, she went to the library and the attendant brought to her the bright, blue-clad volume. "I bore off my prize with glee," she said, "and admire what I have read intensely. What glorious English he does write!"

Lord and Lady Frederick Cavendish read *Westward Ho!* on their honeymoon. William Fulford and his friends at Birmingham read all Kingsley's works aloud at their meetings. "*Yeast, Alton Locke, Hypatia*, and *Westward Ho!* had all been welcomed gladly by the set," said Mrs. Burne-Jones. Edward FitzGerald wrote to Mrs. Tennyson—

I think a really *sublime* thing is the end of Kingsley's *Westward Ho!* (which I never could read through). The Chase of the Ships:

the Hero's being struck blind at the moment of revenge; then his being taken to *see* his rival and crew at the bottom of the sea. Kingsley is a distressing writer to me, but I must think this (the inspiration of it) of a piece with Homer and the Gods—which you won't at all.

Another Great Novelist, one whom FitzGerald was to appreciate far better than he appreciated Kingsley, published the book which was the beginning of his fame in this same year of 1855. Anthony Trollope began his series of Barsetshire novels with *The Warden*, and followed it two years later with *Barchester Towers*, which carried on the story, begun in the earlier book, of the clerical dignitaries and their families living in the famous cathedral city of Barchester. In *Barchester Towers*, Mr. Trollope had the honour of introducing to the readers of England a lady who at once joined the ageless and deathless company which included such of her contemporaries as Miss Betsy Trotwood, Miss Mattie Jenkyns, and Monsieur Paul Emmanuel. Mrs. Proudie, wife of the Bishop of Barchester, made the fortune of the book, although it also had great general interest in the picture it gave of life in a cathedral town.

Readers must have regarded it as a happy coincidence that while Trollope was inviting them to visit the Barchester clergy in their respective dwellings, a writer in *Blackwood's*, in a series of sketches called *Scenes of Clerical Life*, was introducing them to some very different clerical interiors. They perhaps compared the Reverend Amos Barton with Mr. Quiverful, and Mr. Tryan with the Reverend Obadiah Slope. Doubtless they compared Anthony Trollope with the "George Eliot" by whom the *Scenes* were signed, and who, as we know, though the readers of that day did not, was Miss Mary Ann Evans.

The comparison was decidedly in favour of George Eliot. Froude wrote to *Blackwood's* to thank the author most sincerely for the delight they had given to himself and his wife. Dickens expressed his "admiration of their extraordinary merit." "The exquisite truth and delicacy, both of the humour and pathos of these stories I have never seen the like of," he said. Mrs. Carlyle said she read the *Scenes* when they were published in book form

during one of the most (physically) wretched nights of my life; sitting up in bed, unable to get a wink of sleep for fever and sore

throat, and it helped me through that dreary night as well as—
better than—the most sympathetic, helpful friend watching by
my bedside could have done.

Thackeray and Mrs. Oliphant both thought highly of the *Scenes*,
though both felt sure that the conjecture that they were written
by a woman—put forward by a few readers, including Dickens—
was without foundation. Clergymen, including at least one bishop,
recognized the truth and the sympathy shown in these clerical
portraits. Mrs. Gaskell wrote to Charles Eliot Norton, "Read
Scenes from Clerical Life. ... They are a discovery of my own, and
I am *so* proud of them. *Do* read them. I have no notion who
wrote them." Readers laughed over them and cried over them.
"The death of that sweet Milly made me blubber like a boy,"
said Albert Smith, humorous writer and contributor to *Punch*.
"I did not think, at forty, I had so many tears left in me."

Trollope had no such list of compliments to show. He had a
moderate-sized circle of readers, which grew steadily larger as his
books became better known. FitzGerald was his enthusiastic
admirer, and so was George Eliot. "He is so thoroughly wholesome-
minded that one delights in seeing his books lie about to be read,"
she told Sara Hennell. Other "Barsetshire" novels followed
Barchester Towers, and readers grew familiar with the county
Trollope had created, and greeted its inhabitants as old friends.
But when he turned to other scenes and characters they were not
so well pleased. This he did in *The Three Clerks*, 1858. Walter
Bagehot read the book almost as soon as it came out, and wrote
to Miss Eliza Wilson, "It is not nearly so clever as *Barchester
Towers* on the whole." He complained that "whole dissertations
and irrelevant reflections" were inserted to make up the three
volumes. Miss Wilson replied that her family had been reading
the book, and they quite agreed with him.

George Eliot's second book was more successful than her first.
It had, as she said, a popular success, whereas the success of the
Scenes had been mainly a literary one. "Not even Sherlock Holmes
got such a grip of the public mind in 1892 as *Adam Bede* in 1859,"
said R. E. Francillon, who in that year was a young man of
eighteen. The book came out in February, and in April Lady
Rose Fane wrote to her brother, "Mr. Elwin (editor of the
Quarterly) has sent you *Adam Bede* because it is 'making a noise.'
Everyone is reading it."

Prince Albert read it, and thought so highly of it that he sent a copy to Baron Stockmar in Germany. Mrs. Carlyle was again enthusiastic; she found herself, she said, "in charity with the whole human race" when she laid the book down. Shirley Brooks was delighted with it, and Charles Reade declared it was the finest thing since Shakespeare. Mrs. Gaskell wrote to Charles Norton, "I think I have a feeling that it is not worth while trying to write while there are such books as *Adam Bede* and *Scenes from Clerical Life*." Dr. John Brown sent a message of appreciation and a copy of his own book, *Rab and his Friends*. There came news of a cabinet-maker, who declared when he read *Adam Bede* that the writer must have been brought up to the business, or at least have listened to the workmen in their workshop; of a "grave lady" who said she never read novels except a few of the most famous, but had read *Adam Bede* three times running; of another lady who after reading *Adam* went at once and bought copies of that and *Scenes of Clerical Life*. "I wish there might be three hundred matrons as good as she," said George Eliot. A working man wrote to say that he had only been able to get "a hasty read" of *Scenes of Clerical Life* and a glance at *Adam Bede*, and entreated the author to issue a cheap edition; he spoke, he said, for his working brethren as well as for himself. Sir Henry Holland read and re-read *Adam Bede*; by 1866 he had read it four times. "I often read in it, you know, besides," he said, "but it is the fourth time quite through."

On the other hand, FitzGerald protested that he could not read "your *Adam Bedes*." A good many people were shocked at some of the scenes in the book, and sternly put it away. Sir Henry Sanderson says that his father considered George Eliot's works improper, and there were many who shared his opinion. Mrs. Benson, wife of the Headmaster of Wellington College, scandalized her friends by her advocacy of the novels. She let her children read them, and she would thrust *Adam Bede* into the hands of clergymen's wives, and tell them not to mind being seen reading it.

But in spite of the moralists, the book continued to make its way, largely by the help of Mrs. Poyser. The whole reading public quickly became familiar with that sharp-tongued, capable lady; and when, about six weeks after the publication of the book, Mr. Charles Buxton remarked in a speech made in the House of Commons, "As the farmer's wife says in *Adam Bede*, 'It wants to be hatched over again and hatched different,' " there were probably few who heard his speech or read a report of it who did not recognize and chuckle over the quotation.

When the 'sixties opened six of the Great Novelists were still writing. Charlotte Brontë had died in 1855. Thackeray, who had published *The Virginians* in 1859, wrote only one more great novel, *The Adventures of Philip*, before his death in 1863. Dickens' most prolific period was over. But the 'sixties were to see some of George Eliot's finest work; they were to see more "Barsetshire" novels from Trollope; three stories in Mrs. Gaskell's best vein; and, from Kingsley, *Hereward the Wake*.

All these books were widely read and freely discussed. On the whole, probably George Eliot's works were the most popular, though none of them made such a sensation as *Adam Bede* had done. When *The Mill on the Floss* came out, Henry Kingsley, though he had by this time reached the mature age of thirty, added to the list of his literary sweethearts poor, sorely tried Maggie Tulliver, "the noblest of them all, the girl who wore dark night on her head for diadem." Mrs. Benson, the intrepid, read the book aloud to her family. Darwin, in reply to a letter from his friend Fox, wrote—

I did not enjoy *The Mill on the Floss* as much as you, but from what you say we will read it again. Do you know *Silas Marner?* It is a charming little story.

Miss Williams-Wynn did not care for the book, and did not think it at all worthy to be a successor of *Adam Bede*.

It is lengthy, and altogether leaves a disagreeable impression on one's mind. There is much beautiful writing scattered through it, and wonderful painting of character; but it decidedly wearied me.

FitzGerald, as usual, was unappreciative. "I can't read George Eliot, as I presume you can," he wrote to Tennyson. "I really conclude that the fault lies in me, not in her." He read *Barchester Towers* over again with great enjoyment, and he read the other novels of Trollope as they appeared. Trollope's novels were steadily rising in the favour of the reading public, which was beginning to manifest such interest in the fate of his heroes and heroines as marks the stage when these have passed from being mere characters in a book, and have become real living men and women. Lily Dale's love affairs in *The Small House at Allington* and its successors were followed with keen interest, and Trollope in his *Autobiography* says—

From that day to this I have been continually favoured with letters, the purport of which has always been to beg me to marry Lily Dale to Johnny Eames.

Two years before *The Small House*, in 1863, came George Eliot's *Romola*. It was hailed as something more than a novel—as a story that dealt with spiritual issues rather than mortal ones, a kind of Scripture. "Read *Romola*, by George Eliot," wrote the devout, fifteen-year-old Digby Mackworth Dolben to his friend, Robert Bridges. "Be enthusiastic about Savanarola. I am." Mary Gladstone read and re-read it; she

thought it heavy as a novel and somehow not really impressive in an Italian or even historical sense. I mean the scenes and descriptions do not quite fit into the surroundings. Romola is intensely English. . . . But she is very grand, and the scene in which she first bows her will to Savanarola is surely unbeaten by anything George Eliot has ever done. Tito is, of course, the triumph as to character.

By this time George Eliot was a grave and majestic lady, living in dignified retirement at The Priory, Regent's Park, and regarded almost with awe by those who had the good fortune to be admitted to her presence. Miss Betham-Edwards tells how, in 1867, when she was a girl of twenty-one she was taken to the Priory by a friend, and graciously received by George Eliot and Mr. Lewis.

Suddenly Mr. Lewis accosted the great woman with boyishly enthusiastic camaradeship.
"Now, Polly, what say you to this?"
Bishop Proudie, in Trollope's immortal scene, could not have been more thunderstruck at hearing "the wife of his bosom" called a woman than I was then.

It is saddening to remember that at the time when the great "Bishopess" was thus recalled to Miss Betham-Edwards' memory, the lady herself was dead. She died in 1866, while Trollope was writing *The Last Chronicle of Barset*. The time and occasion of her decease we learn from Mrs. Panton, to whom the author confided the story. One day he heard two men at his club talking about her, and saying how they wished she were dead. "I went straight home and killed her, and some day I mean to tell those fellows they incited me to murder."

We may hope, and indeed may believe, that not many readers sympathized with these unkind and relentless gentlemen. The majority had delighted in Mrs. Proudie, and had felt her temper no bar to familiarity. It was she who gave to the Barsetshire novels salt and savour. Robert Louis Stevenson, referring to the scene in which Mr. Crawley bids defiance to the lady in her own palace— the same scene in which the dumbfounded Bishop hears her addressed as a woman—says that it is "epically conceived," and raises the everyday story of Trollope's "inimitable clergymen" to the rank of a work of art.

Carlyle is recorded to have said, in one of his more splenetic moments, that Trollope's works were like alum; but to set against this we have a long list of admirers, including Lord Rayleigh, Thackeray, Lady de Rothschild, and Walter Bagehot. George Eliot read each number of *Orley Farm* as it came out, and admired it very much. Mr. Frederic Harrison said—

We used to look forward to getting "a first read" of a new Trollope, for we knew we should find in it lively pictures of true life, pure women, wholesome families, and men of sterling honour and sound sense.

Meantime Mrs. Gaskell had left off writing social novels, and was giving her readers some delightful tales in the vein of *Cranford*. Of these, the critics placed first *Cousin Phyllis*—that "flawless and radiant idyll," as one of them called it. Cardinal Newman thought *Sylvia's Lovers* the best of all Mrs. Gaskell's stories; and Lady Frederick Cavendish wrote in her diary in April 1866—

Finished *Sylvia's Lovers* in floods of tears, and think it one of the best novels I ever read; but a *cruel* one; a thing it is really bad for one to have a heartache over.

George du Maurier, who knew the district that was the scene of the story well, delighted in the book and loved the name of Sylvia, and when Mary Gladstone paid a visit to Rasthwaite in 1871 her chief interest in it came from its being the scene of *Sylvia's Lovers*.

Mrs. Gaskell's last novel, *Wives and Daughters*, came out in the *Cornhill Magazine* from August 1864 to January 1866. In December 1864, Madame Mohl wrote to Mrs. Gaskell from Paris—

I got the numbers long ago and read the story in two days (such a treat!). . . I have this very evening read the last number of the *Cornhill*, and am as pleased as ever. The Hamleys are delightful, and Mrs. Gibson!—oh, the tricks are delicious; but I am not up to Cynthia yet. Everyone says it's the best thing you ever did.

More and more people read the *Cornhill* as the story unfolded. That charming young lady whom Austin Dobson met on a railway journey, who babbled so prettily about Tennyson and Browning, babbled also of the novels of the day and of Mrs. Gaskell. From the poets the conversation

> shifted to muscular novels,
> With a little digression on prigs.
> She thought *Wives and Daughters* "so jolly."
> Had I read it? She knew when I had,
> Like the rest I should dote upon Molly,
> And "poor Mrs. Gaskell—how sad!"

The "how sad!" refers, of course, to Mrs. Gaskell's sudden death on November 12, 1865. "I am trembling," wrote Bishop Thirlwall, "lest she should have left her last novel unfinished. It is one of the most delightful specimens of the still life novel I have ever read."

It was left unfinished, but only the last chapter remained to be written, and the tenor of that was made quite clear by what had gone before. The final instalment of the story, completed by the editor, appeared in the January number of the *Cornhill*.

The eighteen-seventies found the band of the Great Novelists sadly diminished. Thackeray was dead and Mrs. Gaskell, and Dickens died on June 8, 1870. The great days were nearly over. There was still *Middlemarch* to come, and *Daniel Deronda*; but it was becoming clear that George Eliot was moving farther and farther from the standpoint of the writers of the earlier part of Victoria's reign, who regarded the telling of a story as the main business of a novelist, and was approaching that of the new school by which the story was treated as subordinate to the setting forward of a philosophic theory and the minute dissection of character and motive. Walter Bagehot, when in 1870 he was kept at home by illness for some weeks, would ask his wife or her sister to bring him something to read from Smith's Library; but not George Eliot—that, he said, was work.

Middlemarch was somewhat heavily loaded with philosophical disquisitions, but it had enough story to carry the weight bravely. George Eliot said—

> No former book of mine has been received with more enthusiasm, not even *Adam Bede*: and I have received many deeply affecting assurances of its influence for good on individual minds.

Bishop Thirlwall was among those who delighted in it.

> I have never received a part of *Middlemarch* without reading it straight through, and should always have done so in much less time if it had not been a thing which one savours like some exquisite liqueur.

Lord Acton, who was a George Eliot enthusiast, placed *Middlemarch* very high. There had been a touch of failure, he thought, in the two preceding works, *Felix Holt*, and even *Romola*. "It was *Middlemarch* that revealed to me not only her grand serenity, but her superiority to some of the greatest writers." Florence Nightingale's comment on the book was characteristic. Could not the heroine, she said, have been put to some such work as that of Octavia Hill. Mary Gladstone was only interested in the Dorothea–Casaubon part, which she thought first-rate. Henry Sidgwick believed he could have planned the story much better.

> I don't see why the Dryasdust hero need have been more than, say, thirty-five, and he might have had an illusory halo of vague, spiritual aspirations. The end of the story would have been made just as tragic. The *style* is the finest intellectual cookery.

Middlemarch was Miss Dorothea Beale's favourite of all George Eliot's books. W. L. Courtney says that it was his bedside book when he went through the examination for the Merton Fellowship in 1872. An old lady living at Coventry, after lying awake all night thinking pitifully of Bulstrode, wrote—

> Poor dear creature, after he had done so much for the wretch, sitting up at night and attending on him! *and I don't believe it was*

the brandy that killed him: and what is to become of Bulstrode now—he has nobody left but Christ.

Samuel Butler was almost alone in regarding the book with entire disfavour.

"It is very clever," he said, "but that is a matter of course; nevertheless, her characters are not lovable, and there is something hard about the book which makes it grate upon me, though I do not exactly know what it is."

As the 'seventies went on George Eliot came to be regarded more and more as an inspired prophetess whose works had a message and a significance far above that of the ordinary novelist. Lord Acton regarded her with a reverence that almost amounted to worship. William Archer said that from the time he was about twenty, for ten years George Eliot was probably the paramount influence on his mind. When *Daniel Deronda* appeared in 1876 it was received with the respectful eagerness due to the utterances of a great teacher, but of delight in it as a story there seems to have been very little, though Miss Jane Harrison says that at Cambridge she and her fellow-students used to wait outside Macmillan's shop for each new number. Mary Gladstone read and re-read it. In May 1879 she wrote in her diary, "Finished *Daniel Deronda* for the second time with much admiration. It is an underrated book." Charlotte Yonge said—

It seems to me that she [George Eliot] could represent, but not create, and that when she had lived with a world she did not really know, her ideals were absurd, as in *Deronda*.

Yet Dr. Adler, the Chief Rabbi, appreciated the book for "the fidelity with which some of the best traits of the Jewish character have been depicted," and a large number of other Jewish readers joined in his appreciation. But the public in general probably agreed with Anthony Trollope when he said—

I doubt whether any young person can read with pleasure either *Felix Holt*, *Middlemarch*, or *Daniel Deronda*. I know that they are very difficult to many who are not young.

Swinburne was much more severe. "Having no taste for the dissection of dolls, I shall leave Daniel Deronda in his natural place, above the rag-shop door."

FitzGerald remained constant in his distaste for George Eliot and her works. He was growing old now, and his eyes were failing, so that he had to employ someone to read to him.

> I set my Reader last night on beginning *The Mill on the Floss*, he wrote in 1873. "I couldn't take to it more than to others I have tried to read by the Greatest Novelist of the Day; but I will go on a little further. Oh, for some more brave Trollope!"

There was to be very little new "brave Trollope" forthcoming, and none equal to the old. Trollope's admirers had to be content with reading that over and over again. FitzGerald consoled himself with *The Eustace Diamonds*, which, he said—

> interest me almost as much as Tichborne. I really give the best proof I can of the interest I take in Trollope's novels by constantly breaking out into argument with the Reader (who never replies) about what is said and done by the People in the several Novels. I say, "No, no, she must have known she was lying! He couldn't have been such a fool!" etc.

George Eliot, who during the later years of her life read little fiction, made an exception in favour of "bits of Mr. Trollope, for affection's sake." She died on December 22, 1880, and Lord Acton wrote to Mary Gladstone—

> It seems as if the sun had gone out. You cannot think how much I owe to her. Of eighteen or twenty writers by whom I am conscious that my taste was formed, she was one. In problems of life and thought that baffled Shakespeare her touch was unfailing.

The age of the Great Novelists was over. Kingsley had died in 1875 and Trollope in 1882. But their works remained, to form for many years to come the main provision for a large body of readers. Other prophets arose and had their followings, but the true Victorian could not be drawn from his allegiance. For him the Great Novelists always came first, the rest fell into rank behind them.

CHAPTER XIV

A YOUNG VICTORIAN'S LIBRARY

THE boys and girls whose childhood fell within the second half of the nineteenth century had good reason to consider themselves prime favourites of that department of Dame Fortune's establishment which is charged with the distribution of books; for during that period were handed out gifts unique and precious, which those lucky young Victorians held for their own and bequeathed as a great heritage to their sons and daughters. Up to the time of the Queen's accession books for young people had come in but slowly, and of the meagre store only one here and there had possessed character or originality. But as the years of the reign went on the numbers increased, the quality rose, and the masterpieces appeared; and we watch the boys and girls gleefully adding treasure after treasure to the inheritance they had received from their fathers.

The most valuable part of this inheritance had come, not by right of succession, but by annexation. The young people, while their own stock of literature had remained scanty, had been used to supplement it by reading the books belonging to their elders. When books specially designed for juvenile reading began to appear in considerable numbers, most of them left off doing this. But there were some grown-up books they could not make up their minds to leave behind—notably *Pilgrim's Progress*, *The Arabian Nights*, *Gulliver's Travels*, and *Robinson Crusoe*. They insisted on keeping these and adding them to their own particular store, and gradually the fathers and mothers gave up their claim and the transfer was complete.

There were also certain of the works which, before Victoria's time, had been written for the young, that were decided to be worthy of preservation. Some of these were school books; others were such specimens of the intensely moral and improving type of story (favoured during the eighteenth and early nineteenth centuries) as had, in spite of their morality and their improvingness contrived to make themselves favourites with young readers, and among these were *Sandford and Merton*, *The Fairchild Family*, Miss Edgeworth's *Moral Tales*, and *The Swiss Family Robinson*.

The list given by James Wilson (who was born in 1836 and died Canon of Worcester in 1931) of the books read by his brothers and sisters and himself during their childhood may be taken as a representative one, such as might have been obtained from almost every early Victorian family where the children's education and general reading were carefully supervised. Here is the list: Mrs. Markham's *History of England*, Pinnock's *Greece* and *Rome*, the *Bible*, *Pilgrim's Progress*, *Gulliver's Travels*, *Robinson Crusoe*, *The Fairchild Family*, *Sandford and Merton*, Maria Edgeworth's *Tales*, and, at a later stage, the works of Sir Walter Scott. To this list many new books were added as time went on, but the original ones were only very slowly discarded. Some have survived to the present day.

If we take these books in the order of their popularity as indicated by the number of copies circulated, those published by Mr. Pinnock undoubtedly come first. "Have you ever heard the name of Pinnock?" counsel asked George Meredith, who was a witness in a case brought by a certain James Pinnock (apparently no relation to his illustrious namesake) in 1890, against Chapman and Hall. "Not since the days of my youth," was the answer, "when I learnt his *Catechism*." Almost every man and woman, whose childhood had been passed, as Meredith's had been, under the rule of Victoria, might have replied in substantially the same terms. Mr. Pinnock was an enterprising gentleman who had been quick to see how the vogue for school books written on the plan of question and answer could be turned to advantage. Miss Richmal Mangnall's *Historical and Miscellaneous Questions for the Use of Young People*, published in 1800, had become extremely popular, and so had other books written on the same plan, such as *The Child's Guide to Knowledge*. Mr. Pinnock took over Mangnall's *Questions* and issued it as one of his series; and he set a whole company of writers to work to prepare similar books on almost every imaginable subject—history (ancient and modern), geography, science, theology, as well as that wide and inclusive department of knowledge classed as "miscellaneous." These he issued, usually at the price of ninepence, and they quickly found their way into almost every schoolroom.

At the beginning of Victoria's reign the popularity of Mr Pinnock's catechisms was at its height, and for another thirty years it showed no sign of waning. "We very old pupils," wrote Miss

Frances Mary Buss, who was ten years old when the Queen came to the throne, "can carry our minds back to the time when the *Guide to Knowledge* and Mangnall's *Questions* were the chief standard school books." At the Mount School for Girls, founded by the Society of Friends in 1831, Mangnall's *Questions* was on the list of school books for at least thirty years. Izzy Tindall, afterwards Mrs. Joshua Rowntree, was among the pupils set to imbibe its wisdom. So general was the use of this compendium of knowledge that when, in 1855, Thackeray told his young readers in *The Rose and the Ring* that the Princess Angelica "could answer half a dozen Mangnall's *Questions*, but then you must take care to ask the right ones," he had no misgivings that his allusion to the famous schoolroom classic would not be understood and enjoyed.

When the 'seventies came they found Mr. Pinnock still the chief, though not the sole, purveyor of mental nourishment for the schoolroom. His little books were still selling by thousands, and boys and girls all over the country still looked on him as the uncomfortably omniscient director of their studies. Henry Newbolt pored over Pinnock's *Greece* and Pinnock's *Rome* until he knew them both almost by heart—as James Wilson had done nearly twenty years before him. Miss Frances Gray, at her preparatory school, was absorbing from Mangnall's *Questions* and *The Child's Guide to Knowledge* a store of miscellaneous knowledge which one hopes she found useful in later years in her position of Principal of Westfield College. Henry Sanderson, at the advanced age of six, was making acquaintance with the same works, and feeling slightly staggered when, on opening *The Child's Guide*, he was met by the comprehensive question, "What is the world?" Miss Cecily Steadman, too, had entered on the well-trodden educational path that led through Mangnall and Pinnock, though later she turned into the newer road opened by Miss Dorothea Beale and Cheltenham Ladies' College. Even vacuous youths of the type that produced inane young gentlemen like Mr. Potts of *Molly Bawn*, were being so well drilled in Pinnock that they retained a vague memory of him for some years after they left school. "I was christened Plantagenet," said Mr. Potts proudly. "Good sound, hasn't it? Something to do with the Dark Ages and Pinnock, only I never remember what."

But as the 'seventies drew towards their close the glory of the universal instructor began to wane, and Miss Lilian Faithful expresses the views of many of her contemporaries when she says—

The preceding generation also had *The Child's Guide to Knowledge*, Mrs. Markham's *History*, Mrs. Marcet's *Conversations by Land and Water*, and Mangnall's *Questions*. We inherited these lesson books, but a new era was approaching, and we resented what our elders had accepted meekly enough, and scorned the priggish children who were introduced as asking intelligent questions, and who appeared genuinely anxious to learn.

Mrs. Markham's *History* was, for at least a generation, almost as popular as Mangnall's *Questions*. It was written at the request of Mrs. Markham's son, Richard, a clever little boy of ten, who had tried to read Hume and found it beyond him. He implored his mother to write a history that he could understand; and she accordingly produced this work, beginning with the Ancient Britons and arriving finally at the fourteenth year of Queen Victoria. She wrote also a *History of France* and a *History of Germany*. These works, it soon appeared, met the needs of many other children besides little Richard Markham, for before very long they were to be found in a large number of schoolrooms, and many boys and girls were learning from them about the things that happened in the ages long ago—with the most unpleasant parts left out, for Mrs. Markham did not think it right to show children the worst side of the villains of history if it were possible to avoid doing so.

They learnt too, which perhaps made the book additionally interesting, something about Mrs. Markham's three children, Richard, George, and Mary; for Mrs. Markham, although she had abandoned the form of question and answer beloved of Mr. Pinnock, encouraged her children to ask questions on anything contained in each particular section which they did not understand; and these questions, with her answers to them, she printed in full at the end of the section. Richard asked thoughtful and intelligent questions, such as, "Were there no learned men in England before Alfred's time?" which enabled his mother to give a dissertation on Gildas, Bede, and Scotus. George was chiefly interested in the structure of the ancient ships and the arms used in battle, and for his sake various illustrations were inserted which increased the attractiveness of the book. Mary was rather frivolous, and wanted to know how Alfred managed to carry a book in his bosom. But even such questions Mrs. Markham turned to account by using them as a text for a full and accurate description of the costume of the period.

Canon Wilson, Sir Henry Sanderson, and Miss Lilian Faithful all in their schoolroom days learnt their history from Mrs. Markham. Florence Nightingale studied the *History of France* with her governess, and found later, when she visited France, that she had learnt enough from it to make her visit pleasant and profitable. Ouida must have known the *History of England* well, and found in it certain dramatic possibilities, for in one of her less flamboyant stories she tells of two little children living in a Devonshire vicarage who, when the unaccustomed snow came to their valley one Christmastide, were moved to act the scenes pictured by Mrs. Markham, showing the French retreat from Moscow. Samuel Butler shows us poor little Ernest Pontifex studying the *History* with his governess in his dismal schoolroom. He probably hated it as he hated all his lesson books, since he was liable at any moment to be examined on their contents by his very unpleasant father and soundly whipped if his answers proved unsatisfactory. There must have been many other Victorian children who had almost equally disagreeable associations with Mrs. Markham, for, up to the later days of the great Queen, even loving parents believed that the more children were whipped the faster they would proceed on the way of learning. The family of Edward White Benson, whose study of Mrs. Markham began twenty-five years later than Ernest Pontifex's, regarded her *History of England* with a mixture of awe and dislike. Whether this was due to painful associations such as his we are not told; but when in 1873 they came to live at Lincoln, on their father's preferment as Canon of Lincoln Cathedral, and discovered in the cloister a stone marking the grave of the learned lady, their chief feeling seems to have been one of relief that she would write no more histories. Mrs. Markham has, however, a gallant champion in Dame Ethel Smyth.

From Mrs. Markham I learned all the history I knew till the day dawned for loving Shakespeare, and I consider these two together could defy the universe as quickeners of an historical sense in the young.

There was another book, called *Little Arthur's History*, written by Lady Callcott in 1835, which was to be found in many school-rooms. It was simpler than Mrs. Markham's, and was often used as preparatory to that work. Mr. Arthur Waugh, Miss Steadman, Lord Sanderson, and Mr. Joseph Chamberlain all gained their first ideas of history from it.

The name of Colenso was not quite as familiar to young Victorians as were the names of Pinnock and Mrs. Markham. But when, in 1862, the outcry arose against the "heretic bishop," there were many young ladies and gentlemen, as well as boys and girls still at school, whose thoughts at once went back to the thick, dumpy volume with its many pages of closely printed exercises, from which had been taken the sums that they had worked on smudgy slates, often with groaning, sometimes with tears. Colenso's *Arithmetic* had appeared in 1843, and it testifies to an increase in the attention given to the teaching of arithmetic. Even girls were allowed to go a little farther than the first four rules, though there was still a prejudice against the subject in the minds of conventional mammas, who considered it unladylike. By 1862 Colenso had established itself so firmly as a textbook that even the bishop's heresy did not serve to dislodge it; though some young ladies brought up on High Church principles—like Miss Yonge's unruly Angela Underwood—excused themselves for their arithmetical failures by declaring that the book was a shocking one, not fit to touch, so of course the sums came wrong. No allurement, no imprisonment, said Angela, with a pleasing sense of martyrdom, should make her consent to truckle to a heretic. Her steadier sister, Robina, who had worked "innumerable problems out of Colenso," reasoned with her, but in vain.

Coming now to the story-books, we find that Canon Wilson's list includes the names of all those that were most widely read during at least the first few years of Victoria's reign. Most popular of all were *The Pilgrim's Progress*, *Robinson Crusoe*, and *The Arabian Nights*. On these the early Victorians were brought up, as their fathers had been before them. A very long list could be made of biographies and autobiographies in which one or more of these books is mentioned as having been read during childhood. Everyone seems to have read *Pilgrim's Progress*—except James Anthony Froude, whose father had such a horror of Dissenters that he would not have Bunyan's book in the house, and Edward Burne-Jones, of whom his wife said—

How he came to miss it I do not know, but so it was, until by the time he first saw it the names in the story jarred upon him so much that he would not read it.

It was a great favourite in large families, where its characters came to be looked upon almost as familiar playmates. Lucy Lyttelton and her brothers and sisters exulted in a copy of *Pilgrim's Progress* unabridged and delightfully illustrated. In the patriarchal colony of the Leaf family at Streatham, where in the 'sixties William Leaf, wholesale dealer in silks and ribbons, ruled over his three sons and their families, it was well known; the children, says Walter Leaf, a grandson, looked upon Apollyon "as a specimen of somewhat grim humour." The family of the Reverend James Lynn, rector of the remote Cumberland parish of Crosthwaite, received it with modified enthusiasm, being prejudiced against it because their father attempted too definitely to point the moral. It was the second book Walter Besant read for himself—the first was *Robinson Crusoe*. "The immortal *Pilgrim's Progress* was my book of books," says Thomas Cooper. Thomas Burt read it at the house of an aunt who lived two miles from his own home. She would not lend him her copy, so he used to rush off during his short periods of leisure to read, if it were only for a few minutes, the enchanting book.

Not as a dream or an allegory, but as solid literal history did it present itself to my boyish mind. I believed every word of it. My pious aunt, wishful to know how I had been impressed, was greatly shocked to find that in the famous encounter between Apollyon and Christian I declared my sympathies to be wholly on the side of the evil one.

Robert Louis Stevenson put *Pilgrim's Progress* "not indeed in the inner circle of my intimates," but in the front rank of "a good troop of dear acquaintances." He gained more delight from *The Arabian Nights' Entertainment*, which he remembered first reading in "the fat old double-columned volume with the prints."

I was just well into the story of the Hunchback when my clergyman grandfather (a man we counted pretty stiff) came in behind me. I grew blind with terror. But instead of ordering the book away, he said he envied me. Ah, well he might!

Lord Rosebery wrote in his copy of *The Arabian Nights*, "This is the copy we all read out of as children." W. E. Henley lighted by some happy chance upon a copy, and at once life "became touched to eternal issues and tinctured with magic." The little Lynns "received its wonders with trembling." William Morris revelled in it. It was one of the few story-books that Christina Rossetti read in her childhood, and one of the few that brought some rare snatches of happiness to Charlotte Brontë's neglected little heroine, Jane Eyre, in hers.

As for *Robinson Crusoe*, we will quote the words of George Borrow, written about 1845. He had been recalling the day, more than twenty years earlier, when he had been introduced to the "wondrous volume," which had so fascinated him that he had ever since been a keen observer of its influence over other young minds. It was, he said—

a book which has exerted over the minds of Englishmen an influence certainly greater than any other of modern times, which has been in most people's hands, and with the contents of which even those who cannot read it are to a certain extent acquainted; . . . a book . . . to which, from the hardy deeds which it narrates, and the spirit of strange and romantic enterprise which it tends to awaken, England owes many of her astonishing discoveries both by sea and land, and no inconsiderable part of her naval glory.

The Swiss Family Robinson was generally regarded with tempered enthusiasm, as being a weak imitation of the great Crusoe epic. Some children enjoyed it because it suggested to them the fascinating game of imitating the life of the stranded family; as it did to Hughes' Tom Brown, who read it before he was eight years old and dreamt of building a house for himself in the branches of a great elm that grew by his father's stables. Many, like Henry Sanderson, were annoyed with the story because everything that was needed turned up just at the right moment, and there were none of the ingenious contrivances that made the joy of De Foe's book.

The passion for Scott came, usually, with these Victorian boys and girls, a little later than the passion for *Robinson Crusoe*—except in the case of such an insatiable reader as William Morris, who, realizing that only by beginning early was there any chance of his getting through all he intended to read, was at four years old already deep in the Waverley Novels. But come it almost invariably did. The parents of these children were among those who remembered vividly the stirring days when the Waverleys were appearing, and enthusiasm was rising higher and higher. They had lived joyfully under the sway of the Wizard of the North, and they brought up their children in the same allegiance. The children responded eagerly. They seized upon the novels and were ready to take them over as their own property, as they had done with *Pilgrim's Progress* and the others. But this the older folk would by no means allow. Their rights in Sir Walter were far too precious to be surrendered. So the claims of both were recognized, and young and old read their Waverleys in amicable enjoyment. "For many years," says Philip Henry Wicksteed (born 1844), "Scott, read by my father as few could read him, was part of the life of the household." "We had been brought up on the novels of Sir Walter Scott," says Miss Frances Gray; and William Archer tells us that when he was a boy, in the late 'fifties and early 'sixties, the name of Sir Walter was held in reverence in the household, and "the children were turned loose at an early age into the fair domain of the Waverley Novels, as into a garden where no poisonous plants were to be feared." George Eliot, writing in 1871, said—

I began to read him when I was seven years old; and afterwards when I was grown up and living alone with my father, I was able to make the evenings cheerful for him during the last five or six years of his life by reading aloud to him Scott's novels. . . . It is a personal grief, a heart wound to me, when I hear a depreciatory or slighting word about Scott.

Such pronouncements might be multiplied. All through the reign of Victoria the spirit of each generation was being kindled at the torch of devotion carried by its elders. Sir William Orchardson says that he was introduced to Scott by his father reading aloud to him *The Black Dwarf*, which so enchanted him that he went on to *Ivanhoe*, which he found even more fascinating, and then to the rest of the Waverleys. Sir Sidney Colvin declares that he can never be grateful enough to his mother for setting him on to read *Rob Roy* to her when he was eight years old. "The other Waverleys followed," he says, "and subsequent years have only deepened and confirmed my delight in the imaginary world

of which I was thus early made free." Lord Rosebery began at
the age of eleven with *The Legend of Montrose*, which his mother
read to him in the Christmas holidays of 1858, while he was
suffering great pain from burns received from an accident during
a game of snapdragon. In the household where Mr. Maurice
Baring's childhood was spent "the reading of the Waverley Novels
was a divine, far-off event to which all one's life seemed to be
slowly moving." "When you are nine years old," was the promise
made to him and his sisters, "you shall read *The Talisman*." First
one sister and then another attained the longed-for age and entered
into its proud privileges, and by the time the little brother's ninth
birthday came they had read "all Walter Scott, except, of course,
The Heart of Midlothian, which was not, as they said, for the
J.P. (*jeune personne*), and *Peveril of the Peak*." The tutor of the
young Leafs, at Streatham, used what was perhaps rather a doubtful
means of stimulating his pupils' interest in the Waverley Novels.
He gave them dictation lessons from those works. "I still recall,"
said Walter Leaf many years later, "one passage from *The Antiquary*
which was thus stamped on my memory."

Not all these boys and girls felt for Scott the reverent admiration
with which children belonging to High Church families were
taught to regard him. They thought of him as the great romancer,
the magician who could open to them delights undreamt of before.
It was this magic which caught up twelve-year-old Henry Sidgwick,
and sent him with a volume of *Waverley* to sit enchanted on the
stairs while hue and cry was made for him to take his part in a
tableau for which the audience was waiting. It was this magic
which, as Sir Francis Burnand tells us in *My Time*, kept two
small boys awake night after night in their school dormitory beds
while the more fortunate one, who had read Sir Walter's novels,
recounted the history of Ivanhoe and Guy Mannering to his friend
who had not. Miss Faithful says that by the time the 'eighties
came Scott was not as universally read by boys and girls as by their
parents; but it was not until near the end of Victoria's reign that
the falling off became at all considerable.

Midway between school books and books read purely for
entertainment came Macaulay's *Essays*. "From Eton and Harrow
down to an elementary school in St. Giles's or Bethnal Green,"
wrote John Morley in 1881, "Macaulay's *Essays* are a textbook."
Textbook is perhaps scarcely the right term to describe a work

which intelligent young Victorians read with extreme delight. "I was very much under the spell of Macaulay's *Essays*," said Walter Leaf. Lucy Lyttelton read them when she was fifteen years old, and, says Mr. John Bailey, her brother-in-law, who edited her diaries—

they were with her, as with so many of us, in spite of youthful Royalist feelings "desperately exasperated" by Macaulay's whiggery, the first, or almost the first, grown-up book to be appreciated.

Miss Elizabeth Wordsworth, when she was fourteen years old and at school at Brighton, got hold of Macaulay's *Essays* and read some of them with great interest. Lord Rosebery came to them even earlier. He was only eleven when, wandering round the library at Chevening, he quite by chance took down Macaulay's *Essays* and "fell at once under the wand of the enchanter." He began with the essay on Milton, and went straight on through the three volumes, not understanding all that he read, but delighting in "the eloquence, the grasp and the command of knowledge, the irresistible current of the style." "And to that book," he said, "I owe all the ambitions and aspirations I have ever indulged in."

A few years later another boy, of even higher gifts and greater future fame, was reading Macaulay's works. Lord Balfour has told how his mother gave him the posthumous volumes of Macaulay's *Miscellaneous Writings*, then recently published, and how he became at once a fascinated admirer—

His style delighted me. I thought his dialectics irresistible. His gift of narrative carried me away; the things he wrote about invariably interested me; in short, he supplied much of the mental nourishment I desired in the exact form that best suited my very youthful appetite.

All this time the new story-books were coming in, and the young Victorians were not so preoccupied with the old ones as to fail in giving these fresh arrivals a hearty welcome. For the boys there were books of adventure. Scott had quickened their taste for the romantic and the unfamiliar, and a company of lesser writers were working to satisfy it. Fenimore Cooper sent over his Leatherstocking stories from America, and at home Marryat, Mayne Reid, Ballantyne, and Kingston provided a large and varied selection. Robert Louis Stevenson said that when he was a boy he loved best stories about highwaymen; a Jacobite would do, but a highwayman was his favourite dish. He had a friend who

preferred the Malabar coast in a storm, with a ship beating to windward, and a scowling fellow of Herculean proportions striding along the beach; he, to be sure, was a pirate.

Walter Frith wanted plenty of imagination and adventure. Miss Faithful declared for a smuggling story. All these tastes could be satisfied by the works that were being so generously provided, and William Morris, Walter Besant, Lord Kilbracken, Lord Balfour, Sir Sidney Colvin, and Sir Oliver Lodge are among those who have testified to the delight with which in their boyhood they read these books of adventure. Smedley's heroes read them, and so did Hughes' Tom Brown and Henry Kingsley's Charles Ravenshoe. Girls, too, received them with rapture. In those days, as Miss Faithful has reminded us, the gulf between boys and girls was strongly marked by the books provided for each. All the greater, therefore, was the joy with which a girl of an adventurous turn of mind laid hands on the books belonging to her brother, even though by doing so she risked incurring a pained rebuke for her unladylike tastes. Dora Alison, of Miss Yonge's *My Young Alcides*, made use of a period of convalescence to insist on hearing Marryat's stories read aloud. Miss Broughton's Nell L'Estrange probably followed the more usual plan of dispensing with the permission of the higher powers, and making an unauthorized acquaintance with the young lady in *Midshipman Easy*, whose declaration that "to shake hands with a man made a cold shiver run down her back" she quoted with much appreciation.

In our own day, competing with the story of adventure for the favour of the young reader, comes the story of school life. The boys and girls of early Victorian days were but scantily provided with literature of this type. The girls had only *The Governess* and its few feeble imitations until America sent the *Katy* books. The boys had nothing that could be called a school story until *The Crofton Boys*, by Harriet Martineau, appeared in 1841. This was a distinctly more interesting book than *The Governess*, less rigid in its conventions and with some well-told episodes. It had even touches of humour. But its boy characters were merely puppets, and it was grievously overloaded with its moral. The boys for whom it was intended received it, apparently, without much enthusiasm, though some grown-up readers praised it warmly. George Eliot said—

What an exquisite little thing that is of Harriet Martineau's, *The Crofton Boys*. I have had some delightful crying over it. There are two or three lines in it that would feed one's soul for a month;

and she proceeded to quote some pages she specially admired. *The Crofton Boys* survived as a book for children's reading for a good many years. Maurice Baring says that in 1883 it was given him for a prize, and he adds, "It is very difficult for me to understand now how a child could have enjoyed the intensely sermonizing tone of this book, but I certainly did enjoy it."

Other writers were slow to follow Miss Martineau's example, and no other notable boys' school story appeared until 1857; and then came *Tom Brown's Schooldays*. The young Victorian was quick to see that here was the real thing, and that Tom Brown and his schoolfellows were boys like themselves who could be received as friends and comrades. The book appealed to the sporting, open-air instincts of the natural boy, as well as to his love of fair play, his loyalty, and his manliness. The moral, though it was there (Hughes said that his motive in writing the book was to preach a sermon), was not offensively evident, and there were pages that could safely be skipped by wary readers bent on avoiding it. Kingsley, writing to Hughes in June 1857, said that he had puffed the book everywhere he went, but—

I soon found how true the adage is that good wine needs no bush, for everyone had read it already, and from everyone, from the fine lady on her throne to the redcoat on his cock-horse and the school-boy on his forrum (as our Irish brethren call it) I have heard but one word, and that is that it is the jolliest book they ever read. Among a lot of redcoats at the cover-side, some very fast fellow said, "If I had had such a book in my boyhood I should have been a better man now," and more than one capped his sentiment frankly. Now isn't it a comfort to your old bones to have written such a book, and a comfort to see that fellows are in a humour to take it in?

John Godley (Lord Kilbracken), as the time approached when he was to be a "schoolboy on his forrum" at a great public school, took from *Tom Brown* his notion of the life before him, and felt distinctly inclined towards it. Mr. Cecil Torr read the book in

1866, when he was in his teens. Octavia Hill read it soon after it was published, when she was eighteen years old. "I think the book one of the noblest I ever read," she declared.

Tom Brown was the first of a series of books destined to shine with peculiar brilliance in the library of the young Victorian, and to attain, if not immortality, yet a great and honoured age. It is a significant fact that, with regard to several of these books, the older generation attempted something akin to the act of annexation which had given the young ones the acknowledged primary rights in *Robinson Crusoe* and its fellows. But in no case did they succeed. The books were so obviously young people's books that their claim could not be set aside. The elders might—and did—read and enjoy them. Holman Hunt said that he read *Tom Brown* with delighted interest. Tennyson read it aloud to his wife while they were on a tour in the north of England in 1857, and they both enjoyed it thoroughly. Walter Bagehot read it in 1858. Mr. Cecil Torr says he remembers his father and an old-fashioned doctor discussing the book. The doctor contended that Dr. Arnold, for all his fame as a schoolmaster, did not know how to bring up his sons, since Matthew turned out a free-thinker, and Tom became a Roman Catholic. Madame Mohl, who before her marriage had been the clever, attractive Miss Mary Clarke, daughter of Mr. Clarke of Westminster, criticized the book rather unkindly. The author, she said, "shows, unknown to himself, the intense empty-patedness of boys, and fancies he is showing them to advantage."

How far the next notable school story owed its origin to *Tom Brown* is not certain, but the relation of one to the other is plain. It was inevitable that there should be some counterblast to the cheerful, rousing note sounded by Thomas Hughes; for sentimentalism had come into fashion, and there was a large and increasing body of readers who prided themselves upon their emotional reactions; who loved to shed the tear of sensibility, and whose highest praise bestowed upon a work of art was "So touching!" or "So sweet!" These delicately constituted persons were, in the summer of 1858, tearfully delighted with *Eric; or Little by Little*, the work of Frederick Farrar, a young classical master at Harrow. Mr. Farrar had embodied his recollections of King William's College, in the Isle of Man, where he had been a pupil in a story founded on the Awful Example principle of *The Fairchild Family* and other moral books of that era. His schoolboys had none of the hearty, natural enjoyment of mischief that characterized Tom and his companions; they did not tread the up-and-down pathway, through one scrape into another, by which the ordinary schoolboy light-heartedly progresses. The bad boys— and they were very bad—went steadily downhill, sinning without zest and with visible depression. The good boys preserved a saintly —yet cheerless—demeanour, and found a morbid satisfaction in provoking scenes with their unregenerate schoolfellows—scenes in which speeches of heartrending eloquence were made, floods of tears shed, and, in extreme cases, kisses exchanged. Nearly all these boneless young gentlemen—the bad and the good—came to unhappy ends, and the reader was called upon to stand by several death-beds and to weep over wasted lives and broken hearts.

It seems strange that such a book should have found favour with a youthful audience, but it did. Many boys read it, probably even more than read *Tom Brown*. "*Eric* has received the warm encomiums of the boys and masters here," the author wrote from Harrow; and his son quotes many letters from young as well as from adult admirers, all testifying to the immense pleasure and profit the writers had received from reading this depressing tract on school life. It is true that the *Saturday Review*—the Saturday Wasp the badly stung Mr. Farrar called it—published a scathing notice of the book. It is true, also, that many old boys of King William's College cried out on Farrar for villifying the school they held in affectionate remembrance. "I put it to any King William's College man whatever whether he would recognize the College by the description given in *Eric*," said T. E. Brown; and he declared, "We repudiated it with indignation." But Canon Wilson, who entered the school in 1848, a little later than T. E. Brown, admitted that "Farrar's *Eric* was no caricature of this school, though it was a caricature of the human boy."

In the second edition, which was very soon demanded, Farrar apologized for any harm that his book might have done to the College, but neither the attack nor the apology injured the circulation of *Eric*. When the author's next book, *St. Winifred's*, which was a trifle more robust than *Eric*, and contained only one death-bed scene, appeared in 1865, it was rapturously received. Probably some part of the popularity of the two books, or at least of the popularity as evidenced by their sales, was due to the fervent admiration of fathers and mothers and uncles and aunts who persisted in giving them as birthday and Christmas presents; but there seems no doubt that the young people really read and enjoyed them. For the next thirty years almost every young Victorian whose parents took any interest in his reading was supplied with copies of *Eric* and *St. Winifred's*.

So long as sentimentalism persisted, this type of story flourished. Mr. E. E. Kellet, the author of *Fashion in Literature*, says that he has known people unable to control their emotions while reading the final pages of *Eric* or *Misunderstood*. The two works are aptly classed together, for *Misunderstood*, by Florence Montgomery, published 1869, is almost as harrowing as *Eric*, though pleasanter to read. It is about a motherless little boy named Humphrey, whose father is inclined to think him rough and unfeeling when really he is craving for love. He has a little brother, Miles, whom he adores, and who adores him. Miles is gentle and affectionate, and everybody's favourite; he is constantly being led into mischief by the more adventurous Humphrey, who finally dies in saving his brother's life.

It was possibly of these two works that Professor Conington was thinking when he discussed the children's books of the day with Miss Elizabeth Wordsworth, and confessed that he was sometimes set off crying by them in a London club or no matter where. Mrs. Panton said that *Misunderstood* made her laugh, but she must have been exceptionally hard-hearted. It is a little disconcerting to find that both Mr. George Du Maurier and Mr. Charles Lutwidge Dodgson (or, as most of us prefer to call him, Lewis Carroll) thought highly of Miss Montgomery's morbidly sentimental story. Du Maurier, who was illustrating the book, wrote to Carroll—

I am, like you, a very great admirer of *Misunderstood*, and cried pints over it. When I was doing the last picture I had to put a long white pipe in the little boy's mouth until it was finished, so as to get rid of the horrible pathos of the situation while I was executing the work. In reading the book a second time (knowing the sad end of the dear little boy), the funny parts made me cry almost as much as the pathetic ones.

Lewis Carroll, however, may well be forgiven a lapse into sentimentality, since he provided a delightful and efficient antidote against it for other people. In 1861 he wrote for one of his many little girl friends, Alice Liddell, that unique and fascinating story

Alice in Wonderland. It was passed from one to another in the circle of his friends—children and adults—and everyone who read it was enchanted by it. It must be published, they declared; and in 1865 it was published. Thus the children of England received one of the most marvellous and delightful gifts that has ever been given to them. They read the book eagerly and appreciatively. Perhaps they did not realize as fully as did their elders its rare quality. The adventures of little Alice, walking unperturbed through a topsy-turvy world, merely formed a thrilling extension of their own experiences. So had every child walked from his baby-hood, finding strange new phenomena at every step, and learning to regard with philosophic calm the many incomprehensible and even ridiculous arrangements ordained by parents and grown-up persons in general in the world around him; which helps us to understand what the little girl, of whom Lewis Carroll himself tells us, meant when she said, in answer to a question as to which she liked best, *Alice in Wonderland* or *Through the Looking Glass* (which followed four years later), "Oh, yes, I've read both of them, and I think (this more slowly and thoughtfully) that *Through the Looking Glass* is more stupid than *Alice's Adventures*. Don't you think so?" She certainly did not mean the same as did Henry Sanderson when he said that *Alice* was read to him before he was nine years old, and he thought it very silly.

Lewis Carroll sent the first presentation copy of *Alice* to Miss Alice Liddell, the second to Princess Beatrice, then eight years old. What the little princess thought of the book is not recorded, but obviously her royal mother read and was entertained by it, for according to the oft-told story (which all appreciative readers of Lewis Carroll must insist on believing, however often it is contradicted) she asked that the author's other works might be sent to her and received with astonishment *A Syllabus of Plane and Algebraical Geometry*, *The Formulae of Plane Trigonometry*, *An Elementary Treatise on Determinants*, and other learned mathe-matical dissertations. The reason why it is incumbent on loyal readers to accept this story is because it shows Her Majesty as so satisfactorily representative of a large number of her subjects who had undergone an experience similar to hers. *Alice* would not be quite the same to any of us (at least to the grown-ups) without the memory of the shock of amused realization that came when we recognized, standing behind the White Rabbit and the Mad

Hatter, the Queen of Hearts and the rest, the grave figure of a learned professor—a man who lived on familiar terms with the terrifying symbols and formulae of the higher mathematics. It added another touch of the same delightful incongruity of which one was conscious when, on looking at the baby in the Duchess's arms, one discovered it to be a pig.

Very soon Alice became the friend of thousands of English children. Even the little ones who had not yet learnt to read looked at the delightful illustrations by Sir John Tenniel, and became familiar with the demure little maiden, her hair kept in place by the Victorian comb, her short-sleeved frock protected by the inevitable Victorian pinafore. Mr. Austin Dobson expressed the feelings of all readers of the book when he said of her—

> Nought save Chaos and old Night
> Can part you now from Tenniel.

There were a few children who took up a superior attitude, and affected to look down on *Alice*. Theodore Lorn, aged thirteen, of Justin MacCarthy's *A Fair Saxon*, when asked if he had read *Alice's Adventures*, replied, "I have just looked into it. I don't care much for that sort of thing. Children's stories are all so dull and silly." Cardinal Newman was not nearly so superior as Master Theodore. When he paid a visit to Dean Church at Whatley, in 1870, he made himself quite at home with the children and compared notes with them, said their father—

about children's books, which has ended in their sending him, and he very heartily accepting, one of their books of nonsense, *Alice's Adventures in Wonderland*, which he did not know, and they thought he ought to.

The book had in it something to delight all ages. "It is one of the very few books in the world that can be read with pleasure by old and young," said Walter Besant. Shirley Brooks, editor of *Punch*, delighted in it to the end of his life. "To see him the centre of a group of wide-eyed youngsters reading his favourite poem, *The Jabberwock*, or *Alice's Adventures*, was to see him only as the biggest youngster among them." Henry Kingsley, at thirty-five, found *Alice* "a charming book," and of *Through the Looking Glass* he wrote to the author, "I can say with a clear head that your new book is the finest thing we have had since *Martin Chuzzlewit*." Mary Gladstone read *Alice* when she was eighteen, and enjoyed it thoroughly, and when *Through the Looking Glass* came out she pronounced it "delightful, quite equal to the other." Ellen Terry says that she and her sister Kate, when they were small girls, read *Alice*, and so did every member of the Terry family and in later years their children. The children of Archbishop Benson were brought up on Lewis Carroll's two books, and so was that other family of Bensons, of whom Sir Frank Benson says, "Lifelong trails were blazed for us by *Alice in Wonderland*, Lear's *Book of Nonsense*, *Shock-headed Peter*, and *Swiss Family Robinson*." George Tyrrell, afterwards Father Tyrrell of the Modernist movement, made, he says, quite a reputation for himself by reciting in 1871, when he was eleven years old, the *Looking Glass* poem about the "aged, aged man a-sitting on a gate." "Ever after I was a standing dish at these almost monthly festivals, and got to be as well known as the town clerk."

Miss Gertrude Thompson, the artist, said in 1878 that *Alice* had long been one of her pet books and she knew it nearly all off by heart. Annabel Huth Jackson read both books in the late 'seventies, before she was ten years old, and "adored them, finding them extraordinarily funny." Somewhere about the same time Maurice Baring was adventuring on *Alice*—the first book he ever read for himself. And while these children were poring over these two treasures from their library with delighted appreciation, cultured and scholarly men and women were also feeling their fascination. Miss Wordsworth has told us that they divided with the Gilbert and Sullivan operas the interest of Oxford society, and in 1873 a Cambridge tutor set his pupils for Latin elegiacs the poem beginning—

> 'Twas brillig and the slithy toves
> Did gyre and gimble in the wabe.

In 1885 some verses appeared in *Sylvia's Home Journal*, signed "One who loves Alice," which were highly appreciated by many readers who also loved Alice. The author was Miss E. Manners, and one of her verses ran—

> We climbed the mantelpiece and broke
> The jars of Dresden china;
> In Jabberwocky tongue we spoke,
> We called the kitten Dinah.
> And, oh! how earnestly we planned
> To go ourselves to Wonderland.

Long before this *Alice* had attained the honour, bestowed upon only a few of our most eminent classics, of having some of its phrases accepted as serviceable additions to everyday language. "Jam yesterday and jam to-morrow but never jam to-day" passed almost into a proverb, and few people to whom the words "I doubt it" were addressed failed to add, "Said the carpenter and shed a bitter tear." "So much the better-better-BETTER as the White Queen says," wrote James Smetham, and "Curiouser and curiouser, said Alice," was the comment of one of Mrs. Hungerford's heroines when the story of a midnight adventure was being told her; while William de Morgan, in *The Old Man's Youth*, told of a coachman who took "a view like that of the father in Jabberwocky, that the avoidance of danger was a soldier's first object to consider. He was to heed well jewjub birds, and shun the frubious bandersnatches."

One point that must have told in favour of *Alice* with young people was that it had no moral. Not even the most ingenious of parents or governesses could turn it into an instrument of edification or instruction. It had a real and important part in helping to banish the too obtrusive moral which had devastated and was still to devastate so many potentially charming children's books. Something had been done towards this good work before *Alice*. Thackeray, in *The Rose and the Ring*, 1858, had made an effective beginning, but he had done so by deriding the moral rather than by leaving it out; and in the end the good were rewarded and the bad punished in the traditional fashion.

There was another book, also entirely destitute of a moral, which appeared in its first form in 1846, and should have been mentioned before, except that it has so great an affinity with *Alice* as to make it almost obligatory to consider the two together. This was Edward Lear's delightful *Book of Nonsense*. In some ways it anticipated *Alice*; the "Pobble who has no toes," whose

> Aunt Jobiska made him drink
> Lavender water tinged with pink,
> For she said, "The World in general knows
> There's nothing so good for a Pobble's toes,"

would have been quite at home in the company of the Jabberwocky, the Gryphon, and the Mock Turtle; so, indeed, would the whole of Lear's entrancing company—

the small Olympian Bear,
And the Dong with its luminous nose;
And the Blue Baboon who played the flute,
And the Orient Calf from the Land of Tute,
And the Attery Squash and the Bisky Bat.

They delighted many of the same children as revelled in *Alice*. Both the Benson families read the book. Mr. Chichester Fortescue, afterwards Lord Carlingford, wrote to Lear about "A first cousin of mine, a certain Mrs. Tisdall, whose children have been feasting on *The Book of Nonsense*." The Francillons, who lived at Cheltenham, and whose father was a personal friend of Lear's, were enthusiastic over it. Robert Francillon says that once when Lear was visiting at their house he, his brother, and his sister were delighted eye-witnesses of the production of some of the first pages of *The Book of Nonsense*. He says, too, that Lear used to tell a story of how, soon after the book was published, he was travelling in a railway carriage with, as fellow-passengers, a family who were reading a copy of the book and highly enjoying its fun. Presently he heard the father telling his children that the book was written by the Earl of Derby, and that "Lear" was an anagram of "Earl." The author found this more than he could bear. He intervened politely, explained that he had written the poems, and offered his card. But the gentleman remained unconvinced. "I have it on the very best authority," he said.

The young Victorian, although he delighted in these moral-free books, had not arrived at the stage at which he definitely resented the presence of a moral. He was only beginning to feel a little ruffled when it took a too prominent place. Often he managed to ignore it. He ignored it almost completely in *Water Babies*, which had appeared two years before *Alice*. The moral was foremost in Kingsley's thoughts when he wrote the book, and he tried very hard to make it permeate the story. "I have tried," he wrote to F. D. Maurice—

in all sorts of queer ways to make children and grown folks understand that there is a quite miraculous and divine element underlying all physical nature. . . . And if I have wrapped up my parable in seeming tom-fooleries, it is because so only could I get the pill swallowed by a generation who are not believing with anything like their whole heart in the Living God.

His wrapping up was more effectual than he intended it to be, for there were some people who could get at neither the story nor the moral.

"Read to them [her younger brothers] the beginning of Kingsley's mad book, *The Water Babies,*" wrote Lady Frederick Cavendish in her diary, "the only comprehensible part, the rest being an entangled jumble of allegory, fairy-tale, and natural history. Very dream-like and crazy."

Dr. Whewell said that he didn't care for *Water Babies,* and couldn't make out what it was about. No child, he declared, would understand it. But if the children did not understand it, some of them at least read and enjoyed it. Mr. E. F. Benson tells how, when he was a small boy of eight or nine, Mrs. Kingsley (who was his godmother) gave him a copy of *Water Babies,* which he found "an enthralling book." "May I ask if you have read *The Water Babies?*" wrote Mrs. Gatty, author of *Parables from Nature,* to Mrs. Moberly. "I ask everyone, for it has enchanted me to such an extent that I dip into it again and again as a sort of refreshment." After such a recommendation, we may feel sure that Mrs. Moberly introduced the work to her large and book-loving family in the house in College Street, Winchester—if it was not already well known there.

Kingsley's other two books, *Heroes* and *Westward Ho!,* were also great favourites with the young Victorian. Lady Frances Balfour says that her daughter, when she was a small child, was obsessed by *Heroes,* "an immortal work for children." Kingsley himself described *Westward Ho!* as "a most ruthless, bloodthirsty book (just what the times want, I think)." What Kingsley called its ruthlessness and bloodthirstiness made it acceptable to the young and the adventurous, and its high courageous spirit suited the temper of a nation that was, at the time the book was published, full of pride in the deeds of its fighting men.

By the time the 'seventies came many authors had realized the importance of the young Victorian as a reader. Stories of adventure and stories of school life, quiet domestic stories and thrilling tales of mystery, stories moral and stories nonsensical, stories pathetic and stories mirthful—all came in abundance to enrich his library. Children's periodicals, which contained much entertaining and instructive matter as well as fiction, increased and multiplied.

Many of these stories were excellent and deserved to be read, as they were, with gusto. To give a list of them here would be neither interesting nor useful; to deal at length with each would be impossible. We will take one book, which may fairly be called the gem of this period, to show the kind of gift that was being bestowed on the young Victorian of the 'eighties.

It came when to those who loved stories the prospect seemed a little unhappy. There were writers in plenty, too many, so pessimistic readers were inclined to think. But they produced no masterpieces. All the great Victorian story-tellers were dead. Science was attracting the readers who once gloated over novels; the triumphant days of fiction, said the prophets, were over.

"We are to look for no more Sir Walters," wrote Mr. Augustine Birrell in *Obiter Dicta*, "no more Thackerays, no more Dickens. The stories have all been told. Plots are exploded. Incident is over. In moods of dejection these dark sayings seemed only too true. Shakespeare's saddest of sad lines rose to one's lips: 'My grief lies onward and my joy behind.' Behind us are *Ivanhoe* and *Guy Mannering*, *Pendennis*, and *The Virginians*, Pecksniff and Micawber. In front of us stretch a never-ending series, a dreary vista of *Foregone Conclusions*, *Counterfeit Presentments*, and *Undiscovered Countries*. But the darkest watch of the night is the one before the dawn, and relief is often nearest to us when we least expect it. All this gloomy nonsense was suddenly dispelled, and the fact that really and truly, behind this philosophical arras, we were all inwardly ravening for stories, was most satisfactorily established by the incontinent manner in which we flung ourselves into the arms of Mr. Robert Louis Stevenson, to whom we could almost have raised a statue in the market-place for having written *Treasure Island*."

Mr. Birrell spoke for young readers and for old. The book was essentially a boys' book, but men of all ages became boys in their enthusiasm for it. The editor of the *Saturday Review* declared that it was the best boys' book that had appeared since *Robinson Crusoe*. Lord Rosebery read it, and Mr. Gladstone, having seen it at his house, could not rest until he had obtained a copy for himself. In a letter to its author, Mr. Edmund Gosse said—

Miss Gladstone was telling me the other day that her father had read *Treasure Island* over and over, and had tried to make Lord Hartington read it—but complained, "He won't read anything, not even *Treasure Island* and *Sister Dora*."

"This is the kind of stuff a fellow wants," declared Andrew Lang. Lord Balfour has told how, one afternoon in the year 1883, Randolph Churchill came up to him in the House of Commons, and said he had just returned from Eton, where everybody was reading with the utmost enjoyment a new novel of adventure by Robert Louis Stevenson called *Treasure Island*. He advised Lord Balfour to get a copy of the book without delay—which he did. The Headmaster of Mr. Maurice Baring's preparatory school read *Treasure Island* aloud to the boys, and in a list of books he had read, which he made a little later, Mr. Baring wrote opposite the name of this masterpiece of Stevenson's, "Perfect book."

Tom Brown, Water Babies, The Book of Nonsense, The Rose and the Ring, Alice in Wonderland, and *Treasure Island,* with many others that would have served to make notable a less opulent age—all these were bestowed upon the young Victorians within the space of thirty years. Has any like period in our history given to its young readers in such royal abundance?

CHAPTER XV

BOOKS FROM MUDIE'S

SOME time during the year 1840 a small shop was opened in King Street, Bloomsbury—now Southampton Street. Its proprietor was a young man of twenty-two named Charles Edward Mudie, active and ambitious and bent on making his business a success. He dealt chiefly in newspapers, but he sold books too, and was ready for any new venture that seemed likely to be profitable. He tried publishing, beginning with Emerson's *Essay*, which he called *Man Thinking*, and this attracted the notice of some of the young students living in Bloomsbury. The London University had lately been established, and the neighbourhood was beginning to be overrun with eager young men whose chief need was books. A good many of these came into Charles Edward Mudie's shop, and found the proprietor as eager and as book-loving as themselves. Soon it occurred to Mr. Mudie that to lend books to these not too affluent young students would be a useful and a profitable undertaking, and with the promptness that was natural to him he at once made a start. First, he brought to the shop his own private collection of books, and before a day had passed every one had been borrowed. Then, taking pains to find out what kind of works were really needed, he gradually collected a stock that was highly appreciated by his young customers. His shop became the general meeting-place of a small group of enthusiastic readers.

I was one of the not very numerous circle of readers who gladly availed themselves of what was then a unique collection, and who were additionally attracted to King Street by the intelligence and amiability of their owner,

wrote Francis Espinasse, and he mentions that among the books he borrowed were the works of Theodore Parker and of Emerson, and Margaret Fuller's periodical, *The Dial*. Young Richard Hutton, the future editor of *The Spectator*, was then a student of University College and a frequenter of Mr. Mudie's shop, and David Masson, author of the *Life of Milton*, was also often to be seen there.

The success of this venture caused Mr. Mudie to resolve to

extend his library, and to become a lender rather than a seller of books. He was a prudent man, and doubtless before he took any decisive steps he considered carefully the condition and prospects of lending libraries in England. The great days of William Lane and the Minerva Press were over. The growth of periodical literature with its serial stories by popular writers, and the custom of publishing works of fiction in monthly parts, had turned many borrowers into buyers. There were cheap editions to be had of scientific, historical, and poetical works, but new issues were still highly priced, and novels were almost invariably published in three volumes at ten shillings and sixpence a volume.

It was still impossible, therefore, for any but very wealthy readers to buy all the books they needed, and libraries were a necessity. The older establishments, such as Hookham's of Bond Street and Booth's of Regent Street, had a large connection among readers of the better class and did very well in a steady, unenterprising fashion. There were libraries of a sort in most towns, large and small, throughout the country, but a considerable proportion of these resembled the establishment situated in a small street off the Tottenham Court Road, where Mr. Mortimer Knag, of *Nicholas Nickleby*, "let out by day, week, or year the newest-old novels, whereof the titles were displayed in pen-and-ink characters on a sheet of cardboard swinging at his door-post." Mr. Mudie knew all about libraries of this type. Had there not been, in connection with his father's book and paper shop at Chelsea, a library which was a higher development of that of Mr. Knag, and had not his own youth been spent in its service? But it was not such a shop as his father's that Charles Edward saw when he looked into the future, nor were his visionary customers at all like the nursemaids and shopboys, the small tradesmen's wives, and the grubby children to whom he had handed out soiled volumes, and whose pennies he had received in payment. His library should not cater for boys who, like young Herbert Spencer, brought their "occasional pence" and asked for *The Castle of Otranto* and the works of Mrs. Radcliffe; nor for flighty damsels like Mrs. Henry Wood's Affy Hallijohn, who came for third-rate love stories, which turned their heads and made them dream of marriages that would transform them into ladies; nor of little girls of seven or eight, who persisted, as Mrs. Catherine Gore said she did at that age, in demanding *Ernest Maltravers*, and only after a long and serious discourse from the shocked old lady behind the counter, consented to take *Fatherless Fanny* instead. At first, indeed, such customers might find their way to King Street, but in Charles Edward's visions of the future greatness of the House of Mudie they had no part. That House should be built upon the great middle class. Mr. Mudie felt that of this class he had a just and instinctive understanding. He knew their tastes and their capacity, he knew what would shock and what would please them, and this knowledge he would use to bring them in, from the greatest to the least. He saw the vast population that lived in City streets and squares and suburban villas, over thriving shops, and even in West End mansions, flocking to his doors. It is, perhaps, unlikely that he clearly foresaw the time when the box from Mudie's would be an institution at most country houses, and when branches of the main establishment would be found in almost every provincial town. But since there is no greatness without vision, some vague picture of the vast extension to come must have flitted before the eyes of Charles Edward Mudie, and given to the opening of his modest library in King Street the significance of the first strategical move in a great campaign.

Mr. Mudie knew that the books with which his library was already stocked would attract only the small body of readers who read to satisfy a real intellectual curiosity. The larger public wanted simply to be interested and amused—which meant that they wanted novels. And here came in a difficulty. Mr. Mudie was a Dissenter, a prominent member of his denomination. Busy as he was, he found time for regular attendance at chapel, where indeed he sometimes preached. Novels were held by most members of the Dissenting community to be works of the Evil One. But the bookseller was too intelligent and too much a man of the world to hold this doctrine in its entirety. Good novels he believed he might, with a clear conscience, supply to his customers; bad novels, those which had the slightest immoral tendency—no. He was firmly resolved that with such he would have nothing to do, and he called his library Mudie's *Select* Library to indicate that he reserved a right of choice in the books that he provided.

From the beginning the venture went steadily forward towards success. The small collection of books grew from hundreds to thousands. A subscription of a guinea a year enabled readers to borrow one volume at a time from the library; and inveterate novel-readers who were anxious to keep up with the fashionable literature of the day found themselves able to supply their needs more cheaply than they had ever done before.

It was probably some two or three years after the library was opened that William de Morgan, then a very small boy, came one day with his mother from their home in Gower Street near by to change the books she had borrowed. He stood with his chin resting on the counter, and gazed at the shelves upon shelves of enchanting volumes that extended before him. He saw a tall gentleman step out from the back of the shop and hand his mother a three-volume novel; and as they turned to walk away his mother whispered to him, "That was Mr. Mudie." The young bookseller was already a well-known and, in his way, a famous person. His dream was fulfilling itself, and the readers of London were in ever-increasing numbers flocking to his doors.

One of the earliest subscribers was Miss Dorothea Beale, then a girl of sixteen living at her father's house in Bishopsgate. Herbert Spencer, who was in students' lodgings near by, says that he came to Mudie's, "then a thriving infant in Southampton Row," for the novels which he liked to read in bed after a day of mental exertion. Edward FitzGerald had books sent regularly to him at Woodbridge, and Tennyson's two brothers, Frederick and Charles, visited the library when they were in town. Thomas Hughes, F. Denison Maurice, Anna Swanwick, and the Wedgwood brothers were also early subscribers. Sir John Franklin, a few days before he started on his last Arctic expedition, came into Mr. Mudie's shop to choose books for the voyage.

Most of the subscribers came for novels. The novel was, as Robert Louis Stevenson said, "the staff and stay of Mr. Mudie." But the astute bookseller did not rely solely on fiction. He took pains to keep up his collection of books for students and thinkers, and he bought in considerable numbers the newest works on history and biography. Occasionally one of these scored a success even greater than that of a popular novel. Macaulay's *History*, of which Volumes I and II were published in 1849, is an example. Macaulay had maintained that history need not be dry and uninteresting. "I shall not be satisfied," he had said, "unless I produce something which shall for a few days supersede the last fashionable novel on the tables of young ladies." He succeeded in doing this, and in delighting more serious readers as well. Three editions of his *History* were called for in the first six months, and eighteen thousand copies were sold. Lady Frances Balfour says that there is a tradition in her family that

the first volume was cut and read aloud after breakfast without a break until the luncheon hour; after which the reading was resumed until the shades of evening drew on.

Mary Ann Evans read the *History*, and wrote to Sara Hennell—

I am delighted to find that you mention Macaulay, because that is an indication that Mr. Hennell has been reading him. I thought of Mr. H. all through the book as the only person I could be quite sure would enjoy it as much as I did myself. I did not know if it would interest you. Tell me more explicitly that it does.

Sara Coleridge said she had finished "Macaulay's highly attractive volumes, the second of which has an enchanting interest." School-boys read it for pleasure, not as a task. Seventeen-year-old Charles Lutwidge Dodgson wrote from his school at Richmond complaining that he had "not yet been able to get the second volume of Macaulay's *England* to read." Edmund Yates, then a young Post Office servant of eighteen, read it, and so did young Dr. Priestley, who had just come back from his honeymoon, and was living in Portman Square waiting for patients. Middle-aged business gentlemen grudged the time that must be given to their families while those fascinating volumes remained unread. Thackeray, writing to *Punch* in the name of Mr. Spec, bewailed the tyranny which obliged papa to escort his offspring to children's parties—

You must go. If you are dying of lumbago, if you are engaged to the best of dinners, if you are longing to stop at home and read Macaulay, you must give it all up and go.

Lord Auckland said that he had hated one of his best friends, whom at any other time he should have embraced on both sides of his face, for coming in one evening and hindering the reading of the book. Seventy-two-year-old Mr. Brontë read it at Haworth, and eighty-two-year-old Miss Edgeworth at Edgeworthstown, both with keen enjoyment. It was all very well for Carlyle to reply grudgingly to Francis Espinasse's praises that Macaulay "never said anything not entirely commonplace," though he was certainly "a very brilliant fellow"; and the sage's sarcastically meant comment, "Flow on, thou shining river," was really a very apt description, not only of the author's style, but of the manner in which the book made its bright, irresistible way through the country, to the profit of everybody concerned, including Mr. Mudie.

Exactly how many of the copies used by eager readers came from the library in King Street we do not know, but probably a good many, for when the third and fourth volumes of the *History* were published in 1855, Mr. Mudie took two thousand four hundred, and these he at once put into circulation.

"Letters and criticisms still pour in," wrote Macaulay, in January 1856. "Praise greatly predominates, but there is a strong admixture of censure. I can, however, see no sign that these volumes excite less interest than their predecessors."

The censure came chiefly from scholars who disagreed with Macaulay on his reading of historical facts. A few readers, however, complained of a falling off in the charm of the narrative.

"I have only read about a hundred pages of Macaulay," wrote Matthew Arnold. "I thought my chariot wheels went heavier than when I was reading the first two volumes."

Mrs. Oliphant criticized somewhat tartly, "Everybody admires him, of course, but nobody believes him, as far as my experience goes."

But the volumes sold in even greater numbers than the earlier ones, and the demand for them at the libraries kept all available copies in circulation, and Mr. Mudie was satisfied.

By this time Mudie's Select Library, having outgrown the accommodation of its early home, was more suitably housed in fine and spacious premises in New Oxford Street. Mr. Mudie had taken the bold step of removal in 1852, and again his enterprise had been justified. His business increased rapidly; the number of his subscribers exceeded twenty-five thousand; and in the book-selling world his name had become a power. His announcement that he meant to take a large number of copies of any particular book was the best advertisement the work could have.

"My own first production was so honoured," said Mrs. Oliphant, "and I confess it seemed to me in those days that the patronage of Mudie was a sort of recognition from heaven."

In 1854 Miss Mitford, writing to a friend, said that such had been the demand for her new work, *Atherton*, that Mr. Mudie "had four hundred copies in circulation and found them insufficient." Of *Livingstone's Travels*, published in 1857, Mr. Mudie took two thousand copies. Concerning *Adam Bede*, George Eliot recorded in her Journal on February 6, 1859, that Mudie had taken five hundred copies on the publisher's terms. "At first he had stood out for a larger reduction, and would only take fifty, but at last he came round." On March 8th she wrote, "Mudie has sent for two hundred copies additional." On March 26th he "thinks he must have another hundred or two of *Adam*—has read the book himself and is delighted with it." When *The Mill on the Floss* came out in 1860, Mr. Mudie took two thousand.

Mudie's was now sending out parcels of books regularly to subscribers in the country who could afford this luxury. "A box for the country to be worth anything costs five guineas subscription, and then there's the carriage to and from London," lamented one of Miss Fothergill's Yorkshire heroines. But Smedley's wealthy young Midland squire, Harry Coverdale, could well afford this indulgence for his wife, and we read how Alice Coverdale, feeling very low-spirited after a lonely day while her husband was out hunting—

opened a parcel of books from the library, and began upon a new novel by that very talented lady, Mrs. Bluedeville, and read how a fair and gentle girl, brought up by a select coterie of fiendish relations, and subjected from infancy to a series of tortures sufficient to have expended the stoutest negro, developed under these favourable circumstances into a perfect Houri of Paradise, with the additional attraction of possessing the mind, manners, erudition, and phraseology of an old Divine of the Church of England. This interesting young martyr, released from her educational Bastile, and turned out to grass for a brief space in a pleasant meadow wherein pastured a gallant but very moral officer of dragoons, naturally falls in love with the same, who fortunately does not resent the liberty. Angelica, taken up from her month's run, and put to work much too heavy for her, becomes better and better and better, until as might be expected she overdoes the thing, and getting too good to live, has nothing left for it but to die, which she accordingly does on the arrival of the post which brings an account of the bold dragoon having fallen a victim to his dauntless courage, which, leading him to kill sixteen mounted

Sikhs in single combat, had failed to preserve him from the vindictive fury of the seventeenth evil-disposed survivor.

"Strange to say," adds Mr. Smedley, "this talented work, delightful as it was, failed to render Alice much more cheerful."

The sorely tried, meekly enduring heroine seems to have been a feature of the library novels of that day. Mrs. Austin, writing to M. Guizot in December 1853, said—

> *The Head of the Family*, by Miss Mulock, has some merits . . . but there is too much affliction and misery and frenzy. The heroine is one of those creatures, now so common (in novels) who remind me of a poor bird tied to a stake (as was once the cruel sport of boys) to be shied at till it died. Only our gentle lady writers at the end of all untie the poor battered bird, and assure us that it is never the worse for all the blows it has had—nay, the better—and that now, with its broken wings and torn feathers and bruised body, it is going to be quite happy.

Mrs. Jeune, wife of the master of Pembroke College, called this work "a pretty chaste little novel." She apparently was satisfied with the "happy ending," but to some readers there seemed little to choose between such an ending and that of the Mrs. Bluedevilles who consigned the heroine to an early grave. "I never read the history of a consumptive heroine twice," said Thackeray; and Harriet Martineau inveighed against "metaphysical, sentimental novels" such as *The Ogilvies*, another work by Miss Mulock. Poverty was the least of the trials that beset these interesting young martyrs; it was, indeed, scarcely to be regarded as a trial, but as an ennobling condition infinitely superior to gross wealth.

> For I've read in many a novel that unless they've souls that grovel,
> Folks *prefer* in fact a hovel to your dreary marble halls,

sang Calverley.

Miss Mulock was very popular in the 'fifties and 'sixties, especially after the publication of *John Halifax, Gentleman* in 1856. R. E. Francillon says that when he was a boy everybody was reading this book. It gave rise to endless arguments on the question, "What is meant by the term gentleman?" which had been discussed by Newman in his *Idea of a University* and by Ruskin in *Modern Painters*, and was to be raised again by George Meredith in *Evan Harrington*. By some people *John Halifax* was held to

have answered the question conclusively; others were contemptuous, even derisive. "The author wants to show her blame of
the love of money and finery, and shows all the time the importance
she attaches to it," said Mme. Mohl.

Henry Sidgwick was one of those who thought highly of Miss
Mulock's powers.

"I saw Miss Mulock the other day," he wrote to his sister.
"She looks pleasant and sympathetic, yet hardly capable of the
powerful delineations of passion one meets with in her books."

William de Morgan, on the other hand, found the blameless
and suffering heroines of this popular writer simply boring. He
and Burne-Jones once amused themselves by playing a game which
they called "Cartoons." Burne-Jones drew a procession of stout,
crinolined women in bonnets and shawls, and he and de Morgan
both wrote verses inspired by the picture. de Morgan created it
as an illustration to Dante's *Inferno*, the figures representing

> The Heroines of Romance who expiate
> Here, in this circle, mawkishness above,

and he put into their mouths their mournful confessions of identity.
Some of Miss Mulock's heroines thus bemoaned themselves—

> "Yea, I
> Was Agatha's Husband's wife, an awful bore,
> A woeful and abominable bore."
> "And I was 'Mrs. Halifax, Lady,' " cried another.
> Then a third and smaller one,
> "And I was Muriel in the self-same novel
> As she who last addressed thee." Then they all
> With one accord set up a mournful song,
> "Go tell Miss Mulock to ha' done and make
> Night hideous with her bores no more."

A large proportion of the novels that filled the shelves of the
circulating libraries were after Miss Mulock's pattern. They were
designed especially for the reading of young ladies. "Unidea'd
melodrama for unidea'd girls," growled the eccentric Dr. Sampson
of Charles Reade's *Hard Cash*; and one of Ouida's dashing young
guardsmen contemptuously described the

mild, religious, and respectably twaddling fiction of the milk-and-
water, pious-tendency, nursery-chronicling, and grammar-dis-
regarding class, nowadays indited for the mental improvement of

a commonplace generation in general, and growing young ladies in particular.

Yet, mild as it was, some parents and guardians deemed that this fiction required still further dilution before it reached the innocent damsels for whom it was intended. When Miss Twinkleton, of *Edwin Drood*, came to London to take charge of her old pupil, charming Rosa Bud, the two took lodgings in Southampton Street, once the home of the Select Library; and it was doubtless from that same library, in its new home near by, that they obtained the novels which the discreet governess read aloud to cheer the ladylike dullness of their evenings.

But Rosa soon made the discovery that Miss Twinkleton didn't read fairly. She cut the love scenes, interpolated passages in praise of female celibacy, and was guilty of other glaring pious frauds. As an instance in point, take the glowing passage: "Ever dearest and best adored," said Edward, clasping the dear head to his breast, and drawing the silken hair through his caressing fingers, from which he suffered it to fall like golden rain, "ever dearest and best adored, let us fly from the unsympathetic world and the sterile coldness of the stony-hearted, to the rich warm Paradise of Trust and Love." Miss Twinkleton's fraudulent version tamely ran thus: "Ever engaged to me with the consent of our parents on both sides, and the approbation of the silver-haired rector of the district," said Edward, respectfully raising to his lips the taper fingers so skilful in embroidery, tambour, crochet, and other truly feminine arts; "let me call on thy papa ere to-morrow's dawn has sunk into the west, and propose a suburban establishment, lowly it may be, but within our means, where he will always be welcome as an evening guest, and where every arrangement shall invest economy and constant interchange of scholastic acquirements with the attributes of the ministering angel to domestic bliss."

It is no wonder that pretty Rosa began to lose her spirits; but Mudie's came to the rescue. Quite by accident she lighted (doubtless while visiting the Select Library) on some books of voyages and sea adventures; and as she was beginning to take a tender interest in a certain gallant sailor who lived in Furnival's Inn near by, these were, to her, more enthralling than any love story. Miss Twinkleton read them aloud, and

made the most of all the latitudes and longitudes, bearings, winds, currents, offsets, and other statistics; . . . while Rosa, listening intently, made the most of what was nearest to her heart. So they both did better than before.

It was particularly unfair to leave the love out of these innocuous novels, since love was the chief ingredient and that which gave the flavour to the whole. It was all very well for highly educated young ladies, like Charles Reade's Miss Julia Dodd, to be indignant because a novel strongly recommended by a literary journal proved when it arrived from the library to be "an ignoble thing; all flirtations and curates." Flirtations and curates were what the ordinary young lady liked—or was supposed to like. Some people were beginning to lay the blame for this milk-and-watery fiction at the door of Mr. Mudie. It was he, they said, who fostered and encouraged it by refusing to admit to his library any story that showed life as it really was. There was some truth in this charge, but it was not wholly true; for most of the best novels of the day were to be found in the Select Library, as well as a large number of the feeblest. Mr. Mudie admitted *Adam Bede* and *Ruth* when a considerable section of the reading public held up its hands in horror at these two masterpieces. He excluded *The Morals of Mayfair*, by Mrs. Edwards, presumably because it told of the love affairs of certain actresses. It is less easy to see why he refused *The Ordeal of Richard Feverel* in 1859, though it is true that a good many people were shocked at the book's outspokenness. His reasons for declining to admit a copy of Charles Reade's *Cream*, which contained the two stories, *The Autobiography of a Thief*, and *Jack of All Trades*, he gave in a letter to the Press. *The Autobiography*, he said, appeared to him "of less than average ability, quite unworthy of Mr. Reade's high reputation, or of a place in any select library"; and he declared that if Reade would write a work with "anything like his old delicate and sparkling freshness of style and feeling," he would cheerfully "give a good round sum for the first edition."

There was sometimes a little unpleasantness at the Oxford Street establishment when a subscriber asked for a book that the proprietor had banned, and was told by a very polite attendant that a select library could not possibly circulate such a work. It was perhaps an indignant subscriber or, more probably, an indignant author, who in 1860 wrote to the *Literary Review* complaining that Mr. Mudie was unfair in his choice of books for his library. Mr. Mudie replied by a letter in the *Athenaeum*. He pointed out that he had from the first reserved the right to exclude any books he considered unsuitable, and declared that he was guided in his choice entirely by moral considerations. Nevertheless, he submitted that the large number of books he bought each year proved the wide range of the works in his library. Since January 1858 he had added to it 391,083 volumes made up as follows: History and Biography, 87,210; Travel and Adventure, 50,572; Fiction, 165,445; Miscellaneous, including Science, Religion, and the principal Reviews, 87,856.

These figures show to what an enormous extent the library had grown. It was, in fact, on the way to becoming a national institution; and the complaints of a few dissatisfied subscribers and authors could not overthrow or even appreciably injure it. In this same year of 1860 Mr. Mudie enlarged his premises by building a great hall, such as "would be considered a handsome assembly room in any provincial town." The walls of this hall were lined with books, and light iron galleries gave access to the upper shelves. In 1861 it was estimated that the library included 800,000 books, and that 10,000 passed in and out of its walls every day.

The cost of building the hall proved, however, too great for Mr. Mudie's resources, and in 1864 the library became a limited company. Half the shares were held by Mr. Mudie, and he retained the sole management, so that there was no change in the conduct of the business. He still bought freely all such books as seemed to him suited to the tastes and harmless to the morals of his large public.

The task of selection during the 'sixties must have been a difficult and a strenuous one. Not only were works coming from Dickens, George Eliot, Anthony Trollope, Charles and Henry Kingsley, Mrs. Gaskell, Meredith, Tennyson, Browning, and Matthew Arnold, but a host of lesser writers was sending out novels in quick succession. A rage for sensationalism had set in, and Mr. Mudie must have been hard put to it to gratify this taste, and at the same time to preserve his library from the taint of doubtful literature.

Wilkie Collins may be said to have set the fashion with his *Woman in White*. It appeared first as a serial in *All the Year Round* in 1860. Miss Eliza Chambers, daughter of the author of *Vestiges*, said—

When *The Woman in White* was creating a great sensation, my twin wrote to Wilkie Collins saying she could not wait any longer and must know the fate of Laura, etc. Wilkie Collins replied, "I beg to assure Miss Chambers solemnly that nobody about whom she is interested and over whom the undersigned can exercise benevolent control shall come to any harm. If she will look at the number published to-morrow she will see that Laura is *not* murdered, and in another week she will know that Anne Catherick *is* caught. In the same two numbers Miss Halcombe's whereabouts is satisfactorily ascertained and Miss Halcombe's recovery positively asserted.

When it appeared in three-volume form there was a rush for it at the libraries. Prince Albert read it and approved. Thackeray said he was engrossed by it from morning to sunset. Gladstone recorded in his diary on October 18th—

I did not get to the play last night from finding *The Woman in White* so very interesting. It has no dull parts, and is far better sustained than *Adam Bede*, though I do not know if it rises quite so high. The characterization is excellent.

FitzGerald read it again and again. "Now I turn again to Mudie," he wrote in 1866. "It is time to read again *The Woman in White*; a masterpiece in its way, I do think." In 1867 he wrote, "I have to my very great sorrow finished *The Woman in White* for the third time." He thought of having a herring-lugger he was building named "Marion Halcombe," "after the brave girl in the story." Swinburne thought Marion "a glorious woman," and delighted in Count Fosco. Lord Rayleigh read the book with enjoyment. "Papa deep in *The Woman in White*," recorded Lucy Lyttelton in July 1861. Even Mrs. Oliphant went so far as to admit that the story was "a marvel of workmanship." There were *Woman in White* cloaks and bonnets, *Woman in White* waltzes and quadrilles. The book had, said John Forster, a pre-eminent success.

Mr. Wilkie Collins naturally hastened his efforts to procure a second triumph. But his next two novels, *No Name* and *Armadale*, though they were widely read, fell far short of the success of their predecessor. Bishop Thirlwall read *Armadale* as it came out in the *Cornhill* in 1863.

"I have read *Armadale*," he wrote, "drawn on by curiosity to see how such a very complicated skein is to be unravelled, but with very little enjoyment. Miss Gwilt is a tragic Becky Sharp, but immensely below her prototype. On the whole I consider this class of novels as an unhappy invention, creating an insatiable demand which must be met by less and less wholesome food."

After a few more instalments had appeared he wrote—

We seem to be nearing land in *Armadale*. Is it not marvellous that anybody could have conceived it possible for Miss Gwilt to write such a journal? It is a comfort to think that she cannot go on much longer, and that almost the only doubt remaining is whether she is to poison or drown herself.

Edward FitzGerald waited until he could borrow the completed story from Mudie's. "Absurd as it is," he said, "so near being very good, I only wished it were a dozen volumes instead of two."

The Moonstone (1868) repeated the triumph of *The Woman in White*. Swinburne went into raptures over it, and compared Serjeant Cuff to Inspector Bucket of *Bleak House*. Walter Leaf, who read it some years after its publication, declared that he had "a day and a night of rapture over *The Moonstone*, which I am still inclined to look on as almost the best detective story ever written." The author in his preface to the second edition said—

The welcome accorded to the story in England, in America, and on the Continent of Europe was instantly and universally favourable. . . . Everywhere my characters made friends and my story aroused interest.

Miss Clack, the "Evangelical hag," as Swinburne called her, was a special favourite, and her *Narrative* did much towards giving the book its great success. Mr. Mudie had all he could do to supply his subscribers' demands for this second triumph of Mr. Wilkie Collins'.

Readers who liked something even more thrilling than *The Woman in White* asked at Mudie's for the novels of Le Fanu. His *The House by the Churchyard* and *Uncle Silas* were published in 1863 and 1864 respectively. They had the weird quality that could produce a sense of terror, growing by slow degrees until it became almost intolerable, by means of quiet suggestion and matter-of-fact narrative. By the general public their subtlety was little appreciated. Wilkie Collins' more facile methods of causing the flesh to creep it found far more enjoyable. But for those who loved the painful rapture of suspense, slow-mounting and mysterious, Le Fanu's stories had a strong fascination. Once begun they could not be laid down. Many readers had an experience similar to that which Henry James records of Oliver Lyon in *The Liar*, who arrived on a visit to a country house, and found in his room

the customary novel of Mr. Le Fanu—the ideal reading in a country house for the hours after midnight. Oliver Lyon could scarcely forbear beginning it while he buttoned his shirt. Perhaps that is why he not only found everyone assembled in the hall when he went down, but perceived by the way the move to dinner was instantly made that they had been waiting for him.

James Payn was proud of having brought Le Fanu's works to the notice of Prince Leopold, Duke of Albany—

I had the satisfaction of introducing him to the works of Le Fanu, and his admiration of the author (so strangely neglected by the general public notwithstanding the popularity of some of his imitators) vied with my own.

It is interesting to know that George Eliot's *Silas Marner* could arouse in some readers an excitement of suspense equal to that caused by the famous sensational novels. Mrs. Panton says—

It was just at the time when *Silas Marner* had come out, and everyone was reading that most exquisite book. Papa had it from Mudie's, and I read it aloud to him while he worked. He was tantalized by the mystery of the disappearance of Dunstan, but I would not allow him to look at the end. "Well, no one who has this copy shall wait as long as I have done to know what happened to the fellow," he said when the book was finished; and he wrote at the bottom of an early page just what had happened. The copy afterwards went to Mr. Cresswell, who adored novels and read as many as any lovesick miss. He was furious, and there was a sharp quarrel between him and my father, and it was some time before he forgave the offence.

In the same year as *Silas Marner* came a book which must have cost Mr. Mudie some anxious thought before he allowed it to join the select company in his library. This was *East Lynne*, by Mrs. Henry Wood. The difficulty was that the heroine was not one of the blameless damsels to whom Mr. Mudie's readers were accustomed. She started in the early chapters as *the* very pattern of all that the Select Library approved, but less than half-way through the book she became an erring wife. True, she underwent such buffetings and tortures as few heroines, even those of Miss Mulock, had suffered before her, and died while her afflictions were still at their height. But it was clear that the author intended her to be an object of compassion, not of utter reprobation. Would British mothers see in this a danger to their daughters' innocence? and would they overlook what might be considered the indelicacy of certain passages? George Meredith, as reader to the firm of Chapman and Hall, to whom Mrs. Henry Wood had submitted her work, strongly advised its rejection. "Foul," he called it, "in the worst style of the present taste." In the end it was accepted by Bentley's, and as soon as it was published its phenomenal success began. A good many readers of education and taste gave it high praise. Harriet Martineau said—

I am amazed at the power and interest of *East Lynne*. I do not care how many murders or other crimes form the foundation of plots if they are to give us such stories as this. I wish I possessed a hundredth part of the author's imagination.

Mary Howitt wrote enthusiastically to Mrs. Wood—

I cannot tell you how high an opinion I have of *East Lynne* as far as I have read it in the monthly parts; but this I will say; that you have only to publish the work with your name attached to it, and you will at once become famous.

Lord Lyttelton declared that *East Lynne* was the most interesting book he had ever read, and that the chapter *Alone for Evermore* was "one of the finest and most pathetic chapters in the whole realm of English fiction." Henry Sidgwick did not admire the book; in lamenting the falling off in Millais' pictures he said, "His inspiration seems now about the level of Mrs. Henry Wood's novels."

There was a long and enthusiastic review of *East Lynne* in *The Times*, and this must have helped to confirm Mr. Mudie in the conviction that he had done wisely in not rejecting Mrs. Wood's story. Equally reassuring must have been the report of an incident which occurred during a tour to the Holy Land made in 1862 by the Prince of Wales, with Stanley, who was now Professor of

Ecclesiastical History at Oxford and Canon of Christ Church, as guide and director. The party made some stay in Egypt, and one day an expedition was planned to visit the tombs. The Prince declined to join it, and when the others returned they found him sitting outside the tent smoking and reading *East Lynne*. He insisted on Stanley reading it too, which the Canon did in three sittings, and "stood a tolerable examination on it." The Prince's interest in *East Lynne* remained keen, and on the next evening he and Stanley, with two other members of the party, had an amusing discussion on the book, cross-examining each other on its contents. "I came off with flying colours," said Stanley, "and put one question which no one could answer—with whom did Lady Isabel dine on the fatal night?"

When the party reached Athens they took on board a fresh cargo of novels, including *The Channings*, another story by Mrs. Henry Wood, and Bulwer Lytton's *Strange Story*. The books were probably sent from the Oxford Street Library, for we have it on the authority of W. S. Gilbert, in the *Bab Ballads*, that by this time its enterprising proprietor had extended his activities beyond the shores of his own country, and that

> New volumes came across the sea
> From Mr. Mudie's libraree.

The sanction of an authority even higher than that of the Prince of Wales was given to another work of sensational fiction published in 1862—Miss Braddon's *Lady Audley's Secret*. Queen Victoria read and admired it. From this book also the blameless heroine had disappeared. Lady Audley, with the face of an angel, was a monster of deceit and cold-blooded selfishness, and when she pushed her husband down a well had apparently no qualms except that she might be found out. The reader almost from the beginning was allowed to see the true character of the blue-eyed, golden-haired little beauty, and there was no attempt to make him sympathize with her in her wickedness; and the punishment meted out to the poor lady was inhumanly terrible. The sex question was entirely absent from the book, which perhaps explains why many Victorian mothers allowed their daughters to read it, regarding its cheap sensationalism as less harmful than the beautiful sincerity of *Ruth*. Miss Betham-Edwards, who was almost exactly contemporary with Miss Braddon, and read all her stories as they came out, attributed her great popularity to the "wholesomeness and cleanness" of her novels—

Therein vice is never sugared. No page, no sentence tempts youthful readers to lift the hidden veil, to attain the knowledge that is as the poison of asps, "a stumbling-block before the children." Can any writer desire a nobler epitaph?

This eulogy sounds, perhaps, a little overstrained and meaningless, but it shows the estimation in which Miss Braddon was held by her own generation. *Lady Audley's Secret* had an enormous success. In three months eight editions were sold. William Tinsley, its publisher, in his *Random Recollections*, says—

I was in the habit of going to Mudie's and the Library company almost every day in the week during the rage for *Lady Audley's Secret*, and it was seldom that I left one or both of the houses without an order for the book.

Mrs. Panton, discussing the authors whose books she had loved in her youth, said, "The dearest of all to me was the wonderful Miss Braddon"; and Henry Sidgwick, writing to his sister from Margate in 1873, informed her—

I subsist chiefly on a kind of fish called Margate Dabs . . . and on Miss Braddon. Yes, I have decided that they really are more improving to the mind than Mrs. Henry Wood's.

These two ladies went on industriously writing novels until the former had about fifty volumes on the shelves of Mr. Mudie's library, the latter about forty. Their public never failed them. The critics were often scornful, but that had no influence on the sales.

"The *Saturday Review* sent me down by post Mrs. Wood's last novel, *Elster's Folly*, to review," wrote Mrs. Lynn Linton in 1866, "and I could not but cut it up. . . . Mrs. Wood is to me a very, very shallow writer, a shallow observer of society, and a puerile and vulgar one, and I have said so."

Next came Ouida; and a gust of excitement, half delighted and half fearful, shook the reading public while her first novel, *Held in Bondage*, circulated among them during the summer of 1863. For here all the cherished Victorian conventions were reviled and flouted; Victorian restraint and propriety were replaced by voluptuous licence. Here were men, magnificent fellows, guardsmen for the most part, splendidly handsome, fabulously wealthy, super-humanly strong and gifted; owning no law but the law of what they called honour. Here was a heroine who was a beautiful fiend, lost to all sense of virtue or of shame. The richness and warmth of Ouida's work made Miss Mulock and Mrs. Wood, and even Mr. Wilkie Collins, seem dull and chilly; and it had a romantic daring and passion that some readers found more attractive than the higher qualities of *David Copperfield*, *Vanity Fair*, and *Adam Bede*. There had been nothing at all like *Held in Bondage* except Lawrence's *Guy Livingstone*, and that seemed almost brutal in tone beside the exotic grace of Ouida.

Strathmore came next, and then *Chandos*, *Under Two Flags*, *Idalia*, *Puck*, *Moths*, *Two Little Wooden Shoes*, and others. All through the 'sixties and 'seventies the stream went on. There was no doubt in anybody's mind that the books were decidedly immoral. Few ladies owned to having read them; even matrons put them quickly out of sight when visitors appeared. To young people they were strictly forbidden. Nevertheless, there were many young people who knew more about these delightful wicked books than did their elders. If by any chance it became known that a copy had found its way into youthful hands, there was consternation among the grown-ups. Mr. Maurice Baring recalls the horror of his governess when she was told that a French lady, misled by the commonly held belief that all British books were highly moral, gave a translation of *Moths* to her young daughter. Yet the young people, it would seem, managed to extract some moral teaching from these pernicious works—at least in retrospect. Lady Frances Horner, in *Time Remembered*, has told of her mother who was a young lady in the 'sixties, and who thirty years later still loved to hear Ouida's novels read aloud, and was moved to tears by such passages as "He bounded on to the stage—over the heads of the stupefied throngs—and gazed with a hungry glare on the snowy loveliness palpitating beneath the shimmering gauze." "He is very noble, dear—what I admire in Ouida is that Vice is Vice and Virtue is Virtue," she would murmur to her inwardly protesting daughter.

Lord Strangford attacked Ouida's earlier works almost savagely in the *Pall Mall Gazette*, and the general public took their views largely from this article. Many read Ouida's stories chiefly because it seemed a daring thing to do, and gained from them only a confused impression of riot and luxury and immoral conduct. Others went to them prepared to be horrified, and consequently were horrified. So the conviction that Ouida's books were full of a mysterious wickedness that permeated everything she dealt with grew and strengthened. Gissing shows us a "musty and nervous City clerk" darkly warning a friend against taking his wife to Paris because of the exceedingly undesirable company into which, according to Ouida, a visit to that capital would introduce her.

Lady Dorothy Nevill thought Ouida's books "showed brilliant talent." Shirley Brooks gave the view of the ordinary robust type of male reader when he wrote, "Reading Miss de la Ramée's *Idalia*, terrible rubbish, yet much of it readable." Charles Reade found her, Mr. Robert Buchanan tells us, quite unreadable. "I well remember his impatience when, taking up a novel of Ouida, and being pestered with a certain abominable iteration about an 'Ariadne,' he sent the book flying across the room before he had finished the first chapter." Yet Burne-Jones said he remembered Ruskin and Cardinal Manning "routing on their knees amongst some books to find *The Dog of Flanders*, which they loved; getting covered with dust and searching with enthusiasm," and he owned that he himself admired certain passages in the novels.

And what of Mr. Mudie? Did he see Ouida as a chronicler of evil unspeakable, a perverter of the morals of youth? All we can know is that he bought her novels. Perhaps he had now not quite as free a hand as formerly, or perhaps the public demand for the books was too strong for even such an autocrat as he to resist. At any rate, there they were on the shelves of the establishment in Oxford Street, and obliging assistants handed them out to subscribers without protest or comment.

The rage for Ouida continued into the 'eighties, although as time went on the legend of her wickedness faded somewhat and her flamboyancy became a little tiresome. Neither she nor any other of the sensational novelists had the qualities that make the works of the Great Novelists immortal. Lord Lytton, whose books had been immensely popular in the early part of Victoria's reign, was, said Mr. Mudie, little in request during the 'sixties, while "no sets of books were so rapidly worn out as those of Charles Dickens." By the 'sixties, too, a new class of book had come into favour. "The fairy tales of science, as narrated by a Huxley or a

Darwin," said Mr. Mudie, "are beginning to be as eagerly demanded as the latest productions of Miss Braddon or Mr. Wilkie Collins."

Mr. Mudie had, it is clear, a steady though comparatively small body of subscribers who were interested in the non-fictional part of his library. "Some Travels and Biographies from Mudie's are nearly all I read now," wrote FitzGerald in 1861. Rossetti went there for Lord Braybrook's edition of *Pepys' Diary*. Mrs. Melladew, of Cuthbert Bede's *Muttons and Mattins*, who reproved her daughter for not having "even cut the leaves of that new edition of *Alison's History*, in which I am sure you would find more solid reading than in those Mudie tales," might have reflected that probably the *History*, too, came from Mudie's; for Messrs. Blackwood, the publishers, had found great cause for rejoicing in the large and continuous demand for the book made by the libraries.

Poetry, too, was well represented at the Oxford Street establishment. When the volume containing Tennyson's *Enoch Arden* and other poems was published in 1864, Mr. Mudie showed his faith in the poet by ordering two thousand five hundred copies, the largest order ever known to have been given for a volume of poems. His faith was justified, for the book had a great success. Sixty thousand copies were sold in a few months, and the demand for it at the libraries was almost as great as the demand for a popular new novel. Matthew Arnold, writing to Dykes Campbell, said, "I agree with you in thinking *Enoch Arden* itself very well done—perhaps the best thing Tennyson has done." George Richmond, the artist, tells how in 1864 he was staying with Dean Liddell of Christ Church at his home near Orme's Head, where he was painting the Dean's portrait. The Dean read aloud in the new volume in the evenings "while I drew and the girls sewed," and when he came to the passage that describes Enoch coming back and looking through the window "he fairly broke down."

In 1870 Mr. Mudie made one of his few miscalculations. Disraeli, having deserted authorship since 1847, now returned to it, and published *Lothair*. Mr. Mudie ordered fifteen hundred copies, and then, finding the book much talked about, another fifteen hundred. But the demand quickly died down, and the larger part of the three thousand volumes went to join the worn-out and unwanted books in the cellars of the Oxford Street establishment. Henry Sidgwick said he did not think *Lothair* equal to the best of the earlier works, but it was very light and amusing. FitzGerald called it "a pleasant magic lantern." Mary Gladstone considered it "snobbish and trash," but that was probably prejudice. "None of us, I believe," said John Morley, "were ever able to persuade Mr. Gladstone to do justice to Disraeli's novels," and Mary naturally followed her father. But Disraeli, although his fame as a statesman had eclipsed his fame as an author, had still some ardent admirers on the literary side, and his early books were still widely read. Stanley thought *Tancred* "exceedingly clever and interesting," and re-read it on the steamer when he travelled to Alexandria in 1862. Shirley Brooks said of it, "What good things there are in this!" Mortimer Collins declared—

One thing is quite clear to any reader of *Henrietta Temple.* Disraeli is the ladies' premier. No Prime Minister of England ever wrote such a charming love story, or any love story at all, so far as I can remember.

Mark Rutherford quoted Anthony Trollope as saying that

Disraeli's works smelt of hair oil, and they got much of their savour from Lytton. But then the original compound was at least the very finest Macassar.

Lady Dorothy Nevill said that Disraeli told her he was once getting into a hansom cab when the driver suddenly opened the trap-door at the top and called down, "I know who you are, sir, and have read all your books, bar *Lothair.*" Warmest of all was the praise that came from Ellen Terry—

I love Disraeli's novels, like his tie brighter in colour than anyone else's. It was *Venetia* that first made me see the real Lord Byron, the real Lady Byron too. In *Tancred* I recall a description of a family of strolling players, which seems to me more like the real thing than anything else of the kind in fiction. It is strange that Dizzie's novels should be neglected. Can anyone with a pictorial sense fail to be delighted by their pageantry? Disraeli was a heaven-born artist, who, like so many of his race . . . had an unerring instinct for the things the Gentile acquires by labour and training. The world he shows us in his novels is big and swelling, but only to a hasty judgment is it hollow.

But in spite of a few false steps, Mudie's Select Library continued to go forward with speed and certainty. Its vans were to be seen all over London; it had connections in almost every provincial town. "Briareus-handed Mudie," said Edward Fitz-Gerald. There were very few people who were, as Canon Ainger put it, "unspotted from Mudie's." When Planché, in his burlesque of *The Bride of Lammermoor*, made Edgar conclude the curse with which he cursed the faithless Lucy with the words—

> May Mudie never send you a new book!!
> And may you never get a sober cook!!!

the audience was perhaps more affected by the penultimate than by the ultimate article of the denunciation, since all did not employ cooks, but all probably hoped for new books from Mudie's.

The 'seventies opened with a new writer competing for the favour of the younger and more frivolously minded section of the reading public. Miss Rhoda Broughton, the twenty-seven-year-old daughter of a Staffordshire clergyman, had produced in 1867 a novel called *Cometh Up as a Flower*, and had gone on since at a great rate with *Not Wisely But Too Well*, *Red as a Rose is She*, and others with similarly appealing titles. She was not, like Ouida, considered "wicked," but her works were looked upon as slightly improper, and not such as a modest and well brought up young lady should read; "though honestly," said Mrs. Panton, who read a good many of them during her young ladyhood, "I never could understand why. They are always entertaining, and leave a good taste behind." The early works were published anonymously, and there is a story, which Miss Broughton's friends loved to tell in later years, that her father had once strictly forbidden her to read her own novels.

Very soon her books were being constantly asked for at Mudie's. Herbert Spencer borrowed *Cometh Up as a Flower* soon after it was published, and read it, as it was his habit to read novels, late at night; then went to sleep and dreamt that he was in the midst of a large circle of his friends, one of whom asked him, "O, have you seen the Reverend Mr. So-and-So's story called *The Lily*? It is the most beautiful moral essay I ever read." "Ah, I see," replied Spencer; "a sermon that cometh up as a flower."

Mr. Gladstone, it is recorded, was once seen in the library of his club so absorbed in *Red as a Rose is She* as to be deaf to all that was going on around him. His daughter read the book, and thought it "well written, but flippant to excess." Mary Gladstone also read *Second Thoughts*, which she described as "an innocent but racy novel." Professor Sidgwick complained that Miss Broughton "imitated her own natural untamedness *ad nauseam*"; and there is certainly a rather cloying sameness about her stories. But the improprieties of her books—or what the Victorians considered as such—became fewer as she grew older and wiser, and her reputation improved; so that there was no sting in the story she once told about herself, that she had seen some copies of her books on W. H. Smith's bookstall at Liverpool Street Station marked "Rhoda Broughton, soiled but cheap." Sir Frank Benson has told us that when in her girlish and gushing days she was introduced to Professor Jowett, she greeted him with "Oh, Mr. Jowett, I am so glad at last to meet you. How do you like my last book?" "Not at all, not at all," replied the uncompromising Master of Balliol, who—rather surprisingly—had evidently read the work in question; "too much bread-and-butter and kissing in it." Against this criticism we may set that of Monsieur Jusserand, who said that *Cometh Up* was the only novel he had read in English that had real passion.

"It is perchance the worst evil of modern novel-writing (and I fearlessly accuse George Eliot as chief offender)," declared Mortimer Collins, "that the favourite heroine is the silly girl— somebody who cometh up as a flower, or throweth her husband down a well."

This indictment of George Eliot was probably provoked by the success of *Middlemarch*, published in 1873. Rosamund Vincey was certainly a silly girl, and so was Celia Brook; and Dorothea, too, might be called silly, if she were judged only according to her worldly wisdom. But they were girls such as none but a genius could have created, and *Middlemarch* was certainly one of George Eliot's masterpieces.

Spite of resolutions not to read at all, the volume of *Middlemarch* from Mudie's tickles me like a trout, and at last George Eliot lays me gasping on the grass,

wrote James Smetham, and he went on to a long, subtle, and enthusiastic criticism of the book.

It is true, however, that in the hands of weak imitators the heroines of George Eliot and other great writers did turn into silly and, what was worse, uninteresting girls. Mr. Mudie's shelves were crowded with volumes by third-rate authors who had won a little temporary popularity by diligently attempting to copy the style of notable public favourites. But he kept plenty of room for writers of the first rank also, and he had not lost the instinct which taught him how to choose just the books that would please the majority of his subscribers. Fanny Kemble was delighted with his selection.

"I then went to Mudie's and took a three months' subscription for Fanny [her daughter]," she wrote in 1877, "sending her down Charles Kingsley's *Life and Letters*, and Captain Burnaby's *Ride Across Asia Minor*. Of all the devices of our complex and complete civilization, I think this huge circulating library system one of the most convenient and agreeable; to be able for twenty-one shillings to have for a quarter of a year ten volumes of excellent literature for one's own exclusive use seems to me a real privilege and a capital return for one's money."

There was, however, a minority of dissatisfied subscribers. The old charge against Mr. Mudie had never been dropped. He was still being accused of exercising over the contents of his library a too strict moral supervision which favoured the spread of an unreal and feeble literature, and many authors complained bitterly of his unfair treatment of their works. Of these, Mr. George Moore was the most indignant and the most outspoken. In 1885 he wrote a pamphlet which he called *Literature at Nurse*, in which he set forward his grievances. Two years before, he said, he had published a novel called *Modern Love*. It had been favourably reviewed by the entire Press, but Mr. Mudie had refused it on the ground that two ladies living in the country had written to say they disapproved of its morals. Mr. Moore's next novel, *A Mummer's Wife*, had been published in a cheap edition at six shillings. When it was asked for at Mudie's Library, the assistants had explained that it was an immoral production, and therefore could not be issued. Mr. Moore compared his book with others that had been admitted to the library—*Nadine* by Mrs. Campbell Praed, *A Romance of the Nineteenth Century* by W. H. Mallock, *Foxglove Manor* by Robert Buchanan, *Puck* and *Moths* by Ouida, and *Phillida* by Florence Marryat. Against these, he said, the charge of immorality might much more justly be brought than against *The Mummer's Wife*.

The librarian rules the roost, he crows and every chanticleer pitches his note in the same key. . . . And in accordance with his wishes English fiction now consists of either a sentimental misunderstanding which is happily cleared up in the end, or of singular escapes over the edges of precipices, and miraculous recoveries of one or more of the senses of which the hero was deprived, until the time has come for the author to bring his tale to a close. The novel of observation, of analysis, exists no longer among us. Why? Because the librarian does not feel as safe in circulating a study of life and manners as a tale concerning a lost will. . . . We must write as our histories, our biographies are written, and give up once and for ever asking that most silly of all silly questions, "Can my daughter of eighteen read this book?"

Mr. Edmund Gosse took a similar view of the influence of the libraries. Authors, he said, were suffering from

the disease which we may call Mudieitis, the inflammation produced by fear that what you are inspired to say, and know you ought to say, will be unpalatable to the circulating libraries, that "the wife of a country incumbent," that terror before which Messrs. Smith fall prone upon their faces, may write up to headquarters and expostulate.

But the Select Library was proof even against such attacks as these, the more so since, as Mr. Edmund Gosse intimates, an ally was now in the field who was working heartily with Mr. Mudie to keep from the public such books as were calculated to injure its morals or to taint its beliefs. Mr. W. H. Smith, junior partner in a prosperous bookselling business, had in 1846 conceived a plan for setting up bookstalls at the principal railway stations, to supply the need for "something to read" on a long journey. The venture had been highly successful, and by 1862 bookstalls were established on almost every important line. It then occurred to Mr. Smith that he might profitably establish some kind of circulating library in connection with these bookstalls. A book could be borrowed and a deposit paid at the station from which the passenger started; it could be returned when he reached his destination, and the deposit, less a small deduction, repaid. At first Mr. Smith thought of working this library in connection with Mudie's, but that proved to be impracticable. He made his own collection on the same lines as those of the Select Library. He had been brought up according to the strictest Wesleyan principles, and his ideas of morality were as uncompromising as Mr. Mudie's own, so the rejected of Oxford Street could not hope for acceptance at Paddington or Waterloo.

Mr. Smith soon realized, as Mr. Mudie had done before him, that his chief reliance must be on fiction, and he took a step which had a considerable influence on the prevailing practice of issuing novels in three volumes at ten shillings and sixpence each. For some time there had been dissatisfaction at this practice, and clear-sighted publishers and authors had seen that it could not much longer be upheld. The librarians were naturally in favour of retaining it. "As soon as a book is published in a cheap edition it ceases to be in demand," said Mr. Mudie. But Mr. Smith, in his efforts adequately to supply his bookstalls, caused cheap editions to increase and multiply. He bought the copyright of some of the works of Charles Lever, and these were issued by Chapman and Hall in the covers that later became so familiar and gave the name of yellow-backs to the series. This venture turning out highly successful, he dealt in the same way with works by other authors. His example was followed by various publishers, with the result that a goodly supply of cheap editions was put on the market, though new volumes by popular authors continued to be published in three-volume form.

The increase of cheap editions was a far more serious danger to the circulating libraries than any attack from hostile critics could be. But even that danger Mudie's triumphantly met and overcame. The library was firmly established as a national institution, secure against the shocks that overthrow less stable structures, and an abiding witness to the Englishman's need and love of his books.

CHAPTER XVI

THE NEW WOMAN

WHAT is the effect upon the women of a country of living under the rule of a queen rather than of a king? Was there any change in the mentality of Englishwomen when the accession of Queen Victoria gave them what for more than a hundred and twenty years they had not known, a sovereign of their own sex? These are hard questions, and an attempt to answer them would open up a fascinating piece of research. But without any very deep inquiry it may safely be said that the knowledge that a woman holds the highest position in the land must, consciously or unconsciously, affect the outlook of many other women, and seem to them to justify their most soaring ambitions and their most extravagant claims. Said *Punch* in 1850, when the question as to who should succeed Wordsworth as Poet Laureate was being discussed, "Hasn't somebody said that a woman ought to have the place, specially as a woman wears the crown?"—expressing by reference to a special instance a general notion that existed in many minds.

The ambitions and claims of the aspiring women varied according to the individual. One desired equality with man in educational advantages, another free entrance to the learned professions. A third claimed a share in the government of the country. A fourth demanded the removal of all conventional restrictions laid on women with regard to dress and manners and mode of living. A fifth rebelled against the marriage bond, and clamoured for a new code of female morality. From the working of the forces striving for these varying "rights" emerged the New Woman, who is an undoubted product of the reign of Queen Victoria.

The term New Woman denotes for most people a blatant female who made herself conspicuous and at the same time absurd by going about loudly demanding her "rights," denouncing man as her natural enemy, affecting an uncouth singularity in dress and manners, and generally transforming herself into as unlovely and unfeminine an object as nature would permit. It is true that there were women of this type, true also that they had their function and value in the evolution of a great movement. But the real New Woman was a being of a far higher order and a finer imagination than these. She was the woman who saw that she and her sisters had, under existing conditions, no reasonable chance of doing their best work and making their largest possible contribution to the world's welfare and happiness; who, courageously and hopefully, stepped off the beaten, easy track and forced a way through the thick growth of prejudice and established custom to the open regions where free development was possible. She had no sex antagonism, and accepted gratefully the help which many men ungrudgingly gave her. She did not regard herself as a martyr or a marvel, but simply as a woman trying to show the world that a woman could do a piece of hard and honest work, and do it well.

It is not claimed that the rule of Queen Victoria was solely or even largely responsible for the emergence of the New Woman; it is only suggested that it was a contributory cause hastening the process. The Queen herself would have been horrified if it had been suggested to her that she had had the smallest part in forwarding the movement she detested. In 1860 she wrote to Mrs. Theodore Martin—

The Queen is most anxious to enlist everyone who can speak or write to join in checking this mad wicked folly of Women's Rights, with all its attendant horrors, on which her poor, feeble sex is bent, forgetting every sense of womanly feeling and propriety.

This was her precept, but it was not supported by her example. She herself, strongly as she would have disclaimed the title, was really a New Woman in so far as she felt within herself powers that could not be satisfied by the ordinary woman's round. She, being in a position to do so, insisted on her "rights," took an active part in the government of the country, did the work of a man, and did it to admiration. So it came about that two widely differing bodies of Englishwomen owed some of their inspiration to their Queen's influence—the "early Victorian" ladies, conventional and proper even to prudishness, who were guided by her precepts; and the eager, rebellious innovators, who were encouraged by her example.

Both these bodies had a considerable influence on the books that were read during the first fifty years of Victoria's reign. Each had a literature of its own which it read diligently, and each inspired a literature descriptive of itself which was read with zest by friends and by opponents. Numerically the party of the New Woman was insignificant. Public opinion was strongly, even violently against her. Sydney Dobell spoke for an overwhelming majority of his fellow-countrymen when he expressed his satisfaction at the

noble rebuke begun by our great Laureate in the *Princess*, continued in the *Idylls*, and echoed more or less audibly by nearly every great man of our day.

The ideals of the orthodox party were well summed up in a series of books written by a certain Mrs. Ellis, which were immensely popular, and were constantly quoted with respectful admiration. They were known as the *Women of England* series, and included *The Daughters of England*, *The Wives of England*, and others. They insisted strongly on man's superiority. "The first thing of importance," so the Daughters of England were instructed, "is to be content to be inferior to men—inferior in mental power in the same proportion that you are inferior in bodily strength." This being so, they must not expect or desire any great advantages with regard to education. Mrs. Ellis discussed the education suitable for women under three heads—cleverness, learning, and knowledge. Cleverness she defined as "dexterity and aptness in doing everything that falls within the sphere of ordinary duty," and this she considered the most important of the three for girls in the middle rank of life. Rich women with servants had not so much need of it. For learning she took Dr. Johnson's definition, "Skill in language or science." "I confess I do not see the value of languages to a woman," she said; and as for science, women might learn enough to render them more companionable to man—"an intelligent listener is all that he requires." Knowledge is "that acquaintance with facts, which in connection with the proper exercise of a healthy mind will necessarily lead to general illumination." The facts which Mrs. Ellis had in mind seem to have been such as might be acquired by a diligent study of Mangnall's *Questions* or some similar repository of knowledge, though they might include some information concerning the political and social affairs of the country. But—and here Mrs. Ellis was explicit—this was to go no farther than was necessary to render the Daughters of England "intelligent listeners" to the views of their male relatives.

Concerning the duties of a wife, Mrs. Ellis was eloquent—

It is the privilege of a married woman to be able to show by the most delicate attentions how much she feels her husband's superiority to herself—not by mere personal services . . . but by a respectful deference to his opinion, and a willingly imposed silence when he speaks.

It is true that some people laughed at Mrs. Ellis. *Punch* poked fun at her frequently. Thackeray, in *The Book of Snobs*, having given a burlesque account of the paragraphs that appeared in the daily papers describing the Court dresses of Lady Snobky and her daughters, went on—

Oh, Mrs. Ellis! O mothers, daughters, aunts, grandmothers of England, this is the sort of writing which is put in the newspapers for you. How can you help being mothers, daughters, etc., of Snobs so long as this balderdash is set before you.

But even those who laughed were in agreement with the main principles enunciated in the worthy lady's books. Thackeray certainly was. His Amelia was obviously brought up on Mrs. Ellis, and so were a good many more of the sweet and docile heroines of Victorian fiction. Tennyson did not entirely repudiate Mrs. Ellis, although his conception of the relations between man and woman, set forward in *The Princess*, was immeasurably nobler than hers. Yet in some passages, such as that in which the Prince describes his mother—

> Not learned, save in gracious household ways,
> Not perfect, nay, but full of tender wants,
> No Angel, but a dearer being, all dipt
> In Angel instincts, breathing Paradise,
> Interpreter between the Gods and men,
> Who look'd all native to her place, and yet
> On tiptoe seem'd to touch upon a sphere
> Too gross to tread, and all male minds perforce
> Sway'd to her from their orbits as they moved
> And girdled her with music.

Tennyson perpetuated the old unhappy convention, showing woman in the twofold aspect of domestic servant and haloed saint; a convention as obstructive to women who were eager to go out into the common ways of the world and learn and work and fight their own battles as was that set up by Mrs. Ellis. Tennyson's picture of a woman's college, too, hindered instead of helped the movement for the higher education of women. It removed the whole question of the higher education of women to the realm of fantasy, and made it appear unreal and slightly absurd; so that when later a proposal for the establishment of a woman's college was put forward, Miss Elizabeth Sewell—and doubtless others also—said, a little scornfully, that it sounded like *The Princess*.

There was another poem, published the year before Tennyson's, that dealt with the woman's question in a more practical fashion. This was Arthur Hugh Clough's *The Bothie of Tober-na-Vuolich*. It told the story of a holiday reading party of Oxford undergraduates in a Highland village. Its main purpose was to glorify work—honest, hard, manual toil—and it specially insisted on the value of such work for women.

> Oh, if our high-born girls knew only the grace, the attraction,
> Labour, and labour alone can add to the beauty of women.

The poem did not gain any great popularity, though Kingsley reviewed it very favourably in *Frazer's Magazine*, or, as he put it, "celebrated the birth of Clough's *Bothie* with penny whistle and banjo." Clough wrote to Emerson—

> In England I shall not be troubled with a very onerous weight of celebrity. Mr. Kingsley, a chief writer in *Frazer*, devoted the whole of a cordial, eulogistic article to the Pastoral and has made it tolerably known; but the *Spectator* was contemptuous; and in Oxford, though there has been a fair sale and much talk of it, the verdict is that it is "indecent and profane, immoral and communistic."

To girls brought up on Mrs. Ellis some of the passages in the *Bothie* may well have appeared shocking, but those who were longing for freedom to live in their own way must have welcomed the forthright, practical manner in which Clough proposed to set them to work.

> You young girls, who have had such advantages, learnt so quickly,
> Can you not teach? O yes, and she likes Sunday-school extremely,
> Only it's soon in the morning. Away! if to teach be your calling,
> It's no play, but a business: off! go teach and be paid for it.
> Surely that fussy old dowager yonder was meant for the counter;
> Oh, she is notable, very, and keeps her servants in order
> Past admiration. Indeed, and keeps to employ her talent
> How many, pray? to what use? Away, the hotel's her vocation,

Lady Sophia's so good to the sick, so firm and so gentle,
Is there a nobler sphere than of hospital nurse or matron?
Hast thou for cooking a turn, little Lady Clarissa? in with them,
In with your fingers! their beauty it spoils but your own it enhances.
For it is beautiful only to do the thing we are meant for.
But they will marry, have husbands and children and guests and
    households—
Are there then so many trades for a man, for women one only,
First to look out for a husband, and then to preside at his table.

"For it is beautiful only to do the thing we are meant for" might
almost be taken as the motto of the Woman's Movement. "In
spite of Mrs. Ellis, there are women whose mission it is *not* to be
good housewives," said Lawrence in *Guy Livingstone*; and these
women were encouraged in their rebellion against what had always
been regarded as a natural law by the *Bothie*.

The friends of the movement, however, were few and its
opponents many. Even some of those women who had themselves
demonstrated their right to be considered as the intellectual equals
of men were unwilling to support the claims of their sex to work
outside the domestic circle. Mrs. Jameson, who was an authority
on art and the author of several well-known books, said—

All this business of *women's work* seems to me in a strange state
and quite out of joint. They cannot and will not do their own
work, and they want to do other people's. Why is this? And it is
true of all classes.

Mrs. Oliphant was strongly opposed to the movement, and Miss
Charlotte Yonge thought it was doing more harm than good.
When, in 1868, Miss Mozley was preparing an article, to appear
in *Blackwood's*, on the changes in the position of women during
the past fifty years, John Blackwood wrote to her—

I always find that it is really accomplished women like yourself
... who are least disturbed about the Rights of Women. The Rights
of Women papers that I see are almost invariably as badly composed
as doubtless their unfortunate husbands' dinners are cooked.

Some of the elder women were more staunch. Harriet Martineau
and Mrs. Norton and Mrs. Somerville upheld the woman's cause
gallantly, in defiance of Mrs. Ellis. But the great fight was to be
fought not by them, but by a valiant company of their younger
sisters who, during the early years of the Queen's reign, were

growing up from girlhood to womanhood in various parts of the country. Most of them were girls of the upper middle class who had, through exceptionally favourable circumstances or their own insistent efforts, managed to obtain a better education than that which was generally considered suitable for young ladies—such an education, for example, as Surtees tells us in *Ask Mamma* fell to the lot of the three Yammerton girls—

They were very highly educated—that is to say they could do everything that is useless—play, draw, sing, dance, make wax flowers, bead-stands, do decorative gilding and crochet work; but as to knowing how many ounces there are in a pound of tea, or how many pounds of meat a person should eat in a day, they were utterly, entirely, and elegantly ignorant. . . . Not one of them could write a letter without a copy, and they were all very uncertain in their spelling—though they knew to a day when every king and queen began to reign, and could spout all the chief towns in the kingdom.

The future champions of the Woman's Movement were educated on lines far different from these. By the ladies of their acquaintance they were probably described as "blue"—a term which for most people brought up a vision of an angular female resembling the learned Miss Virginia, aunt of the hero of *Verdant Green*, "sitting stiff and straight, with her wonderfully undeceptive 'false front' of (somebody else's) black hair, graced on either side by four sausage-looking curls . . . spectacles on nose, and dictionary in hand." To be reputed "blue" seriously impaired a young lady's chances of marriage. Men, as Mrs. Ellis had explained, did not care for learned wives. Miss Geraldine Jewsbury, in her novel, *The Half-Sisters*, dealt vigorously with this article of the popular creed—

What is the most stringent caution ever offered to young women to lead their life by? It is "Do not do so-and-so, do not say so-and-so before *men*, they do not admire it." When it was the question about giving women education, "Men do not like learning in women" was the grand argument used. . . . Then their gentleness and softness, "so lovely," are preached up in all the books written with the purport of teaching the women of England to do their duty.

But these ardent young pioneers did not regard marriage as the only, or even as the most desirable and interesting, career for

women, and they remained undismayed even when the still more
damaging epithet "peculiar" was added to that of "blue."

One of the earliest of the pioneers was Florence Nightingale.
She and her sister had, as was usual with girls of their rank, been
educated by a governess at home, but she had also learnt much by
reading with her scholarly father. She could read Greek, Latin,
and Italian, and had studied mathematics and a little philosophy.
At the time of the Queen's accession she was seventeen, and was
longing to use her energy and her rare abilities in some useful
work. She remembered always February 7, 1837 as the day when
"God called her to His service." She read eagerly and widely,
especially such books as dealt with social conditions and ideals of
social service. She was deeply interested in the works of Carlyle
and Kingsley and in Disraeli's *Sybil*. A story called *Anna: or
Passages in the Life of a Daughter at Home*, by a Miss Sarah
Stephens, seems specially to have appealed to her by its bearing on
her own problems. It told of a large family of girls who led a life
very like her own, with little to do except amuse themselves,
practise their music and drawing, pay visits, and be pleasant. Anna
Mowbray, the eldest daughter, was restless and unhappy because
she was denied opportunities of using the powers she felt she
possessed in the service of God. Florence Nightingale, as she read
the book, marked and commented on certain passages, and it was
clear from these comments that she could not accept the conclusion
at which Anna Mowbray arrived—that it was possible to lead a
satisfying life within the limits of a young lady's home. She still
desired a wider field, and still read and studied diligently, so that
when the opportunity came she was ready.

Another girl, Frances Power Cobbe, was in 1837 at a very
select and expensive boarding-school at Brighton. "In the curri-
culum of this school," she said, "at the bottom of the scale were
morals and religion, at the top music and drawing—miserably poor
music, too." She remembered once having had thirteen pages of
Woodhouselee's Universal History to learn by heart; and she recalled
also a course of nine lectures, each dealing with a different science.
When she left school and returned to her home in Dublin, this
training had so far destroyed her natural delight in things intellectual
that she resolved, "I will not trouble myself ever again with
learning anything, but read novels and enjoy myself all the rest of
my life." But this mood did not last long, and soon she was reading

all the works on scientific and philosophical subjects that she could find in her father's library or borrow from the public libraries of Dublin. Finally, she settled down to a close study of religion and religious evidence, with the result that she became and remained for the rest of her life a Deist, having strong sympathy with the Unitarians. Her father died in 1857, and then she came to London. She became an ardent advocate of women's rights and an opponent of vivisection; she did splendid work in connection with ragged schools and workhouses; and she wrote and spoke with tireless energy in favour of the causes that she advocated and on moral and philosophic subjects.

In a remote Cumberland parish another girl was growing up who, although in 1837 she was only fifteen years old, was already in open rebellion against the limitations that her circumstances imposed upon her. Her name was Eliza Lynn; her mother was dead, and her father, the rector of the parish, left his family to bring themselves up for the most part as best they could. Eliza was the eldest, and she educated herself and did what she could to help the younger ones. She had a strong masculine intellect and a restless ambition, and was resolved to push her way in the great world. In 1845, when she was twenty-three years old, she at length succeeded in persuading her father to let her go to London, and there she worked and struggled until she won a moderate reputation as a journalist and writer of novels. She was an ardent advocate of Woman's Rights, and she joined herself to the small band that was working with enthusiasm for the cause.

By this time there were some signs of advance. In 1848 Queen's College was opened with the object of training teachers for work in secondary schools, and a group of eager girls assembled, ready to take full advantage of their new privileges. Among them were Frances Mary Buss and Dorothea Beale. Both these girls came from homes where books made part of the family life, and both inherited from their forbears a tradition of wide and generous culture. Frances Mary Buss had, as she said, "revelled in books" from her childhood. She has told how, when she was thirteen years old, she saved up her money to buy each volume of Miss Strickland's *Lives of the Queens of England* as it came out, and stole away to enjoy it by herself, reading slowly and carefully, and making notes as she went along. When she was fourteen she began to teach in the school for girls that her mother had opened in Camden Town, and it was clear at once that she had found her vocation. Dorothea Beale did not make such an early start, but in her case too the vocation was evident. She was seventeen when she came to Queen's College; before that she had been the teacher of her younger brothers and had read voraciously, subscribing to both the London Library and Mudie's for supplies. She early decided that her work in life must be to do what she could for the higher education of women, and she never moved from that decision, although, as she said—

The want of ideals depressed me. If I went into society I heard it said, "What is the good of education for our girls? They have not to earn their own living."

She became a teacher at Queen's College in 1856, but left in 1857 to take the post of Headmistress of the Casterton Clergy School; so she did not come in contact with a girl who entered in 1858, and who was to be one of the pioneers in opening the medical profession to women. This girl, Sophia Jex-Blake, came up at eighteen from her home at Hastings, full of life and vigour and high spirits, and with a strong inclination to revolt against the limitations which a strict Evangelical upbringing had imposed upon her. She had no clear idea of what she wanted to do, but she longed for useful, satisfying work. She had not had much chance to read, except the improving books and religious publications that her father favoured. Novels he condemned as "mainly trash," and scientific works as tending to infidelity. But once released from his authority and settled in London, Sophia was able to obtain the food her eager mind required, and she read omnivorously.

One of her fellow-students at Queen's College was Emily Hill, and through her Sophia came to know Emily's sister, Octavia, who was engaged in just such a piece of useful, practical work as she herself coveted. Octavia Hill was at this time twenty-one years old. She was the daughter of a corn merchant, who had lost his fortune and had died leaving his wife and his five little daughters almost penniless. Fortunately, Mrs. Hill's father was ready to help them, and the little girls grew up happily at a cottage in Finchley, until the offer of a post in connection with the Ladies' Guild, which was opening a workroom where Polish refugees were to be taught painting on glass, brought Mrs. Hill to London. Octavia, though she was only fourteen, came to the workroom to learn this art. She had been a happy, merry little girl, but she had taken the family troubles seriously, and was now over-grave for her years. But the life at the Guild, where there was much merriment and laughter as well as lively discussion on all sorts of religious, social, and political questions, did her good; and a girl she met there, and who became her special friend, did her more good still.

This girl was Emma Cons, whose high spirits were considered by some people to be reprehensibly hoydenish. They were really only the outcome of a hopeful, courageous temper and a fine physical constitution. Emma Cons was no mere hoyden, as she proved later in the magnificent work she did in turning the "Old Vic" from what Kingsley tells us it was in 1850 into the centre of education and culture and healthy enjoyment for working people that it afterwards became. She and Octavia Hill worked heartily together. They read the same books, and went together to lectures given by Kingsley, Maurice, and Thomas Hughes. When a workroom was opened for teaching toy-making to poor girls, Octavia was put in charge of it. The work and responsibility were heavy, and told upon her health, but she found time to read books on the economic questions that so deeply interested her, Miss Graham's *London Labour and the London Poor* and Charles Kingsley's *Cheap Clothes and Nasty* and *Alton Locke* among them; and she read also Myers' *Lives of Great Men*, Maurice's *Philosophy*, and Carlyle's *Cromwell*, with all the works of Ruskin, whom she knew personally, through his interest in the Guild.

Her friendship with Sophia Jex-Blake brought her new interests.

"I have been giving some book-keeping lessons to Miss Jex-Blake," she wrote in 1860. "She is a bright, spirited, brave, generous young lady, living alone in true bachelor fashion. It took me three nights to teach her."

In return, Sophia gave Octavia lessons in Euclid, and for a time they were close friends.

In 1860 Ruskin bought and rebuilt some dilapidated houses in the neighbourhood of Cavendish Square, and put Octavia Hill in charge of the property. Emma Cons turned rent-collector, and the two girls, neither of them yet twenty-three years old, began with enthusiasm the work in which they were to accomplish great things.

Meanwhile, Sophia Jex-Blake also had chosen her life work. She would be a doctor, and she would not be daunted by any of the obstacles which in 1860 seemed to make such a decision simply ridiculous. She found it difficult to decide how best to carry on her campaign, and in 1865 she decided to visit the United States to learn what she could from Dr. Elizabeth Blackwell, who had taken her degree in the States, and had given several lectures on medical matters in England, with the object of bringing in women recruits.

But the cause was not doomed to wait for Sophia Jex-Blake's return. Another champion was in the field; a champion who was backed by a very resolute friend, and even more effectually by a convinced and enthusiastic father. The champion was Elizabeth Garrett, the friend was Emily Davies, and the father was Newson Garrett, merchant, of Aldeburgh, Suffolk. Elizabeth Garrett was a girl of brilliant intellectual powers, a serious outlook on life, and an attractive personality. She was the eldest of a large family, and her sister Millicent (afterwards Mrs. Fawcett) always remembered how on Sunday evenings she used to take the youngest brother on her knee and gather the rest round her "while she talked on just what was uppermost in her own mind at the time—Garibaldi and the freeing of Italy from the Austrians, Carlyle's *Cromwell*, Macaulay's *History of England*, and modern political events and persons." It was her friend Emily Davies who first awoke in her the desire to take an active part in the woman's campaign; and it was Dr. Elizabeth Blackwell's lectures that turned her thoughts to medicine.

Emily Davies was the daughter of a Lancashire clergyman, and, like Frances Mary Buss and Dorothea Beale, was devoting all her energies to the cause of higher education for women. She saw what a great thing it would be for that cause if the clever young student from Suffolk could show herself capable of taking a medical degree and could force her way into the ranks that up till then had been occupied only by men. So she gave her friend all the help and encouragement she could, and at the same time worked hard with meetings, committees, pamphlets, and petitions, first to get girls admitted to the University Local Examinations (which came to pass in 1864), and then to found a woman's college at Cambridge. She wrote a book, *The Higher Education of Women*, in which she tried to show that while the idea persisted that women's chief business in life was to please men no progress could be made; but if all concerned in education proposed to themselves a worthier aim—that of "seeking in every human soul that divine image which it is their work to call out and develop"—questions of sex would cease to hamper their efforts.

One of the most gallant in the band that worked with Emily Davies was Barbara Leigh Smith, daughter of the wealthy Mr. William Smith, Member of Parliament for Norwich, and cousin of Florence Nightingale. She was a beautiful, talented girl, seven years younger than her famous cousin, and filled with a gay hopefulness that made her an ideal comrade. She married in 1857 Dr. Eugéne Bodichon, and henceforward spent only half of the year in England, but she still managed to do a great deal of work for the cause.

These and many others who worked and hoped with them were the progenitors of the New Woman in her finest and most gracious development. The story of how they fought and struggled and proved their capacity by doing thoroughly and effectively one piece of hard work after another cannot be told here. For purpose of this book it is only necessary to recognize them as women of intellect and culture, who loved books and set a high value on the help these could give to their cause. Through their influence, books whose reading required real intellectual exertion became familiar to a wide circle of women readers. Many of these books were naturally of an educational and professional character, but the pioneers of the Woman's Movement did not stop at these. They read widely and eagerly. They were keenly interested in the scientific and theological questions raised in those stirring days, and were not content to take their opinions on *The Origin of Species* and *Essays and Reviews* from their menfolk, as most women were. Politics they studied with enthusiasm, and they read with delighted gratitude the article by John Stuart Mill in the *Westminster Review* in which women's right to vote at all political elections was vigorously and convincingly maintained. The Female Political Association was formed, with Frances Cobbe and Emily Davies among its earliest members. Henceforward the fight for the vote became an important part of the woman's campaign.

Those women who were not entirely in sympathy with the campaign found a good deal to cavil at in Mill's article. Mrs. Oliphant spoke scornfully of "Stuart Mill and his mad notion of the franchise for women." Charlotte Brontë wrote to Mrs. Gaskell—

Your words on this paper express my thoughts. . . . When I first read the paper I thought it was the work of a powerful-minded, clear-headed woman, who had a hard, jealous heart, muscles of iron, and nerves of bend-leather; of a woman who longed for power and had never felt affection. . . . I believe J. S. Mill would make a hard, dry, dismal world of it; and yet he speaks admirable sense through a great portion of his article—especially when he says that if there be a natural unfitness in women for men's employment there is no need to make laws on the subject; leave all careers open; let them try; those who ought to succeed will succeed, or, at least, will have a fair chance—the incapable will fall back into their right place. He likewise disposes of the "maternity" question very neatly. In short, J. S. Mill's head is, I dare say, very good, but I feel disposed to scorn his heart.

In spite of their more serious preoccupations, the New Women found time for light reading, and grew as enthusiastic over a good novel as they did over John Stuart Mill. Sophia Jex-Blake read *Jane Eyre*, and wrote to her mother—

There never was such a book as *Jane Eyre*—of its kind. Talk of "finding"—that finds me through and through continually. How people *dare* speak ill of such a book!—I suppose they simply can't understand it. Its grand steadfastness and earnestness and purity is something glorious. I read and read and re-read it as I never could another novel, and how it helps me!

"I do so love a novel," confessed Emily Davies, and she managed to read most of those that were worth reading, old and new. "I have been reading down here a novel or two—*Tancred*, *Ruth*, *Quentin Durward*," she wrote in 1867, when she was staying with Madame Bodichon at her country home. The philosophical George Eliot advised the even more deeply philosophical Sara Hennell (both of them sympathized warmly with the Women's Movement) to get *The Shaving of Shagpat* for idle reading. Octavia Hill delighted in Mrs. Gaskell's stories and in *Tom Brown*, and she read also most of the best poetry of the day. Frances Cobbe was a great lover of novels, and confessed to being deeply interested in *The Silence of Dean Maitland*. Margaret Todd, a younger colleague of Sophia Jex-Blake, who wrote novels about the student life of the 'seventies, shows us this second generation of New Women delighting in *Rhoda Fleming*, *Villette*, *Adam Bede*, *The*

Scarlet Letter, and even *Moths*. The New Woman enjoyed heartily the amusements and even the frivolities of life, but she had learnt to keep them in their right place.

The New Woman had at first attracted little public notice, but with the 'fifties began that campaign of ridicule and detraction which soon caused the name to signify, in the ears of the careless majority, a being as absurd as she was unpleasant. This was due partly to the extravagances of some ardent but misguided advocates of the cause; partly to the bitterness of a small band of women opponents who honestly believed that these enlightened leaders of a new movement were going about to disgrace and degrade their whole sex. Mrs. Lydia Bloomer, who came from America in 1851, and as her contribution to the equality of the sexes advocated the wearing by women of a garment fashioned on the lines of the trousers worn by men, was responsible for a good deal of the ridicule that began to be poured upon the New Woman. When we remember the cumbrous and impeding female garments then in fashion, we cannot but see that there was some sound sense as well as symbolic aptness in the proposed innovation; but the publicity methods of its upholders turned it into a joke that was too good to be missed. For more than a year *Punch* was full of "Bloomers" and "Bloomerisms," and all chance of the matter being seriously considered was lost.

Among the most determined enemies of the Woman's Movement was Eliza Lynn, now Mrs. Lynn Linton. She had been its ardent advocate, and she still declared her adherence to its main principals as far as equality of education for men and women and legal rights for wives were concerned. But she thoroughly disapproved of the methods employed to gain these ends, and she thought that the whole sex was painfully deteriorating in consequence of the greater freedom that was being claimed for it. In her novels her views were expressed with harshness and bitterness. George Meredith advised Messrs. Chapman and Hall to reject Mrs. Linton's novels because of her "abhorrence of the emancipation of young females from their ancient rules." Charlotte Brontë said she had not read *Amymone* or *Azeth*, but had "seen extracts from them which I found literally impossible to digest. They presented to my imagination a Bulwer Lytton in petticoats—an overwhelming vision."

In *The Rebel of the Family* Mrs. Linton gave an exaggerated picture of a Woman's Rights advocate of the most blatant type. This very unpleasant lady was made to declare that—

> The struggle between us and man is just the struggle between light and darkness—the divine element in humanity and the diabolical. . . . Let them use their great brutal muscles in the subjugation of nature. Let them be the hewers of wood and drawers of water—the miners and sailors and rough handicraftsmen they were meant to be—while we take up our natural duties as law-makers, politicians, artists, leaders in all moral and intellectual questions whatsoever.

In another novel, *Christopher Kirkland*, Mrs. Linton gave her views on the New Woman in detail. The book, although it told the life story of a man, was largely autobiographical, and along with many bitter comments on the movement in general there were some unworthy sneers at individuals. "Most of them, in the early days, were not only plain in person, but ill-bred in manner," said Christopher Kirkland. "Women's Rights are Men's Lefts was truer then than now." Concerning the medical students, his remarks were especially vitriolic—

> But few young women had clanked into the dissecting room. Miss Garrett, the two Misses Blackwell, and Dr. Mary Walker are all that I remember. The aftermath of flirting, tousled, pretty young creatures—foolish virgins of eighteen or nineteen—had not then sprouted into being.

His own wife turned out to be "a Woman's Rights woman from head to heel," and she made his life so completely miserable that, although he acknowledged she had many good qualities, the time came when he could bear it no longer, and they separated.

Christopher Kirkland's views of the unprepossessing exterior of the New Woman were shared by the public in general, which pictured her as not unlike the picture which R. E. Francillon gives of Mrs. Lynn Linton herself in the early 'seventies— "stern-eyed and spectacled, a typical school ma'am." As a matter of fact, there were many who were extremely attractive, and without a trace of the "school ma'am." Emily Davies was fully alive to the value of appearance in helping on the cause. She rejoiced because Miss Garrett looked "exactly like one of the girls whose instinct is to do what you tell them," and at a meeting held to advocate the admission of girls to the University Local Examinations she took care to have "three lovely girls for the front row," in spite of the contention of her friend and colleague, Miss Isa Craig, that those who upheld so worthy a cause had a right to have "Mission" stamped on their foreheads. Miss Davies was wiser. Perhaps in her extensive reading of the novels of the day she had come across such passages as that in *Mona Maclean*, where a young man says of a beautiful girl, "If all *emancipées* were like Miss Colquhoun, I would get a book and go round canvassing for Women's Rights to-morrow."

Early in 1868 there began to appear in the *Saturday Review* a series of articles on *The Girl of the Period*. They were not signed, but there was a strong suspicion which grew quickly to be almost a certainty that the author was Mrs. Lynn Linton. The articles were even more bitter and offensive than the attacks made upon the New Woman in Mrs. Linton's novels, and were intended to show the baneful effects that the cry of "emancipation" had had upon the female sex in general.

The Girl of the Period is a creature who dyes her hair and paints her face as the first article of her personal religion; whose sole idea is plenty of fun and luxury; and whose dress is the object of such thought and intellect as she possesses. . . . No matter whether, as in the time of crinolines, she sacrificed decency, or as now, in the time of trains, she sacrifices cleanliness; no matter, either, whether she makes herself a nuisance and an inconvenience to everyone she meets. . . . With purity of taste she has lost also that far more precious purity and delicacy of perception which sometimes means more than appears on the surface. What the *demi-monde* does in its frantic efforts to excite attention, she also does in imitation.

Such a way of life, the writer went on to say, led to bold talk, unseemly jesting, slang, love of pleasure, indifference to duty, the inordinate desire of money, and a horror of all useful work.

It is clear that it was not the type of New Woman that Emily Davies and Frances Mary Buss were striving to bring into being that Mrs. Linton had before her eyes. She had noted that, as was perhaps to be expected, some women had taken advantage of the measure of freedom that the efforts of others had secured for them to throw off all wholesome restraint and claim the right to do as they pleased. The crudities and extravagances of this set appeared to Mrs. Lynn Linton so monstrous that she could not see beyond

them. A good many other people were in like case, for the Girl
of the Period made herself much more conspicuous than did those
other girls whose thoughts and energies were given to the work
they were trying to do. Kingsley, ten years before the *Girl of the
Period* articles appeared, had attributed many of the worst features
of the new freedom to the teaching of Emerson. He had spoken
with severe reprobation of those

strong-minded and emancipated women, who prided themselves on
having cast off conventionalities, and on being rude and awkward,
and dogmatic and irreverent, and sometimes slightly improper;
women who had missions to mend everything in heaven and earth
except themselves; . . . every one of whom had, in obedience to
Emerson, "followed her impulses," and despised fashion, and was
accordingly clothed and bedizened as was right in the sight of her
own eyes, and probably in those of no one else.

The fiction of the day abounds in references to the unpleasant
female whose portrait had been drawn in the *Saturday*. "What
does a London girl talk of to-day?" asked an irate gentleman in
Justin MacCarthy's *Dear Lady Disdain*. "Radicalism and blasphemy, nothing else." In Lord Lytton's *Kenelm Chillingly*, written
in 1873, and dealing with a period a few years earlier, the hero,
writing to his father, said—

I don't think nearly so many young ladies six years ago painted
their eyelids and dyed their hair; a few of them there might be,
imitators of the slang invented by schoolboys and circulated through
the medium of small novelists; they might use such expressions as
"stunning," "cheek," "awfully jolly," etc. But now I find a great
many who have advanced to a slang beyond that of verbal
expressions—a slang of mind, a slang of sentiment, a slang in which
very little seems left of the woman, and nothing at all of the lady.

Of a girl of the opposite type, one who would "grace and adorn
any civilized era," Kenelm Chillingly says emphatically, "Among
'Girls of the Period' Cecilia Travers cannot be classed."

The articles in the *Saturday* made a great sensation, and many
women waxed furious against the unknown writer. Mrs. Lynn
Linton told how a celebrated authoress whom she met at an
evening party said to her, "I refuse to take your hand unless you
can first assure me you did not write that odious article, *The Girl*

of the Period." "As an authoress yourself you must be well aware that you are asking me an unpardonable question," replied the undaunted offender.

I, for one, burned with indignation over the really abominable articles on my sex which culminated in *The Girl of the Period*, and were generally supposed to have been written by a man,

said Mrs. Panton, who at the time of the publication of the articles was a girl of twenty. She learnt later that the writer was Mrs. Linton.

Mrs. Lynn Linton was looked upon by us with suspicion and dislike, first, because she had just electrified the world with her odious article, *The Girl of the Period*, and secondly, because she had produced *The True Story of Joshua Davidson*, a book I learnt to thoroughly enjoy and appreciate, but which we heard most emphatically condemned, and were not allowed to read. I saved up my money to buy a copy, and I have it still.

The True Story of Joshua Davidson did not deal with the woman question. It was the story of a youth who devoted himself to the service of the poor, who went among thieves and ruffians and prostitutes and such unpleasant people, of whose existence young ladies were supposed to have no knowledge. "A truly refined mind will seem to be ignorant of the existence of anything that is not perfectly proper, placid, and pleasant," declared that supreme authority on ladylike behaviour, Mrs. General of *Little Dorrit*. But one of the effects of the Women's Movement was the insistence of young ladies on learning some of the ugly facts of life that had hitherto been hidden from them. Some desired this knowledge through a healthy, others through an unhealthy, curiosity; many desired it because they longed to help their unfortunate sisters and brothers. Josephine Butler's great campaign on behalf of the unhappy company of prostitutes was soon to begin, and many philanthropic movements were afoot in which women were eager to take their part. If they were to do this efficiently, they must know many things of which so far they had been kept ignorant, and they read eagerly the books that would give them this knowledge. The social and political novels of Disraeli and Dickens, Kingsley and George Eliot and Mrs. Gaskell taught them much; and a development of these, to be known later as the problem novel, and of which *Joshua Davidson* was an example, excited their keen interest. The problem novel did not deal with those social evils which legislation or a change in conditions could remedy. It was concerned with moral questions which must be answered by the individual and by society at large, and which called for a change of heart rather than a change of circumstances. An early example of such a novel was Mrs. Gaskell's *Ruth*. Miss Mulock's *A Life for a Life*, Charles Reade's *Hard Cash*, William Black's *In Silk Attire*, Trollope's *The Vicar of Bulhampton*, and Wilkie Collins' *The New Magdalen*, with many others of the same class, came later.

The more closely the New Women studied the problems of the day, the more ardently they desired for their sex a position of power and influence which would enable it to be an effective force in national affairs. To many women it seemed that the only way to this lay through the vote. The activities of the Female Political Association were increased, and pamphlets such as Barbara Bodichon's *Reasons for and against the Enfranchisement of Women* were circulated. John Stuart Mill had been elected Member of Parliament for Westminster in 1865, and had introduced a bill for giving votes to women, which, although it had been thrown out, had received enough support to encourage him to continue his efforts. In 1869 he wrote a pamphlet of some hundred pages which he called *The Subjection of Women*. Its purpose, he said, was to show

that the principle which regulates the existing social relations between the two sexes—the legal subordination of one sex to the other—is wrong in itself, and now one of the chief hindrances to human improvement, and that it ought to be replaced by a principle of perfect equality, admitting no power or privilege on the one side, nor disability on the other.

The argument that followed was clear, logical, and closely reasoned, and the case for those women who wished to enter the professions and occupations hitherto reserved for men was put with vigour.

Let us consider women only as they already are, or as they are known to have been; and the capacities which they have already shown. What they have done, that at least, if nothing else, it is proved that they can do. When we consider how sedulously they are trained away from, instead of being trained towards, any of the occupations or objects reserved for men, it is evident that I am taking a very humble ground for them, when I rest their case on what they have actually achieved. For, in this case, negative evidence is worth little, while any positive evidence is conclusive. It cannot be inferred to be impossible that a woman should be a Homer, or an Aristotle, or a Michael Angelo, or a Beethoven because no woman has yet actually produced works comparable to theirs in any of those lines of excellence. This negative fact at most leaves the question uncertain and open to psychological discussion. But it is quite certain that a woman can be a Queen Elizabeth, or a Deborah, or a Joan of Arc, since this is not inference but fact. Now, it is a curious consideration that the only things which the existing law excludes women from doing are things which they have proved that they are able to do. There is no law to prevent a woman having written all the plays of Shakespeare or composed all the operas of Mozart. But Queen Elizabeth or Queen Victoria had they not inherited the throne could not have been entrusted with the smallest of the political duties of which the former showed herself equal to the greatest.

The Subjection of Women naturally aroused the wrath of those who were opposed to Mr. Mill's views. Herbert Spencer maintained that there could be no equality between the sexes since Nature had imposed such a heavy handicap on women. Mrs. Oliphant continued to regard the idea of votes for women as madness. "Confound the fellow!" wrote Mr. John Blackwood; "he writes as if mankind, male and female, were equally stocks and stones, or, if positively not equal at first, to be made so by the teaching of him—Mill. The man is blinded by arrogance." Professor Lorimer of Edinburgh University defended Mr. Mill's proposals against the charge that the admission of women to the professions would bring about an undesirable familiarity between the sexes. "I cannot see," he said, "why greater harm should come of men and women meeting at their occupations than at their amusements—such as croquet and riding parties." But this defence availed nothing with those who, like Queen Victoria, were determined opponents of the Women's Movement as a whole. Her Majesty was particularly outraged at the idea of women being admitted to the study of medicine.

To propose that they should study with *men*—things which could not be named before them—certainly not in a *mixed* audience

—would be to introduce a total disregard of what must be considered as belonging to the rules and principles of morality.

The women in whose cause Stuart Mill was working welcomed his pamphlet with joy and gratitude. "Have you seen Mill's *Subjection of Women?*" wrote Sophia Jex-Blake to Dr. Lucy Sewall, one of the friends she had made during her stay in America. "Your father would delight in it. I mean to send him a copy as a remembrance." Mrs. Millicent Fawcett, then living in London with her blind husband, said—

I regarded it as a very great honour when we were invited from time to time to dine with Mr. Mill and his stepdaughter, Miss Helen Taylor, at Blackheath.

"My saint and hero, the author of *The Subjection of Women,*" was the ecstatic ejaculation of Miss Gibson, one of the earliest students of the new woman's college. For there was a woman's college now, established at Hitchin, and preparing students for the examinations of Cambridge University. At Oxford, too, classes for the higher education of women were being formed, and a movement for establishing a woman's college going forward. The cause of higher education was prospering. Frances Mary Buss was the Headmistress of the North London Collegiate School which she had founded in Camden Town, and Dorothea Beale was the Principal of Cheltenham Ladies' College, which had been opened in 1856. Girls were learning to put aside the feeble literature that had hitherto contented them, and read books of real intellectual value. Miss Beale was inspiring her pupils with her own love of Browning's poetry. Professor Seeley was lecturing on English to the students at Hitchin, and, said Miss Gibson, this was looked upon as "a signal honour and great opportunity, for *Ecce Homo* was to many of us the book of the day."

Yet all these signs of advance, encouraging as they were, were confined to the few. The mass of the women of England still lagged far behind. Parents were unwilling to let their daughters take the examinations which had been opened to them. That popular Congregational minister, Mr. Beecher, of *Phoebe Junior,* refused to allow his daughter to enter for the Cambridge Local because "the connection might think it strange to see her name in the papers," and might "think he meant to make a schoolmistress of her, which he thanked Providence he had no need to do."

This second reason was the one which weighed most heavily with the majority of parents; it was still looked upon as something to be ashamed of that a girl should earn her own living. To fill the university colleges that had been opened was even more difficult. The founders had to use personal persuasion to obtain as pupils a few promising girls whose success, it was hoped, might induce others to come forward.

The lower middle class had scarcely been touched. Kingsley's words in *Two Years Ago* were as true in 1870 as they had been in 1857. A good many people were trying to help these girls, but were finding them very difficult to reach, since their poor smattering of education had served to give them a distinct distaste for any literature other than trashy novels. There were many girls who, like Matilda Cookson of *Mona Maclean*, openly avowed that they hated "*Lycidas* and *Hamlet* and everything else I read at school." It was only after months of patient effort on the part of a cultured woman acquaintance that it could be said of Matilda, "She has read *Sesame and Lilies*, has been much struck by that quotation from Coventry Patmore, and at the present moment is deep in *Heroes*."

Public opinion, although it had made a large advance from the position in which Mrs. Ellis would have entrenched it, still lagged far behind the front lines of the pioneers. In 1876 Miss Charlotte Yonge published a book which she called *Womankind*, and though its ideals were higher and finer than those upheld by Mrs. Ellis, the old view of women's position was to a large extent maintained. Miss Yonge condemned the way in which so many young ladies passed their time—"A little note-writing, a little vase-dressing, a little practising, a little reading, a little croquet, a great deal of chatter, and, worst of all, much running in and out among near neighbours"; but she did not suggest that release from this trivial and unsatisfying round of occupations could be obtained by taking up some useful work outside the home. She advised that at least a couple of hours in the forenoon should be spent in reading "something sensible," and that girls should go up for the Cambridge Local Examinations, but she warned them that they could never hope to compete with men—

A woman of the highest faculties is, of course, superior to a man of the lowest; but she never attains to anything like the power of a man of the highest ability.

It is a little surprising that Miss Yonge even admitted the value of the university examinations, for she had always stoutly maintained that home education supplied all that was necessary for a girl's training. "Home education is far more valuable intellectually and morally than any external education," she had said when she was applied to for help in establishing the woman's college. "Superior women will teach themselves, and inferior women will never learn more than enough for home life." In her *Pillars of the House* she showed her gifted little artist, Cherry Underwood, drawing two cartoons which symbolized with considerable aptness the views of a large number of devout and intellectual people on the question of the higher education of women.

One was a kind of parody of Raffaelle's School of Athens, all the figures female, not caricatures, but with a vein of satire throughout. The demonstration on the floor was an endeavour to square the circle; some of the elder ladies were squabbling, some of the younger furtively peeping at themselves in pocket-mirrors, or comparing ornaments; some in postures of weariness, one gazing eagerly as if responding to some signal, another mimicking her teacher, a third frowning at her rival's success. There was no air of union or harmony, but something of vanity and vexation of spirit pervaded all.

The companion was arranged on the same lines, but the portico was a cloister, and the aisle of a church was dimly indicated through a doorway. The figures and occupations were the same, but all was in harmony. The maidens, though mostly in secular garb, wore the cross; the central figure, in matronly beauty, was portioning out the household tasks, while in the place of the harsh, or sour, or tyrannizing, disputatious ladies were women, some in hood and veil, but others in ordinary dress, all dignified and sweet, while the damsels were smiling happily over their employments, for the most part the same as before, but in a different spirit. The demonstration on the floor was no longer impossible. It was the circle of eternity spanned by the Cross; the quizzing and teasing had ceased, the loiterers were at their needlework; the rivals were united.

Cherry's brother suggested that the cartoons might do for *Punch*, but the others cried shame, and Cherry explained that they were meant to teach the same lessons as Tennyson's *Princess*, only going further into life.

I mean that, while woman works merely for the sake of self-cultivation, the clever grow conceited and emulous, the practical harsh and rigid, the light or dull vain, frivolous, deceitful by way of escape, and it all gets absurd. But the being handmaids of the Church brings all right; and the School of St. Sophia develops even the intellect.

It was this view of the question that made Christina Rossetti doubtful of the expediency of establishing a woman's college that was not under the direction of the Catholic Church, and that caused Dr. Pusey to be violently opposed to the project. Mrs. Gatty thought the experiment dangerous. "*Frivolity* is sooner cured than *conceit*," she said. Even George Eliot, although she supported the plan, hesitated to give to girls full intellectual opportunities. "When you talk to young people and teachers you *will* advise against indiscriminate reading," she said to Emily Davies.

The measure of success that had attended the New Woman's efforts to prove herself capable of high intellectual development had increased the bitterness with which a certain section of her opponents regarded her. Mrs. Edwards, in her novel, *A Blue-Stocking*, published in 1880, puts into the mouth of one of her characters a description of the New Woman as she appeared to a considerable number of her contemporaries.

The Modern Blue-Stocking acknowledges few things that cannot be weighed in the balance or observed in the spectroscope. Of your own soul, if you are weak enough to fancy you possess one, she will tell you that it is but a distillation through the vegetable and animal worlds from inorganic matter. She talks familiarly of atoms, molecules, and the argument from experience, wears her hair, if she is pretty, in a fringe upon her forehead, and invariably writes humanity with a big H.

This charge of irreligion did much towards making the way of the New Woman hard and painful, and keeping the doors she was striving to enter sternly shut against her. One of the most passionate and moving pleas that had been made on her behalf was contained in a book called *The Story of an African Farm*, which came from South Africa in 1883. The name of its author was given as "Ralph Iron," and it told the story of a girl, clever, ambitious, sensitive, full of life, and conscious of power. She was of English parentage, but was brought up on an African farm, and in spite of all her efforts she could not find her way to the fuller, more satisfying life that she desired; and she ended in unhappiness and disaster. The book is full of appeals for the removal of those barriers which cut off such women as she from the work for which they craved.

> When we ask to be doctors, lawyers, law-makers, anything but ill-paid drudges, they say, "No; but you have men's chivalrous attention; now think of that and be satisfied! What would you do without it?" They say women have one great and noble work left them, and they do it ill. That is true; they do it execrably. It is the work that demands the broadest culture, and they have not even the narrowest. . . . If we are not fit, you give us to no purpose the right to labour; the work will fall out of our hands into those that are wiser.

The first very small edition of the book was published early in 1883; a second larger edition came in July of the same year, but the book only slowly became known. The third edition appeared in 1887, with the author's real name, Olive Schreiner, on the title-page.

Mr. Forrest Reed, in *The Eighteen-Eighties*, says that *The Story of an African Farm* gave rise to the Woman's Rights Novel, the Religious Doubts Novel, and the Sex Novel.

> "To myself," he says, "the book appealed profoundly, and in an ancient copy lying on the table before me, quite a jungle of marked passages remains to show me where I was moved, if not, alas, to show me why."

Edith Nesbit was a great admirer of the book and a friend of the author. Mary Gladstone recorded in her diary on May 26, 1885, that she had talked to Mr. Myers about Olive Schreiner, the authoress of *An African Farm*. Later in the same year she received a letter from Professor Sidgwick, in which he said—

> *An African Farm* is oddly crude and young, but full of promise from its freshness and force. I hope she will not go the bad way of Rhoda Broughton and imitate her own natural untamedness *ad nauseam*.

To many people *The Story of an African Farm* seemed to afford additional proof of the irreligious tendencies of the New Woman. *The Spectator* headed its review of the book, *An Agnostic Novel*, and careful parents forbade their children to read it. Mrs. Huth Jackson says that while she was at Cheltenham Ladies' College—

Girls smuggled in *The Story of an African Farm*, then just out. The whole sky seemed aflame and many of us became violent feminists. (I was one already.)

Mrs. Jackson was one of a generation that was growing up in familiarity with the ideals of the Woman's Movement, and which was to see something of its further development. So far, the influence of the New Woman had made itself effective only within a small circle. She had not succeeded in revolutionizing the literary taste of the women of England. It is probable that Mr. Mudie noticed no difference in the demand for light novels made at his library. But she had made it possible for such of her sisters as had aspirations towards a higher culture to satisfy their longings. She had opened a path which, though it was not free from many and painful obstacles, could yet be trodden without a struggle at every step. She had encouraged those who came after her to go forward in a high and courageous spirit, and with a fine disregard of detraction and ridicule.

> Dare to be learned, dare to be blue,
> Ours is a work that no others can do.

CHAPTER XVII

THE AESTHETES

A BOOK has lately been published in praise of J. M. Turner, on landscape painting. I have read it all through with the greatest delight. It is by Ruskin, who is a child of genius certainly.

Thus, in 1844, wrote Benjamin Jowett, from Balliol College, Oxford, of the first volume of *Modern Painters*; but he did not realize that the book was far more than a eulogy of Turner or a treatise on art. It marked the opening of a compaign that was to have large, and in some directions startling, developments. The campaign was to be directed against the dullness of spirit that made man insensitive to the loveliness, both in nature and in art, that he might enjoy, and made him, of choice, surround himself with things drab and ugly and uninspiring. It was to be directed, in short, against that habit of life and thought which Matthew Arnold, nearly twenty years later, branded as Philistinism.

The watchword of the campaign was Beauty, and in the name of Beauty those who took part in it did many things which to sober-minded people appeared highly reprehensible. They were often scornful and intolerant, they allowed themselves a liberty which sometimes reached licence, they sacrificed to Beauty much that good men held to be of higher worth; and finally, some of them took the dire step that leads from the sublime to the ridiculous. But they were aflame with the glory of their cause, and they attacked the enemy country with high and sustained courage; and if they did not capture its innermost stronghold, they at least took possession of a large portion of its territory.

The advance was made on many and various lines, and one of them lay through books. When twenty-five-year-old John Ruskin opened the campaign by way of the first volume of *Modern Painters*, the immediate result was to bring many who were already lovers of Beauty to his side. The second and third volumes, published in 1846 and 1860 respectively, brought many more; and the forces gathered. Wordsworth, now an old man of seventy-three, gave the book his rare praise. Tennyson, still an unrecognized and needy poet, was too poor to buy the book, so went about trying to borrow it. Octavia Hill also could not afford to buy it, so she borrowed a copy from the author, and wrote out long extracts from it in a note-book. Cardinal Wiseman lent his copy to a young art student named Telfer, and allowed him to pass it on to a fellow-student, Holman Hunt, for twenty-four hours. Hunt sat up most of the night reading it, and even then could not finish it. "But of all its readers," he said, "none could have felt so strongly as myself that it was written expressly for him."

James Smetham praised it almost rapturously—

There is a passage in the second volume of *Modern Painters*, Theoria, the Service of Heaven, which I have half chanted to myself in many a lonely lane, and which interprets many thoughts I have had.

Both the Brownings spoke and wrote about *Modern Painters* with enthusiasm, and so did Sir Henry Taylor. Charlotte Brontë and Mrs. Gaskell agreed in admiring it warmly. George Eliot read it aloud to Mr. Lewis, to the delight of both; she told John Morley later that the second volume had made a deep and lasting mark on her mind. Miss Mitford went into raptures over the work. Sara Coleridge wrote to her friend, Miss Morris, "A book which has interested me much of late is a thick volume by a graduate of Oxford whose name is Ruskin"; and, most impressive tribute of all, the thick volume was seen by those privileged to attend the famous breakfast parties of the eighty-year-old poet, Samuel Rogers, lying upon the table of that arbiter of literary taste.

This influential support gave young Mr. Ruskin a high position as an authority on matters of art, and caused all those who were in revolt against material or spiritual ugliness to look to him for help and direction. Among such was the body of ardent young men who, in 1848, banded themselves together to form the pre-Raphaelite Brotherhood. Their watchword, like Ruskin's, was Beauty. Their aim was to break away from the conventionalities and falsities that, as they believed, were corrupting modern art, and go back to the practice of medieval times, before Raphael, when artists drew their inspiration directly from nature, and did not imitate each other. There were seven members of the Brotherhood, all of them very young; Dante Gabriel Rossetti, the chief among them, was only twenty. A few older men, including Ford Madox Brown and Coventry Patmore, were, although not members of the Brotherhood, in close sympathy with it. All of them worked industriously, painting pictures and writing poems, but they made few converts. The Brotherhood was attacked and derided on every side, and its works became a byword. Here was a case, the smarting young geniuses thought, for a pronouncement by an authoritative voice. They appealed to Ruskin, and he, recognizing that they too served Beauty, came to their help. He wrote a letter to *The Times*, upholding their ideals of art, and he afterwards published a pamphlet explaining and justifying pre-Raphaelitism. As a result the scoffers scoffed less loudly, and the movement began slowly to gain ground. Ruskin and the pre-Raphaelites fought side by side.

Meantime Ruskin had written two more works—*The Seven Lamps of Architecture*, 1849, and *Stones of Venice*, 1851–53, in which he had given his ideas on beauty of buildings. These, too, were enthusiastically received by the elect few. "I congratulate you on the approaching publication of Mr. Ruskin's new work," wrote Charlotte Brontë to her publisher. "If *The Seven Lamps of Architecture* resemble their predecessor, *Modern Painters*, they will be no lamps at all, but a new constellation—seven bright stars, for whose rising the reading world ought to be anxiously agaze."

Only a small proportion of the general reading public concerned itself with the new constellation, though to the elect it seemed very bright indeed. The *Stones of Venice* received more attention. Lady Louisa Stuart, who was a Ruskin worshipper, read it with rapture. Millais thought that the last two volumes surpassed anything that had come before them. F. W. Robertson thanked a friend "most gratefully" for sending him the book to read. "There are no writings which, at the present moment, offer such interest to me as Ruskin's," he said. Charlotte Brontë gave it a splendid panegyric. She wrote to Mrs. Gaskell—

The *Stones of Venice* seem nobly laid and chiselled. How grandly the quarry of vast marbles is disclosed! Mr. Ruskin seems to me one of the few genuine writers, as distinguished from the book-makers, of this age. His earnestness even amuses me in certain passages; for I cannot help laughing to think how utilitarians will fume and fret over his deep, serious (and as *they* will think), fanatical reverence for Art. That pure and serene mind you ascribed to him speaks in every line. He writes like a consecrated priest of the Abstract and Ideal.

A good many people did, as Charlotte Brontë had foreseen, fume and fret over the *Stones of Venice*. Mr. Ruskin had entered on the first of the four stages into which William de Morgan, in *The Old Man's Youth*, divides his career; that is, he had become "an object of literary ferocity to the standard art critics." Mr. Slocum the head of the school of art attended by young Eustace Pascoe, of de Morgan's story, gave it as his opinion that Mr. Ruskin was an ass, and encouraged his pupils to make fun of him. Critics of a higher standing expressed the same sentiment, less crudely perhaps, but with more bitterness and publicity. Thus far Mr. Ruskin had done little towards overthrowing the idols of Philistia. The Honourable Mrs. Twistleton was outraged because, in some lectures on architecture given at Edinburgh, Ruskin had dealt severely with some of the popular artists of the day. "He is the maddest and most prejudiced creature that ever wrote on art," said the lady. "Think of his setting down Flaxman as having done nothing worth doing! and so calling him 'a lost mind.' One applied the phrase rather to the judge than to the judged."

Carlyle was among those who laughed and made to laugh at the book. Fanny Allen, sister of John Allen, wrote to her sister concerning *Stones of Venice*—

Carlyle amused me yesterday by his summing-up of the moral of the book—that you must be a good and true man to build a common dwelling-house.

Kingsley, too, found in Ruskin's works matter for a jest. In a rhyming letter to Thomas Hughes he wrote—

> Leave to squeamish Ruskin
> Popish Apennines,
> Dirty stones of Venice
> And his Gas-lamps Seven;
> We've the stones of Snowdon
> And the lamps of heaven.

Herbert Spencer had admired *Modern Painters*, but he found in *Stones of Venice* nothing but "sheer barbarity."

I opened it with raised expectations. My faith in Mr. Ruskin's judgment was at once destroyed. Henceforward I paid no attention to his works. Doubtless Ruskin has a fine style, writes passages of great eloquence, and here and there expresses truths, but that one who has written and uttered such multitudinous absurdities should have acquired so great an influence is to me both surprising and disheartening.

But in spite of the laughter and the irritation of those to whom the new doctrines made no appeal, it soon became clear that Ruskin was advancing towards the second position which, according to Mr. de Morgan, he was to hold—that of "an Apostle whose sayings it was blasphemy to contradict." Young people especially gave him whole-hearted and reverent allegiance. When William Morris went up to Oxford in 1853 he found the whole University talking about the new teacher, and soon he and the little Anglo-Catholic group to which he belonged were eagerly reading *Stones of Venice*; and Ruskin became for them all, we are told, both hero and prophet. They read *Modern Painters*, and placed it alongside *Past and Present* as "inspired and absolute truth." They read the *Edinburgh Lectures* which had aroused the ire of Mrs. Twistleton, and were struck not so much by Ruskin's high-handed treatment of the older artists as by the praise he gave to the young painter and poet, Dante Gabriel Rossetti and to the other members of the pre-Raphaelite group. Here were names which they had never heard before and which promised new delights. They managed to get hold of a copy of the pre-Raphaelite magazine, *The Germ*, which contained Rossetti's poem, *The Blessed Damozel*, and this they "read and re-read for ever." Rossetti became another of their heroes, and pre-Raphaelitism their artistic creed, though Ruskin remained their first and great inspiration.

"Ruskin has published the second volume of his *Stones of Venice* entitled *Sea Stories*," wrote Edward Burne-Jones. "His style is more wonderful than ever; the most persuasive oratory we ever read. His acme is to come. There never was such mind and soul so fused through language yet. It has the brilliancy of Jeffrey, the elegance of Macaulay, the diction of Shakespeare had he written in prose, and the fire of—Ruskin—we can find no other."

It was largely the aesthetic impulse that came through the works of Ruskin and Rossetti that made Morris and Burne-Jones give up their idea of being ordained priests of the English Church and decide to follow what seemed to them the equally high and noble calling of the artist.

Edward Burne-Jones came down from Oxford in 1856 still an

ardent Ruskin worshipper, and eager to make the Macdonald sisters sharers in his delights.

"Ruskin's lectures had reached us from Oxford through my brother Harry," said Georgina Macdonald. "*The Seven Lamps* was the next wonderful experience, and then on to the *Stones of Venice* and *Modern Painters*. . . . Every book by Ruskin that Edward possessed was brought round to me before breakfast the morning after we were engaged—a royal gift."

In 1857 Morris and Burne-Jones settled in London, and joined with other members of the Oxford group who were bent on taking part in the war that was being waged against all that was ugly and ignoble in the life of the day. They soon contrived an introduction to Ruskin, who looked very kindly on these ardent disciples. Ruskin was fully enthroned now as "the Apostle whose sayings it was blasphemy to contradict," and was known even among the Philistines.

One of the inevitable consequences of this enthronement was that he became the fashion. All who aspired to be considered cultured or artistic professed (if they did not possess) an intimate knowledge of his books and an enthusiastic agreement with his principles. Their over-emphasized worship proved irresistible to the mockers, and jests and caricatures made Ruskin's name familiar to a good many people who would never have thought of opening *Modern Painters* or *Stones of Venice*. He began to appear in the fiction of the day. Ouida made fun of the tourists who visited celebrated buildings "Ruskin à la main," and "prated of severity and purity"; and in *Harry Coverdale* we are introduced to "a tall, gaunt, blue woman, rejoicing in a red nose and a long, fluent tongue," who, at one of Lady Tattersall Trotmont's famous soirées, discoursed on "various hackneyed pseudo-literary topics," "among them *the* Oxford Graduate (viz. Turner's single and singular disciple, wonderful Mr. Ruskin) and pre-Raphaelitism."

Oxford was a stronghold of Ruskin worship, and year by year sent out fresh recruits to join in his crusade. There was a red-headed, unruly young genius named Algernon Swinburne who came up in 1856, and who proclaimed himself Ruskin's devoted admirer; and two years afterwards came a quiet, thoughtful lad named Walter Pater, who was still more completely under the master's spell. James Addington Symonds, a frail but brilliant youth who came up to Balliol in 1858, was also to have his place among the forces that fought for Beauty.

William Morris, in London, was working with apparently inexhaustible energy at architecture, painting, and literature. In 1858 he published a volume of poetry, *The Defence of Guinevere and other poems*, most of which he had written while he was at Oxford. The little volume, although at first its influence was felt by only a small circle, became a source of inspiration to the leaders of the Aesthetic Movement. In 1858 Morris married, and built for himself a house on Bexley Heath, which in its design, its decoration, and its furnishing was to be as beautiful as he and his associates could make it. The difficulty that they found in obtaining furniture, wall-paper, and draperies that were not ugly, conventional, and of poor workmanship pointed to a state of things that seemed to cry aloud for remedy; and he determined that it should be remedied. He established a factory for the manufacture of furniture and fabrics, and he put all his energy and his enthusiasm into his efforts to produce lovely colours and beautiful shapes. His wall-papers and chintzes, his chairs and tables, his glass, his patterned silks and linens were all designed by artists and carried out by skilled workmen whom he encouraged in every way he could to take a pride in their labour. Burne-Jones joined with him in the enterprise, while William de Morgan at the same time was experimenting with pottery and was producing tiles and vases and bowls of rare and ravishing beauty.

The effects of Ruskin's teaching and Morris's work began to be noticeable. Before the 'sixties came to an end there were signs in many of the houses of the upper and middle classes of a complete revolution of taste. Heavy and depressing ugliness was giving place to lightness and grace and softly glowing colours. Mrs. Humphry Ward, in *The Marriage of William Ashe*, described the house of Lady Tranmore, which

reflected the rising worship of Morris and Burne-Jones. . . . Her walls were covered with the well-known pomegranate or jessamine or sunflower patterns; her hangings were of a mystic greenish blue; her pictures were drawn either from the Italian primitives or their modern followers.

Against such a background the fashionable dress of the day, the crinoline and elaborately arranged hair, seemed stiff and ungainly, and the pre-Raphaelite ladies adopted a more graceful and flowing style. Mary Howitt, who, Quakeress as she was, was on friendly terms with the principal members of the group, wrote to her daughter in June 1861, telling of "a great pre-Raphaelite crush" she had been to where "the uncrinolined women with their wild hair, which was very beautiful, their picture dresses and rich colouring, looked like figures cut out of pre-Raphaelite pictures." At Oxford, university society was gradually transforming itself in accordance with the new aesthetic principles. Morris wall-papers and reproductions of Burne-Jones pictures found their way into pleasant academic drawing-rooms. Plain, straightly cut gowns, with a string of beads for ornament, took the place of more elaborate *toilettes* at the evening parties where *The Defence of Guinevere* and Ruskin's new book, *Sesame and Lilies*, were appreciatively discussed; and there was a general feeling that the movement was going forward.

Sesame and Lilies helped more perhaps than any previous work of Ruskin had done to make the principles of that movement familiar to the general public. It was quite a short book, consisting only of two lectures, the first called *Of Kings' Treasures*, treating of reading, the second called *Of Queens' Gardens*, treating of ideals for girls and women. In a preface to a later edition Ruskin said, "If read in connection with *Unto This Last* it contains the chief truths I have endeavoured all my past life to display." It was easy to read, and its statements, if startling, were expressed in plain language without the allusions and technicalities that made *Modern Painters* a little puzzling to the uncultivated reader. It penetrated farther into Philistia than any other sally made by the crusaders had yet done, and it was also a favourite book with many young people who lived outside the boundaries of that unenlightened country. There were a few who, like Mr. Robert Bridges, then seventeen years old, resented Ruskin's telling them what they should like or dislike. There were others who, like Lady Rose Fane, found *Sesame and Lilies* rather amusing.

"I wish you would tell me what you think of Ruskin's last book," wrote Lady Rose to her brother Julian. "I see the *Saturday* demolishes it very much. I thought there was a good deal of nonsense in it, put so charmingly that one liked it better than a great deal of sense. Mamma cannot get over the nonsense; but I do not mind that, and I think the denunciations of *everything* in the Carlyle style are very amusing. What on earth does he mean by the title?"

But most people read it in the spirit that made Lady Theodore Martin (who before her marriage was Miss Helen Faucit, the famous actress) say, "What an exquisite thing it is! How much I thank Ruskin for it!"

At Oxford Lady Rose's criticism would have seemed almost irreverent, for there Ruskin was still "the Apostle whose sayings it was blasphemy to contradict." Each successive body of undergraduates brought new worshippers. Walter Pater was a don now, living quietly in his rooms at Brasenose College, reading and studying, and writing with slow, fastidious care the books which were to be in themselves models of the beauty he loved. Algernon Swinburne had left Oxford in 1860 without taking a degree, and after some travel in Italy had settled in London. There he lived in close association with Rossetti, and Morris and Burne-Jones whom he had met at Oxford; and, almost at the same time as *Sesame and Lilies*, appeared his poem, *Atalanta in Calydon*.

It made an immediate sensation. Its lyrics had the strange, exciting note that had not been heard in poetry since Shelley, and, like Shelley, Swinburne flouted all accepted beliefs and conventions, religious, moral, and social. It was clear that for him, as for Ruskin, the motive power was an intense love of Beauty, but the vision that possessed him glowed and palpitated with a febrile loveliness that gave to his work a quality very different from anything to be found in *Modern Painters* or *Stones of Venice*. It startled, shocked, puzzled, and enraptured all in one. It took away the breath of a large number of its readers, but those who retained their powers of articulation were numerous enough to raise a storm made up partly of delight, partly of horror. Ruskin, the critic of revered and unquestioned authority, declared that it was "the grandest thing ever done by a youth." Morris was lukewarm. Burne-Jones and Rossetti admired it fervently, and so did Rossetti's sister, Christina. At Wallington Hall in Northumberland, the home of Sir Walter Trevelyan, the progress of *Atalanta* was watched with the warmest interest, and there was much rejoicing when favourable notices appeared in the Press. Lady Trevelyan was strongly pre-Raphaelite in her sympathies, and the house was a favourite meeting-place of the Brotherhood.

Sissie Frith was one of the few young readers who did not care for *Atalanta*. R. E. Francillon was enraptured with it.

"There was no possible minority of even a single voice," he says, "when one evening in 1865, still remembered as if it were yesterday, I, with my brother who then shared my lodgings, and another *habitué* of Mitre's Court, feasted together on *Atalanta*."

From the Philistines came an outcry of shocked and pained disapproval; not that many of them read the poem, but they heard it talked about as atheistic and immoral. The voices of those who blamed were, however, almost lost in the voices of those who praised. The classical subject of the poem made the atheism less noticeable than it would have been had the theme been a modern one, and the enchanting lyrics could scarcely fail to delight any reader who had the least feeling for poetry.

By this time another champion had appeared who was laying about him, not in the spirit of reckless defiance that moved Swinburne, but with a calm deliberation of aim that did great execution. Matthew Arnold's ironic thrusts were dealt on behalf of intellectual and moral rather than natural beauty. He loved the calm graciousness of Greek forms of art and the satisfying perfection of classical verse, both ancient and modern. He was not a pre-Raphaelite nor a follower of Ruskin; indeed, in the *Essays in Criticism* with which, in 1865, he opened his attack, he dealt rather severely with some of Ruskin's theories and modes of expression. But he had set himself to do battle with what was mean and sordid and ugly in the life of his day, and so far he was in agreement with all the aesthetic company. James Smetham read the essay on Eugenie de Guérin, and thought it interesting and clever. Mrs. Humphry Ward says—

As a girl of sixteen I became a resident in Oxford. Up to then Ruskin—the *Stones of Venice* and certain chapters in *Modern Painters*—had been my chief intellectual passion. . . . About 1868 I first read *Essays in Criticism*. It is not too much to say that the book set for me the currents of life.

In the *Essay on Heinrich Heine*, Arnold introduced and explained his use of the term Philistine and made his indictment against the powerful middle class. The middle class was not in the habit of reading Matthew Arnold, but its members heard of this attack on their ranks, and many of them read *Heinrich Heine* and talked about it indignantly to others. There were some readers, and those not only among the Philistines, who thought that Arnold affected too superior and lofty an air in his criticisms; but his urbanity, his ease, and his ironical humour saved him from giving real offence, and he continued to tell his countrymen unpleasant truths in a pleasant manner in another series of Essays, in *Culture and Anarchy*, 1869, and *Friendship's Garland*, 1871. His poetry was read at first by only a small circle of thoughtful, intellectual people, but it had its authentic message to the men of his day, and gradually it gained a wider hearing. In 1858 Walter Bagehot read the newly published *Merope*, and thought it "clever, but too much 'high art' and not enough addressed to the common feelings and minds of ordinary people." Twenty years later Matthew Arnold wrote to his sister—

It is curious how the public is beginning to take my poems to its bosom, after long years of comparative neglect. The wave of thought and change has rolled on until people begin to find a significance and an attraction in what had none for them formerly.

Eighteen-sixty-five had been a memorable year for the Aesthetic Movement. It had seen the opening of three several attacks, by way of *Sesame and Lilies*, *Atalanta*, and *Essays in Criticism*. Eighteen-sixty-six saw a pitched battle. In August of that year Swinburne published his *Poems and Ballads*. It was received with a storm of reprobation that rose quickly to fury. To the majority of readers it seemed that here were immorality and blasphemy, not veiled as in *Atalanta*, but open and unashamed. There was a minority which was enraptured, almost intoxicated, by the sheer poetic beauty of the strange verses. William Hardman wrote to his friend, Edward Holroyd, telling him of the publication of the volume and the uproar that it had caused—

Truly this volume of Swinburne's is a strange medley. It contains some passages worthy to rank among the noblest in our language, while three parts of it are the foulest beastliness. Biting lips, lithe limbs, supple flanks, hair that stings and burns, and kisses—by Jove, it would be curious to count up the kisses in the book, for I am sure there are ten times as many in the 344 pages as there are in the same number of pages from the most erotic work ever before produced.

John Morley reviewed *Poems and Ballads* in the *Saturday Review* for August 4th. He condemned the book utterly, as unfit to be read, and denounced its author as an "unclean, fiery imp from the pit" and "the libidinous laureate of a pack of satyrs."

Ruskin read the review, and was much disturbed. He, with another friend of Swinburne's, called on Moxon, the publisher, to consult with him as to what could be done. The publisher was in terror lest the Public Prosecutor might call him to account, and received with the utmost relief a proposal to transfer the work to another firm. A publisher, John Horton, was found who was willing to take the risk, and the sale of the book went on. The outcry was redoubled. *Poems and Ballads* was denounced as an outrage against religion, morality, and decency. John Malcolm Ludlow, the Christian Socialist, demanded insistently that the author should be prosecuted. Friends besought Ruskin to use his influence with Swinburne to procure the withdrawal or modification of the poems. "Swinburne is infinitely above me in all knowledge and power," replied Ruskin, "and I should no more think of advising him than of venturing to do it to Turner if he were alive again." He recognized in the audacious and turbulent young man the true poet, and knew that Swinburne, like himself, worshipped the pure spirit of Beauty. The extravagances, the irreverences, the offences against good taste, even the uncleannesses, were the outcome of a youthful devotion to Beauty, so passionate that it took no thought of anything but its object.

The young people—such of them as managed to read *Poems and Ballads*—were nearly all on Swinburne's side. We hear how at Oxford the book "simply swept us off our legs," and how at Cambridge the undergraduates joined hands and marched along singing *A Song in Time of Revolution* and *Dolores: Our Lady of Pain*. A stanza of the latter poem may be quoted—

> O lips full of lust and of laughter,
>   Curled snakes that are fed from my breast,
> Bite hard, lest remembrance come after
>   And press with new lips where you pressed,
> For my heart too springs up at the pressure,
>   Mine eyelids too moisten and burn;
> O feed me and fill me with pleasure,
>   Till pain come in turn.

Walter Leaf says that his friend Sidgwick, although in ordinary conversation he stammered, could recite Swinburne "for ever," and that another undergraduate friend, Edmund Gurney, "also had a passion for Swinburne." "Like most of my contemporaries who had any taste for poetry, I was carried away in my youth by his [Swinburne's] poetry," says Sir Frederick Pollock. Parents did what they could to protect their children from the contamination of his works. They brought up their boys and girls to regard him with horror, and as far as was possible kept the poems out of their way. Yet somehow the young people managed to get hold of them, and the succession of Swinburne's worshippers remained long unbroken, weakening only with the 'nineties.

If abuse could have killed *Poems and Ballads*, it would quickly have died. Following John Morley in the *Saturday* other eminent critics reviewed the book in a tone of scornful disgust, and the lesser ones followed with shriller and more violent abuse. Swinburne answered in a furious article called *Notes on poems and reviews*, but his defence in the eyes of outraged readers only tended to prove him utterly shameless.

Having read Mr. Swinburne's defence of his prurient poetics, *Punch* hereby gives him his royal licence to change his name to what is evidently its true form—SWINEBORN—

was *Punch's* answer to this outburst; and *Punch* expressed, as it so often did, the feeling of the majority of its readers.

Swinburne's raptures of melody and passion must—if they were ever admitted—have sounded strangely in the aesthetic drawing-rooms where gracefully attired ladies and gentlemen discussed Ruskin's theories of art with admiring reverence, or listened to a mystic sonnet by Rossetti, or gazed delightedly upon the wan and wistful maidens depicted by Burne-Jones. Swinburne was not really a pre-Raphaelite, although he was associated with the pre-Raphaelite leaders, and although, like them, he was in revolt against convention and in search of pure beauty. Morris's *Jason*, which was published in 1867, was much more to the taste of the aesthetes than was *Poems and Ballads*. It was nine years since the appearance of *Guinevere*, and Morris was known far better for his furnishings than for his writings; but *Jason* took the country by storm—not only the inner circle of those who shared Morris's aesthetic ideals, but also the great public beyond. Only that crochety critic, Edward FitzGerald, raised his voice in contradiction of the general verdict. "I tried to read *Jason*," he grumbled, "but *No Go*."

Jason was followed by *The Earthly Paradise*, which appeared in four parts between 1868 and 1870, and which some readers had the temerity to compare to the four *Idylls* published in 1869. Mary Howitt said—

> I have vastly enjoyed Mr. Morris's poems, and it is a pleasure to me to think of him in his blue blouse and with his earnest face at the Firm, and feel that he is a great poet. Tennyson's poetry is the perfection of art and truth in art. Morris's is nature itself, rough at times, but quaint, fresh, and dewy beyond anything I ever saw or felt in language.

Bishop Thirlwall and the "young friend" to whom he wrote his letters both read each part of *The Earthly Paradise* as it came out.

> "Some of my very pleasantest hours last summer were spent in Morris's *Earthly Paradise*," wrote the young friend, "and I am looking forward to the second volume."

When the second volume came the bishop wrote—

> Though I have only just opened the new part of the *Earthly Paradise*, I feel sure you need be in no fear of disappointment. Morris is one of those poets who will always be true to themselves.

John Addington Symonds wrote to Mrs. Clough—

> In this sleepy weather and among your sea caves you should read the *Earthly Paradise*. I wonder if you do. It is *langweilig* but genuine. I want to make the man get to his point faster and be a little more stern. But his delicate pathos, as of a loose-stringed, softly stricken lute, and his sweet natural pictures are very charming.

Symonds was by this time beginning to be known as a writer both of verse and of prose. His style, judged by the standard that Ruskin had set up, was too ornate and mannered for true beauty, but he was a sincere and earnest adherent of the aesthetic movement, and the aim that he set before himself, "to live resolvedly in the Whole, the Good, the Beautiful," was in accordance with its highest teaching.

All through the 'seventies the aesthetic cult grew stronger, and its votaries tended to show more and more the outward signs that distinguished them from their fellows. At Oxford, Miss Wordsworth has told us, it was the day of green serge gowns and Morris papers.

Every lady of true culture had an amber necklace, sleeves tight below the elbow and puffed above, and all the scraps of yellowish lace she could lay her hands on to trim her dress.

The literature of the aesthetes was growing, and a philosophy of life founded ultimately upon Ruskin's principles but with variations and developments that carried it outside the limits of his plan was being evolved. Ruskin himself had for some years given up writing books bearing directly upon the movement. He had devoted himself almost entirely to the consideration of economic problems and to the writing of those books which have been referred to here in the chapter "The Two Nations." The spirit and aim of the author had not altered, but his books were no longer of primary interest to those who called themselves aesthetes.

In 1869 he was appointed Slade Professor of Fine Art at Oxford, and there to some extent he took up again the aesthetic side of his work. Oxford was still loyal to him. The undergraduates flocked to his lectures, and the rest of the University society read them with eagerness when later they were published. Lord Cave, who went up to Oxford in 1874, said that he attended Ruskin's lectures, and had some thought of joining the party of undergraduates who, under the Slade Professor's direction, were making a road to Hinksey. Among those who did join it was a young man whom Sir Frank Benson—also an undergraduate at the time— describes as a "lazy, lumbering, long-haired, somewhat sallow-faced individual, with a greeny-brown coat and yellow tie." His name was Oscar Fingall O'Flahertie Wills Wilde, and he had been greatly impressed by Ruskin's lectures. Nobody in Oxford thought very much of Mr. Wilde, but he thought a great deal of himself, and was indeed a very clever young man, and destined to take a conspicuous part in the movement that Ruskin had begun.

The man who at this time was attracting most notice in Oxford was Walter Pater. He was still living his quiet, studious life, writing his exquisite prose, and labouring to perfect it in every detail with pre-Raphaelite care. His was an ideal which differed widely from that of Ruskin and that of Swinburne. He saw Beauty as something transient, pure, and perfect, untouched by human passions and having no bearing upon moral conduct. In 1868 he had published an *Essay on Aesthetic Poetry*, which had been inspired by Morris's *Guinevere*. In 1873 came a collection of his essays, published under the title of *Studies in the History of the Renaissance*. Mrs. Humphry Ward, then twenty-three years old, and living at Oxford, says—

> I recall very clearly the effect of that book, and of the strange and poignant sense of beauty expressed in it, of its entire aloofness also from the Christian tradition of Oxford, its glorification of the higher and intenser forms of aesthetic pleasure, of passion in the intellectual sense—as against the Christian doctrine of denial and renunciation. It was a gospel that both stirred and scandalized Oxford. The bishop of the diocese thought it worth while to protest. There was a cry of Neo-paganism, and various attempts at persecution.

Pater taught the love of art for art's sake, because from art man could obtain the highest form of enjoyment that life was capable of yielding. The present moment, he said, was all that man could be sure of; it was the "sharp apex" between "two hypothetical eternities." Man's problem therefore was "How such actual moments as they pass may be made to yield their utmost by the dexterous training of capacity." To him the answer was, through the appreciation of art. The acceptance of this solution of the problem meant that life must be lived on a high plane of intellectual effort and must be free from all grossness and mean cares. It would, nevertheless, be a life whose chief aim was self-gratification.

The publication of *Studies in the History of the Renaissance* caused real pain to many who were devout as well as beauty-loving. The book did not reach the great reading public, but by thoughtful and intellectual people it was discussed with intense and serious interest. What were the implications of this new aesthetic doctrine, and to what would it lead? There were some who accepted Pater's principle of obtaining the greatest enjoyment from each moment as it passed, but who did not accept his solution of the problem that it raised. In that same year of 1873 Lord Lytton published his *Kenelm Chillingly*, and the words that he put into the mouth of his hero, lately down from Oxford, perhaps express the views of a party in the University that held a view opposed to Pater's.

"According to aesthetics," said this grave young scholar, "I believe man arrives at his highest state of moral excellence when labour and duty lose all the harshness of effort—when they become the impulse and habit of life; when, as the essential attributes of the beautiful, they are, like beauty, enjoyed as pleasure. . . . A lovely doctrine, not perhaps so lofty as that of the Stoics, but more bewitching. Only very few of us can practically merge our cares and our worries into so serene an atmosphere."

The lady to whom he spoke—the intellectual, cultured wife of a country clergyman—gave him the answer which the Church was consistently giving to the aesthetes in all such discussions, "Some of us do so without knowing anything of aesthetics and with no pretence to be Stoics; but, then, they are Christians."

Pater himself took no part in the discussions his book had aroused. He lived his retired life in Oxford in his own fastidiously aesthetic fashion among a group of friends who had the same tastes if not exactly the same opinions as his own. They read Rossetti and Ruskin and Morris, and when Swinburne's drama, *Bothwell*, came out in 1874 they, with the greater part of the reading public, welcomed it with enthusiasm, though Morris did not like it, and Henry Sidgwick called it "a mass of uninspired verbosity." John Addington Symonds said, "I do not think anything greater has been produced in our age, in spite of its inordinate length and strange affectation of style."

When, four years later, the second series of *Poems and Ballads* appeared, it roused no such storm as had raged in 1866. Swinburne had modified his youthful extravagances, and readers were now free to delight in the pure poetry of his marvellous verse without being disturbed by the consciousness of an unclean taint breathing through it. Yet he never entirely outlived the reputation that his earlier works had gained for him. Many earnest, religious people still thought of him with horror as Morley's "unclean, fiery imp from the pit." Others regarded his early excesses with something of the indulgence given to a brilliant, wayward child, and spoke of him in the tone of Mr. George Augustus Sala, the journalist, who (as Sir Edmund Gosse reports) in returning thanks for the toast of "Poetry" at a public dinner, did so in the names of "the clever (but I cannot say moral) Mr. Swinburne, and the moral (but I cannot say clever) Mr. Tupper"; which double thrust must have delighted his audience. Mr. Tupper, as might be guessed, was not one of Swinburne's admirers; yet, like the rest of the world, he knew something about *Poems and Ballads*, for in his *Autobiography* he quoted from *Dolores*, remarking with his usual unashamed self-righteousness, "I have always been stupidly prone to prefer 'the lilies and languors of virtue' to the 'roses and raptures of vice.' "

As denunciation slackened, the lighter and more teasing strokes of ridicule fell on Swinburne ever more thickly. Parodists could not resist the temptation offered by the strong individuality of his style, and even his most sincere admirers read the parodies with relish. One of the best of these was *The Octopus*, published in 1872 in a Cambridge University magazine called *Light Green*, and written by an undergraduate, Arthur Hilton. It was inspired by the octopus in the Crystal Palace Aquarium, and its last verse ran—

> Ah! thy red lips, lascivious and luscious,
>   With death in their amorous kiss,
> Cling round us and clasp us and crush us
>   With bitings of agonized bliss;
> We are sick with the poison of pleasure,
>   Dispense us the potion of pain;
> Ope thy mouth to its uttermost measure
>   And bite us again.

Mortimer Collins, in his novel *Two Plunges for a Pearl*, caricatured Swinburne as Swynfen—

the favourite poet of the ladies and the pre-Raffaellites, a little man built like a grasshopper, but with energy enough to inform the bodies of both Anak and Chang. It was hard to criticize Swynfen's face for the vast amount of bright yellow hair that he wore wherever hair would grow; but his eyes, small and deep sunk, were of an intense blue, like the first flame of a lucifer match. Swynfen firmly believed himself the greatest living poet, and his fury if anybody ventured to doubt this was exquisitely amusing.

Swinburne's eccentricities of appearance and manner had made him one of the best-known and most talked-of figures in London, and the dark rumours that were everywhere whispered of dissipations and excesses added interest to his notoriety. But the time was quickly coming when he was to be faced with a rival—one who understood far better than he did the art of attracting public notice.

Oscar Wilde came down from Oxford in 1878, and settled in London. He became known as a writer of poems and articles in various magazines, but these, although they were clever and witty, would not of themselves have given him notoriety. That came from his personal eccentricities. He went about London dressed in a velvet coat, knee-breeches, a loose shirt with a turned-down collar, and a long-floating tie of some unusual shade. He wore his hair long, and often carried a lily or a sunflower in his hand. He loved to pose, and at evening parties would sometimes stand in a rapt attitude as if absorbed in the contemplation of a beautiful vision unseen by the grosser eyes of those around him. He affected a scorn of all that was homely and commonplace, and a high-souled devotion to Art, spelt always with a capital A. Beauty he proclaimed to be his watchword, as it was the watchword of all the aesthetes, but his was a special and limited form of beauty—a frail, tenuous, unhealthy growth, in which was displayed the decay, not the fulfilment of vital forces.

He soon had a large following, including many who came from the ranks of the Philistines. Where Ruskin and Morris had by long and patient effort gathered in ten converts, Wilde by his spectacular methods attracted a hundred. For thirty-four years the crusade in the cause of Beauty had been going on, and great advances had been made, but the innermost strongholds of Philistia had not fallen. The books and the pictures of the leaders of the campaign had required some mental effort—often, also, some travail of spirit—before they could be understood and appreciated, and only a comparatively small number of readers were willing to take these necessary pains. Yet there were probably few who were unaware that such a crusade was in progress. The gibes of the newspapers and the jokes of *Punch* would alone have sufficed to tell them that. They were conscious that they were being called to make their surroundings and their habits—their whole way of life—more beautiful, but the idea seemed to most of them visionary and unattractive. Nevertheless, the fact that such an idea existed in their minds made their response the readier when the appeal was made in a more inviting form. When Ruskin had said, "Art, properly so called, is no recreation. To advance it men's lives must be given and to receive it their hearts," that seemed to them a hard saying, and one which called upon them to take a great deal of trouble for something which they were not sure was worth having. When Morris said—

> O fools! and if ye could but know
> How fair a world to you is given,

they did not take the reproach to themselves and open their eyes and look about them; and his austere, practical dictum, "Have nothing in your houses that you do not know to be useful or believe to be beautiful," involved too many heartsearchings and sacrifices to be taken seriously. But according to Mr. Oscar Wilde no such effort or such sacrifice was necessary. It was all a matter of posings and yearnings and sighings and raptures. Ideal beauty lay in blue china and peacocks' feathers and Japanese fans and flowing raiment of peculiar shades. One showed oneself a true disciple by gazing entranced at a sunflower or a lily, by rhapsodizing over pale cheeks and sunken eyes and wasted limbs, and turning with a shudder from rosy health. When Oscar Wilde, in a sonnet addressed to Ellen Terry in her character of Henrietta Maria, compared her to Helen of Troy—

> In the lone tent, waiting for victory,
> She stands with eyes marred by the mists of pain,
> Like some wan lily, overdrenched with rain,

the response required was obvious. All the aesthetic young ladies proceeded to make themselves as much like wan lilies as their countenances and contours permitted; poetic appreciation could go no further. It is true that, as Sir Henry Newbolt has told us, when Oscar Wilde presented a copy of his poems to the Oxford Union Library, its rejection was moved by Professor Elton on the grounds, "not that the poems are thin—and they *are* thin," "not that they are immoral—and they *are* immoral," but because they "are for the most part not by their putative father at all, but by a number of better-known and more deservedly reputed poets." He showed conclusively the extensive plagiarisms of which Wilde had been guilty; his motion was carried, and the volume was, presumably, returned to its owner. But such considerations as these did not affect Mr. Wilde's disciples; nor did *Punch's* verdict—

> Aesthete of Aesthetes!
> What's in a name?
> The poet is wild,
> But his poetry's tame.

At first this new aesthetic school professed unbounded devotion to the older leaders of the movement. They "adored" the works of Ruskin, and were "ravished" by the pictures in the Grosvenor Gallery—an exhibition which Sir Coutts Lindsay had caused to be established in 1877, primarily for the purpose of introducing to the public the works of the pre-Raphaelites, who were not in favour with the Academy. Ouida gives the Philistine view of this gallery when she makes two of her guardsmen drop in "to lounge away an hour, chiefly for the great entertainment and fun afforded to persons of sane mind by the eccentricities of the pre-Raphaelite gentlemen." Miss Braddon's aesthetic young ladies, on the other hand, held that no works of art worthy of notice existed outside this delectable gallery. They went further, and yearned for "a Temple with a single Watts or Burne-Jones or Dante Gabriel Rossetti, which one could go in and worship quietly in a subdued light." These young ladies belonged to "the peacock-feather school of art." They wore short-waisted gowns with broad sashes of "pale pinks and olive greens, tawny yellows and faded russets," and insisted on talking of Swinburne's latest tragedy and Ruskin's theories of art to uninterested young gentlemen who, "on being pushed hard, believed there was a biggish swell of some such name among the Oxford dons," about whom they could not reasonably be expected to know anything, since they belonged to Cambridge.

It was not long, however, before the more advanced members of the Oscar Wilde group began to take up a superior attitude towards Ruskin. *Modern Painters* was all very well, but it was out of date. Ruskin preached a gospel that had been superseded. He had, in fact, as far as they were concerned, reached the third stage indicated by William de Morgan, and had become "a fogey with a niche in the Temple of Orthodoxy." "Passionate Brompton" and "intense Kensington" had no further use for him.

The novels of the day abound in pictures of these devotees of the highest aesthetic culture. They still paid some homage to Rossetti and Swinburne, and wild-haired, haggard maidens recited *The Blessed Damozel* at evening parties with great effect. But their most fervent admiration was given to Oscar Wilde, and the poets— they were many—who aspired to follow him. Miss Rhoda Broughton, in *Second Thoughts*, shows one of these interesting young aspirants who had written a poem which he wished to read to an attractive young lady—not of the aesthetic cult—for whom he cherished what he believed to be a wild and desperate passion. In a drawing-room which contained such Philistine abominations as an india-rubber plant and lustres under green shades he bravely began, "Ho! sick-sweet beryl eyes"—then murmured, "Surely there is nothing so beautiful as disease." But he could not go on. The surroundings were incompatible with high poetry. "It should be read," he plaintively breathed, "to the low, pale sound of the viol or virginal; with a subtle perfume of dead roses floating about while the eye is fed with porphyry vases and tender Tyrian dyes."

More fortunate was Mr. Blanchet, of Justin McCarthy's *Miss Misanthrope*. He had an adoring sister who lived as companion to the wealthy young lady to whom the poems were to be read, and this sister saw to it that all incongruous articles were removed from the drawing-room, the blinds drawn, and one shaded lamp arranged to throw its light on the figure of the reader.

Mr. Blanchet had never read Shakespeare, considered Byron below criticism, and could hardly restrain himself on the subject of Browning. . . . His poems belonged to what might be called the literature of disease. In principle they said to corruption, "Thou art my father," and to the worm, "Thou art my mother and my sister." They dealt largely in graves and corpses and the loves of skeletons, and the sweet virtues of sin and the joys of despair and dyspepsia. They taught that there is no truth but paradox. Mr. Blanchet read his contribution with great effect, in a voice now wailing, now threatening, now storming fiercely, now creeping along in tones of the lowest hoarseness.

The reading concluded with the stanza—

> I asked of my soul—What is death?
> I asked of love—What is hate?
> I asked of decay—Art thou life?
> And of night—Art thou day?
> Did they answer?

The young lady to whom the poems were read was unable to extract any meaning from them, and was considerably bored by the recital. But she was of a kindly disposition, so she promised the poet that she would pay for the publication of his works. A sumptuous edition was prepared—vellum paper, rare typography, wide margins, costly and fantastic binding, lavish illustration. The volume was freely distributed among the poet's friends, and a few copies—possibly—were sold. It lay on the drawing-room tables of aesthetic ladies in company with various other slim and ornamental booklets of the same type. It was passed from one to another, and gushing readers prophesied for it an assured immortality; until the next long-haired poet managed to get his poems published and became in his turn the little idol of the hour.

We might be inclined to regard the descriptions given by the novelists as mere amusing exaggerations were it not that the memoir writers of the day also bear witness to the amazing habits of these Oscar Wilde aesthetes. Mr. Robert Francillon, for example, describes an evening party at the house of Mr. George Robinson, in Gower Street, where he saw

a youth carrying throughout a whole evening, in melancholy silence, a tall white lily, with whose droop he was evidently doing his best to bring his own figure into imitation. At this same house a young woman, dressed as it seemed to me in nothing but an old-fashioned bathing-gown and an amber necklace, whom I was asked to take to the supper room, returned to my inquiry of what I could get for her the lugubriously toned answer, "I seldom eat!" And these words were all I could win from her, then or thereafter.

If Mr. Francillon went—as he almost certainly did—to a performance of the Gilbert and Sullivan "new and original aesthetic opera," *Patience*, produced on April 3, 1881 at the Opera Comique, he must have thought of the young gentleman with the lily while he listened to the too fascinating hero of the play, the poet Bunthorne, singing to an adoring circle of twenty lovesick maidens—

If you're anxious to shine in the high æsthetic line as a man of culture rare,
You must get up all the germs of the transcendental terms and plant them everywhere. . . .
Though the Philistines may jostle you will count as an apostle in the high æsthetic band,
If you walk down Piccadilly with a poppy or a lily in your medieval hand.

Patience was a complete and most delightful skit on the later phases of the aesthetic movement. There were the rival poets (who stood primarily for Swinburne and Wilde, although traits of other writers were introduced)—Bunthorne, the "fleshly poet," yet "soulfully intense," and Archibald Grosvenor, the Apostle of Simplicity—

A pallid and thin young man,
A haggard and lank young man,
A greenery-yallery, Grosvenor Gallery,
    Foot-in-the-grave young man.

There were audacious parodies of Swinburne's verse—

> What time the poet hath hymned the writing maid
> Lithe-limbed, quivering on amaranthine asphodel.

There were the twenty lovesick maidens, whose dress and make-up was copied from Burne-Jones' picture, "The Triumph of Love," headed by Jane in a black Japanese dress after Whistler. They had once worshipped the military, but were now possessed by the aesthetic ideal. They had the Oscar Wilde school's horror of bright tints, and its curious conception of high art as a hotchpotch of things remote and unusual. "Red and yellow! Primary colours! Oh, South Kensington!" exclaimed Jane, looking with horror on the uniforms of the dragoons. "We didn't design our uniforms, and we don't see how they could be improved," retorted one of the gallant warriors. "No, you wouldn't," was Jane's withering reply. "Still, there is a cobwebby gray velvet, with a tender bloom, like cold gravy, which, made Florentine fourteenth century, trimmed with Venetian leather and Spanish altar lace, and surmounted with something Japanese—it matters not what—would at least be Early English."

Patience drew the whole town, including Suburbia. The aesthetic craze had reached its height; society was divided into those who worshipped and those who scoffed; and for both the witty, tuneful play had its attraction. Oscar Wilde himself was present on the first night, sitting in the stalls, and received with good humour the chaff that was poured upon him from the gallery. Mary Gladstone went to see the opera in July, and recorded in her diary that she enjoyed it much, in spite of the heat. "An enchanting opera of Sullivan's," she called it, "and the greatest triumph for aestheticism which it was meant to bring to shame." Exactly what she meant by "a triumph for aestheticism" is not quite clear, unless it was that aestheticism had inspired the two collaborators to the creation of a masterpiece. *Patience* did not bring the movement to shame, it associated it with inextinguishable laughter. It certainly helped to kill aestheticism, but at the same time raised an enduring monument to its memory.

There were other causes also tending to the decline of the craze. Its very extravagance was wearing it out. Oscar Wilde, brilliant as he was, had not the force that could sustain and vitalize it. In the late 'eighties it drooped; in the early 'nineties, when newer crazes arose, it died.

The true Aesthetic Movement survived the decay of its degenerate offshoot, and though it gradually ceased to exist as a distinct activity, it cannot be said to have died, since the results that it achieved remained as a permanent influence in English life and literature. Throughout the 'eighties these results were to be seen in a more general appreciation of aesthetic literature and a growing desire to banish the elaborate ugliness that disfigured so many homes. Young readers still thrilled to the passion of Swinburne. Mrs. Annabel Huth Jackson says that while she was at Cheltenham College one of the girls brought back after the holidays a copy of *Poems and Ballads*, and "half the house went mad over it, and copied out most of the book since we could not afford to buy it." Miss Lilian Faithful concludes her account of undergraduate life at Somerville College, Oxford, in 1883, with the words, "The Oxford bells are ringing, and we are reading *Atalanta in Calydon* for the first time, and life is very good." Mrs. Hungerford shows the charming heroine of *Molly Bawn*— which was, in the 'eighties, delighting a large number of readers— wandering sadly in the woods one autumn afternoon, when "Swinburne's exquisite lines rose involuntarily to her mind—

> Lo, the summer is dead, the sun is faded,
> Even like as a leaf the year is withered.

When *Tristram of Lyonesse* appeared in 1881 it was received with almost universal appreciation, though there were still some who cried out against its glorification of sensual love. It did not succeed in breaking down Morris's distaste for Swinburne's poetry. "I have made two or three attempts to read it," he said, "but have failed—doubtless my own fault."

Morris's own works, both in prose and in verse, were still being widely read. George Richmond, the artist, declared that when he visited Oxford in 1879, Morris was there the most popular poet, and Sir Henry Newbolt, who was an undergraduate at the University in 1882, says that he read there the whole of Morris's works, poetry and prose.

Walter Pater, too, kept his small circle of devoted admirers. In 1885 he published *Marius the Epicurean*, the fruit of twelve years' quiet, intense, and loving labour. It did not attract the general reader, and it raised less discussion than *Studies in the History of the Renaissance* had done. At Oxford it was received with reverence. "If Jowett was our major, Pater was our minor prophet," says Sir Arthur Quiller-Couch; "we had all, of course, read *Marius the Epicurean.*" Some readers, like David Hogarth, were disappointed in it, finding its characters lacking in life and its phraseology vague. Henry Sidgwick wrote—

Have been reading *Marius the Epicurean* with an adequate amount of serene satisfaction. I think it is a success—as much a success as Pater is capable of. . . . In short, it is a "bland" and "select" book, "gracious" certainly, if not exactly "opulent," and its preciosity, though a salient feature, is not offensive.

What Sidgwick called preciosity appeared to the true lovers of Pater as perfection of style and polished beauty of phrase, and to them the book was a delight. Among them was Canon Coles. "No one," we are told, "who heard him read the account of the Eucharist in *Marius the Epicurean*, or a poem of Robert Bridges, could doubt that he was made happy by beautiful literature."

Ruskin, the writer to whom beyond all others the Aesthetic Movement owed its inspiration, was ending his great career in sad retirement; but he still had his devoted followers, whose faith in the power and beauty of the gospel he preached never wavered. To the new generation growing up it might seem that he had reached Mr. de Morgan's fourth stage, and had become "a successful candidate for a niche in the Temple of Oblivion." But the doors of that temple never closed upon him, and the light of his teaching still shone out, though he himself was in shadow.

CHAPTER XVIII

PUNCH

Punch started on the course which leads to that august eminence reserved for national institutions almost at the same time as did Mudie's Select Library, but quickly outdistanced his less nimble companion, advancing by leaps and bounds, while the other marched steadily along. It is at first a little difficult to see why, in his case, the goal was so quickly and easily attained. Other comic journals had attempted the same achievement and had failed. There was *Figaro in London*, for example, which ran from 1832 to 1839, and *Fun*, which reached its fortieth year (1861–1901). They were excellent periodicals of their class, and in the lists of their contributors appear the names of several of the writers who helped to make *Punch* famous. But they never wielded *Punch's* authority, nor learnt his secret of perpetual youth. They were just ordinary journals that flourished for a season, then died.

The name, it is true, was a good one, and may have helped to attract readers. Every Englishman had known Mr. Punch from his childhood, and had none but mirthful recollections of the conjugal drama in which that very irascible gentleman took the leading part. "Punch" was reminiscent, also, of a beverage much esteemed by convivial Victorians. "Punch with a lemon in it," as someone remarked when the name was suggested at the meeting where the original prospectus was drawn up, and "gay, fat Mark Lemon" occupied the chair. But the name of itself could not make the paper.

The time was not specially favourable to the launching of a comic journal. There was widespread poverty and unrest. Tractarianism and the Chartists, O'Connell and the Corn Laws occupied men's minds and made them, one would have thought, disinclined for laughter. We are forced to fall back upon the explanation, indefinite but convincing, which has often been given before. *Punch* owes its success and its pre-eminence to the possession of a quality which (as the Captain in *Utopia, Limited,* asserted concerning the flirtations of soldiers with pretty young ladies) is "particularly English."

It was four years after the accession of Queen Victoria that the little hump-backed gentleman, with his hooked nose and his high-peaked cap, made his first mocking bow to the public in presenting to them the opening number of *Punch*; and a new social force came into action. It has been said of the Victorians that they took themselves too seriously, that they never knew when they were making themselves ridiculous, but saw themselves always as imposing figures playing their parts on the world's great stage. Thus has a more enlightened, or possibly a more frivolous, generation arraigned its forbears, and whatever weight the culprits —such few of them as remain—attach to the charge, they can at least reply that the age which so offended provided its own antidote. For *Punch* spared neither fault nor foible, and in dealing with pomposity, pretentiousness, false dignity, or any other form of hypocrisy he was especially relentless. Duke or dustman, it was all the same to him, except that he was tenderer to the dustman. "*Punch* laughs at everybody but the workpeople," observed Mrs. Beecher Stowe during her visit to England in 1853, when she was, of course, provided with the works of the English censor. Many very important persons must have winced at his gibes, and fumed, at least inwardly, at the impertinence of this upstart and self-constituted social authority. But there was no outcry, and the victims, at least most of them, nourished no real ill-feeling against Mr. Punch.

For a time the public scarcely realized the importance of the new publication. Walter Frith said that he bought the first number at a small newsvendor's shop off the Edgware Road, and being much delighted with it he went the next week and asked for the new number. "Oh, I haven't taken it again," said the shopkeeper. "I don't believe there'll be no more numbers out." But Frith found another newsagent who was less pessimistic, and henceforward he took the paper regularly week by week; and when he had become a famous R.A. and a married man with a family, *Punch*, as his daughter tells us, was "a part of the household" and a joy to all its members.

Soon there were many households of which the same thing could be said. William de Morgan, in his story, *The Old Man's Youth*, tells how, when Mr. Pascoe died somewhere about 1865, he left behind him a complete set of *Punch* from the beginning up to the date of his death, entered in the auctioneer's catalogue as "perfect." Robert Louis Stevenson says that he found among the grave and old-fashioned books in his father's library four odd volumes of bound numbers of the work. Lord Rayleigh, his son has told us, was "a diligent reader of *Punch*." It went regularly to the Gladstone household, and from scattered remarks in their *Lives* and *Reminiscences* we gather that it went also to the homes of Charlotte Brontë, George Richmond, James Wilson, Lady Frances Balfour, and Dame Ethel Smyth. Canon Ainger was for many years a regular and admiring subscriber.

Punch was to him a delight from cover to cover. At his breakfast on Wednesdays, as he sat with the paper in his hand, he would suddenly be seen to shake with inward laughter, and when his nieces, anxious to share his mirth, would ask the cause, he would do his best to tell them, but, instantly repossessed by merriment, would relapse into his chuckles of enjoyment.

Few, even among the most eminently correct Victorian families, hesitated to admit *Punch*. Mr. O. F. Christie, in his *Transition from Aristocracy*, quotes the words of a provincial journalist—

It was the first paper we ever saw which was not vulgar. It will provoke many a hearty laugh, but never call a blush to the most delicate cheek.

Not everybody was of this journalist's opinion. Sophia Jex-Blake's father, who was a rigid Evangelical, considered that *Punch was* vulgar. Coventry Patmore entirely disapproved of the paper, and regarded it as dangerous to the morals of youth. In 1864 he wrote to his little daughter, who was away at school—

Mrs. Marshall, you tell me, doubts whether *Punch* is good reading for you. I am quite of Mrs. Marshall's opinion, and I am sure your mama would have been so too. I cannot tell how you can be so "very, very sure" that mama would let you, when, to the best of my recollection, I would never have a copy of *Punch* in the house.

A few days later, in reply to another letter, he wrote—

I am delighted to hear that Mrs. Marshall agrees with me in detesting *Punch*. I daresay an odd number of *Fun*, with a parody of the *Angel* in it, may have got into the house, and that it was given to you and Bertha to cut up—as a proper punishment for having "cut up" me.

Punch, as well as *Fun*, had "cut up" Coventry Patmore's poem, *The Angel in the House*—which may have had something to do with its author's distaste for the publication.

On this question of the suitability of *Punch* as reading for the young, opinion was much divided. Mr. Cecil Torr says that his grandfather wrote to his father—who had encouraged both his sons to cull wisdom from Mr. Punch's pages—saying—

My object in giving him the Bible was to get *Punch* out of his head. *Punch* may be well enough for grown people, but surely very improper as a foundation for a child.

Edmund Yates' godmother, a worthy old spinster lady, held somewhat similar views as to the effect of a course of *Punch* on the immature mind.

What with his *Pickwick* and his *Punch* I wonder the boy hasn't softening of the brain. I'm only sorry my Uncle Beilby is not alive to give him a good talking to.

Uncle Beilby was a former Bishop of London. What would have happened had his lordship been available to administer the required talking to remains problematical; failing it, Mr. Yates remained all his life a faithful reader both of *Pickwick* and of *Punch* with, as far as could be judged, no disastrous results.

On the other hand, the father of Sir Francis Burnand kept up what his son calls the laudable practice of sending him a copy of the paper in which they both delighted, week by week, all through his schooldays. Sir Edward Parry has told us that each Sunday morning during his childhood he and his brother used to be summoned to the room where their father had just finished breakfast, and that a feature of the delightful half-hour that followed was

a careful examination on our weekly studies of the pages of *Punch*, which my father held rightly to be the earliest nursery textbook of history and sociology for the English child.

Mr. Cecil Torr, who seems, in spite of his grandfather's remonstrance, to have remained a diligent reader of *Punch*, would have agreed with Judge Parry, for he declares that by those early studies he stocked his memory with facts that history books ignore. Mrs. Panton said that a great deal of the all-round information she possessed she had gained from *Punch* and the daily papers. *Punch* was indeed, and is, a very trustworthy encyclopedia of general information on social matters. He neglected nothing, from politics to costume, and he was very careful that his detail should be correct. When, in 1868, Mr. George Du Maurier made a sketch for the paper of Miss Frith playing croquet with a curate, he was very particular as to the tilt of her sailor hat and the points of white braid that trimmed her skirt. William Black, in his *In Silk Attire*, shows Nelly Featherstone, a comedy actress, who, on being invited to visit at a grand country mansion, "bought the current number of *Punch* and dressed her hair and herself in imitation of one of the ladies of that periodical." She went somewhat astray over colour, for there *Punch* gave her no guidance, but nevertheless she managed to make a considerable impression on the family lawyer, and to reduce the supercilious servants to a state of respectful amazement.

All public men made a point of seeing *Punch* regularly, and we may imagine that in the early days, before they were inured to its particular form of criticism, that it was with some trepidation they opened each weekly number. And yet, even while in uneasy imagination the victim listened to the laughter that was coming from readers all over the country, he felt that there were some compensations. To be caricatured by *Punch* was a distinction; it meant that he had in a sense "arrived." So he learnt to laugh himself, not only at Mr. Punch's criticisms, but also at the clever way in which the little gentleman seized upon his personal peculiarities and made them contribute to the success of his indictment. Old Lord Brougham, said Lord Carlisle, used to congratulate himself that "those *Punch* people" "never get my face and are obliged to put up with my plaid trousers." Miss Betham-Edwards said that she gained her first idea of Lord John Russell by seeing him represented in *Punch* as a tiny figure almost dwarfed by an enormous hat. Disraeli's personality lent itself to caricature, and week after week *Punch* presented him to its readers under different guises; so that once a little girl, on meeting him for the first time, greeted him with the words, "I know you. I've seen you in *Punch*." If a public man had no outstanding peculiarity of appearance, Mr. Punch invented one for him. Sir Algernon West once asked Tenniel why Palmerston was always represented with a straw in his mouth. The reply was that it was difficult to give a likeness of him that would be definitely characteristic, so that the artist was obliged to supply something that the public would recognize. John Bright, Tenniel added, was always shown with a broad-brimmed Quaker hat and an eye-glass—neither of which he ever wore. Miss Eliza Wilson remarked on the straw in the mouth and the hat on one side of the Palmerston cartoons, recognizing these as emblematic of the statesman's "light and airy way of meeting difficulties"; and she noted the cartoon of 1851, in which his shipwrecked government was represented as being saved by the "Exhibition" steamer.

Punch had his favourites among the Victorian statesmen, and Mr. Gladstone was one of them. Mary Gladstone recorded in her diary that on November 10, 1880, Mr. Ruskin lectured at Oxford on *Punch*. The lecture was "deliciously delicate and merry, and yet full of moral lessons"; and in the course of it the lecturer said, "*Punch* consistently idolizes Mr. Gladstone." This did not mean that Mr. Punch had never made his readers laugh at the great statesman's expense; but the laughs had been kindly, and when the chance came to exhibit him in an heroic light Mr. Punch had taken it. Yet criticism, direct and unhesitating, was not wanting when occasion called. The sad and dignified comment on the fall of Khartoum carried with it keen reproach. Lady Frances Balfour wrote in her journal on February 5, 1885—

Punch had a cartoon by Tenniel the week before of General Gordon meeting Sir Herbert Stuart with the words "At Last!" So certain seemed the relief of the town. Another cartoon appeared the week of the news with the tragic words "Too Late!"

There were some readers who, although they themselves welcomed Mr. Punch gladly when he paid his weekly visit, yet thought it scarcely seemly that the little hump-backed gentleman should consort with the dignitaries of the Church. One day, when John Allen was dining at Lambeth Palace a lady asked the Archbishop if he read *Punch*. "Allen thought this was a misplaced question," said Edward FitzGerald; "but I think the Archbishop ought to see *Punch*, though not to read it regularly, perhaps."

This seems to indicate that FitzGerald would have favoured a nicely adjusted scale regulating the time which members of the priesthood might, without scandal, spend in the company of Mr. Punch. To archbishops would be allowed only short and occasional interviews, and these would increase in duration and frequency as the lower ranks of the clergy were approached. With such a scale in operation, Canon Ainger would have had some joyless Wednesday breakfasts, and Bishop Colenso—who also avowed a strong preference for *Punch*—would have been similarly deprived of enjoyment. John Allen, who seems to have read the paper fairly regularly, might have been allowed to go on as he had begun; and the Rector of Ipswich, of whom Miss Betham-Edwards relates that he used occasionally to get a number of *Punch*, and never failed to bring it to her father's house that the family there might enjoy it also, would certainly have remained unaffected.

The High Church party did not always find the paper pleasant reading. Mr. Punch was a convinced anti-Puseyite, and during the early years of his censorship there was scarcely a number that did not hold the High Church party up to derision in a manner that often went beyond the limits of seemly if caustic comment which the little gentleman had set for himself. Francis Burnand said that all he knew of Puseyites and Puseyism he learnt "from the columns of Mr. Punch, who at that time seemed to consider it a duty to go out of his way to denounce the High Church movement."

All the notable movements of the day, in their turn, received a share of Mr. Punch's notice and mockery. The scientific controversy early engaged his attention. There were jokes concerning mesmerism and *Vestiges*, and an account of a meeting of the British Association where "Professor Luddyfuddy read an ingenious paper on the probable length of the whiskers of the Aborigines of ancient Jericho." In 1861, while the warfare concerning Darwin's *Origin of Species* was at its fiercest, Mr. Punch summed up the situation in verse—

> The *Vestiges* taught
> That all came from naught
> By "development" so called "progressive,"
> That insects and worms
> Assume higher forms
> By modification excessive.

Then Darwin set forth
In a book of much worth
The importance of "Nature's selection,"
How the struggle for life
Is a laudable strife
And results in "specific distinction."

Am I satyr or man?
Pray tell me who can,
And settle my place in the scale,
A man in ape's shape,
An anthropoid ape,
Or a monkey deprived of its tail?

When the aesthetic movement took possession of the town, Mr. Punch invented two "greenery-yallery" young men, whom he called Maudle and Postlethwaite, to represent the extreme type of the followers of Oscar Wilde. Du Maurier's illustrations showed these devotees with long hair, haggard faces, and studiously unconventional costume. They had all the most admired tricks of the true Oscar Wilde aesthete. Postlethwaite, for example, was shown entering a pastrycook's shop and calling for a glass of water, in which he placed a lily he had brought with him and sat soulfully gazing at it, refusing all other refreshment. Week by week these two young men disported themselves before *Punch's* large circle of readers, until they became familiarly known and were referred to as common acquaintances. "A youth whose name was not Postlethwaite or Maudle, though it might have been either," said Mr. Francillon, describing the young gentleman with the lily, whom he met at an evening party. Sometimes the caricature was broader, as when, during the hot summer of 1881 while all London was going to see *Patience*, *Punch* showed a costermonger aesthetically adorned, and under the picture the lines—

Twopence I gave for my sunshade,
A penny I gave for my fan,
Threepence I paid for my straw—forrin made,
I'm a Japan aesthetic young man.

For more than a year the jokes were kept up, and the inhabitants of "passionate Brompton" were shown asking each other such questions as "Are you intense?" or "discoursing upon high art with a certain hungry look of ineffable yearning towards the infinite." *Punch* had a part in bringing the Oscar Wilde cult to its downfall.

If we go to Mr. Punch for information as to what people were reading in the days of Victoria, he will not fail us, though we shall learn more by noting implications and references than by looking for direct statements. If an author is frequently mentioned by *Punch*, we know that he has become an object of interest to a considerable section of the public, even though, as in the case of Bulwer Lytton, the references to him are derisive and uncomplimentary. *Punch* did not like Lytton, and lost no chance of gibing at him and at the people who read his books. When *Zanoni* was published in 1842, the caustic little critic remarked—

It is not true that the hero of Sir E. L. Bulwer's new novel is, as usual, a portrait of himself. The report arose from a notion that the title of the work is the Italian form of Zany or Za-ninny.

In 1845, when a new edition of the novel was published, *Punch* commented more at length—

To Sir B. Lytton. You dedicate the last edition of *Zanoni* to Gibson the sculptor in these words, "I, artist in words, dedicate to you, artist whose ideas speak in marble, this well-loved work of my mature manhood. I love it not the less because it has been little understood and superficially judged by the common herd. It was not meant for them." Now, Sir Edward, this is not fair to the circulating libraries. It is all very well to talk of the "common herd" and say "it was not meant for them," with a curl of your fine lip; but you know it was meant for everybody who could pay threepence for the perusal of the volumes—and very popular it has been, especially with ladies' maids and milliners. Why are you always complaining? The public read your novels; the publishers pay for them; you are a lion at dinners, a thing to point at in the streets.

Your admirer (within limits), PUNCH.

We may imagine that Mr. Punch's—very limited—admiration of Sir Edward Bulwer Lytton did not prevent him from feeling a gleeful satisfaction in publishing Tennyson's lines, written in 1846, in reply to the novelist's *The New Timon*. Tennyson had lately accepted a State pension, and Lytton—mistakenly believing him to be already possessed of ample means—had attacked him savagely. Tennyson retorted with equal bitterness—

> And what with spites and what with fears,
>   You cannot let a body be,
> It's always ringing in your ears,
>   "They call this man as good as me."
>
> .   .   .   .   .
>
> A Timon you! Nay, nay, for shame:
>   It looks too arrogant a jest—
> The fierce old man—to take his name
>   You bandbox. Off, and let him rest.

In a very different style were *Punch's* references to Dickens, which came in almost every number. Their familiar and affectionate tone represented very justly the feeling of the nation towards its great humorist. There were many cartoons in which his characters figured; for example, there was Tilly Slowboy nursing Cobden's Baby (Free Trade) and crooning to it, "Dids its Dukes of Richmonds say it was a humbugs!" There were items of news in *Punch's* well-known style—

> We learn at Truefitt's that there has been an immense order for packing and transport from Boz, who has resolved to gratify the seventeen thousand American young ladies who have asked for locks of his hair. Two ships will start on April 1st.

Mrs. Gamp and Mrs. Harris were represented as correspondents of the *Morning Herald* and the *Evening Standard* respectively, and in number after number they delighted the readers of *Punch* by conversations after this fashion—

> Mrs. Gamp: I tell you what it is, Mrs. 'Arris, *The Times* is a hinfamous fabricator.
> Mrs. Harris: So it is, my dear; and as for that nasty, hojus *Punch*, I'm disposed to scratch 'is hi's out a'most. What I ses, I ses; and what I ses I stick to.

Carlyle *Punch* treated with a bantering kindliness which must have been peculiarly irritating, though perhaps it was wholesome, to a prophet who took himself so seriously. It doubtless conduced to his looking on the paper as an entirely frivolous organ which usurped the attention that should be given to matters of more moment. Espinasse recorded that the sage

complained of the interest which his countrymen took in what to him were the merest trivialities of literature, and that when he last visited the fatherland he was pestered with questions as to who it was that wrote this, that, and the other thing in *Punch*.

Perhaps some inquisitive Scot was tactless enough to ask who wrote, in the introduction to the 1840 volume—

The attar of *Punch* is—*Punch* knows it—destined to save and to sweeten Mr. Carlyle's "decadent generations," to arrest them by sweet intoxication in their railway speed to final perdition.

Or—even worse—possibly there were inquiries as to who was responsible for the mock police-court report that appeared after the publication of the *Latter Day Pamphlets* in 1850—

Yesterday a gentleman of the name of Thomas Carlyle was brought up before Mr. Punch charged with being unable to take care of his own literary reputation—a very first-rate reputation until a few months past—but now in consequence of the reckless and alarming conduct of the accused in a most dangerous condition; indeed, in the opinion of very competent authorities, sinking. A policeman gave evidence in the course of which he said that the accused "delighted to crack and dislocate the joints of language and to melt down and alloy sterling English into nothing better than German silver." Mr. Carlyle was found guilty, but was released on the surety of two publishers of the highest respectability on the condition that he was not to be allowed to put pen to paper.

Macaulay received his share of notice. *Punch* gave ironical praise to the extreme detail of the *History* and predicted the contents of the fiftieth volume; and he repeated, with a suave yet galling air of kindly patronage, the charge of inaccuracy which more seriously critical readers were making. In one of his *Provincial Letters* he wrote—

Mr. Macaulay has just looked in to lunch. Seeing that he had some papers under his arm, I naturally asked him what they were. It appeared that they were proof sheets (just received from Messrs. L———) of the next volume of his *History*. He was good enough to let me glance over them; and though, of course, I should not pretend to criticize his magnificent style, I was able to point out a few grammatical and historical mistakes which he instantly corrected.

Mr. Punch kept his eye on the lesser writers also, and dealt them a passing stroke or approving pat on the back as seemed best to his omniscience. Mrs. Ellis was satirized in the "Unprotected Female" series. Charlotte Brontë, writing to her publisher concerning a parcel of books, said she awaited it

in all reasonable patience and resignation, looking with docility to that model of active self-helpfulness *Punch* friendly offers the "Women of England" in his "Unprotected Female."

There were various shrewd hits at Harrison Ainsworth's romances, which were extremely popular. Mr. Punch showed very neatly the value he put upon them by his comment upon an arrangement made for the publication of one of them, between the author and Henry Colburn, publisher of the *New Monthly Magazine*—

Says Ainsworth to Colburn
"A plan in my pate is
To give my romance as
A supplement gratis."
Says Colburn to Ainsworth
"'Twill do very nicely,
For that will be charging
Its value precisely."

Punch acknowledged the popularity of *Uncle Tom's Cabin* in one of the early numbers of 1853, which contained an illustration described as "A Swell's Homage to Mrs. Stowe." "A *must* read *Uncle Tom*," said the languid young gentleman in the picture, "because People one meets begin to talk of Mrs. Hawiet-beastowe. A Countess would pasist last night in asking me about haw book. Bai Jove! A was completely flaw'd, A wished myself, or haw, in France."

When *The Woman in White* was coming out in monthly numbers, and many people were finding it impossible to go to bed until the breathless perusal of the latest instalment was completed, Mr. Punch showed his sympathy with these midnight orgies by an illustration depicting Mr. Tomkins absorbed in the thrilling pages, and Mrs. Tomkins, "an awful apparition" in nightdress and nightcap, appearing at the door. "Pray, Mr. Tomkins, are you never coming upstairs? How much longer are you going to sit up with that Woman in White?"

Ouida received a few shrewd yet good-natured thrusts. Her special type of aristocratic hero was delightfully caricatured by a drawing showing the high-born Sabretache of *Held in Bondage*, most magnificent of a magnificent company, appearing to carry two milking-pails, which were really suspended from a yoke borne by a woman who walked behind him.

Behold the haughty Sabretache as he walks down the High Street—cold, sarcastic, unbending as ever, and with more than his usual stateliness, for he sees the lovely Violet and her lady mother coming towards him.

Thackeray was a regular contributor to *Punch*, so gave instead of received the stripes under which the others winced. In April 1847 he began a series of articles which he called *Punch's Prize Novelists*. His choice of victims gives us some information regarding the fiction which was being widely read at the time. He parodied, most happily, Lord Lytton, Charles Lever, G. P. R. James, Mrs. Gore, and Disraeli, and *Punch's* readers received his papers with delight.

Of parodies Mr. Punch produced an unfailing supply. He laid hands with equal readiness on the works of a great writer or a little one, provided both were well known to the public. Tennyson's *May Queen* became a plaintive ode to the Exhibition of 1851, and *The Old Woolsack* retained all the lush sentimentality of Eliza Cook's *The Old Armchair. Uncle Tom's Cabin* provided material for *The Political Topsy*, and *Alice in Wonderland* became *Alice in Blunderland*.

But *Punch* not only made sport of literary masterpieces, it produced them. We have seen how Hood's *Song of the Shirt* moved the whole country in 1843. In 1845 came a contribution of a very different character in the form of a series of articles by Douglas Jerrold, called *Mrs. Caudle's Curtain Lectures*. They were very clever and very funny, and they were a fortune to *Punch*. Douglas Jerrold used to go radiant to the *Punch* monthly dinners, while the *Lectures* were sending up the circulation at a rate that delighted the editor and the other contributors round the table. Mrs. Caudle was shown as an ignorant, narrow-minded woman bent on making a show before her neighbours, and getting the best of everything for herself and for her children. In the privacy of the marital bedchamber she attacked her husband with coaxing and tears, with screams and hysterics, with complaints and abuse, stopping at nothing to gain her ends; until the poor man was ready to promise anything and give anything for a little peace.

Mrs. Caudle's arguments, her pathetic descriptions of the ill-treatment she received and the wrongs she endured, her illustrations and her epithets were irresistibly comic, and all England laughed. Yet there was a serious side to it, too. The *Lectures* showed conclusively the estimation in which the ordinary domestic woman was held by the male population. Allowing for the exaggeration natural to humorous writing of this kind, it was still clear that the general conception of such a woman's intelligence, aims, and methods of getting her own way was a very low one; and unfortunately it was probably more or less correct. The *Lectures*, said Emily Davies, proved the enormous need for a change in the education of girls of the middle class.

It is no wonder that many women were indignant at the laughter and jokes with which their husbands and fathers and brothers greeted Mrs. Caudle. Douglas Jerrold received

a very pathetic though not very well expressed letter from an aggrieved matron who appealed to him to discontinue or modify the *Caudle Lectures*. She declared they were bringing discords into families and making multitudes of women miserable.

The first lecture of the series gave great offence to Mrs. Pascoe, of *The Old Man's Youth*. When her husband read aloud the laments of Mrs. Caudle over the black satin gowns and bonnets for the girls, and "no end of things" that she might have bought with the five pounds Mr. Caudle so foolishly and wickedly lent to a friend, Mrs. Pascoe saw nothing humorous in the passage, and when her husband declared, "That's just like you, Cecilia," she was so incensed that she managed later to destroy the offending number; thus obliging Mr. Pascoe to obtain another, that his set of *Punch* might remain complete.

There was another lady who resented the implications of the *Lectures* as strongly as did Mrs. Pascoe, and who was able to make her resentment more widely known. This was Mrs. Anne Marsh, one of the popular minor novelists of the day. At the time of Mrs. Caudle's appearance Mrs. Marsh was engaged on a new novel, to be called *Emilia Wyndham*. It was one of the "persecuted heroine" type to which Mrs. Janet Ross so strongly objected. *Emilia Wyndham*, she said, was a kind of martyrology, such as made one doubt "whether any torments the heroine would have earned through being naughty could exceed those she incurred by her virtue." A large proportion of these torments came through a selfish and unworthy father, who made the life of his daughter, and still more of his wife, almost unbearably miserable. Mrs. Marsh had obviously set out to show that there were detestable husbands as well as detestable wives, and that the *Lectures* gave an unfair, because one-sided, view of married life. She made this intention quite clear by a passage in which she said—

Any vulgar penny-a-liner can draw Mrs. Caudle and publish her in a popular journal; and with such success that she shall become a byword in families, and serve as an additional reason for that rudeness and incivility that negligent contempt with which too many Englishmen still think it their prerogative, as men and true-born Britons, to treat their wives.

Punch was not slow to reply. A correspondent, he said, had directed his attention to a criticism of the *Caudle Lectures* appearing in *Emilia Wyndham*, and this criticism he pretended to quote—

"What," said Emilia, her peach-down cheek glowing with emotion. "You do not like Mrs. Caudle? Well, I never. Woman as I am, I adore it. All the springs—the springes I should rather say—of woman's nature are so deliciously, so delicately developed in that love of a book. 'Twould have beguiled Eve herself in her banishment. . . . Well, if ever I marry," and Emilia looked with ecstatic wickedness in the eyes of her lover, "I should wish no better bridal present than Mrs. Caudle, bound in Hymeneal satin."
Henry—what could he do?—instantaneously whipped his arm round Emilia's waist, and looking in her blue orbs, exclaimed in a voice tremulous with passion, "Emilia, thou shalt have it."
There is much more after this fashion in the book, to which we refer the curious reader. We can only add that the publishers are desirous of informing "those about to marry" that Emilia's suggestion has been acted upon, and that Caudles bound for bridal presents may be had at the shortest notice.

The imitation—it can scarcely be called parody—of *Emilia Wyndham*, both style and sentiment, was most happy. *Punch* had deftly parried the enemy's stroke, yet without malice. Mrs. Marsh was doubtless furious; yet the subsequent sale of *Emilia Wyndham*, which rapidly became a "best-seller," was certainly not injured— was probably greatly helped—by *Punch's* mocking notice.
The next year brought the first of another notable series of

contributions to *Punch* in Thackeray's *Snob Papers*, which were addressed to "The Snobs of England: by one of themselves." "It is impossible for *any* Briton, perhaps, not to be a snob in some degree," said Thackeray; and it seemed, indeed, as if a large number of Britons took a personal interest in the papers. Each, as it appeared, became a subject of general discussion. Some people were angry and reviled the writer, but most laughed and admired. Mrs. Norton said that the paper on *Clerical Snobs and Snobbishness* reminded her of Elia. When the papers were collected and published as *The Book of Snobs* in 1847, the volume had a very large sale. "*The Book of Snobs* made Thackeray's fortune in one year," said John Allen. William Rossetti delighted in it. "William is reading Thackeray's *Book of Snobs* to the Collinsons in the evening," wrote Christina Rossetti, who was with him on a visit to that family; and after her return she wrote, playfully begging him not to begin the book all over again.

No writer rose up in defence of the snobs as Mrs. Marsh had done in defence of the women. In most of the novels of the day, indeed, Mr. Punch was treated very kindly, and referred to in terms of admiration and friendship. The number and variety of these references bear witness to the paper's wide circulation. Surtees, in *Ask Mamma*, showed a party at a country house who, having exhausted their small talk at dinner, must fall back on the latest number of *Punch* as a subject of conversation for the rest of the evening. de Morgan's Mr. Pascoe kept a number on the drawing-room table of his charming house at Chelsea, ready to provide a diversion when visitors were a little heavy on hand. It found its way to the stately, secluded mansion where Maud Ruthyn, the beautiful young heiress of Le Fanu's *Uncle Silas*, lived her lonely life. When Peter Ibbetson, of Du Maurier's story, called at his uncle's house in St. James's Street, the servant handed him *Punch* to ensure his being well entertained while he waited for the master of the house. Helen Melladew, of *Muttons and Mattins*, found it in the waiting-room of the Brighton doctor whom she had come to consult about her throat, and Miss Braddon's Ida Palliser discovered it in the sitting-room of a cottage by the Thames. Whyte-Melville evidently considered *Punch* the invariable companion on a railway journey. In *Market Harborough* he showed the Honourable Crasher regaling himself with the paper, and courteously handing it to his fellow-traveller; and in

Kate Coventry he showed two fashionable ladies, aunt and niece, settling themselves comfortably in a first class carriage, and arranging all the paraphernalia "without which no well-bred woman can travel a hundred yards," after which Aunt Deborah took up her knitting and niece Kate her *Punch*, and was delighted to find there "a portrait of a dandy, the very image of Frank Lovell"—her reigning admirer. Ouida showed a companion picture of a gilded youth departing from his private tutor's to take up a commission in the Guards—

Off he went by the express, with his portmanteau lettered "Granville de Vigne, Esq., —th, P.W.O. Hussars"; off with *Punch* and an Havanna to amuse him, on the way to much more than Exeter Barracks—on the way to Manhood.

Doubtless under these circumstances Mr. Granville de Vigne found all *Punch's* jokes brilliant. Later he might be in the unhappy case of that other young man, of Hawley Smart's *Breezie Langton*, who, after the fascinating companion who had beguiled the first part of his journey had alighted, "tried *Punch*, voted it gone to the bad, getting duller every week. Turned up his nose at one of Leech's happiest efforts."

Still another young man, one of Miss Braddon's all-conquering heroes, read *Punch* by an Italian lake where he was spending an ecstatic honeymoon with the bride he had torn from the arms of a rival; while Ouida's Cornet Arthur Chevasney, of the Dashers, after settling himself under a tree in Kensington Gardens, took out *Punch* to while away the moments until his lady-love should appear. "All military men," declared Thackeray—

"from Field-Marshal the Duke of Wellington downwards read *Punch* in every quarter of the globe; and to the many heroes to be found in that gallant army *Punch*, the universal railer, takes off his hat and says, 'Heaven save them!'"

Schoolboys too, said Thackeray, "many scores and thousands of them, read and love *Punch*; may he never write a word that shall not be honest and fit for them to read." It is clear that, even by strict Victorians, Mr. Punch was never accused of writing such a word; or Miss Charlotte Yonge would not have shown, as she did in *Pillars of the House*, a pile of numbers of *Punch* lying on the window-seat of the dormitory in Lance Underwood's Anglo-Catholic cathedral school.

The habit of saying, when something particularly amusing happened or a specially good joke was made, "It's good enough for *Punch*," began in these early days. John Addington Symonds, when the poems he had written at Harrow were lost, wrote home saying, "My case would do for one of the *Authors' Miseries* series in *Punch*, I think." Pretty, unprincipled Susie Crabtree, of Miss Sarah Tytler's *Buried Diamonds*, said of a charge (justly) brought against her, "What a story it will be to tell, that I was taken up—actually taken up—for robbing my husband's bank! Poor little me a burglar! It is a subject for *Punch*"; and one of Hawley Smart's heroes declared proudly that he had made a conundrum which was "good enough to send to *Punch*." Mr. Punch was, however, very particular as to the contributions that he accepted. He rejected W. S. Gilbert's *Yarn of the Nancy Bell* on the ground that it was "too cannibalistic" for his readers' taste; and Thackeray, even, was requested to discontinue his series of *Miss Tickletoby's Lectures* when it became evident that these were not being appreciated by the public.

Yet, with all his care, Mr. Punch found that he could not please everybody. There were some superior people who looked down, or affected to look down, on the paper from the height of a great intellect. "Have you seen my *Snob Papers* in *Punch*?" asked Thackeray one day, when he was in the company of the not easily approachable George Borrow. "It is a periodical I never look at," replied the other; and there was silence. George Borrow had perhaps some right to assume a lofty attitude, but there were those who did so without his justification. "Read *Punch*!" said one such gentleman to Mrs. Panton, in the hearing of Shirley Brooks, "I thought no one ever did anything but look at the pictures." "They never do when they can't read," growled the affronted editor.

It was Shirley Brooks, too, who replied to a certain ill-mannered acquaintance who had declared that of all the London papers he considered *Punch* the dullest. "I wonder you ever read it." "I don't," was the unwary reply. "So I thought from your foolish remark," said the editor crushingly.

There were some people who did not read *Punch*, not because they objected to the paper, but because they never read anything.

George Richmond tells how he was once painting the portrait of a gentleman of the "Dundreary" type and trying to keep up a conversation meanwhile. One subject after another was introduced, but elicited only a vacuous comment from the sitter. At last, in desperation, the artist said, "The last number of *Punch* was very amusing. Have you seen it yet?" "No-a," was the reply, given with a yawn. "I'm not a bookwo-r-r-r-rm." There were others who avoided it because they had a vague idea that a humorous paper must necessarily be indecorous; like the Oxford don who asked Thackeray if *Punch* were not "a ribald publication."

But those who did not read *Punch*, and those who read and disapproved, form together a minority so small that it did not affect the claim of the paper to be recognized as a national institution. Emerson, visiting England in 1847, so recognized it. His considered and sympathetic estimate justly described the *Punch* of that period, and may be with equal justice applied to the paper in its later developments—

Punch is equally an expression of English good sense as the London *Times*. It is the comic version of the same sense. Many of its caricatures are equal to the best pamphlets, and will convey to the eye in an instant the popular view which was taken of each turn of public affairs. Its sketches are usually made by masterly hands, and sometimes with genius; the delight of every class because uniformly guided by that taste which is tyrannical in England. It is a new trait of the nineteenth century that the wit and humour of England, as in *Punch*, so in the humorists, Jerrold, Dickens, Thackeray, Hood, have taken the direction of humanity and freedom.

CHAPTER XIX

EIGHTEEN-EIGHTY-SEVEN

THE Year of Jubilee. The girl queen was now a plump little old lady, with nothing strikingly majestic about her except the personality that had dominated England for fifty years. The boys and girls who had thrilled to her accession were approaching that seventieth milestone that marks the recognized termination to life's journey. They and their sons and daughters showed clear signs of the Queen's long dominance, and were, for good or for ill, the products of Victorianism. In the grandchildren might be discerned some tendency to resist the all-powerful influence, though so far without any very obvious results.

For those older readers among the Queen's subjects there had been numberless adventures of the mind and of the spirit during the years they had lived under Victorian rule, and of many of these adventures the books that stood on their shelves served as memorials. There were, for example, the volumes of Tennyson, which marked for a multitude of readers the first awakening to a sense of what poetry really was, of how it could strengthen and inspire, as well as delight with its beauty and music. The strictures passed by loftily severe critics on Tennyson's poetry, and especially on *The Idylls of the King*, affected the ordinary Victorian reader not at all. He thrilled to the high ideals set before him, and had nothing but reverence for the moral teaching which some critics derided as trite and Pharisaical. He delighted in the exquisite music of the more exalted passages, and found the flatter stretches of narrative restful, not tiresome. He entered, happy though awed, into the lovely land of faëry that Tennyson opened to him. Many of the readers who welcomed the Queen's Jubilee had, like Sir Henry Newbolt, been in their boyhood denizens of the "dim, rich city of Camelot"; to comparatively few of these had it happened, as it happened to him, that through Browning's magic "a great part of Camelot fell in ruins."

Those few, however, proclaimed the might of the wizard Browning with the ardour of converts to a rare and mystic cult. Browning Societies multiplied and flourished. There was one at Oxford, of which Henry Newbolt was a member during the four years he spent at the University as an undergraduate, and to which J. W. Mackail, W. L. Courtney, Mark Pattison, Arnold Toynbee, Henry Sidgwick, Mrs. Margaret Woods, and Rhoda Broughton also belonged. Mrs. Janet Courtney describes the Encoema garden-party of 1886, where the poet in his doctor's robes sat under a tree in the gardens of Worcester College surrounded by a respectful circle of his feminine admirers.

At Cambridge there was equal enthusiasm. The poet himself, so Mr. E. F. Benson tells us, once attended a meeting of the Cambridge Browning Society, and a young lady of Newnham, who was an enthusiastic member, ventured to ask him to come to tea with her and a few friends after the proceedings. Browning came, and found about a dozen worshipping girls, who besought him to allow them to place a crown of roses on his white locks, to which he good-naturedly consented. After tea his circle of adorers gathered round him, and at their request he began to read *Serenade at the Villa*, but catching sight of his rose-wreathed head in a mirror he broke into jovial laughter. "My dear young ladies, shall I not read *The Patriot* instead? It was roses, roses all the way."

Girton, apparently, had a Browning Society of its own. Mrs. Panton says—

I know the Browning Societies used to amuse him [Browning], and he was particularly tickled by the solemn dissolving of the Browning Society at Girton; a girl I knew from her "long-clothes" stage was the treasurer, and when the Society came to an end the treasurer voted that the money in hand should be spent on chocolate. Much to the wrath of the authorities, the matter reached the ears of Mr. Punch, and an account of the episode was given in Browningesque metre that caused the unrighteous to laugh and drew scorn on Girton generally.

In London the original society flourished, and countless others sprang up in the suburbs that were rapidly spreading around the city. Scarcely a district but contained a few enthusiasts who met together, wrote papers that were read aloud and earnestly discussed, studied line by line and word by word the works of the poet whom they reverently styled the Master, and triumphantly brought to light all sorts of hidden treasure. It was said by some that Browning was a little embarrassed by this microscopic survey of his utterances, and that once, replying to an admirer who had written to ask the meaning of a certain passage, the old poet (he was seventy-five in this year of Jubilee) wrote in despairing exasperation, "There was a time when God knew what it meant and I knew what it meant, but to-day only God knows what it means." But this was probably an invention of the mockers, for there were many mockers still, though most thoughtful and intelligent readers, even if they were not personally attracted to the poet, acknowledged that he was giving to the age guidance and inspiration that met its needs. Mary Gladstone, although she had written in her diary on March 9, 1877, "Dinner at Mr. Colvin's, handed in by old Browning (disliked him more than ever), we talked about *The Ring and the Book* and *Abt Vogler*," had since learned to appreciate his poetry, and in 1887 was an active member of a Browning Society. Mr. Ottley, at one time curate at Hawarden, opened her eyes, she said, to the beauty of the poet's verse.

I used to struggle over him, reading him aloud to Gerty and Adelaide, till the Ottley period (1876–80) when, Arthur having sowed the seeds, I went Browning mad.

Almost as ardent and uplifted in their devotion as the Browningites were the Meredithians, though they were not equally numerous. George Meredith had published his first book of poems in 1851, and his first story, *The Shaving of Shagpat*, in 1856, and during the following thirty years all his great works, both in poetry and prose, had appeared. For a long time he had been ignored, except for the usual small band of enthusiasts that a really good writer gathers round him, however indifferent the rest of the world may be. Meredith said that only two of his readers appreciated *The Shaving of Shagpat*, but that was definitely an under-statement. William Hardman wrote to Edward Holroyd—

The story of Bhanavar the Beautiful is a miracle of imagination. The punishment of Khipil the Builder is rich in fun. The concluding chapters ending in the baldness of Shagpat are unutterably grand and terrible. But read the whole with a pipe in thy mouth, reclining in slippered ease when the toils of the day are over. If it does not arride and console thee, then shall I indeed be amazed.

Sir Frederick Pollock says that while he was at Eton—1858–63— his tutor put into his hands *The Shaving of Shagpat*, "an immortal joy to those who love it," and among these he includes his friend,

George Trevelyan the younger. *The Ordeal of Richard Feverel*, published in 1859, and later probably the most popular of Meredith's works, made its way slowly. Carlyle says that Mrs. Carlyle disliked it at first, and flung it on the floor, but took it up again and read some pieces aloud to him. "The man's no fool," was his comment, and on that she resumed her reading and persevered to the end. *Evan Harrington* came next, in 1861. William Archer tells us that his grandfather, James Morrison, read and appreciated it "at a time when the name of Meredith meant nothing to the ordinary novel reader." Edward Clodd, John Addington Symonds, Hugh Chisholm, Sir Frank Lockwood, Justin MacCarthy, Henry Sidgwick, and Robert Louis Stevenson were also among his early admirers; and, very slowly, a small company gathered, made up largely of young readers who looked to Meredith as the supreme literary artist of the day. Justin MacCarthy, who was twenty-nine when *Richard Feverel* was published, says—

We of the very, very select group, most of us quite unknown to each other, who had read *Richard Feverel* and gone into delight over it, were perfectly certain that the novelist we fancied we alone had discovered, or at all events had been the first to discover, would come one day to the front and receive the world's full recognition. We had still a long time to wait; but the group of admirers grew larger and larger, and the admiration became more and more intense.

Throughout the 'sixties and 'seventies, he acknowledges, there were but small signs of this anticipated triumph—

I feel well assured that if a meeting of George Meredith's enthusiastic admirers could then have been summoned, in some mysterious way, from all parts of Great Britain and Ireland, it might have assembled in some London hall of very moderate dimensions.

That this estimate came near the truth was proved by the small sale of Meredith's books. Henry Sidgwick, in 1865, read *Emilia in England*, then recently published, and it had, he said, such an effect on him that he employed his spare cash in buying up the man's other works. He had no difficulty in obtaining second-hand copies of these for a shilling each. Nearly twenty years later Robert Louis Stevenson wrote indignantly of *Rhoda Fleming*—

"that wonderful and painful book long out of print, and hunted for at bookstalls like an Aldine." *Rhoda Fleming* was first published in 1865, and there must have been some copies in circulation in 1880, for Mary Gladstone says she read it in that year and liked it exceedingly.

One reason for Meredith's failure to gain popularity may have been that given by J. A. Symonds in a letter written to Henry Sidgwick in 1869—

I have finished Meredith's *Richard Feverel*. . . . The man affects me terribly. I quite see why, in spite of his being one of our greatest novelists, he is not read. The sense of pain produced by *Richard Feverel* is intense. My mind ached at passages. I was stifled and had to stop reading. . . . What is terrible about George Meredith is that he feels it as a poet, and stands aside from it as an ironic showman.

To read Meredith was, for readers brought up on the works of the Great Novelists, a somewhat severe intellectual exercise. His novels were not simply stories, in the sense that the novels of Dickens and Thackeray were stories. They set forward, with great precision and subtlety, a reasoned philosophy of life; and the style was often so allusive and epigrammatic that the closest attention on the part of the reader was required. It was this, even more than the painful intensity of which J. A. Symonds spoke, that prevented Meredith from reaching the great general public which comes to a novel for relaxation and entertainment.

Yet the cult of Meredith was slowly spreading, and the Year of Jubilee found him exalted to much the same place among novelists as Browning occupied among poets. His admirers, like the Browningites, were inclined to look upon those who did not share their appreciation as beings of an inferior order of intellect. "In the late 'eighties and early 'nineties," says Mr. Arthur Waugh in his *Hundred Years of Publishing*, "it was regarded as a hall-mark of literary taste to be accounted a Meredithian"; and Mr. Alan Bott, in *Our Fathers*, notes as one of the characteristics of the young intelligentsia of 1887 that they "claimed to understand Meredith." Slowly but with assured right of passage Meredith was mounting to the eminence where he was to occupy one of the places left empty by the deaths of the Great Novelists of earlier Victorian days.

Another novelist was also on his way towards that height. Thomas Hardy was in the comparatively early stages of authorship, for he did not begin to write until twenty years later than George Meredith. His early works had a moderate popularity. He tells how, when he was living at Surbiton in 1875, he and his wife saw "with unusual frequency during their journeys to and from London ladies carrying about copies of *Far From the Madding Crowd* with Mudie's labels on their covers." Coventry Patmore greatly admired *A Pair of Blue Eyes*, and said it ought to have been written in verse, and Robert Louis Stevenson gave it as an example of a fine dramatic novel. But Hardy's philosophy of life was even less to the taste of the general Victorian reader than was Meredith's. To him it seemed to consist wholly of pessimism and gloom. The Victorians liked happy endings. They have been taunted as desiring that all stories should end with a jingle of wedding bells, and it is true that a great many of the second- and third-rate novels did appear to have for their sole theme the leading of one or more couples by devious ways to the altar; true, also, that the writers who supplied these unfailing nuptial terminations did so in response to an obvious demand from their readers. But this desire for a happy ending did not come solely from a facile or conventional attitude towards life's problems. It came partly from the optimism which the tremendous advance their age had made in almost every direction had encouraged, partly from a sincere reverence for an over-ruling Providence, which rejoiced to see demonstrated, even if somewhat crudely, how that Providence was working for good in the lives of men. Moreover, it must not be forgotten that almost if not quite as many of the popular novels of the day culminated in death as in marriage—*The Heir of Redclyffe, The Newcomes, Villette, The Old Curiosity Shop, The Mill on the Floss, East Lynne*, and *Eric*, for examples. The Victorians were willing to accept death, if it came in heroic, beautiful fashion, as a suitable and happy ending; the tears they shed for Little Nell were not tears of revolt. But they did demand that virtue and innocence should be rewarded either by happiness in this world or by an assured passing to the joys to come, and undeniably they preferred the former. The dealing out of nuptial joys to pairs of much-tried lovers—such as took place in the last chapters of *Shirley* and *Martin Chuzzlewit, Framley Parsonage*, and *Frank Fairleigh*—delighted them exceedingly. Nor was it only the mass of readers—the Philistines—who demanded this happy ending; men of fine taste and high intellectual powers were equally insistent. Darwin said that a law ought to be passed against novels ending unhappily, and Thackeray said he never dared to re-read *The Pirate* or *The Bride of Lammermoor* or *Kenilworth* because the end is so unhappy. Burne-Jones felt very strongly on the subject. "Don't lend me any sad stories," he said, after reading *Anna Karenina—*

no, not if they are masterpieces. I can't afford to be made miserable. Look, tell me it ends well and that the two lovers marry and are happy ever afterwards, and I'll read it gratefully.

And on another occasion—

I don't mind being harrowed, but then it must be in lofty rhyme or verse heroical—great kings and queens—and then I like it very much, but I can't bear a tale that has in it a woman who is knocked about and made miserable and mad and thrown away on a wretch and is altogether heart-breaking. I like such a one after due troublesomeness and quite bearable anxiety to marry the hero and be happy ever after.

William Morris would not read *Anna Karenina* because of its miserable ending. Mary Gladstone found it "very clever and exciting," but "a wretched, melancholy, tragic novel, with marvellously delicate human insight, but surely, I earnestly trust, with too low a view of our nature."

Publishers recognized how largely a happy ending increased the chances of a book's success. When, in 1885, a young writer from the Isle of Man discussed the plot of his first novel with the editor of the *Liverpool Weekly*, in which it was to be published in instalments, the editor warned him—

If you kill that man you'll kill your book. Give no more than the public will take from you to begin with; by and by they'll take what you give them.

The writer—Mr. Hall Caine—though loth to give up what he considered the fitting climax of his highly sensational story, recognized that probably the editor knew best what suited the public taste. His novel, *The Shadow of a Crime*, proved to be just what a large class of readers required. He followed it up in 1886 with *A Son of Hagar*; and when the Year of Jubilee came Mr. Hall Caine was on his way, not indeed to the eminence reserved for the Great Novelists, but to that dizzier and more perilous height where popular idols are temporarily enthroned.

On the eve of the Jubilee appeared another writer, who was to join and outstrip him in the ascent of that giddy peak. In February 1886 Miss Marie Corelli, a young lady twenty-two years old, published *A Romance of Two Worlds*. It provided a new kind of sensationalism, and its mixture of the occult and the melodramatic took the public fancy. Oscar Wilde's criticism—accepted and perhaps intended as a compliment—given in a letter to the author, may be regarded as an adequate summing up of the book's qualities. "You certainly tell of marvellous things," he said, "in a marvellous way." It was reviewed only in four papers, and none of the notices were more than ten lines long. "The book will make no converts, but considered as a romance pure and simple, it may entertain its readers not a little," said one. "Miss Corelli," said another, "would have been better advised had she embodied her ridiculous ideas in a sixpenny pamphlet. The names of Heliobas and Zara are alone sufficient indications of the dullness of this book." The *Pall Mall* called it "an audacious novel"—which it certainly was. Yet in spite of slighting criticisms, an immediate rush was made for the book. Mr. Mudie and the other proprietors of circulating libraries sent urgent and repeated demands to the publishers for more and still more copies. One man, we are told, wrote to the author telling her that the book had saved him from committing suicide; another said that it had arrested him in his progress towards atheism. A woman wrote, "I feel a better woman for the reading of it twice; and I know others, too, who are higher and better women for such noble thoughts and teaching."

Later in the same year came *Vendetta*, which was an Italian story, full of hatred and murder and tombs and blood-curdling midnight adventures. "It marches on to its awful finale with the grimness of a Greek play," said Mr. Bentley, its publisher; and he declared that parts of it, such as the supper scenes, were as good as if Bulwer had written them. Mary Gladstone read *Vendetta* in February 1887, while she was recovering from a serious illness, and commented in her diary, "goodish plot, but rot rather otherwise." The general reading public thought it a wonderful and exciting novel, and bought it by thousands. *Thelma*, which appeared in the Year of Jubilee, was less sensational, but had a love story of harrowing sentimentality and quickly became as popular as its predecessors. Miss Corelli had certainly added further thrills to an already exciting year; and among the crowds that waited to see the Jubilee procession there might have been seen many who refreshed themselves during those weary hours with snatches of such mental nourishment as could be obtained from her works. Others—though not so many—regaled themselves with *The Shadow of a Crime* and *A Son of Hagar*. During the months that followed, the progress of Miss Corelli and Mr. Hall Caine towards the heights of popularity went on with amazing celerity. In drawing-rooms and back-parlours and kitchens, in offices and workshops, readers of both sexes and all ages were to be found, neglecting their friends and their duties for the sake of these authors' enchanting works. It was scarcely possible to find a railway carriage, during those times of the day when railway carriages were crowded, in which there were not at least two or three people reading with absorbed attention these masterpieces of sensationalism; or to listen to scraps of conversation in theatres or restaurants without hearing the names of Marie Corelli and Hall Caine. The lady, we are told, numbered among her fervent admirers Theodore Watts, Tennyson, and Ellen Terry; while T. E. Brown was an enthusiastic champion of his fellow-Manxman, and never ceased to extol his works.

It is to be noted that in these later Victorian novels—those of Meredith and Hardy equally with those of Marie Corelli and Hall Caine—the social questions, so prominent in the great works of the previous forty years, were almost entirely disregarded. This did not mean that the Victorian no longer took any interest in those questions; it meant that he was beginning to regard them from a different point of view. Just as philosophy and scientific method had invaded the province of story-telling, so had they transformed the manner of treating social questions. Writers no longer appealed to the hearts and consciences of their readers, and tried to move them to the remedy of particular ills through pity and a sense of the duty they owed to the oppressed. Men's consciences now were to be directed by their intellects. The aim was to formulate a system which should regenerate society as a whole. Carlyle and Ruskin had preached this gospel and had prepared the way, but they had suggested no practical scheme by which it could be put into effect. The new type of book was meant to appeal to pure reason, and presented its arguments in a logical, not an emotional fashion.

The first notable example was Henry George's *Progress and Poverty*. The author was a man of English descent living in Philadelphia, where the book was first published. It began with the statement that the material progress of a country did not, as it ought, lead to a diminution of poverty, but rather to its increase. The reason for this Henry George believed to be the practice of holding land as private property, which affected adversely the laws governing the distribution of wealth. Private ownership of land, he said, must lead to the enslavement of the working classes; and the remedy he proposed was to make the land common property. In 1881 the book was published in England, and in February 1882 its author wrote—

Paul, of Kegan Paul, Trench and Co., says that it is the most astonishing success he *ever* knew. When they first got it out no one would touch it. They laughed at the idea of selling an American book on political economy. It was a long while before they got rid of twenty copies. Then, as he says, purely on its own strength, the book, to their astonishment, began to make its way. Their first edition was out early in December 1881. They have got another; that is going faster, and they anticipate a big sale.

The Times gave *Progress and Poverty* a favourable review occupying five columns, with the result that at the end of the afternoon following its appearance every available copy of the book had been sold.

It quickly attracted the notice of readers interested in social questions. "It was Henry George's *Progress and Poverty* which first arrested Philip Wicksteed's attention and drew his eager and enterprising intelligence to the economic problem," wrote Wicksteed's biographer. Mary Gladstone said she read the book "with feelings of deep admiration. Felt desperately impressed, and he is a Christian." She wrote to Burne-Jones about it, and he replied—

Yes, I know *Progress and Poverty*, and admire greatly its nobility of temper and style. But its deductions—O, I knew all that long ago. It is a book that couldn't more persuade me of a thing I knew already.

Morris was heartily in sympathy with Henry George; his arguments supported the Socialism that Morris had for some time been teaching. Mark Rutherford said—

The rights of man are once more to the front, and the basis of one of the ablest books on political economy that has been written for many a day.

James Stuart, who was a professor at Cambridge, and also managing director of Colman's mustard factory at Norwich, gave *Progress and Poverty* only a qualified approval. He felt, he said, when he had finished reading it, that "the man is a true man, and it would do one a great deal of good to spend a day or two with him"; but he went on—

I think the main fault of his book is in expecting that the position of society can be really changed by forcible action. On the whole I think the most useful part of George's book is his feeling statement of the difficulties and evils there are, and the *fact* that he proposes such a drastic remedy. There are a good many economic fallacies, and the remedy has much to condemn it. But it will wake people up and make a good many people feel uncomfortable who ought to feel so.

The book did wake people up, and aroused a great deal of discussion. Henry George came to England, and he and his supporters toured the country, lecturing and enlarging on the principles advocated in *Progress and Poverty*. They had a mixed reception, but they gained a considerable following, especially among the poorer classes, who were ready to welcome any scheme that promised an improvement in their condition. In January 1883 Mr. Joseph Chamberlain wrote to Lady Dorothy Nevill—

Have you read two books lately published—*Progress and Poverty* by Henry George, and *Land Nationalization* by A. Walton? They come to the same conclusion, "l'ennemi c'est le propriétaire," and they advocate the same remedy, namely, confiscation of property in land. I am told that these books are being eagerly read by the working classes, and the feeling in favour of drastic measures is growing.

Some people thought that all these books and lectures and newspaper discussions were doing the working man more harm than good. George Gissing, the novelist, was decidedly of that

opinion. Gissing was not concerned with social reform in the way
that Disraeli and Dickens and Mrs. Gaskell had been. He did not
attack abuses, or suggest plans for the improvement of material
conditions. He showed life as he saw it; and the feature in the life
of the uneducated classes which most powerfully affected him was
their entire lack of intellectual interests and amenities. In *Thyrza*,
published during the Year of Jubilee, one of the characters, a
young and enthusiastic factory proprietor, says—

With the mud at the bottom of society we can practically do
nothing; only the vast changes to be wrought by time will cleanse
that foulness by destroying the monstrous wrong that produced it.
What I should like to attempt would be the spiritual education of
the upper artizan and mechanic class. At present they are all but
wholly in the hands of men who can do them nothing but harm—
journalists, socialists, vulgar propagators of what is called free
thought. These all work against culture, yet here is the field
waiting for the right tillage. I often have in mind one or two of
the men at our factory in Lambeth. They are well-conducted and
intelligent fellows, but save for a vague curiosity, I should say
they live without conscious aim beyond that of keeping their
families in comfort. They have no religion, as a matter of course;
they talk incessantly of politics, knowing nothing better. But they
are very far above the gross multitude. I believe such men as these
have a great part to play in social development—that, in fact, *they*
may become the great social reformers, working on those above
them—the froth of society—no less than on those below. . . .
Suppose one could teach them to feel the purpose of such a book
as *Sesame and Lilies*.

But although he touched sympathetically on the lives of the
poor working men, Gissing's chief preoccupation, almost his
obsession, was with the lower middle class. He had been born into
that class, and had grown up in fierce revolt against the conditions
of the life he had to live. He hated its ugliness, its lack of gracious
observances, its muddle and uncleanliness; most of all he hated
the low intellectual and spiritual level on which its members
complacently lived. His works give a complete and convincing
picture of one of the most unpleasing types of Matthew Arnold's
Philistine as he was in late Victorian days. Gissing does not concern
himself with remedies for the things that cause him so much
disgust; he does not suggest that more money would bring about

a change for the better. He shows, indeed, in *Demos* a family of prosperous artisans whose inheritance of a fortune degrades instead of raising them. In his novel, *In the Year of Jubilee*, he describes a home in the genteel suburb of De Crespigny Park, Camberwell, where live Arthur Peachey, a City clerk with a good salary, his wife, and her two unmarried sisters. They are in fairly comfortable circumstances and able to keep two servants, but they are ill-bred and ignorant. All three sisters

could "play the piano"; all declared—and believed—that they "knew French"; Beatrice had "done" Political Economy; Fanny had "been through" Inorganic Chemistry and Botany. The truth was, of course, that their minds, characters, and propensities had remained absolutely proof against such educational influences as had been brought to bear on them. That they used a finer accent than their servants signified only that they had grown up amidst falsities, and were enabled by the help of money to dwell above stairs instead of with their spiritual kindred below.

The house was comfortless, disorderly, and unbeautiful, and filled with harsh and wrangling voices. There was nothing to indicate that its occupants took any interest in the things of the mind or of the spirit—

The only books in the room were a few show volumes which belonged to Arthur Peachey, and half a dozen novels of the meaner kind wherewith Ada sometimes beguiled her infinite leisure. But on tables and chairs lay scattered a multitude of papers; illustrated weeklies, journals of society, cheap miscellanies, penny novelettes, and the like.

Even when some show of culture was made by members of this class it was, according to Gissing, only a sham. There was a friend of the Peacheys, a certain Samuel Barmby, who aspired to be considered a man of literary tastes. He had collected a number of books, and on his shelves

Herbert Spencer jostled with Charles Bradlaugh, Matthew Arnold with Samuel Smiles; in one breath he lauded George Eliot, in the next was enthusiastic over a novel by Mrs. Henry Wood; from puerile facetiae he passed to speculations on the origin of being, and with equally light heart. Save for *Pilgrim's Progress* and *Robinson Crusoe* he had read no English classic; since boyhood, indeed, he had probably read no book at all, for much diet of newspapers rendered him all but incapable of sustained attention. Whatever he seemed to know of serious authors came to him at second or third hand. . . . He was used to speak of *In Memoriam* as "one of the books that have made me what I am."

The attitude of the ordinary family of the lower middle class towards poetry is described by Gissing in a letter to Sir Edmund Gosse, with reference to Sir Edmund's *Tennyson—and After*. The letter was written in 1892, but it deals with the writer's experiences during a period that included the Year of Jubilee.

I have in mind a typical artisan family, occupying a house to themselves, the younger members grown up, and in their own opinion very far above those who are called "the poor." They possess perhaps a dozen volumes; a novel or two, some bound magazines, a few musty works of popular instruction or amusement, all casually acquired and held in no value. Of these people I am able confidently to assert (as the result of specific inquiry) that they have in their abode no book of verse—that they never read verse when they can avoid it—that among their intimates is no person who reads or wishes to read verse—that they never knew of anyone buying a book of verse—and that not one of them, from childhood upwards, ever heard a piece of verse read aloud at the fireside. In this respect, as in many others, the family beyond doubt is typical. They stand between the brutal and the intelligent working folk. There must be an overwhelming number of such households throughout the land, representing a vast populace absolutely irresponsive to the work of any poet.

Gissing did not, however, dwell exclusively on the ugly and sordid side of life. In *The Private Papers of Henry Ryecroft* he gives a beautiful and gracious picture of a man of education and intelligence who, through a fortunate legacy, was able to withdraw from the bitter struggle for daily bread, and spend the closing years of his life in beautiful surroundings and in the company of the books he loved. His book-room looked out over the River Exe, and there he stored his old favourites and the new volumes that his improved means enabled him to buy. He mentions his Gibbon, his great Cambridge Shakespeare, Heyne's *Tibullus*, *Jung Shilling*, Cicero's Letters, *Pausanius*, Dahn's *Die Könige des Germanen*, Walton's *Life of Hooker*, Homer, Virgil, the *Anabasis*, *Correspondence between Goethe and Schiller*, Saint Beuve's *Port Royal*, Marcus Aurelius, and *In Memoriam*.

But Henry Ryecroft was a scholar and a writer, and therefore cannot be considered as entirely representative of the ordinary cultured reader of his day. We require rather to find a man well educated and intelligent, yet whose life has been spent in the world of business rather than in the study, and whose reading has been the recreation of his leisure hours and has had no bearing on professional or monetary advancement. Such a one was our friend Edward, whom we met in the year of the Queen's accession. Now, when he was past seventy, he looked back over those fifty years, which in their outward circumstances had been quiet, hard-working, and prosperous, yet had seen many high and exciting spiritual and intellectual adventures. He sat in the pleasant room which was called his study, though all the household came and went there freely, and he looked at the bookshelves which lined its walls with deep, affectionate satisfaction. They were all there, the books that he had met on his journey and which had become his close friends. The great poets and the great prose writers of past ages were there, well beloved and treasured, but even closer to him were the books of his own age, those that had been born into the world he knew and were, in a special sense, his own kin. The good time that he had foreseen in the beginning of Victoria's reign had come, and books in abundance had been set before eager readers. In the early days, while his large family had been growing up, it had not always been easy to buy all the great works as they came out, but he had managed to possess himself of all those that specially attracted him; and now by their help he could recover the years that were lost, and live again through those moments of exalted emotion and keen delight that had made the joy of his youth and manhood. On one shelf stood the *Tracts*, with Newman's sermons, and other works connected with the great Oxford Movement; those never failed to stir in him the old passionate, mystic devotion. Next them came social treatises, from Carlyle and Ruskin to Henry George, bringing back hot youthful enthusiasms, and the more sober efforts of later years to help cure the nation's ills. *The Descent of Man*, *The Origin of Species*, Huxley's *Lay Sermons*, and Herbert Spencer's *Synthetic Philosophy*, even the long-forgotten *Vestiges*—they were all there, and, looking at them, he was back again in the thick of the contention that had roused such fierce emotions throughout the country. He remembered how he had gradually come over to the side of the men of science, realizing that they were not attempting to destroy but to illuminate the truths that faith had taught, and how after that, in the midst of the commotion raised by *Essays and Reviews* and *The Pentateuch*, he had remained calm, accepting the books as legitimate, if ill-advised criticism.

There was a shelf for the poets, all worn by constant reading, especially Tennyson, Browning, and Matthew Arnold. All had given him thrilling moments, but now, in his old age, Arnold seemed to come closest to him; in this changing, hurrying world, which sometimes a little bewildered him, Arnold's wise, lovely verses seemed to give him the help and inspiration he needed. "Toil unsevered from tranquillity," "Saw life steadily and saw it whole"—he often said such lines over to himself, and they gave him back serenity and poise. Arnold's prose works stood on the shelf with those of Ruskin and William Morris and Symonds and Pater, and Edward could always spend an enchanted hour in taking down one after another of these and reading passages marked by him long ago, which had helped to develop in him that delight in beauty which—and especially now, when some other powers of enjoyment were failing him—gave him his moments of rarest, most exquisite pleasure.

A large section was devoted to the novelists, for Edward loved a story, and was not content, when one specially pleased him, to return it to the circulating library and see it no more. There were all the works of the Great Novelists, and a good many by obscure writers who had never won general recognition. Dickens, the well beloved, was represented by a beautifully bound library edition, and also by piles of tattered and worn paper-covered numbers; for Edward could never bring himself to part with the original copies, which he had bought as they came out, and almost every one of which recalled some incident or circumstance connected with its first reading. The works of Meredith and Hardy too were there, but Edward as an old-fashioned Victorian could not take them to his heart. He admired but did not love them.

Nearest to his hand as he sat at his table at the large, sunny window were the books published during the last few years, which so far he felt he had not fully made his own. There was *John Inglesant*, which he had read many times since his eldest son, who was the vicar of a church in a northern manufacturing town, had written telling him what high praise it had won among the Anglican clergy, as well as from laymen of fine literary taste, such as Mr. Gladstone and Lord Acton. As Edward turned over its pages, and re-read the account of the devoted community of Little Gidding, the enthusiasms of his youth came back to him, and he remembered how, after one of Newman's sermons at Oxford, he had felt a strong impulse to give himself to a life of contemplation and prayer. The impulse had passed, but still the contemplative life had a strong attraction for him, and the calm, restrained beauty of *John Inglesant*, even when it told of acts of turbulence and violence, drew him to it again and again. How different it was from some of the books that were coming from Russia, so astonishingly clever, yet so full of sordid misery, so destructive of one's sense of harmony and beauty in human life. How different, too, from the sinister glitter, the ugly decadence that was beginning to show itself in the journalism and topical writings of the day. Henry James's *The Bostonians*, though it did little towards restoring one's enthusiasms, yet gave a sane and balanced view of life and made no outrage upon the emotions; it delighted the intellect by its clever analysis, and the literary taste by its fine individual style. Edward was glad to reflect that the number of James's admirers in England was increasing; it proved that sensationalism, in spite of Hall Caine and Marie Corelli, was not having things all its own way.

That reminded him of another book lying on the table before him, *Called Back*, by Hugh Conway, which had put his wife and his daughter Emily into a state of great excitement during the last two or three days. They had entreated him to read it, telling him that all the world was talking of it. He smiled as he thought of Caroline's literary enthusiasms. She delighted in novels, and was one of Mr. Mudie's most regular visitors; but her taste had improved, and though she still inclined to the sentimental and the sensational, she rejected really trashy novels, and enjoyed thoroughly the works of Dickens, Thackeray, George Eliot, and Miss Charlotte Yonge. It was perhaps Miss Yonge's books that had influenced her most strongly, and had led her, as they had led many other girls of her class and circumstances, to desire and strive for a home well-ordered and harmonious, where the attempt to reach lofty ideals was made through the carrying out of small, everyday duties. She still liked "pretty" poetry, which term she applied to the shorter lyrics of Tennyson, Longfellow, Mrs. Browning, and Adelaide Procter. Edward had not been able to

426 THE VICTORIANS AND THEIR BOOKS

imbue her with a taste for serious literature. He had not, it is true, tried very hard, for he was a man of his time, and at the beginning of his married life had held the common early Victorian notions concerning woman's intellect and the pursuits for which she was best fitted. But he was receptive and open-minded, and as time had gone on he had assimilated many of the new ideas and had been ready to put them into practice. All his ten children—the six daughters equally with the four sons—had had the best education it had been in his power to give them, and no restrictions had been placed upon their reading. He had tried to help them to a literary taste which would reject what was poor or harmful, but he had left them free to choose. In his house there had been no hiding of forbidden novels in bandboxes under Sunday bonnets. Caroline had often been a little shocked at the books her daughters had been allowed to read, and especially at the literature of the New Woman movement which one daughter who had had a medical training, and another who was teaching in a high school for girls, had brought into the house. But she had the Victorian habit of submission to her husband's judgment, and she comforted herself with the thought that one of her daughters, at least, had tastes in literature similar to her own. Emily, the eldest, had shown no desire for a college education or professional training, but was content to stay at home with her mother, and the two spent many comfortable hours reading and weeping over *Thelma* and *Donovan* and *Little Lord Fauntleroy* and *Not Wisely But Too Well*.

Edward thought of all these things as he sat in the midst of his books, with the enchanting *Called Back* lying unopened before him. Great works would still be coming from the press when he was no longer there to read them; but he had trained up, he hoped, a little company of Victorian readers who would be in all things worthy of the name. Some lines from his well-loved Matthew Arnold came into his mind—

> Children of men! not that your age excel
> In pride of life the ages of your sires,
> But that ye think clear, feel deep, bear fruit well
> The Friend of man desires.

INDEX